REVOLUTION IN THE AIR

{ The Songs of Bob Dylan Vol. 1: 1957–73 }

CLINTON HEYLIN

Constable • London

To Sean Body, a gentleman-editor of the old school

Cover image: *Forever Young: Photographs of Bob Dylan*, DaCapo Press, New York. Photograph copyright Douglas R. Gilbert.

Constable & Robinson Ltd
3 The Lanchesters
162 Fulham Palace Road
London W6 9ER
www.constablerobinson.com

First published in the USA 2009 by Chicago Review Press Inc,
814 North Franklin Street, Chicago, Illinois 60610

This edition published in 2010

First published by Constable
an imprint of Constable & Robinson Ltd, 2009

A copy of the British Library Cataloguing in
Publication Data is available from the British Library.

ISBN: 978-1-84901-296-6

3 5 7 9 8 6 4 2

Printed and bound in the EU

{ Contents }

||||| JUVENILIA (1957–60) |||||

Hibbing:

Minneapolis:

||||| 1963 |||||

▌▌▌▌ 1964 ▌▌▌▌▌

||||| 1965 |||||

▌▌▌▌ 1966 ▌▌▌▌▌

▌▌▌▌ 1967: I ▌▌▌▌▌

▐▌▐ 1967: II ▐▐▌▌

▮▮▮ 1968–9 ▮▮▮▮

▮▮▮ 1970–1 ▮▮▮▮

▌▌▌▌ 1972–3 ▌▌▌▌

{ Seems Like an Intro }

My songs are just me talking to myself. . . . [The] songs are just pictures of what I'm seeing – glimpses of things. – Dylan to Ray Coleman, May 1965

I write all this stuff so I know what I'm saying. I'm behind it, so I don't feel like I'm a mystery. – Dylan to Lynne Allen, December 1978

It's not for me to understand my songs. . . . They make sense to me, but it's not like I can explain them. – Dylan to Denise Worrell, November 1985

People can learn everything about me through my songs, if they know where to look. They can juxtapose them with certain other songs and draw a clear picture. – Dylan to Edna Gundersen, September 1990

In April 1964, on the brink of breaking through to the mainstream, Dylan told *Life* magazine's Chris Welles, 'I am my words.' Coming from the man who had just written 'Chimes of Freedom' and 'Mr. Tambourine Man,' it represented a statement of artistic intent as deliberate and self-conscious as Rimbaud's 'I is another.' Dylan has many achievements from forty-five years in the limelight, but it is as a crafter of songs – on the page, in the studio, and onstage – that he is most likely to be remembered.

Yet the output of this most prodigious of song-poets remains mired in misinformation that constrains a full analysis and appreciation of his achievement. Put plainly, too many writers are starting with the whole issue of 'What does it mean?' when no one has yet resolved the *means* by which the most remarkable artist of his era built his array of oral poetry wrapped in song. It is high time an actual order to the work was established: a context that may yet allay the catastrophe and confusion of which its practitioner remains so fond (and which he once told Ray Coleman was 'the basis of [his] songs').

Even though there seems to be an unending variety of Dylan books – good, bad, and indifferent – no one has quite met the challenge of documenting every one of his songs with the aim of providing an authoritative history of the most multifaceted canon in twentieth-century popular song. To see the wood and not just the trees, we should perhaps start with a big bonfire of 'books about Bob.' Too many have been written by the chronically misinformed, the mercenary, and the magpie. And when the smoke begins to clear, we shall see a large stack of songs tottering in the wind, in need of shoring up with a few solid facts.

As both his output and his popularity have continued to grow – lest we forget, the man has recently had *two* transatlantic number-one albums in the space of twelve months – the whole thing seems to have struck others as just too damn daunting. It initially seemed that way to me. Having compiled a provisional chronological list of every known original Dylan song (excluding instrumentals), I discovered it totalled six hundred compositions. With so many songs, an ever-renewing fan base tuning in, and the ongoing pandemic of disinformation that is the Internet, a 'just the facts' history of every song from composition to recording and/or performance seemed like a necessity.

Accepting that 'the song is the thing' was just the first step. I was determined to organize this array of songs from Dylan's pen in the order in which they were *written* – not the order in which they were recorded or released. Only then could I start to tell the stories behind those songs not from the outer realms of speculation, but from the centrality that is their compositional history. At the end, there would hopefully be six hundred vignettes that amounted to a whole worth much more than its constituent parts. Maybe it wouldn't be the greatest story ever told, but it would provide the evidence necessary to blow away any other claimant to the singer-songwriters' crown of thorns.

I should perhaps state at the outset that *Revolution in the Air*, despite its allusive title, is *not* an attempt to emulate Ian MacDonald's commendable work on The Beatles' songs *and* their context, *Revolution in the Head*. Yes, it is an attempt to tell the story of an artist through his art. But in the process, I seek to show that Dylan's work is a whole lot more than a series of period pieces confined to their milieu. Hence, *Revolution in the Air* alludes not only to one of Dylan's most perfectly realized songs ('Tangled Up in Blue'), but also to something he said to journalist and author Charles Kaiser in 1985: 'I've never looked at my stuff or me as being part of a certain age or an era.' The spirit underlying the best of these songs is intangible, ever moving, just out of reach. Even when one is acting as the guide.

In a (doubtless forlorn) attempt to slacken the grip of the sociologists on the study of not just Dylan, but popular literature, folk songs, and mass culture, I hope to remind readers that the songs are the product of one man from a particular time and place. He wrote the songs in a specific order, and they reflect both lesser and greater concerns. He did not write to, as it were, change the world. Even if he did. The songs repay such a forensic approach precisely because many continue to stand up, to defy the ebbing tides of trendiness that have washed away many of his peers' more earnest efforts.

By sorting the historical wheat from the sociological chaff, I hope to give readers a sense of how the songs acquired the internal strength to take on a life of their own, and how their creator had the artistic will to see them through. The changes he has gone through are all here, burnished by the alchemy of song. And to *feel* those changes, all one really needs to do is return to the songs, hopefully with a fuller understanding as to the where, when, and why of how they came about.

||||▌|▌|▌||||

Having already written extensively (exhaustively?) about the author of this inestimable body of song – though not for the past decade – I have returned to find the world of Dylan experts, would-be academics, and online know-it-alls in a greater stew than in the days when the Internet had yet to compound every crackpot theory, crank story, or distorted fact into an endemic diaspora of misinformation. Even when one so-called expert produced an encyclopedia on the man, it turned out to be an almanac of prejudices founded on precious little original research: a bringing together of *mis*information, not an organized compendium of facts, methodical and managed.

The question I kept asking myself was, why had no one tackled the *songs* in a systematic way when the likes of XTC and the Clash [!] had both been the subjects of such studies? Sure, there had been an occasional foray into the sixties catalogue, as a means to reiterate the received wisdom of others and collect a bountiful publisher's advance. And there always seems to be room for another hundred-best Dylan songs piece in those periodicals that continue to feed fans of a once-fecund form.

There has even been an intelligent and genuinely original attempt to look at the early, folk-infused songs: *The Formative Dylan: Transmission and Stylistic Influences, 1961–1963*, by the academically inclined Todd Harvey. But Harvey stops short of contemplating every song, even from the years that concern him, or putting them in the order in which they were written. So even here, I had to start again and reassemble the work, though many of the early songs put the 'formulaic' in formative.

With the Beatles, MacDonald was able to keep things neat, concocting a rise, a plateau, and a fall. Such neatness would be anomalous in Dylan's case. Unlike other sixties contemporaries for whom subsequent decades have been one sustained, slow decline, he has continued to produce not just a quantity of songs but also, at times, songs of commensurate quality. And as of 2006, he has six hundred notches on his belt.

With a body of work this expansive, the quality has necessarily been uneven (and not just in the later years). So the reader must expect to veer from a work of genius to the genuinely gauche and back again in the twinkling of an eye. Dylan has always liked to upset the carts of preconception. That too has probably scared off some potential chroniclers. It has certainly scared off a few publishers, for whom the inevitable solution – two volumes – was a bridge too far.

Thankfully, the symmetry of Dylan's career to date could not have provided a neater divide, separating into two parts my detailing of these exercises in songwriting. The first

5

three hundred songs were all completed by the end of 1973, when Dylan was on the verge of an eagerly awaited return to performance, signing off the years of amnesia (1968–72) with the immortal line, 'Now that the past is gone' ('The Wedding Song'). The 301st song marks the start of an entirely new phase for Dylan the songwriter: 'Lily, Rosemary and the Jack of Hearts,' the first song written for perhaps his most perennially rewarding breakthrough, *Blood on the Tracks*.

Revolution in the Air, though, concentrates on Dylan's sixties output, trickling into the early seventies, when Dylan was still struggling to come to terms with the burdensome legacy of those halcyon days and wondering if he'd *ever* paint his masterpiece. The true surge of songwriting had come at the same time as that of his Liverpudlian peers, with 207 of the 300 songs herein written between 1962 and 1967, a burst of creativity that dwarfs any comparable twentieth-century figure. Organizing such material, given that Dylan then wrote his songs 'in two hours, or maybe two days at the most,' proved a challenge.

Thankfully the documentation has generally been available, if not always at hand. I am constantly gratified to be reminded of how well Dylan's artistic footsteps have been traced by his contemporaries, and how friends and other strangers have seen fit to preserve scraps of paper, tapes of jam sessions, and even diaries to light the way. In many cases, especially in the years before mass acceptance, there are home performances, demos, live tapes, session tapes, and even drafts of lyrics available to the collecting cabal, along with session logs, first-person accounts, and some video. As I was putting the finishing touches to this very volume, I uncovered another batch of 'MacKenzie songs,' drafts of original songs he left at Eve and Mac's house back in 1961, which required a reorganization of that initial section.

One of the challenges with Dylan is that new information

(and new work) continues to come out, constantly forcing rethinks from redoubtable experts. And we can all still experience new perspectives as important influences yield up some of their secrets. Most recently, Greenwich Village girlfriend Suze Rotolo has decided to publish her own memoir of those days, even though it is only fleetingly informative, and woefully edited.

If the lack of any reliable biographical data has forced those obsessed with Shakespeare to look for hidden clues in often-unreliable texts, the budding Dylan scholar has no such excuse. I have tried to maintain a balance between finding patterns in the man's life replicated in his art and out-and-out speculation as to the identity of characters and events in songs. (This is not the publishing equivalent of filmmaker Todd Haynes's *I'm Not There*!) I have also sought to remind myself that the songs' reference points most likely reside in previous Dylan originals or in the traditional folk songs from which he says he 'learned the language [of song] . . . by singing them and knowing them and remembering them.' As he told Mr. Farley on the eve of his first album of the twenty-first century, 'All my songs, the styles I work in, were all developed before I was born.'

Truth be told, Dylan has borrowed rather heavily from that veritable 'tree with roots,' the branches of which have been responsible for Anglo-American folk and blues. As he told journalist Mikail Gilmore in their most recent on-the-record conversation: 'Folk music is where it all starts and in many ways ends [for me]. . . . If you don't know how to control that, and you don't feel historically tied to it, then what you're doing is not going to be as strong as it could be. . . . [Back when I started] you could hear the actual people singing those ballads. You could hear Clarence Ashley, Doc Watson, Dock Boggs, The Memphis Jug Band [*sic*], Furry Lewis.'

Dylan has driven this point home time and time again in

performance, in the cover versions he has recorded at career tipping points, in interviews sincere or surreal, and now in the first (and last?) volume of some highly selective memoirs, *Chronicles*. But still, too much time has been spent finding obscure (and usually dubious) literary references or rummaging through a blues concordance for a line here or there that Dylan has integrated into work of a richer vein, rather than relating that work to (what Dylan continually assures us is) the veritable font of his vision: traditional folk song.

As with Robert Burns, tradition underlies everything Dylan has done. Yet it has never limited the horizon of his vision. And so, hoping to redress an imbalance in Dylan studies (cough), I have highlighted any references to this rich tradition whenever I have come upon them in word and tune. However, at no point do I suggest that Dylan's own songs are mere reconstitutions of what came before (except perhaps in 1961–2, when he had not yet learned to use tradition as a prodding stick rather than a crutch).

The cumulative effect should demonstrate how the influence of the old songs is altogether more profound and more invasive than the more modern forms of music celebrated on Dylan's *Theme Time Radio Hour* radio shows (for which producer Eddie G. should undoubtedly share much of the credit/blame on the selection front), or those occasional literary influences he has admitted. May I divert readers away from the secondary streams that seem to have occupied many a study of this song-and-dance man.

Which is not to say that Dylan hasn't at times self-consciously connected the two traditions: oral and literary. When he says, 'All . . . the styles I work in were all developed before I was born,' he does not *just* mean folk music. He is talking about a way with words present in all his lyrics, as he admitted when talking about Shakespeare (of all people) to an L.A. journalist in 1988, hoping to distance himself from those singer-songwriters who treat him as the originator of the form:

8

> [Some] people think that people who play the acoustic guitar
> and write their own songs are folk singers, but that's not
> necessarily true. They're writing their own songs but they're
> not really based on anything. . . . Ever seen a Shakespeare
> play? It's like the English language at its peak, where one
> line [after another] will come out like a stick of dynamite.
> . . . And folk songs are pretty much the same way.

Even Christopher Ricks, that most respected of literary
scholars, spends barely a handful of pages in his *Dylan's
Visions of Sin* relating Dylan's work to the folk songs and
ballads that provided him with that rock-solid foundation.
(Ricks compounds his sin by quoting from Arthur Quiller-
Couch's *Oxford Book of Ballads*, a source utterly discredited
for more than ninety years.)

If Dylan's own imagination provides the building bricks
underlying the architecture of his songs, then tradition
supplies the mortar. How many would imagine that the
opening line to 1963's 'Percy's Song,' 'Sad news, sad news,
came to me,' was a play on a commonplace convention
found as far back as 'The King and the Abbot,' a sixteenth-
century minstrel ballad? And how many more would imagine
that it was the assimilation of all that inherited tradition that
kept Dylan inspired all the way from 'Song to Woody' to
'The Wedding Song'?

Because Dylan remains first and foremost an oral poet, and a
literary figure only as an unavoidable by-product, an appreciation of the man's achievements and the critical apparatus
necessary to critique his work have rarely comingled. Seeing
him as a literary figure has even led some minor modern
poets – Simon Armitage, who he? – to write condescending
'appreciations' of his art from a supposedly empathic position.

But then, as Nietszche well knew, 'Communication is only possible between equals.'

Dylan himself has preferred to avoid those who equate performance art with poetasters of the page. Even a general disinterest for the passage of his lyrics from performance to page suggests he considers such an exercise as unimportant as a published version of his plays was to Shakespeare. Dylan told a friend back in 1965, 'I have no respect for . . . the literary world . . . [or] the museum types.' Yet there have been times when he has owned up to a certain literary bent, notably back in 1973, when he oversaw the publication of the first authorized edition of his lyrics, *Writings and Drawings*.

At this troubled time, he displayed a genuine interest in its presentation and the accuracy of its contents. Even in *Writings and Drawings*, though, he allowed a number of anomalies to go unexplained, and even introduced a few. The placement of certain unreleased songs seems at first glance somewhat whimsical ('I'll Keep It with Mine' comes in the *Blonde on Blonde* section, while 'Long Distance Operator' is with *The Basement Tapes*, though the songs date from 1964 and 1965, respectively). In fact, a kind of logic *was* applied, albeit based on the date of studio recording, not actual composition. But one can place a good deal more faith in the song order in this book than in *Writings and Drawings*.

A further source of frustration with that original edition of lyrics is that Dylan allowed some of the unreleased songs – specifically ones from the defining years 1965–7 – to be taken from audio transcriptions and not his own memory or manuscript/s. To push the Shakespeare analogy again, these transcriptions are almost in the vein of the so-called 'bad quartos,' cloth-eared and incompetent transcriptions made in haste, replacing a quixotic internal logic with ungarnished gibberish.

In fact, bookleg versions of the same songs, found in the

unauthorized early seventies Dylan songbooks that *Writings and Drawings* was published to counteract, are often superior, despite sometimes being derived from nth-generation bootleg tapes. The official volume's mis-transcriptions have not only remained uncorrected in subsequent editions but have been compounded further. Indeed, in 1985 and 2004, when he again allowed collected editions of his *Lyrics* to go to press – editions of which the printers behind those infamous 'bad quartos' would have been ashamed – it was left to the man's minions to supervise the finished artifact.

Perhaps the most frustrating aspect of these two latter editions of *Lyrics*, both published under Dylan's auspices, has been the way that each revision has led to a *less* precise version than its predecessor. The 2004 *Lyrics* actually omitted all of his poems and sleeve notes and even some songs found in the two previous editions, all the while leaving previous errors uncorrected. Yet a number of bookleg collections of Dylan lyrics continued to introduce songs and variant versions to the (underground) printed word. (One of these collections, *Words Fill My Head*, deserves special commendation.)

As it is, the latest edition of *Lyrics* – perhaps the most frustrating 'Collected Works' since Robert Graves started to lose his marbles and began reorganizing his collected poems according to a senile disposition – contains only about 60 percent of the originals covered here, as well as continuing to include lyrics that are clearly mis-transcribed or annoyingly incomplete. (Where, pray tell, are all the verses to songs as important as 'Call Letter Blues,' 'She's Your Lover Now,' and 'Farewell Angelina'?) As such, although it is not my primary concern, I have duly noted instances where the published lyrics are unreliable or incomplete in some significant way, referring the reader back to the recording or a more reliable published source.

One can't help but conclude that Dylan really doesn't

give a damn about his lyrics being transplanted from their preferred medium. As he told Bruce Heiman back in 1979, 'You can't separate the words from the music. I know people try to do that. But . . . it's like separating the foot from the knee.' He, at least, recognizes the futility of fixing lyrics on a page minus the tune, which will *always* be an inferior experience to hearing the way the man bends words to his will in performance. Because it is in performance that they can *change*; it is where they live and breathe.

He has talked at length about how it is performing these songs that gives his life purpose ('the songs are what I do'), making him *and them* stay young. This makes this song-history as much a work in progress as the songs themselves. It also means that readers are sometimes required to follow the history of a song from, say, its conception in 1964 to its execution (*sic*) at a 2006 *Modern Times* show, only to have to re-immerse themselves in that original milieu. (Told ya it wasn't *Revolution in the Head*.)

Generally I have tried to restrain the obscurantist in me and have confined myself to especially 'noteworthy' reworkings, albeit applied subjectively. I am, after all, primarily concerned with the starting point for the songs: possible autobiographical inspirations; any sources, musical and/or lyrical; the time lag between composition and recording on tape; and indeed each song's relationship to other songs in the canon. The song's survival in performance may not do more than reiterate its original self.

Some of the time, though, performances become an integral part of an ongoing process. As Dylan told Jim Jerome while preparing to take the *Blood on the Tracks* and *Desire* songs on the road for the first time: 'A songwriter tries to grasp a certain moment, write it down, sing it for that moment and then keep that experience within himself, so he can be able to sing the song years later.' The songs move their meanings as much for Dylan as for his audience. By establishing how and when each song came about, one can hopefully tether that movement to something relatively sturdy. Here's hoping.

||||||||||||

Dylan's working methods have changed over the years, but certain constants remain. He has continued to find inspiration in isolation. As he told Ellen Baker, 'Writing is such an isolated thing. You're in such an isolated frame of mind. You have to get into or be in that place.' Suze Rotolo's evocative description of a young Dylan who 'would sit at a table in some cheesy little luncheonette and write . . . in his little spiral notebook while drinking coffee' only holds true to the end of their relationship in March 1964, and maybe not even that late.

By February 1964 he had to write in hotel rooms, in the back seats of cars, or in snatched moments backstage. Over the next decade he tried fleeing overseas, retiring to Woodstock, and disappearing into the desert of Arizona to write – all the time searching for 'the environment to do it in.' (This is the sole subject matter of one of his finest post-accident compositions, 'When I Paint My Masterpiece.') In one infamous instance, as he worked to make an absurdly tight deadline, he even started writing songs in the studio, with quite impressive results – *Blonde on Blonde*.

Other times he took his time, as with the likes of 'Mr. Tambourine Man' and 'Like a Rolling Stone.' Yet quick or slow, in the city or in the country, overseas or back home, the songs generally flowed until 1968 when, as he later put it, 'I was half-stepping and the lights went out.' Interestingly, this happened shortly after he departed from a working practice established early on in his career. Having rarely felt compelled to work out the words first, he began to break this golden rule on the songs he wrote at Big Pink in the summer of 1967, carrying over the practice to the unexpectedly austere *John Wesley Harding*.

But generally Dylan has used the tune as a prop (or often, when trawling tradition, as the germ of an idea). As he told journalist Ray Connolly, 'When I do songs I usually fit the words around the music, and it's the music which determines the words.' He was even more specific to Australian journalist Karen Hughes: 'A melody just happens to appear as I'm playing and after that the words come in and out.' Not a bad way to make a living.

He is generally reluctant to deconstruct his own work – as indeed he should be – even on those occasions when he feels obliged to demonstrate that they *were* conceived consciously and worked on meticulously. The one thing that the combination of a couple dozen song drafts and dozens more studio takes confirms is that Dylan works long and hard on most of his songs, even if he has had to learn the *hard* way not to consider the initial inspiration sufficient to get the song nailed. As he has said, 'The hardest part is when the inspiration dies along the way. Then you spend all your time trying to recapture it.'

This book is necessarily as much about those moments 'when the inspiration dies along the way' as it is about the moments when a song is a home run. The former is as much a part of Dylan's art as the latter. One can learn at least as much about his craftsmanship from a song that he ultimately rejects, like 'She's Your Lover Now,' as from one that came along free and easy, like 'Tombstone Blues.' (I made much the same point in *Recording Sessions*, apropos his studio work, but I'd like to think it holds true here, too.)

Every song has a story. Some can be told over a cigarette. Others require the full gypsy feast. But please do not assume that Dylan's more famous songs necessarily receive the most fulsome entries or have the most interesting histories. All six hundred such histories are required to build up a recognizable self-portrait of this remarkable songwriter. No matter how fascinating the true story of the libeling of William Zantzinger, the slandering of Carla Rotolo, or the eulogizing of Joey Gallo, they are but the pieces in a jigsaw puzzle that is not as yet complete.

Revolution in the Air starts with a boy who hardly seemed to have an original thought in his head, eases into a period when he could almost do no wrong and had the world of song at his beck and call, and then stretches into that (longer) period when he was forced to extract each and every masterpiece like an impacted wisdom tooth. At the end of this process, he emerges as a conscious artist, ready to unleash his mid-seventies masterpieces at a pace almost as dazzling as during that initial heyday. But for that, I'm afraid, one must wait to find out the price of doing all this twice.

– Clinton Heylin, December 2008

Note: Since the completion of this volume, Tim Dunn has updated *The Bob Dylan Copyright Files 1962–2007*. In this rather weighty update are a series of song titles, copyrighted en masse when transferred from Grossman's estate to Dylan's publishing company, in 1988. Credited to Dwarf Music, the long list (some ninety songs) appears to include some previously unknown basement-tape compositions. Aside from 'Dress It Up, Better Have It All' and 'You Own a Racehorse,' it seems there were three other related titles reassigned at this juncture: 'What's It Gonna Be When It Comes Up?,' 'My Woman She's A-Leavin',' and 'Mary Lou, I Love You Too.' A separate reassignment has a song called

'Baby Lou,' which one suspects is simply the previous song under another name. Further information (and maybe even a tape or two) shall hopefully emerge in the fullness of time.

'Do Not Accept Chaos'

{ Some Notes on Method }

It might be helpful if I outline a few factual guidelines before readers hunker down with the first three hundred-weight of songs. So here are some notes pertaining to the criteria for inclusion that I've exercised; what manuscripts I have been able to access; how I have used the Sony studio logs and sessionographies that I and others have compiled over the years; what basis I applied when inserting Dylan's own thoughts and/or those of collaborators and intimates; further notes on the three official collections of lyrics; and, finally, those online resources that might actually steer the reader right, thereby enhancing his or her appreciation of Dylan's – and this – work.

Criteria for Inclusion – A cursory scan of the contents page will tell anybody what is extant and what is not. There are some songs I have listed, even discussed, that do not exist either on tape or on the page, but only in the memory banks of a few fortunate folk (e.g., 'Won't You Buy My Postcard?' and 'Gates of Hate'). There are also, as one *would* expect, some songs (e.g., 'Wild Wolf,' 'My Previous Life,' and others) that we can be confident *were* recorded but have not as yet reached these ears. A number of oft-rumoured songs (the legendary 'Church with No Upstairs,' for one) I have simply omitted, along with every instrumental the man has ever recorded.

Essentially my criteria have been to include only 'songs,' *not* tunes, and to include only those that have a documented title and/or a set of words, no matter how unlikely it may be that the song has survived in some concrete form. If it has been copyrighted to Dylan, it's here; if not, I have used my own judgement. Where there is no title, or the title is itself a matter of dispute, I have treated the song's existence as uncertain unless there is evidence that it was put down on tape (e.g., the basement tape section, where I include copyrighted songs as yet unheard, but omit any example if a rumoured title is all we have).

Manuscripts – Because they go to the very core of Dylan's inspirational way of writing, the few manuscripts that have come the serious student's way represent the most fascinating and potentially revealing of all the material with a direct bearing on his compositional art. So how exactly does he go about writing his songs? Certainly not with a tape recorder in his hand, à la Pete Townshend. A pencil in his hand, yes.

The extant material makes it clear that Dylan generally likes to write songs out in long-hand, only typing them up when he feels he has arrived at some approximation of the finished form. Even exceptions, like 'Subterranean Homesick Blues' and certain *Blonde on Blonde* drafts, where he might start at the typewriter, indicate someone who is likely to rework the results with pen(cil) in hand.

Based on the unrevealing scraps tossed into *The Bob Dylan Scrapbook* and the 2004 edition of *Lyrics*, one might assume that there is a paucity of surviving source material. In fact there are at least five major collections of Dylan's lyrics and poems from the pre-accident years, listed below.

(i) *Poems Without Titles*, circa 1960 – a self-conscious collection totalling some two dozen pages of *vers libre* poems that revel in a new-found freedom from parental control and the joys of a world full of sexy gals.

(ii) *The MacKenzie-Krown Papers*, circa 1961 – an extremely important collection comprising a couple dozen early Dylan songs – some handwritten, some typed out with chords – that were left with, or given to, Eve and Mac MacKenzie, with whom Dylan often 'crashed' in 1961, or Kevin Krown, a friend from the Midwest who traveled to New York at much the same time as Dylan. These were subsequently auctioned by the MacKenzies' son, Peter. Most of the songs appear to date from April to September 1961, though it is possible that some of the typed songs have a slightly later provenance, say fall 1961.

(iii) *The Margolis and Moss Manuscripts*, circa 1963 – the most substantial of the early Dylan collections, the bulk of these papers are in fact typescripts of poems written in the fall of that year, after the completion of the *The Times . . .* LP. Several are concerned with JFK's assassination. Also included are the originals for all eleven of Dylan's *Outlined Epitaphs*, plus draft versions of 'Liverpool Gal' (June 1963), 'I'll Keep It with Mine' (June 1964), and 'Phantom Engineer' (June 1965), which do not date from the same period as the poems (and play) that constitute the bulk of the collection, which was ultimately acquired by Salford singer Graham Nash.

(iv) *The* Another Side *Manuscripts*, circa May–June 1964 – the most important collection of Dylan lyrics and poems to have emerged to date, the *Blood on the Tracks* notebook excepted.

Not only does it provide almost entirely handwritten drafts of most songs recorded on June 9 for that album, but in important instances (like 'To Ramona,' 'Ballad in Plain D,' and 'It Ain't Me Babe'), there are two or more draft versions, allowing a microscopic insight into the process of composition.

Also part of this material is a handwritten draft of 'Gates of Eden' (included in *The Bob Dylan Scrapbook*) and typed versions of all the poems, given the general title 'some other kinds of songs' when a selection was published on the rear sleeve of *Another Side*. An unedited set was later included in *Writings and Drawings* and the 1985 edition of *Lyrics* (though not the 2004 edition). This invaluable resource I have used freely. As a result, I recommend that readers have a copy of *Lyrics* on hand when they get to that part of the book.

(v) *The* Blonde on Blonde *Typescripts / Miscellaneous Manuscripts*, circa February/March 1966 – the most problematic of the early collections simply because the various typescripts and handwritten lyrics have been sold piecemeal at various auctions, years apart, by the original owner, making it hard to establish the size or worth of the material *as a collection*. What it does not provide is a single example of a *Blonde on Blonde* song in the various stages of composition from idea to resolution. But there are around a dozen individual lyric sheets of varying worth, some typed *and* hand corrected, others providing a shorthand version of an almost complete lyric in Dylan's hand.

On the basis of the above material, it does seem clear that Dylan likes to work fast on his songs, often coming up with couplets and bridges when a song's structure is not yet defined. He also appears to have a pretty good idea of when a song has exhausted its potential. The few fragments we have of prototype songs that never became more than this demonstrate generally sound instincts as to what works and what doesn't. These early manuscripts also show how Dylan likes to reuse ideas from songs he has abandoned (see song entries for 'I Hear a Train A-Rollin,' 'Man on the Street,' 'Hero Blues,' and 'Liverpool Gal'; and their corollaries, 'Train A-Travelin',' 'Only a Hobo,' 'It Ain't Me Babe,' and 'I Don't Believe You').

There are also a number of song typescripts from the period 1962–3 that are known to exist, though in most cases they constitute the 'finished' versions Dylan inserted into his own notebooks (and which he clearly consulted when compiling *Writings and Drawings*; see 'I Shall Be Free'). But even after what might be termed his 'New York' period, the occasional typescript or handwritten draft has found its way into the collecting world, notably the frustrating but fascinating 'I'm Not There' draft from 1967.

The manuscripts demonstrate something not necessarily apparent from his recorded and live work – that Dylan is actually an exemplary editor of his own work. Rarely will he substitute an image or a phrase with an inferior one, and when he sees a lyric that needs repair work, his instincts are almost invariably correct. Given the number of times he has exercised 'poor' judgement in the studio when picking takes or songs for release, it is perhaps surprising that he should be so sure of himself when working on the page. Yet the evidence, where available, is pretty conclusive. Oh, for a similar booty from *Oh Mercy!*, though I somehow doubt they'd show those 'missing' verses quoted in *Chronicles*.

It seems inevitable that more and more such material will start to surface now that contemporaries are dying off or bolstering their pensions. Suze Rotolo recently sold some of her personal collection, including a previously undocumented four-page poem about life in prison, written circa 1962. Hopefully much of it will continue to be surreptitiously copied before disappearing into the cloistered confines of the

Morgan Library in New York, where the originals of a great deal of this material – first collected by a wealthy Brooklyn banker named George Hechter – currently reside. Greatly restricted access was one condition of its deposit there.

Studio Logs – A little background: back in 1994 I obtained access to the Sony cardex and what session records were held at their New York archives. Incorporating other original research made into Dylan's non-Sony sessions, musician information from the New York office of the American Federation of Musicians (AFM), and two days' work at the Country Hall of Fame in Nashville, I made the first serious effort to compile a song-by-song record of Dylan's recording sessions, published initially in the fall of that year as *Bob Dylan: Recording Sessions 1960–1994* (St. Martin's Press).

Between writing this book and its publication, Dylan's office decided to provide a Danish dentist and amateur Dylan collector, Michael Krogsgaard, with access to the whole Sony system. The result was a sessionography that he published in nine installments in two Dylan fanzines, first *The Telegraph* and then *The Bridge*, stopping at Dylan's 1990 album *Under the Red Sky*. For reasons best known to Mr. Krogsgaard, he (and *Telegraph* editor John Bauldie) decided not only to preempt my own work by hastily publishing the first part of his researches – so hastily he decided 'Advice to Geraldine,' a printed poem, was an *Another Side* outtake – but to produce this entire sessionography without a single reference to my published book, even when I had self-evidently heard an outtake he had not.

Because of his unparalleled access, Krogsgaard's sessionography has become, in the fullness of time, a valuable resource. But it could have been of greater value still if he had collated his own work with that of the only other person to use Sony's resources, and annotated his session listings with a clear indication of which material he had actually heard (almost none of it, I'd surmise). As it is, there is no way of knowing which material in his sessionography is based solely on studio logs or those AFM sheets he was able to access. Hell, he could even have looked at first-hand recollections from sessions – as I had – that referred to recordings absent from the logs (the acoustic 'Dirge,' f'r instance). 'Above all else, call it research.'

But he didn't do any of this. As a consequence, I have been obliged to cross-reference his sessionography with the now wholly computerized Sony database to make sure that the former tallies with the latter. And although I have adhered to Krogsgaard's session listings when I have no evidence that he has sinned by omission, I have where possible applied a critical discrimination to *his* work that he considered unnecessary with mine. Not surprisingly, his work has sometimes been found wanting. The session sheets to some of the sessions he could not find have also turned up as part of an ongoing review of Dylan studio material by Sony. So, the session information herein is the most accurate of any would-be Dylan researcher.

How useful such information is in deciding the likely order in which Dylan wrote the songs he recorded is a frustrating issue, especially once he starts recording albums in one or two blocks of sessions. With the *Nashville Skyline* and *New Morning* LPs in particular, one is obliged to cast about for other evidence to supply an order in which the songs were most likely composed (i.e., intelligent speculation).

Even though the *New Morning* album was in fact recorded at four separate sets of sessions – in March, May, June, and August of 1970 – the songs themselves seem to have been largely composed in two bursts: one in the winter of 1970, supplying the sessions in March and May, and one preceding and/or coinciding with the June sessions. The songs written in 1969–70 remain the most organizationally and chronologically problematic of those covered in this volume (though we are still on firmer ground than with songs written after 1990).

Performances – In the sixties Dylan's live performances often served as a barometer not for the next album but for the one after that, so fast was the man spinning. As such Dylan's early performance history is an integral part of this narrative, especially the important New York showcases at Carnegie Recital Hall (11/4/61), Town Hall (4/12/63), Carnegie Hall (10/26/63), and Philharmonic Hall (10/31/64), as well as the three Newport Folk Festival performances recently released on DVD. Thankfully – and hats off to Columbia for their foresight – all of these performances were taped professionally and, save for seven songs from the Recital Hall performance, circulate.*

The more attentive reader may in fact notice that in the historical information attached to each and every song, I have sometimes listed the 'first known performance' first, whereas other times the 'known studio recordings' takes priority. This is no typographical accident. It is based on whether Dylan went from composition to performance to recording

---

* Seven more songs from the Recital Hall have recently come into circulation, leaving just seven songs to be unearthed. The full track-listing is as follows (asterisked items remain uncirculated): 'Pretty Peggy-O,' 'In the Pines,' 'Gospel Plow,' '1913 Massacre,' 'Backwater Blues,' 'The Trees They Do Grow So High,' 'Fixin' to Die,' 'San Francisco Bay Blues,'* 'Riding In My Car,'* 'Talkin' Bear Mountain Picnic Massacre Blues,' 'Man on the Street,' 'Sally Gal,'* 'This Land Is Your Land,' 'Talkin' Merchant Marine,' 'Black Cross,' 'He Was a Friend of Mine,'* 'Pretty Polly,'* 'House of the Rising Sun,'* 'The Cuckoo Is a Pretty Bird,'* 'Freight Train Blues,' 'Song to Woody,' 'Talkin' New York.'

or from composition to recording to performance. Though the former instance becomes a rarity once Dylan returns to the arena/s in 1974, audio documentation exists for many songs in this first volume: songs that served as performance pieces while awaiting a studio setting.

And even though he stopped previewing songs to audiences after 1981, Dylan has consistently claimed that the records matter a great deal less to him than his performances. As he said to Jon Bream in January 1978: 'An album for me isn't anything more than a collection of songs . . . written to be sung from the stage. . . . It's always been that way for me . . . . I just put out one album after another. . . . Songs aren't any good really unless they can be sung on stage. They're meant to be sung to people, not to microphones in a recording studio.'

Dylan in His Own Words – As with my Dylan biography – in both guises – I have endeavored to find out what Dylan has had to say about his work both generally and specifically, incorporating his words in the relevant song's history, providing yet another invaluable resource for the congenitally lazy breed of 'rock critic' to cherry pick for this month's 'Why Dylan Matters' feature. In trawling every published interview, onstage rap, written prose piece, and now one rather unreliable memoir, I'd like to think I've brought the reader some insight into how Dylan sees *his* songs.

Some readers may even be surprised at just how much Dylan's voice appears herein, given the contemporary cliché that he is a difficult interviewee and that he never deals in specifics when talking about his work. Dare I suggest, this volume alone refutes that suggestion. Unlike many a contemporary singer-songwriter – even someone as worthy as Neil Young or Van Morrison – Dylan is a well read, articulate artist who under the right conditions and in the right company (Nat Hentoff, Jonathan Cott, Mikail Gilmore, and Robert Hilburn being four of the better examples) can be surprisingly forthcoming about what makes him tick artistically. Just not when writing his own memoir (hence my frequent attempts to refute the basis of any account given in *Chronicles*, even when Dylan is revealing an emotional connection that *is* real).

Eye-Witnesses, Collaborators, and Muses – Because this is *not* a biography, readers will find that I rely less on the verbatim recollections of musicians and muses than previous chronicles do. Where the relationship between a muse and the music seems 'right on target, so direct,' I haven't shied away from explicating that connection, tight or otherwise. But knowing that Dylan is a master of making songs *appear* to equate life with art, I've tried not to overstate the case (especially after seeing what Mr. Haynes did with my supposition that 'She's Your Lover Now' *might* be 'about' a menage involving Dylan, Edie Sedgwick, and Bobby Neuwirth).

A number of folk have been fortunate enough to hear a Dylan song when the ink was still not dry. Where possible I have tried to incorporate their initial impressions. And though it would be 1967 before he started collaborating on songs, a process that lasted well into the nineties, the recollections of these collaborators adds another layer to the portrait of the way Dylan likes to work – even if the songs in question have rarely been commensurate with his best solo work.

Lyrics / Writings and Drawings – I have already given vent on the three official editions of Dylan's lyrics to date. But it should perhaps go without saying that at least one edition would be a useful companion while reading *Revolution in the Air.* And given that the period I cover all but dovetails with *Writings and Drawings*, which Dylan approached in a hands-on way, this is the edition I would recommend. But the songs he recorded in 1973 require reference to either an edition of *Lyrics* or, preferably, the generally excellent *The Songs of Bob Dylan 1966–1975*, an intelligently compiled songbook that provided some additions to the published work on its appearance in 1976.

Internet Resources – Where the Internet *has* proved a boon for fans and scholars alike has been in the way information has been shared, simultaneously reinforcing the view, common among collectors, that the official versions of songs should no longer be seen as the final word when appreciating Dylan's art. Because he attracts (more than) his fair share of fanatics and aficionados, there is certainly no shortage of sites on the World Wide Web providing theories on the songs, though somewhat fewer relate their theories to any actual, factual resource. Nonetheless, the following sites are useful starting points for those readers who wish to dig deeper into Dylan's performance history, session recordings, or lyrical variations.

▐▐▐ *Words Fill My Head* is an absolutely essential addendum to the official *Lyrics*. Starting life back in the early nineties as a privately circulated bookleg, *Words Fill My Head* has continued to expand into cyberspace, all the while accommodating many obvious omissions from *Lyrics*.

▐▐▐ *Still on the Road* is the section of Olof Bjorner's Web site (bjorner.com) that provides a breakdown of Dylan sessions, gigs, and recordings over the years, helpfully organized, easy to access, and regularly updated. Though Bjorner relies heavily (and uncritically) on the work of the usual culprits – myself, Glen Dundas, Krogsgaard – for the more knotty issues, he usually credits his sources and is by far the best starting point for locating such information in cyberspace. Also to be found on Bjorner's site is a section called 'It Ain't Me Babe,' which provides a bewildering alphabetical list of every cover version of a Dylan song that a Swede might know.

▐▌▌▌ The online version of Michael Krogsgaard's sessionography goes up to 1990's *Under the Red Sky*. However, it does not appear that even this version has been updated or corrected from the versions published initially in *The Telegraph* and *The Bridge*. Therefore, it still includes the occasional 'howler.'

▐▌▌▌ *Searching for a Gem* has a subdirectory entitled 'Starlight in the East' with a 'Directory of Bob Dylan's Unreleased Songs' compiled by Alan Fraser. Again, not a great deal of critical methodology in evidence, but a useful checklist of songs, rumoured and real.

▐▌▌▌ bobdylan.com is the official Dylan site, which to its credit offers the lyrics to all songs published by Dylan's music publisher, Special Rider, including so-called 'arrangements,' though it also lists some songs – like 'Kingsport Town' – for which it provides audio excerpts but no lyrics. For those you'll need to turn to, yes, *Words Fill My Head*.

And now, suitably equipped, it is time to return to 1957 and the ample charms of a well-endowed actress, a.k.a. Dylan's first muse . . .

▐▐▐▐ SONG INFORMATION ▐▐▐▐

Published Lyrics – References all three editions of Dylan's lyrics, *Writings and Drawings* (1973) and the two *Lyrics* (1985 and 2004). If relevant, *The Songs of Bob Dylan 1966–1975* (1976) may also be cited. Also cited are the two early 'folk' periodicals that published Dylan lyrics before anyone, *Broadside* and *Sing Out!*; Dylan's first songbook, *Bob Dylan Himself* (1965); and those instances in which the Dylan fanzines *The Telegraph* or *Isis* published a lyric first. For any other lyrical variant, see the *Words Fill My Head* bookleg and/or Web site.

Known Studio Recording – Information is derived from my own *Recording Sessions 1960–1994*, the Michael Krogsgaard sessionography, and an up-to-date printout of the Sony database. The number of takes and the take number released, *where known*, are given. Columbia sessions from November 1961 through January 1966, and March through August 1970, were held in New York; and in Nashville from February 1966 through June 1969. The code for the albums, singles, and CDs on which studio recordings have been officially released is as follows:

45   45 rpm single
AS   *Another Side of Bob Dylan* (1964)
BB   *Broadside Ballads* (1963)

BD	*Bob Dylan* (1962)
BIABH	*Bringing It All Back Home* (1965)
BIO	*Biograph* (1985)
BoB	*Blonde on Blonde* (1966)
BR	*Broadside Reunion* (1972)
BT	*The Basement Tapes* (1975)
FR	*The Freewheelin' Bob Dylan* (1963)
FR ver.1	*The Freewheelin' Bob Dylan* (limited ed. 1st pressing; 1963)
H61	*Highway 61 Revisited* (1965)
INT	*I'm Not There: The Soundtrack* (2007)
JWH	*John Wesley Harding* (1967)
L&T ver.1	*Love and Theft* (limited ed. 1st pressing; 2001)
MGH	*More Greatest Hits* (U.S. title: *Greatest Hits Vol. 2*; 1971)
NDH	*No Direction Home: The Bootleg Series Vol. 7* (2005)
NM	*New Morning* (1970)
NS	*Nashville Skyline* (1969)
PG	*Pat Garrett and Billy the Kid: The Soundtrack* (1973)
PW	*Planet Waves* (1974)
SP	*Self Portrait* (1970)
TBS	*The Bootleg Series Vols. 1–3* (1991)
TIMES	*The Times They Are A-Changin'* (1964)

First Known Performance – Is based on my own research, cross-referenced with Olaf's online listings. If a concert/performance is given in square brackets, this indicates that a recording is not in circulation (or was not in fact made). Where possible, in such instances, a first *recorded* performance will also be given (not in brackets). In a few rare instances first performances have been released officially, on the following CDs/DVDs:

CFB	*The Concert for Bangladesh* (1971)
DLB	*Don't Look Back* (1967) [film/DVD]
L64	*Bootleg Series Vol. 6: Live 1964 Concert at Philharmonic Hall* (2004)
LACH	*Live at Carnegie Hall 1963* (2005)
LAN	Joan Baez: *Live at Newport* (1996)
LATG	*Live at the Gaslight 1962* (2005)
NB	*Newport Broadside* (1964)
OSOTM	*The Other Side of the Mirror: Live at the Newport Folk Festival 1963–1965* (2007) [DVD]
RLC	Joan Baez: *Rare, Live & Classic* (1993)
ROA	The Band: *Rock of Ages* (remastered CD, 2001)
SP	*Self Portrait* (1970)
TLW	*The Last Waltz* (4-CD set, 2002)

1957–60

{ Juvenilia }

Just a dozen documented Dylan originals precede his arrival in New York in late January 1961, when our would-be bard finally moved out of first gear. The dozen songs are separated into the handful of original Dylan lyrics known from his time in various local bands in Hibbing, Minnesota (1–5), and those he supposedly wrote during the year he spent in Minneapolis, ostensibly studying for a degree but in truth immersing himself in some all-night folk-song research (6–12). The recent auctioning of a collection of free-verse poems from his tenure in Minneapolis – entitled *Poems Without Titles* – suggests that he originally thought he might follow in Kerouac's footsteps (as he had already done, following him and Cassady to Colorado, as per *On the Road*). The discovery of Woody Guthrie's autobiography, however, sent him east instead, and gave him a subject for his first serious song, though it turns out that even that breakthrough had been anticipated by an earlier tribute to a certain girl he left behind in the North Country . . .

Songwriting came only after a period of juvenile poetry writing. Dylan claimed to have been a poet from a precociously early age to both Les Crane in February 1965 and Martin Bronstein a year later: 'When I was about eight or nine . . . I actually did write poems at that age, poems, rhymes . . . about the flowers and my mother and *stuff like that.' Father Abraham confirmed his son's early penchant for natural metaphors: 'He was writing poems in high school. He wouldn't show them to anybody, [but] he would show them to me. . . . They were about the wind.'*

However, the earliest poem we have, save for some doggerel on Mother's Day and Father's Day, dates from Dylan's teens – specifically, after he acquired his Harley Davidson 74 motorcycle.* It is in two parts, written on the same scrap of paper, entitled 'good poem' and 'bad poem' at the corners of the page. The former suggests an aptitude for self-analysis surprising in one so young, even if he has not quite mastered the art of Dylanesque rhyme: 'Jimmy, he thinks himself like / Just 'cause he owns a motorbike / He's a little fuzzy kid, not too tall / And boy, is he heading for a fall.' OK, Rimbaud, it ain't.

As to the first song he put down on paper, it was called 'The Drunkard's Son,' which he must have learned from either a Hank Snow 78 rpm, issued in 1950, or the Snow album When Tragedy Struck, not released until 1958. Snow's greatest influence was the Singing Brakeman, Jimmie Rodgers, who died of TB in 1933. Snow went as far as recording an entire album of the man's songs, Hank Snow Salutes Jimmie Rodgers, in 1953 – an album that was still at the Zimmermans' house in May 1968 when Robert Shelton came to call. Dylan later admitted it exercised a profound effect during those formative years:

> When I was growing up I had a record called Hank Snow Sings Jimmie Rodgers [sic] and that's the first clue I had that Jimmie was unique. The songs were different than the norm. They had more of an individual nature and an elevated conscience, and I could tell that these songs were from a different period of time. I was drawn to their power.

---

* The poem about Bobby's Harley was dated 1956 in the recent exhibition at the Morgan Library, but that would make him just fifteen when he was allowed a motorbike. Surely, 1957 is the more likely date.

Rodgers clearly inspired Snow – and by proxy, Dylan – to write material in a similar vein. One song absent from Snow's LP-long salute, though, was one Rodgers wrote with Reverend Andrew Jenkins, 'A Drunkard's Child.' Snow evidently felt he could do something himself with this tale of a child beaten to death by his drunk father, rewriting it as 'The Drunkard's Son.' The young Zimmerman apparently felt he might also make his own version of the song, writing out the lyrics by hand, presumably from that remarkable memory of his.

'The Drunkard's Child' is a rather fitting first lyric to have in Dylan's handwriting. Both Jimmie Rodgers and Hank Snow would remain huge influences on Dylan; though, for all his name-dropping of Rodgers, it has been Snow's work that Dylan has consistently covered, not Rodgers's. (When it is Rodgers's work, it has like as not been drawn from Snow's 1953 tribute album, as with 'My Blue-Eyed Jane' and 'Mississippi River Blues.')

▌▌▌▌ HIBBING ▌▌▌▌▌

{1} SONG TO BRIGIT

Rumoured to be Dylan's first-ever song, circa 1956–7.

The first song Dylan ever wrote – or so he tells us (the song is now lost) – was for French actress Brigitte Bardot. Dylan told Izzy Young in October 1961: 'First song was to Brigit [*sic*] Bardot, for piano. Thought if I wrote the song I'd sing it to her one day. Never met her.' To be fair to Dylan, he has been surprisingly consistent in this claim. In 1964 he informed Nat Hentoff that he wrote the song when he was just fifteen, which would have been in 1956–7. By 1978, he was even prepared to reveal his motivation to Julia Orange: 'I chose Bardot because she had that baby-girl quality and that grown-up woman quality all in one, which tends to attract me.' He was still apparently in a post-*Clara* confessional frame of mind. Assuming Bardot was indeed the subject of his first song, she was by no means the last sex goddess he would depict lyrically, nor the last woman in which he found 'that baby-girl quality and that grown-up woman quality all in one.'

{2} BIG BLACK TRAIN

Possibly written with Monte Edwardson, circa 1957–8; one verse published in Isis: A Bob Dylan Anthology.

{3} HEY LITTLE RICHARD
{4} WHEN I GOT TROUBLES
{5} I GOT A NEW GIRL a.k.a. TEEN LOVE SERENADE

All songs 'home' recordings, circa 1958–9; #3 made by John Bucklen, #4–5 by Ric Kangas. #4 [NDH].

Apparently cowritten with high school buddy Monte Edwardson, 'Big Black Train' was an early attempt at the kind of rock & roll song played by Bobby's first rock & roll band, The Golden Chords. Lines like, 'Well, big black train, coming down the line (x2) / You got my woman, you bring her back to me,' suggest that long, dark trains already held an appeal to Bobby Allen in high school.

By 1958 Bobby Zimmerman, as he now signed himself, had moved on, forming a band and a repertoire of his own. Ex-Golden Chord Leroy Hoikkala recalls how, even then, his friend had a happy knack for changing things around: 'He'd hear a song and make up his own version of it. He did a lot of copying, but he also did a lot of writing of his own. He would sit down and make up a song and play it a couple of times and then forget it. I don't know if he ever put any of them down on paper.' It would appear that he did not, though a couple of home-made tapes by his old friend John Bucklen have him riffing away for the benefit of Bucklen's reel-to-reel.

Played during a 1995 BBC documentary on *Highway 61 Revisited*, 'Hey Little Richard' is little more than a young Zimmerman rhapsodizing about the one man who had shown him a world of possibilities by pounding the shit out of an upright piano. We're still some distance away from anything as evocative as, 'Hey, hey, Woody Guthrie, I wrote a song for you. . . .'

Songs 4 and 5 derive from another home-made tape made during Dylan's high school years. 'When I Got Troubles' was included on the *No Direction Home* soundtrack CD, and a minute-long snippet of 'I Got a Girl' can be found on that soundtrack (the full song apparently times out at two minutes, five seconds). While John Bucklen is rumoured to have considerably more Dylan material on his home-made tapes, the Kangas 'hoard' comprises just four songs.

The full tape (which he recently attempted to auction, apparently unsuccessfully) was recorded circa May 1959, just before high school graduation. According to the description given online, the remaining two songs are a lot less interesting. One is sung by Kangas 'backed' by Dylan; the other is a seventy-second burst of Dylan doing an impersonation of Clarence 'Frogman' Henry (of 'Ain't Got No Home' fame). Since the recording was made at 1 7/8 ips, cassette speed, the quality also leaves a lot to be desired. As for Kangas's claim that 'this is the most important milestone in rock history,' I'm not convinced it's the most important tape Robert Zimmerman made that year.

If 'I Got a New Girl' sounds like a standard teen wish-fulfillment song, 'When I Got Troubles' fits perfectly Dylan's description (to CBS publicist Billy James, barely two years later) of the kinda song he used to write before he discovered Odetta and Lead Belly: 'I never sang what I wrote until I got to be about eighteen or nineteen. I wrote songs when I was younger, [say] fifteen, but they were [pop] songs. . . . The songs I wrote at that age were just four chords, rhythm and blues songs. Based on things that the Diamonds would sing, or the Crewcuts . . . you know, in-the-still-of-the-night kinda songs.'

The single most revealing aspect of the Kangas tape is Dylan's voice, which still has that slightly sweet croon suggestive of Jimmie Rodgers and the Louvin Brothers (much like the two pre-Sun demos Elvis Presley made at the Memphis studio in 1953–4). This trembling tenor he carries over till the following summer, as the May 1960 St. Paul tape demonstrates. But by then he would be taking his cues from the likes of the Kingston Trio and Harry Belafonte, not anything 'that the Diamonds would sing.'

▓▓▓ MINNEAPOLIS ▓▓▓

{6} **ONE-EYED JACKS**

{7} **BOB DYLAN'S BLUES**

{8} **EVERY TIME I HEAR THE SPIRIT**

{9} **GREYHOUND BLUES**

All songs are rumoured to have been written in Minneapolis, circa 1960.

> *I had to play alone for a long time, and that was good because by playing alone I had to write songs. That's what I didn't do when I first started out, just playing available songs with a three-piece honky-tonk band in my hometown. – Dylan to Jonathan Cott, September 1978*

> *Though we know of five 'documented' Dylan originals from the months at the Ten O'Clock Scholar in St. Paul – i.e. before he discovered the Bound for Glory Guthrie – not a single recording*

is known for certain to be in circulation. One song, called either 'One-Eyed Jacks,' according to John Bucklen, or 'Twenty-One Years,' could be on the complete 'St. Paul Tape,' in the possession of one Karen Moynihan. But it seems more likely it is the traditional 'Twenty Years Old,' which Dylan recorded thirty-three years later for World Gone Wrong. Until a dub of Moynihan's May 1960 home-made tape is accessed (see my Recording Sessions 1960–1994), we are reliant solely on John Bucklen's memory for a description of this formative effort:

> He had a list of about 100 songs that he had written, and some of them were really great. I remember one that he did. . . . It goes: 'I'm twenty years old, there's twenty years gone, don't you see me cryin', don't you see me dyin', I'll never reach 21.' Another verse is: 'The Queen of his Diamonds and the Jack of his Knave, won't you dig my grave with a silver spade, and forget my name.' It was one of those tragic things that was appropriate for the time – a backwoods blues folk song.

Another Dylan 'original,' recalled by one of Dylan's Minnesotan friends for the benefit of P. M. Clepper, writing a 1966 feature for the This Week magazine, was called 'Blackjack Blues' and had the verse:

> Yea, yea, yea,
> How unlucky can one man be?
> Every quarter I make
> Old blackjack takes away from me.

But this turns out to be a Ray Charles song that Dylan adapted to his solo folk style and, it would appear, he took the credit, too. Evidently his inclination to take credit for the work of others to blur any debts began early. (Another song he claimed at this time, 'The Klan,' he had learned from a fellow folksinger in Denver.) Another song title remembered by locals he later reused. 'Bob Dylan's Blues' was a generic song title biographer Robert Shelton encountered when interviewing Dylan's Minneapolis contemporaries.

Two other Dylan originals Dinkytowners recalled to Shelton were 'Greyhound Blues' (presumably a reference to the bus company, founded in Hibbing, rather than the animal) and 'Every Time I Hear the Spirit.' The former was mentioned by local folksinger Dave Morton, who also implied he had cowritten it: 'There was a sorority house that Bonny Jean Beecher and Cynthia Fisher [*sic*] belonged to. [It was] there Bob sang a new song called "Greyhound Blues," which didn't last more than a day, but it was a good song. That was one of a bunch of songs that Bob and I made up.'

The other song was an adaptation of a famous traditional Negro spiritual, 'Every Time I Feel the Spirit.' It thus marks the first instance of Dylan adapting a black Baptist spiritual to proclaim his own, more humanistic worldview. Nor did Dylan forget his first such foray, because he later used the opening two lines of 'Every Time I Feel the Spirit' in his fiery December 1961 adaptation of 'Wade in the Water':

> Up on the mountain my Lord spoke,
> Out of his mouth came fire and smoke.

Even at this tender age, he was soaking up the sounds of salvation. As he told Cott, 'When I was first living in New York City . . . they used to have gospel shows there every Sunday, and you could see everyone from the Five Blind Boys, the Soul Stirrers and the Swan Silvertones to Clara Ward and the Mighty Clouds of Joy. I went up there every Sunday.' It was because of that influence, presumably, that he chose to record the likes of 'Gospel Plow,' 'In My Time of Dyin'' (a.k.a. 'Jesus Make Up My Dyin' Bed'), and 'Wade in the Water' in his first year in New York.

And according to 'Spider' John Koerner, 'Every Time I Hear the Spirit' was not the only example of Dylan adapting a spiritual during his time in Minneapolis: 'He was writing some songs at the time but they were like those folksy spirituals that were popular at the time, like "Sinner Man" and things . . . similar to that. . . . He had a very sweet voice [then], a pretty voice, very different from what it is now.' Dylan's rendition of 'Sinner Man,' another revival favourite, can be found on the incomplete, circulating St. Paul tape, albeit in execrable quality. It may or may not stick to its soulful source. But if it was a song Dylan adapted, it was also one of the more popular pieces he played at The Purple Onion Pizza Parlour.

{10} TALKIN' HUGH BROWN

{11} BONNIE, WHY'D YOU CUT MY HAIR?

Both songs performed by Dylan in the fall of 1960, Minneapolis; #10 appears on the first Minneapolis tape, circa September 1960; #11 appears on the so-called Minneapolis Party Tape, May 1961.

{12} SONG TO BONNY

In manuscript, circa winter 1961; published in The Telegraph *#36.*

Songs 10 and 11 are the first 'originals' to appear on tape from the post-Guthrie songwriter. Both appear to have been entirely improvised. As such, they provide early markers of that rare ability Dylan has frequently displayed in the studio and onstage of composing 'on the spot.' In the case of 'Talkin' Hugh Brown,' the tape recorder has been rolling for some time, Dylan firing off a number of Guthrie 'talkin' blues,' before making his roommate the subject of one. He takes great delight in portraying Brown (presumably in his presence) as 'the laziest man in town / Got up this morning and combed his hair / He's so lazy, he just don't go anywhere.' His lyrical barbs became a lot more forensic once he reached New York.

'Bonnie, Why'd You Cut My Hair?' was Dylan's response to a particularly severe haircut administered by girlfriend Bonnie Beecher before a visit home to Hibbing (probably to raise further funds from his estranged father). As Bonnie tells the tale: 'It was an unexpected trip he had to make up to Hibbing and he wanted me to cut his hair real short, real short so that [they] won't know that I wear long hair. He kept saying, "Shorter! Shorter! Get rid of the sideburns!" Then in the door come Dave Morton, Johnny Koerner and Harvey Abrams. They looked at him and said, "Oh my God, you look terrible!" . . . [and] he went and wrote that song, "Bonnie, why'd you cut my hair? Now I can't go nowhere!"' When he returned to Minneapolis the following May, Dylan still remembered the incident and song well enough to record it for posterity, via Bonnie's trusty tape recorder.

Bonnie Beecher probably qualifies as Dylan's first significant song muse. Yes, he had improvised a verse for Echo Helstrom at a high school 'hoot,' and Judy Rubin received a couple of references in a long autobiographical poem composed in Minneapolis, in which he claimed, 'I thought I loved her.' But she is hardly singled out. In the same poem, the young Dylan also enthuses about Carol ('who had tits like headlights'), Barbara (who also 'had big cans'), another Judy (who 'wanted some day to be an actress'), and finally Adele. (This poem is among the set of self-conscious beat poems, *Poems Without Titles*, written in Minneapolis and recently auctioned.)

'Song to Bonny' – apparently written circa December 1960 – appears to be Dylan's first serious attempt to put a real girl into one of his own songs. Not surprisingly, he begins 'Song to Bonny' with a folk commonplace found in the ever-popular 'Knoxville Girl' (and a number of other American narrative songs). But whereas the traditional norm would be to cite both parents, Dylan merely credits his maternal half:

'My mother raised me tenderly / I was her pride and joy. . . .'
(He had already written another poem in 1960 addressed to
'all you mothers.') The tune, though, is not traditional. It is
one of Guthrie's.

Beecher remembers '1913 Massacre' being a regular part
of Dylan's repertoire at the Ten O'Clock Scholar, so perhaps
Dylan chose to set 'Song to Bonny' to this tune *because* it
was one of her favourites. In the lyric he wrote out by hand
for the gal, Dylan makes three attempts at addressing an
intimacy he may never reclaim:

> Hey, hey Bonny, I'm singing to you now,
> The song I'm singing is the best I know how . . .

> Hey Bonnie Beecher I think that you know
> What I am doing and where I must go . . .

And finally:

> Hey, hey, Bonny I wrote you a song,
> 'Cause I don't know if I'll see you again.

Of course, Dylan did continue to visit Bonny (who later
married Hugh Romney, a.k.a. Wavy Gravy), but as this last
couplet does rather suggest, he is half in love with the kind of
hard travellin' that Guthrie had so romantically expounded
in *Bound for Glory*. Dylan liked the idea of being long gone
(he had made the exact same statement in the yearbook of
a female Hibbing student the year he left school). 'Song to
Bonny' would hardly prove to be the last time Dylan wrote
'a song of remembrance of a girl in my mind.' This one,
though, soon mutated into a different kind of song – one that
directly addressed the man whose notion of hard travellin'
held so much allure for the young tyke . . .

1961

{ Bob Dylan }

It seems Dylan arrived in New York the third week of January 1961 and returned home to Hibbing for Christmas the third week in December. In those eleven months, he would write his first set of songs, establish himself at the leading Village folk clubs, sign to Columbia Records, and record his first album. Appropriately, his first 'serious' composition would be about the inspirational figure who brought him to the Big City, the great Woody Guthrie, while his last song of the year would convey a homesickness that still gnawed at him ('I Was Young When I Left Home'). In the interim, he would begin to create a select body of satirical, spoken-word 'talkin' blues,' while at the same time studiously reworking a number of traditional songs at the kitchen table of the MacKenzies, a family wise enough to gather up these uncut gems and file them safely away. As such, though he would record just three original songs for his eponymous debut, there are some twenty-seven documented songs written or recrafted during these eleven months, the bulk of which survive only on the page, in Dylan's spidery scrawl . . .

Published lyrics: Sing Out! *October 1962;* Writings and
Drawings; Lyrics *1985;* Lyrics *2004.*

First known performance: Gaslight Cafe, New York, September 6, 1961.
Known studio recordings: Studio A, NY, November 20, 1961 – 2 takes
[BD – tk.2]; Studio B, NY, May 1, 1970.

We can be pretty sure that 'Song to Woody' is the first song
a nineteen-year-old Bob Dylan wrote after arriving in New
York around January 21, 1961, and that it was inspired by
meeting the great man himself at the imposing Greystone
edifice where he was incarcerated as Huntington's chorea
worked its pernicious poison. Whatever inspiration he got
from Guthrie 'face t face,' it was on a nonverbal level. As
he told playwright Sam Shepard in 1986: 'I never really did
speak too much to [Woody]. He would call out the name of
a song – a song he wrote that he wanted to hear – and I knew
all his songs. . . . I'd go out there. You had to leave at 5:00.
It was in Greystone. . . . Bus went there . . . from the Forty-
Second Street terminal. You'd go there and you'd get off and
you walked up the hill to the gates. Actually, it was a pretty
foreboding place.'

Yet Kevin Krown assured biographer Anthony Scaduto in
1970 that he remembered Dylan singing the song in Chicago
at the turn of the year, before he knew Guthrie personally. For
once we can probably trust Dylan's account rather than that
of his close friend. What Krown almost certainly recollected
(sadly, he's no longer with us to ask) was 'Song to Bonny' (see
above), a song Dylan set to the very same tune – Guthrie's
'1913 Massacre' – clearly the prototype for 'Song to Woody.'

'Song to Woody,' the superior song, postdates 'Song to
Bonny.' Whereas 'Song to Bonny' reads like a note sent from
either Madison or Chicago as New York beckoned, in which
case it predates 'Song to Woody' by at least six weeks (Bonnie
herself cannot recall when exactly she received the lyric),

the later song exudes a persuasive if naive charm borne of reverent respect.

Dylan has consistently claimed he wrote 'Song to Woody' during those first few weeks in the Village, beginning the following October when he told Izzy Young, owner of the Folklore Center, that he had written it in February. This accords with a manuscript copy of the song he left his adopted East Village parents, Eve and 'Mac' MacKenzie, which he annotated with the following legend: 'Written by Bob Dylan in Mills Bar on Bleeker Street in New York City on the 14th day of February, for Woody Guthrie.' He subsequently spoke about the song at length to Gil Turner for a *Sing Out!* profile, in the summer of 1962. In the process he changed the date by a couple of days (the fourteenth was a Tuesday, the twelfth a Sunday) as well as the location of its composition, but even this description was still firmly rooted in the composition's milieu:

['Song to Woody'] was written in the 1960th winter . . . in New York City in the drug store on 8th street. It was one of them freezing days that I came back from Sid and Bob Gleason's in East Orange, New Jersey. . . . Woody was there that day and it was a February Sunday night. . . . And I just thought about Woody, I wondered about him, thought harder and wondered harder. . . . I wrote this song in five minutes . . . it's all I got to say. . . . If you know anything at all about Woody then you'll know what I'm trying to say. . . . If you don't know anything about Woody, then find out.

It should come as no great surprise that the youngster purloined one of Guthrie's 'own' tunes to pay tribute to him. Woody undoubtedly would have approved, having made a lengthy career out of appropriating tunes and even key lines from tradition – like every would-be balladeer from 'Rabbie' Burns to A. P. Carter. Dylan quickly learned to do this, too.

When asked about the practice by publicist Elliott Mintz, he cited Guthrie as someone who 'used to write a lot of his songs from existing melodies.'

Dylan found an immediacy to Guthrie's songwriting that he also discovered, on further investigation, in hundred-year-old ballads. As he told the *LA Times'* Robert Hilburn four decades after expressing this debt in song: 'Woody's songs were about everything at the same time. They were about rich and poor, black and white, the highs and lows of life, the contradictions between what they were teaching in school and what was really happening. He was saying everything in his songs that I felt, but didn't know how to [express].'

Throughout the Never Ending Tour, while still occasionally performing 'Song to Woody' in concert, he continued to idealize the way Guthrie constructed his songs: 'He wanted to bring the news very quick to the people. In those times, whenever a mine collapsed, songs were written about it instantly.' Actually, in the case of '1913 Massacre,' it had taken Guthrie some thirty-two years to write about this particular mining disaster. Hence the opening line, 'Take a trip with me in[to] nineteen thirteen,' like something shown us by the Ghost of Christmas Past. Dylan was impressed by the way Guthrie compacted all the details of a massacre of miners and their families into a four-minute ballad. Displaying a credulity that lingered well into middle age, Dylan took Guthrie's song at face value. In fact Guthrie (and his comrade Pete Seeger) saw nothing wrong with distorting the truth to suit his polemical purpose (Guthrie claims seventy-three children died; in fact it was seventy-three people).

'Song to Woody' was the one original to feature in Dylan's club set that spring. He was not as yet convinced he could or would become more than an interpreter of hallowed tradition. But he remained ever adept at playing the Woody Guthrie Songbook – '1913 Massacre' remained an integral part of a repertoire that allowed for few originals. And when he returned to Minneapolis in May, he refrained from playing 'Song to Woody' to his old friends, while still playing a dozen or more songs derived from the man.

'Song to Woody' disappeared from the live set after he signed to Columbia, as he moved towards the view expressed in his 'Last Thoughts on Woody Guthrie,' written in April 1963, and the 'Letter to Woody,' the sixth 'outlined epitaph,' written in the fall of 1963 and put on the jacket of his third album. In free-form verse he would recall how Guthrie 'taught me / face t face / that men are men . . . an' that men have reasons / for what they do.'

Dylan would still visit Guthrie through 1961, 'bring[ing] him cigarettes, play[ing] songs and . . . just [talking] about this and that.' At the same time, he continued assimilating everything he could from Guthrie's recordings and song-books and from interrogating those who'd known him in his prime. One songbook, *California to the New York Island*, a copy of which he acquired at the Folklore Center in the winter of 1961, he learned by heart, including the intro-duction (by Pete Seeger), which he highlighted in pen, and which cautioned against imitating Guthrie directly. It gave Dylan a set of songs that provided a benchmark for the young imitator, songs like 'Pastures of Plenty,' 'Pretty Boy Floyd,' 'Vigilante Man,' and 'Philadelphia Lawyer.'

{14} **COLORADO BLUES**

{15} **DON'T LET MY DEAL GO DOWN**

{16} **JUST AS LONG AS I'M IN THIS WORLD**

{17} **MEAN OL' MISSISSIPPI BLUES**

{18} **VD SEAMAN'S LAST LETTER**

{19} **ROCKY MOUNTAIN BELLE #2**

{20} **DOWN AT WASHINGTON SQUARE**

All songs extant in manuscript form only, the MacKenzie papers, circa spring 1961.

Those foolish souls (such as I) hoping to document Dylan's early years can thank their lucky stars that the circles he moved in were frequented by chroniclers and hoarders. Folk music has always been about preservation and documentation, and not just of the past. Among those who had a real sense of history were Eve and Mac MacKenzie, with whom Dylan had an open invitation to stay and go as he saw fit. Never one to pass up the opportunity of an obligation-free home-away-from-home, the young Bobby would turn up for days at a time, crashing on the couch. During these protracted stays he would write out lyrics in longhand.

Thanks to Eve and Mac's foresight, almost twenty Dylan 'originals' dating from the spring and summer of 1961 survived long enough to be auctioned at Sotheby's in the early nineties, along with handwritten transcripts of quasi-traditional songs like 'Omie Wise,' 'Mary from the Wild Moor,' 'Satisfied Mind,' 'Way Down the Ol' Plank Road,' 'I'll Be a Bachelor Till I Die,' and 'I Didn't See Nobody Pray.' All of these he was presumably considering as 'possibles' for his club set, though only 'Omie Wise' exists in a 1961 guise (one less song than he managed to perform in 1980). Here, in capsule form, is Dylan's passage from pure imitation to emulation.

He evidently toyed with an adaptation of the traditional blues 'Don't Let Your Deal Go Down' even as he was still sharpening his command of the idiom. In the version he wrote out at the MacKenzies', he conjures up a couple of 'new' verses using some very old folk commonplaces. One of these has the rambling boy telling his girl, 'I be a long time gone,' already a phrase looking for a song. He also references Johnny Cash's not-so-traditional 'Folsom Prison Blues,' writing of how 'momma always told me son.' Thirty-one years later, Dylan gave up trying to improve the traditional original, debuting a terrific electric rendition of the real 'Don't Let Your Deal Go Down' at some antipodean shows.

If Guthrie exemplified the republic of dreams the teenager was reaching back to, so did another, the talismanic Jimmie Rodgers. With 'Mississippi River Blues,' Dylan took an opening verse from the Singing Brakeman and crafted his own variant, one that name-checks his home state (the river now rolls 'way up in Minnesota / down through to the Missouri sands'). Again, it would be another thirty-one years before he covered another of Rodgers's Mississippi songs ('Miss the Mississippi'), for the aborted electric folk album he recorded before (and superseded with) *Good As I Been to You.*

The other lyrical exercises from spring 1961 reveal a Dylan trying on various songwriting hats for size. The 'VD Seaman's Last Letter' represents his attempt to rewrite 'VD City,' one of four Guthrie VD songs Dylan would perform for his Minneapolis friends in December. 'Rocky Mountain Belle #2,' on the other hand, is an attempt to write something similar to the original 'Rocky Mountain Belle,' which Dylan presumably heard from Ramblin' Jack Elliott, who still sang it. After a single verse that manages to rhyme 'love the best' with 'queen of all the west,' and includes a six-line chorus about how the singer likes to think about his mountain belle when 'nobody is around,' Dylan decided that perhaps the song wasn't such a good idea after all.

'Colorado Blues' – mentioned in Scaduto's 1971 biography – is a simple twelve-bar blues alluding to struggles past and gone, drawing on the time spent in Denver and Central City the previous summer. Dylan suggests that Denver is 'a mean old place to stay' but fails to explain why. Nor would a line like 'Central City / ain't no friend of mine' have meant a great deal to anyone save the handful of folk who knew he had spent some weeks there, playing 'Muleskinner Blues' and other songs in a stripper's bar.

'Just As Long As I'm in This World' constitutes another early attempt at a would-be spiritual, Dylan applying a new coat to suggest he has come from the house of hard knocks. The song tries hard to evoke a Pentecostal fervour, the singer suggesting he has 'fiery fingers / I got fiery hands / And when I get to heaven / I'll join the fiery band.' The main thrust of the song is the trouble in the world, Dylan aligning his own interests with those poor folks who hope to get to 'sit on the welcome shore,' a surprisingly apocalyptic message for a twenty-year-old, and a pre-sentiment of 'When the Ship Comes In.' By December he had replaced these formative efforts with rollicking renditions of 'Gospel Plow' and 'Wade in the Water,' brimful with brimstone, and by the following September he was predicting a hard rain of his own.

Also among such detritus are at least three attempts to write a 'New York is a mean ol' town' song, one of which is a long ballad about the Sunday when the weekly communal folksingers' gathering at Washington Square was broken up by the police [see #21]. This infamous event took place on April 9, 1961. Given that Dylan still 'wanted to bring the news very quick to the people,' we can assume that 'Down at Washington Square' was composed in the immediate aftermath, when feelings still ran high downtown. One might also assume that Dylan, new in town and wanting to belong, was at Washington Square on that very Sunday.

And yet a documentary film and the hundreds of photos taken at the Sunday showdown fail to reveal a single shot of the Minnesotan and his Huck Finn hat. Sixteen years later Dylan certainly implied he was a regular at these gatherings, talking about Washington Square as 'a place where people you knew or met congregated every Sunday, and it was like a world of music.' As he remembered it, 'There could be two hundred bands in one park in New York . . . fifteen jug bands, five bluegrass bands, and an old crummy string band, twenty Irish confederate groups, a southern mountain band. . . . There was bodies piled sky-high doing whatever they felt like doing. . . . Poets who would rant and rave from the statues.'

But the more well-to-do residents in the neighbourhood viewed the average folksinger as more of a deadbeat. Finally the police turned up mob-ready one Sunday and warned the folksingers they could only enter the square if they did not use their instruments. According to folk-etymologist Peter Tamony, in a later article about the fracas: 'When unaccompanied singing [then] commenced, the officers undertook to clear the fountain, suppress factional fights and remove all elements from the park.' Folksinger and author Oscar Brand details what happened next in *The Ballad Mongers*:

It was a warm Sunday afternoon. Police were thickly stationed in the park. They wanted no trouble. At first, they tried to move the demonstrators out with courteous shoves. The crowd moved turgidly, and so those left in the rear were vulnerable to most of the shoves. Some of those shoved turned back and protested. This led to more shoves and a few pokes. One hothead even went so far as to swing at a policeman. A few of the finest hurried over to subdue the swinger. A few folk singers hurried back to help their comrade. More police arrived. Someone began to sing. From the middle of the crowd, a banjo picker began to play the chords to accompany the singing. A guitarist joined in. According to the law, singing wasn't illegal, but playing an instrument without a license was. . . . And so [the police] attacked the folk singers. . . . To the great delight of the television and newspaper reporters, a melee ensued directly in front of their cameras.

Having already developed a propensity for exaggeration, exemplified by the tall tales he told everyone about his background, Dylan took another lesson (and the tune) from Guthrie's 'Pretty Boy Floyd': don't let the truth get in the way of a good story. Like a true balladeer, the Dylan of 'Down at Washington Square' set out to print the legend. Relying little on the comic understatement he was about to use to such good effect on 'Talkin' Bear Mountain Picnic Massacre Blues,' he penned a kind of '1961 Massacre,' wherein boys and girls 'dancing in the sun' find themselves on the receiving end of 'a gang of policemen . . . in trucks.' 'A girl with a banjo' is trampled to the ground, and one man is 'beaten by two big men in blue.'

As it happens, closing down Washington Square served as a much-needed economic boost to the Village folk scene. Tourists were now obliged to pay for their folk music fix. Dylan himself, just two days away from his Gerde's debut when the billy clubs came out, had no intention of trying out such songs on the Gerde's diehards. Save for 'Song To Woody,' which was as yet more of a debt acknowledgement than the calling card of Guthrie's heir, he stuck ruggedly to his (musical) roots. Though he appears to have worked long and hard on 'Down at Washington Square,' leaving behind several drafts, there is no evidence it ever made it into his live set.

{21} NYC BLUES/ TALKIN' NEW YORK

Published lyrics [NYC Blues]: Isis #136.

Published lyrics [Talkin' New York]: Isis #44 [draft]; Writings and Drawings; Lyrics 1985; Lyrics 2004.

First known performance: [Gerde's Folk City, September 26, 1961] Carnegie Recital Hall, NY, November 4, 1961.

Known studio recordings: Studio A, NY, November 20, 1961 – 2 takes [BD – tk.2].

A second attempt at a New York song, 'NYC Blues,' appears to coincide conceptually with the Washington Square diatribe (a six-verse draft appears opposite an early version of 'Down in Washington Square'). At one point the mayor is told about some trouble in Midtown and retorts, 'There ain't no trouble / It's all down in Wash[ington] Sq[uare].' The song, though, was never finished. Just one line – 'Seen so many people I never saw before in my life' – was transposed to a different song – 'Talkin' New York' – another lyric bent on trashing New York, which he had started to sketch out by May. This one would survive in his set until 1963 and became his first talkin' blues on record.

The 'talkin' blues' as a genre can be dated at least as far back as 1926, when Chris Bouchillon recorded 'Original Talking Blues.' In *The Formative Dylan*, Todd Harvey suggests that Guthrie probably learned the form from early Carter Family recordings, though I can't raise a single such example. Guthrie himself seemed to write 'em for kicks, penning at least eight such songs between 1937 and 1957. But it was a form common to *all* folkies, and just as commonly adopted by early country singers. As a format it coalesced many elements important to Dylan the young performer. Its rich comic possibilities and every verse containing a long, tapering punch line appealed to the boy's innate sense of delivery and timing. It also required only rudimentary technique on the guitar. Its half-sung, half-spoken manner of delivery released the performing poet in him.

It was Guthrie's talkin' blues persona, along with *Bound for Glory*, that appealed most to the young Dylan. By the time he arrived in New York, Dylan had already executed a number of Guthrie's talkin' blues, even improvising at least one of his own ('Talkin' Hugh Brown'). But it is 'Talkin' New York' that provides the first glimpse of a man who could compose his own bombshells of bile. Just to hear the man intone, 'They gotta cut something!' is to know the reserves of antipathy he was storing up.

According to Dylan, he first began jotting down the lyrics to 'Talkin' New York' as he was hitching back to 'the frostbitten North Country' in May (not to East Orange and another surrogate family, 'Sid' and Bob Gleason, as he implies in the song). When he returned from the Midwest at the end of the month, he wrote out a draft version of the song for the MacKenzies. The song as it stood six months before it was recorded contains its fair share of rough edges, but it demonstrated someone honing his song-writing skills – witness its opening two verses (see also *The Bob Dylan Scrapbook*):

> I rambled to NY one time, came to see a friend of mine
> After I found my way in, couldn't find my way out again . . .
> When I rolled into this here town, two feet a snow covered the ground
> I couldn't find no place to stay, I rode the subway for a couple a days . . .

So at that time he had already started to romanticize those first few weeks. Those days of struggle and strife would come to have an irresistible fascination for the worldly-wise *wunderkind*. As he wrote in Peter, Paul and Mary's *In The Wind* sleeve notes (1963): 'Snow was piled up the stairs / an onto the street.' Or twenty-one years later in a rewritten 'Tangled Up in Blue': 'There was snow all winter, and no heat / Revolution was in the air.' He even dramatizes the situation in *Chronicles*: 'When I arrived, it was dead-on winter. The cold was brutal and every artery of the city was snowpacked, but I'd started out from the frostbitten North Country . . . and icy roads didn't faze me.' Nor, it seems, did New York Town.

{22} CALIFORNIA BROWN-EYED BABY

Extant in manuscript form only, the MacKenzie papers, circa spring 1961; typed version in Isis *#44.*

By the time Dylan returned from Minnesota – via Connecticut – at the end of May, he had been away almost a month. Though she had told him of her plans to make her own trip home to San Francisco, he had apparently expected dancer-girlfriend Avril to hang around. Dylan duly discovered that the possessive streak residing deep in his internal wiring could be defied and disappointed by the kind of independent woman he was attracted to, but couldn't control. Avril was gone. With only a cold, empty apartment to return to, he arrived at the MacKenzies, asking if he could crash there. It was the start of a long stay.

Almost immediately he penned a song to Avril, his California brown-eyed baby. Still deriving most of his favorite tunes from Woody, he set the lyric to 'Columbus Stockade Blues,' one of Guthrie's better-known political songs, and a song he had previously laid down on the so-called St. Paul tape. Dylan wanted to see if the song would do the trick and send Avril scurrying back into his arms. Eve MacKenzie remembers:

> He was insisting on using the telephone. 'I'm gonna call her!' And I tried to stop him. He said he'd call collect, and I said no, that [Avril] was a poor girl and she couldn't afford to take a call collect. . . . But he did call her – maybe it was the next day – and she took the call. And he said, 'I have a song for you.' And he sang 'California Brown Eyed Baby.' I held the phone for him, he sang it, and everybody cried. It was the first time we'd heard him sing one of his own songs.

Avril apparently stayed put. But 'California Brown-Eyed Baby' was one of those rare early originals that did make it into his club repertoire. He told Izzy Young in October that the song 'has caught on,' though, like 'Song to Bonny,' it was largely folk cliches. Dylan still preferred putting real feelings into the songs of others. In fact, when the chance came in early September to record some songs to garner label interest, 'California Brown-Eyed Baby' was not one he elected to set down for posterity. (Terri Thal, girlfriend to Dave Van Ronk, taped a set at the Gaslight for such a purpose, incorporating three originals, but no song to Avril.)

{23} **DEAD FOR A DOLLAR**

{24} **BIG CITY BLUES***

{25} **THE PREACHER'S FOLLY**

{26} **RED TRAVELIN' SHOES**

All songs extant in manuscript form only, the MacKenzie papers, circa summer 1961.

Asterisked (*) item reproduced in typed form in Lyrics *(2004).*

Despite collectors being reasonably well served by recordings of Dylan as a Village club act, it would appear from extant recordings that our callow singer-songwriter took few chances with what he played in the months leading up to his September signing by John Hammond Sr. Even May's two-dozen-song Minneapolis 'Party Tape' features just a single semi-improvised throwaway.

When John Hammond sent Columbia publicist Billy James to interview his protégé after their first Columbia session, Dylan offered this explanation: 'I write a lot of songs and I forget them. As soon as after I write them or sing them out loud. . . . I forget 'em. But . . . when I take the time to write them down I usually sing 'em once in a while.'

'Once in a while' just about sums it up. Most of the songs written at this time attempt to (re)create songs steeped in the dust of a prelapsarian America, the world described in *Bound for*

Glory. As Dylan said in 1997, 'There was an innocence to Woody Guthrie. I know that's what I was looking for. Whether it was real or not, or whether it was a dream, who's to say but . . . after him, it's over.' With those songs given their own clean, typed copy – and 'California Brown-Eyed Baby,' 'Big City Blues,' 'Red Travelin' Shoes,' 'Dead for a Dollar,' and 'The Preacher's Folly' all received such benediction – Dylan would pencil in guitar chords above each song's first verse, suggesting he did not immediately intend to forget them.

The last of these songs has him satirizing a travelling preacher man who asks of others, 'Have you found the way?' only to be struck dead by lightning during one such medicine show. The moral is unclear – God likes electrocuting those who seek to preach the gospel from place to place, perhaps? – whereas 'Red Travelin' Shoes' uses a simple D-A-G chord progression to convey the misery of being left behind by a green-eyed gal. Though he claims he 'never knew a pain could hurt so hard,' actual heartbreaks to date had been few and far between.

'Big City Blues' is told from the vantage point of some-body who can't wait to reach the Big City, not to see his debilitated hero, but because he believes that 'the streets [really] are full of gold.' In its penultimate line, the ingenue even claims he's 'gonna dig me up a [gold] brick / take it to the bank.' Of course Dylan was self-consciously writing for a small urban audience who knew that the streets were really lined with dog shit. As one of the songs Dylan typed up, he probably envisaged 'Big City Blues' having some kind of shelf life, though probably not making an appearance in his collected lyrics forty-three years after the fact.

Of the four songs he typed to a tune, then left behind, 'Dead for a Dollar' is probably the best of the bunch. It tells the tale of a lad who is about to be executed for having shot a man 'for a dollar.' Dylan makes the boy repeat the last words of the man he murdered as the hangman tightens the noose:

'As he fell you could hear him holler / Oh Mary don't weep for me.' As with 'Man on the Street,' written at much the same time, he resists tagging on a moralizing verse, letting listeners reach their own conclusion concerning this dead man's tale.

{27} TALKIN' BEAR MOUNTAIN PICNIC MASSACRE BLUES

Published lyric: Isis #45 [draft]; Writings and Drawings;
Lyrics 1985;
Lyrics 2004.
First known performance: Gaslight Cafe, New York, September 6, 1961.
Known studio recordings: Studio A, NY, April 25, 1962 – 3 takes [TBS – tk.3].

{28} TALKIN' HAVA NAGILA BLUES

First known performance: Gerde's Folk City, September 26, 1961.
Known studio recording/s: Studio A, NY, April 25, 1962 – 1 take [TBS – tk.1].

Taken from a story in the *New York Herald Tribune* (June 19, 1961), 'Talkin' Bear Mountain Picnic Massacre Blues' tells of a chartered boat trip to Bear Mountain that had been abandoned because thousands of counterfeit tickets had been sold to unwitting customers. Dylan told Izzy Young he wrote the song 'overnight, because of Noel Stookey' (the 'Paul' in Peter, Paul, and Mary). One presumes it was Stookey who brought the original story to his attention. Dylan promptly began to construct an altogether more traumatic version of the 'massacre.' Again he entrusted a handwritten version of the song to the MacKenzies, in which the ship actually sinks and the protagonist ends up on the shore, a little the worse for wear:

> As I got up and looked around
> There were people splattered all over the ground

58

Some were on land, some were afloat
Then I took one look at the boat –
Looked like the planters had come.

'Talkin' Bear Mountain' became something of a party piece for Dylan that summer, allowing him to demonstrate his caustic wit in its raw state. Yes, he was sending up some rather easy targets, but the Village crowds loved the song, which provided Dylan with ample opportunity to come on like a folkie Charlie Chaplin. Far more than 'Song to Woody,' 'Talkin' Bear Mountain' was the song that got him noticed in the months preceding his fateful meeting with Columbia producer John Hammond.

The Dadaist 'Talkin' Hava Nagila Blues' started out as a response to absurd song requests. On a good day lasting almost a minute, it lampooned the folk revival and showed a rich absurdist streak running through the man long before he sped up those synapses. But what worked in concert was never going to come across on record. Though the song was recorded at the first *Freewheelin'* session in April 1962, it was the kind of song that would only serve to rubber-stamp a tag like 'Hammond's Folly.'

{29} **DOPE FIEND ROBBER***

{30} **THE GREAT CHICAGOAN**

{31} **I'LL GET WHERE I'M GOING SOMEDAY**

{32} **ROCKIN' CHAIR**

{33} **I HEAR A TRAIN A-ROLLING**

{34} **RAMBLIN' GAMBLIN' BLUES**

All songs extant in manuscript form only, the MacKenzie papers, circa summer 1961.

Asterisked (*) item reproduced in typed form in Isis #44 *and In His Own Words, vol. 2.*

The bulk of the so-called MacKenzie papers appear to date from those summer days when Dylan was still just another scuffling young folksinger. Of the dozen or so songs – talkin' blues excepted – he wrote down between May and September, just one ('Man on the Street') endured long enough to feature in the repertoire Robert Shelton raved about in the *New York Times* in the last week of September. However, Dylan continued working up songs, and sometime in September he compiled a list of a dozen original songs for purpose/s unknown (two versions of the list survive: the earlier appears beneath lyrics to a song called 'Over the Road'; the later on the rear of the 'Ramblin' Gamblin' Blues' lyric).

The list could be a wish list for a debut album, given that it was almost certainly compiled after he met John Hammond at an informal rehearsal for folksinger Carolyn Hester's LP, around September 10. Or it could be that Dylan thought he might have a songbook in him (though *Bob Dylan Himself*, his first songbook, compiled less than six months later, contained just four of the songs listed here). But the most likely explanation to my mind is that he was drawing up a list of songs to play if and when he auditioned for Hammond, as it has long been rumoured he did. If so, Hammond got to hear some or all of the following songs (as listed in Dylan's hand):

1. Dope Fiend Robber 2. Talking Bear Mt. 3. Ramblin' Gamblin' Blues 4. Over The Road I'm Bound To Go 5. California Brown Eyed Baby 6. I Hear A Train a-Rolling 7. Rocking Chair 8. Old Man (John Doe) 9. Get Where I'm Going 10. Woody's Song 11. Talking New York Town 12. Great Chicagonian.

The earlier draft omits 'Rocking Chair' in favour of a song only identified by its initials – 'B.U.P.'

Of these songs, 2, 5, 8, 10, and 11 were certainly all written by the end of August. The others (the mysterious 'B.U.P.' excepted) reside among the MacKenzie papers, but in no other known form. However, because one of them, 'Over the Road I'm Bound to Go,' would become 'Sally Gal' by late September – when the latter was performed at Gerde's – we can date the list with some confidence to that month. It suggests that Dylan at least fleetingly thought he might have an album of original songs in him. If so he was either disabused by the worldly producer or arrived at the realization himself soon enough.

The six songs listed above [#29–34] contain a number of half ideas that later bloomed into song but are for now buried beneath a mountain of commonplaces and clichés. He knew he could do better and so he overhauled 'Over the Road.' Of the songs scribbled down in (or around) September, the time of the list's compilation, 'The Great Chicagoan' is rather more intriguing than earlier adaptations. An attempt to emulate and not just imitate Guthrie, it is based quite obviously on 'Philadelphia Lawyer' – written around 1937, when Woody was singing over at KFVD in L.A. – which had been covered by Ramblin' Jack Elliott on the *Topic* LP Dylan had taken unauthorized loan of from folk music enthusiast Jon Pankake's Minneapolis apartment back in 1960.

'The Great Chicagoan' tells a slightly different, less lucid version of the same story. Whereas Guthrie set his ménage à trois involving a cowboy and 'a Philadelphia lawyer in love with a Hollywood maid' in Reno, Nevada, Dylan sets his in Santa Fe. It features a fair-haired Indian maid, a man from Chicago ('in town . . . buying and selling some land'), plus the same 'wild cowboy' of Guthrie's version. Dylan even lets the lawyer spend a whole verse describing how cowboys are 'a disgrace to all fellow men.' Both Bobby and Woody let the out-of-towner try to woo the maid, unaware that the cowboy has 'listened awhile at the window' and 'could hear every word that they said.' Rather than relating the inevitable showdown, Guthrie cuts straight to Act Five:

> Now tonight back in old Pennsylvania,
> Beneath those beautiful pines,
> There's one less Philadelphia lawyer
> In old Philadelphia tonight.

Dylan adopts the same 'leaping and lingering' technique, save that in his song, it is 'in Chicago City / Down where the lights are so bright' where they're missing a citizen tonight. 'The Great Chicagoan' is more than just the Guthrie song transposed to a new location; it shows Dylan trying to put his own spin on earlier morés. And the number of crossings-out suggests he took writing it very seriously. Yet he must have known that Guthrie was parodying a familiar murder ballad, 'The Jealous Lover,' and thus that he was writing a pastiche of a parody of a form he had yet to master.

A second Guthrie-esque reworking demonstrates a greater sophistication and has a far greater bearing on the work to come. 'This Train Ain't Bound for Glory,' as the song was initially known, took its premise from Guthrie's adaptation of the traditional 'This Train Is Bound for Glory' and reversed it. Like Guthrie, Dylan suggests that there is no place on the glory train for gamblers, hypocrites, or liars. However, instead of midnight ramblers, high flyers, 'rustlers, sidestreet walkers [and] two-bit hustlers' – all of whom were named by Guthrie – Dylan finds a place on his hell-bound train for the cheater (who 'robbed from all the poor'), the rich man (who 'thinks he's better than you and me'), and the parasite (who 'likes to make his money / Off of all of me and you').

Unlike Guthrie, Dylan also tells us why these individuals 'ain't bound for glory.' Indeed, his description of the 'lyer' (*sic*) comes scarily close to describing another wicked messenger:

'Who lied to his fellow man / Who used them for his own needs / To strengthen his own hand.'

He opens 'This Train' with another line from his favourite Johnny Cash song, 'I hear a train a rolling.' By the time he compiles his second list this has become the song's title, while retaining the notion that the 'glory train,' recast as the 'holy slow train' in later years, has a terrible twin running on an entirely different track. Indeed, just over a year later, he would record 'Train A-Travelin',' another song that lists a retinue of damned souls on a train that is rockin' and rollin' all the way down to the pit.

Of course, one shouldn't read too much into the makeshift morality displayed in these tender-years songs. Dylan's enduring capacity for holding a view in one song and the exact opposite in another, written only days later, is another facet he displayed in these September songs. Having portrayed a gambler in 'This Train' as someone who will 'play you against your brother,' almost immediately thereafter he penned a song airily celebrating the rambling gambler ('Over the Road'), only to portray the life of a rambler as a lonesome one in 'Ramblin' Gamblin' Blues,' a counterpoint to his own arrangement of Guthrie's 'Ramblin' Blues' (a.k.a. 'As I Go Ramblin' Round'), itself a jaunty celebration of the 'rambling' lifestyle. (The existence of a Dylan original called 'Ramblin' Gamblin' Blues,' penned less than two months before he recorded his first album, makes it a faint possibility that the 'Ramblin' Blues' recorded at the *Bob Dylan* sessions, long assumed to be Guthrie's, could be a Dylan original).

Dylan arrived at his own 'Ramblin' Gamblin' Blues' via a couple of false starts. Like 'Talkin' New York,' it began life as a 'come all ye' folk song ('Come all you ramblers of the wide open road') that tells the story of a boy 'I once knowed' who was killed on his way back to Utah to see his mother (thus introducing elements of 'Ballad of a Friend' and 'I Was Young

When I Left Home,' two other songs Dylan had composed by year's end).

Having put himself in a blue frame of mind, Dylan grabs onto any image that suits him. Indeed at one point, the song strings together images in such a way that it seems to be four songs at the same time: 'Let me drift down your highway / Highway 51 / I might be gone a thousand years / Behind the rising sun.' None of these lines lead anywhere. Likewise, when he hooks together 'Freight Train Blues' and 'In the Pines,' for the line 'I'll grab me a freight train a hundred coaches long,' the verse peters out with him complaining about 'these mean old nasty ramblin' gamblin' blues.' And when he says he is 'looking for a woman / To ease my ramblin' mind,' we can be sure he remains someone picking fruit from the tree of tradition.

He shows a similar disregard for narrative sense – and a youthful inclination to (mis)appropriate traditional imagery – in two other songs on that September list – 'Rockin' Chair' and 'I'll Get Where I'm Going Someday.' The former is almost a dry run for 'I'll Be Your Baby Tonight,' as he expresses a clear desire to 'go riding in a rocking chair.' Asking for his bottle and his rattle, he imagines someone willing to 'rock and roll . . . fast and slow' in said rocking chair, emulating the kind of wish fulfillment found in Guthrie's 'I Want My Milk (And I Want It Now),' already done by Dylan on the May 1961 Minneapolis Party Tape. 'I'll Get Where I'm Going Someday' suggests he has already tired of such amusements. He insists he's gonna get where he's going – wherever that might be – in six verses, and he 'ain't gonna sit in no red rocking chair.' Again, he envisages a rosy future. Just not yet.

The other song written out at this time – heading the list above, though hardly on merit – is a seventeen-verse ballad told in the first person, concerning a 'Dope Fiend Robber.'

This dope fiend robber is yet another innocent victim of an unfair system, an ex-soldier who had become addicted to morphine after getting shot 'fighting for Uncle Sam.' Unfortunately Dylan seems a little unclear as to what drug our fiendish robber is on, referring to 'white gold' and 'dust inside my bones,' images that would be more apposite if it was heroin to which the ex-soldier was addicted. Needless to say, the dope soon loses his wife and robs a jewellery store. After being demonized by the press – and Dylan daring to rhyme 'morphine' with 'The papers said I was a dope fiend' – he is sent to jail.

He breaks out but kills a guard in the process and is duly 'condemned to die,' at which point it turns out that society is in fact to blame. 'Dope Fiend Robber,' though hopelessly trite, is a revealing precursor to 'The Ballad of Donald White,' written less than six months later, which also shall suggest that the murderer is the true victim. At least we now know why Dylan loved songwriter John Prine's 'Sam Stone,' a far superior ballad on morphine addiction, when he heard it in September 1972.

{35} MAN ON THE STREET

Published lyrics: Writings and Drawings; Lyrics 1985; Lyrics 2004.
First known performance: Gaslight Cafe, New York, September 6, 1961.
Known studio recordings: Studio A, NY, November 22, 1961 – 6 takes
[TBS – tk.2].

Dylan told Cameron Crowe, for the *Biograph* notes: 'I was only doing a few of my own songs back then. . . . You'd just try to sneak them in. The first bunch of songs I wrote, I never would say I wrote them.' A song he did 'sneak in' to club sets was 'Man on the Street,' one of just three originals he recorded for his eponymous debut LP. Though it went unused, the idea stuck around long enough to be recast as 1963's 'Only a Hobo.'

'Man on the Street' was not its original title. The working title Dylan gave to the best of his summer songs was 'Old Man (John Doe),' an overt admission that the source of his own song was that old Almanac Singers standard, 'Strange Death of John Doe,' written by Millard Lampbell in 1941. Lampbell's song begins thus:

> I'll sing you a song and it's not very long,
> It's about a young man who never did wrong.
> Suddenly he died one day
> The reason why no one could say.

In this Second World War 'original,' the punch line was an apposite one: 'Only one clue to why he died / A bayonet sticking in his side.' So it was an antiwar song. And Dylan elects to maintain the mystery underlying the man's death to the end (without telling us how he knew all about this 'old man who never done wrong'). In just four verses he tells the story of a dead man on the sidewalk, ignored by passersby until a policeman arrives and takes the body away. For now, Dylan is content to refrain from the kind of moralizing last-verse that balladeers – ancient and modern – generally can't resist, simply repeating the conventional 'listen to my story' opening, but now in the past tense.

'Man on the Street' suggests that Dylan's eyes and ears were now open to all the world might throw at him. As Sybil Weinberger, best friend to Suze Rotolo (Dylan's then-new girlfriend), told Robert Shelton, 'When we walked down the street, he saw things that absolutely nobody else saw. He was so aware of his surroundings, in every situation, it was almost like he couldn't write fast enough. He would get thoughts and reactions and stop on a street corner and write things down.'

'Over the Road' extant in manuscript form only, the MacKenzie-Krown papers, circa summer 1961.

First known performance ('Sally Gal'): [Gerde's Folk City, NY, September 26, 1961] Oscar Brand's Folksong Fest, WNYC radio, October 29, 1961.

Known studio recordings: Studio A, NY, April 24, 1962 – 3 takes [NDH – tk.1]; April 25, 1962 – 2 takes.

Thanks to a single sheet from the MacKenzie papers – containing a five-verse draft to 'Over the Road' *and* the first draft of Dylan's September song list – we have both the genesis of 'Sally Gal' and a date for when this song was written – sometime in September 1961 (it was debuted at Gerde's at month's end). Discographer Michael Krogsgaard has suggested that 'Sally Gal' is an adaptation of Woody Guthrie's 'Sally Don't You Grieve.' It is in fact an adaptation of 'Over the Road,' which opens with the only verse either song shares with Guthrie's original: 'I am one of them rambling men / Traveling since I don't know when / Here I come and then gone again. . . .'

In the case of 'Over the Road,' though, the song proceeds to pile high examples of the man's rambling inclinations, from 'Whistlin' train running down the track' to 'A ramblin man's his own boss.' The chorus – 'Over the road I'm bound to go / Where I stop nobody knows' – would end up part of two other Dylan constructs in the next couple of months, 'Sally Gal' itself ('Sally says I'm bound to go') and 'Ramblin' Gamblin' Willie' ('Where he's gamblin' now, nobody knows'). But the song itself was forgotten.

'Sally Gal' fits its milieu perfectly. Neither a straight copy of a traditional original nor a bona fide Dylan original, it was never copyrighted by either Leeds Music or Witmark. In fact it had to await inclusion on the *No Direction Home* soundtrack to warrant even 'Trad. arr.' Dylan status. But this is no mere rearrangement. Rather, it is an early attempt to write a 'gonna get you now' song, with some whooping 'look at me ma' harmonica bursts. Another go at emulating Guthrie, it was introduced on Oscar Brand's radio show as something written while travelling with the carnival in New Mexico. Well, not unless he nipped down there between meeting John Hammond and playing Gerde's.

{37} HARD TIMES IN NEW YORK TOWN

Published lyrics: Writings and Drawings; Lyrics *1985;* Lyrics *2004.*

{38} I WAS YOUNG WHEN I LEFT HOME

Both tracks recorded by Tony Glover at Bonnie Beecher's Minneapolis apartment, December 22, 1961 [track 38 – [TBS]; track 39 – [L&T ver.1] + [NDH]].

One might expect a contract with Columbia to have induced Dylan to use the eight weeks that separated John Hammond Sr.'s (possibly apocryphal) audition from his first Columbia session – on Monday, November 20 – to decide which of his own songs made the grade. Still naive about the niceties of music publishing, the young 'un didn't even push Hammond to include any songs he wrote (perhaps because Hammond had already suggested they weren't generally up to scratch).

As Dylan pointed out, the producer 'didn't ask me what I wrote and what I didn't write.' And anyway, Dylan preferred to spend hours trawling through the archive of America's self-styled premier folklorist, Alan Lomax, for whom Suze Rotolo's sister Carla worked, or listening to records at the Van Ronks. And, as he went on to observe, 'The people whose floors I was sleeping on were all into the Country Gentlemen, Uncle Dave Macon, the Stanley Brothers, Bill Monroe. So I heard all that, too.'

Having located a new set of songs he could try out at his first-ever concert (at the Carnegie Recital Hall on November 4), he set about paring them down to the seventeen that were recorded at Columbia a fortnight later.* The process, though, wasn't quite so clinical. At the same time, he was introduced to a number of folk melodies and themes he would store away for a rainy day, one of which was the traditional folksong 'Down on Penny's Farm,' which forms the basis for another 'New York is a mean ol' town' song.

Such was Dylan's concentration on the task/s at hand that he did not resume his transformation of tradition until the process of selection was complete. In conversation with Billy James at the end of his second Columbia session, he admitted, 'I just wrote a new song last week – about New York. I wish I would have recorded it.' The song in question was 'Hard Times in New York Town.' The night after that second session, Dylan was at the MacKenzies for Thanksgiving with new 'fortune teller of my soul,' Suze, at his side. In keeping with long-standing folk tradition, the guitars came out after dinner, as did the tape recorder, and Dylan played Eve, Mac, their son Peter, Suze, and old friend Kevin Krown his latest composition. Four weeks later he did the same for his Dinkytown buddies (this version opens *The Bootleg Series* vols. 1–3).

'Hard Times in New York Town' allowed Dylan to take yet more potshots at the city he had made his own, using the 'Down on Penny's Farm' template. Instead of 'the trials and hardships of sharecroppers, tenant farmers and agricultural workers' (*Sing Out!*, 1963), Dylan inverts the original country/city dichotomy to produce his own urban folk song. That he took a tad more than just the tune from his source is evident from the original's first verse, which runs thus:

---

* Of the eighteen songs Dylan recorded at the sessions on the 20th and 22nd, some nine were previously performed at the Recital Hall.

Come you ladies and you gentlemen, listen to my song,
I'll sing it to you right but you may think it's wrong,
It may make you mad, but I mean no harm,
It's all about the renters on Penny's farm.
It's hard times in the country,
Down on Penny's farm.

And 'Penny's Farm' was in Lomax's collection, f'sure. Alan
himself, in his notes to Pete Seeger's *Darling Corey*, describes
how he 'found this song not at some secret meeting of sharecroppers' union in Arkansas, but in the files of unreleased
masters of the Columbia Phonograph Corporation.' Given
that it also appears on Harry Smith's *Anthology of American
Folk Music*, compiled *entirely* from commercial 78s, it goes
without saying that the Bentley Boys' recording *was* released.
Indeed Dylan could just as easily have heard it from the Van
Ronks' copy of Smith's seminal set.

The song would certainly have made an interesting
counterpoint to 'Talkin' New York.' But it had missed the
boat when it came to his debut offering. And though he
would record 'Hard Times in New York Town' for his music
publisher in January and for Cynthia Gooding's radio show
the following month, by the time he returned to Columbia
in April, the song had been forgotten – as apparently had 'I
Was Young When I Left Home,' a more important song, and
one he didn't even choose to demo.

Dylan may have heard '500 Miles' – Hedy West's adaptation of the terribly traditional '900 Miles' – at Gerde's, or at
one of the many parties the older folkies flung. West herself,
who was married to John Henry Faulk, was part of the
Greenwich Village milieu and well known to Dylan. Since
she did not copyright '500 Miles' until 1961, it seems likely
that her fellow folkie heard the song 'in person.' But Dylan's
song is not just a composite of West's adaptation and their

shared traditional source, '900 Miles' – itself a song Dylan featured in his repertoire back in Minneapolis. 'I Was Young When I Left Home' displays glimpses of the song-poet to come. Presumably it was written in the weeks after that first album was hurriedly assembled, probably as he prepared to go back home. The only known recording is from Bonnie Beecher's Minneapolis apartment just before Christmas.*

Recently given entry to the authorized canon after decades as a mainstay of the Dylan bootleg industry, 'I Was Young When I Left Home' has received not one, but two official outings since 2001, having been first released as a 'bonus' track on a limited-edition version of *Love and Theft* and then as a bona fide track on the so-called soundtrack CD to Scorcese's *No Direction Home*. This recent recognition has not, however, ensured the song sufficient status to gain entry into *Lyrics*, and it remains absent from the 2004 edition (despite being credited on the *No Direction Home* CD as a Dylan original).

So does it deserve to be designated a Dylan original? He evidently thought so, prefacing its one known performance with the claim that he 'made it up on a train' (this spoken introduction, such an integral part of his early persona, has been edited from both official releases). The story as it stands – meeting an old friend who informs him that his 'mother's dead and gone / baby sister's all gone wrong / and your daddy needs you home right away' – is neither Dylan's nor West's. It is the story in '900 Miles.' Dylan, though, should take any plaudits for the song's most evocative lines: 'I used to tell mama some time, when I'd see them ridin' blinds / Gonna make me a home out in the wind,' which in a single couplet encapsulate everything that drove him to New York in the first place. Equally powerful *and* original is

---

* The so-called Minneapolis Hotel Tape was recorded at Bonnie Beecher's apartment, euphemistically referred to as the Beecher Hotel.

'I playing on the track / Ma'd come and whip me back.' which doesn't sound like Beattie Zimmerman, but absolutely puts the listener *there*.

The trip to Minneapolis seems to have reminded young Bob of the home he left behind. On the (admittedly slim) evidence of two masterful ballads written either side of Christmas – 'I Was Young When I Left Home' and 'Ballad for a Friend' – the trip infused him with a deep nostalgia for 'home.' And yet he wasn't quite ready to embrace such persuasive material. Neither song became part of his regular live set or Columbia currency. By the end of January both songs would be left in their North Country locker, even as their author continued to make his home 'out in the wind.'

{39} BALLAD OF THE OX-BOW INCIDENT
{40} WON'T YOU BUY MY POSTCARD?
{41} STRANGE RAIN

All songs rumoured to have been written circa December 1961 / January 1962.

Even with the half a dozen home tapes, studio sessions, and live tapes that document the rake's progress from his Columbia signing on October 26, 1961, to demo-ing songs for music publisher Leeds in mid- to late January, Dylan was writing and discarding songs at such a rate that some fell entirely by the wayside. During a December interview with Robert Shelton – who had his sleeve writer Stacy Williams's hat on – Dylan informed the *New York Times* correspondent that he was writing a ballad on *The Ox-Bow Incident*, presumably after having seen the 1942 film about a cowboy who is unable to stop three innocent travellers from being lynched for murder. Assuming he finished it, this would be the first Dylan song directly inspired by a film, but this is the last we hear of it.

Two other 'lost' songs from this fertile period he mentioned that winter in conversations with Izzy Young and Cynthia Gooding. In February 1962 Dylan informed Gooding on her *Folksinger's Choice* radio show that he had 'once' written a song about a carnival freak, but that he could no longer remember it. Evidently he was still asserting that he travelled with the carnivals:

> I wrote a song once . . . about this lady I knew in the carnival. . . . They had a freak show in it, and all the midgets and all that kind of stuff. And there was one lady in there in really bad shape. Like her skin had been all burned when she was a little baby, and it didn't grow right, and so she was like a freak. And all these people would pay money to come and see [her], and that really got to me. . . . I wrote a song about her a long time ago. And I lost it some place. It's just speaking from first person, like here am I . . . talking to you. It was called 'Won't You Buy Me a Postcard' [*sic*].

'Won't You Buy My Postcard' (surely the correct title) was possibly another song inspired by a film he'd recently seen – in this case Tod Browning's infamous *Freaks* (1932), a Times Square perennial. This would have been about as close as Dylan ever got to the kind of circus performers described above. The song, if it indeed existed, would have been the first time he had written from a female perspective in the first person, though the fragrant 'Dink's Blues,' another song culled from the Lomax archive, was an early favourite in his live set. Eighteen months later, he would utilize the same technique for the fiercely personal 'North Country Blues.'

'Strange Rain' is another oft-rumoured song, evidence of its existence relying on two separate comments made to Izzy Young in February 1962. What is apparent is that the song dealt with atomic rain and fall-out shelters, two subjects

Dylan would return to in the ensuing months, first with 'Let Me Die in My Footsteps' and then with 'A Hard Rain's A-Gonna Fall.'

On February 7, 1962, he first described the song to Young, using it as a way to condemn the quality of modern protest songs: '"Strange Rain" written while Gil [Turner] and I were in Toronto in December 1961. I set out to say something about fall-out and bomb-testing but I didn't want it to be a slogan song. Too many of the protest songs are bad music. Exceptions being "Which Side Are You On?", [and] most of the mining songs are good.'

Evidently the songwriter was using 'strange rain' – as opposed to hard rain – as a metaphor for nuclear fall-out. Two weeks later Dylan was again talking about bomb testing with Young and referred to a song written by Tom Paxton (which Young apparently confused with 'Strange Rain?' in the margin of his notebook). Dylan told him, 'You ought to go to Nevada where all the stuff [i.e., bomb testing] is going on. Go out there, you'll find some strange rain.'

So, a matter of weeks before he penned 'Let Me Die in My Footsteps,' Dylan was looking to say 'something' about 'the bomb' (probably to impress an old activist like Young). Young may already have been talking about compiling an anthology of antibomb polemics. Later in the year he would persuade Dylan to write about the subject in a free-form poem, 'Go 'Way Bomb.' By then, two later songs had crystallized what he wanted to say 'about fall-out and bomb-testing,' leaving 'Strange Rain' to be blown away by the ensuing wind.

Another song written at around the same time was untitled, though he performed it on film in circumstances Joel Agee outlined in a 1996 essay:

In the spring [sic] of 1962, a friend of my mother's introduced me to the folksinger and photographer John Cohen, who was planning to make a documentary film about Kentucky country musicians and needed an assistant. . . . We borrowed a 16mm camera from a friend of his. . . . The trial run took place on top of a second friend's house. We were going to film the roofs of the Village, the sky, the pigeons, each other. But a third friend of John's dropped by, a folksinger named Bob Dylan who was all excited about some new songs he had written and we ended up making a fifteen-minute film of him. . . . He sang one of his new songs, something involving a request for a pillow from a woman who had locked him out of her room.

The film still exists, as its appearance in the recent *No Direction Home* documentary confirms; but it was shot 'silent,' and so this intriguing song is now lost. The fact that Dylan appears to have stepped off the front cover of his debut album suggests the film was shot around January/February 1962, when photographer Don Hunstein's iconic cover was taken.

1962

{ The Freewheelin' Bob Dylan }

Based solely on sheer quantity of songs, 1962 still remains Dylan's most prolific year as a songwriter – he wrote around fifty songs in this twelve-month period, including songs as enduring as 'Blowin' in the Wind,' 'Don't Think Twice It's Alright,' 'Ballad of Hollis Brown,' and 'A Hard Rain's A-Gonna Fall.' It was the year when a lyrical gift only occasionally evident in 1961 blossomed into a veritable garden of earthly delights.

The year saw his craftsmanship undergo at least four transforma-tions, each marked by a breakthrough song of its own. It began with half a dozen demos cut for Leeds Music, in the midst of which resides the remarkable 'Ballad for a Friend,' evidence that he was starting to tap into some real roots. This was followed in early April by 'Blowin' in the Wind,' a song he was initially uncertain about, but which quickly acquired a momentum of its own. In August came his most personal song to date – 'Tomorrow Is a Long Time' – his first serious attempt to address heartbreak from an adult perspective.

And in late September he shattered the template for popular song forever with the startlingly ambitious 'A Hard Rain's A-Gonna

Fall.' The following month he appeared on the front cover of Sing
Out! *magazine, heralded as the finest young songwriter to have
emerged since Guthrie. But he still had yet to complete his second,
all-original album. To do that he would need to soak up almost as
much from a single month immersed in the London folk scene as he
had from two years in New York.*

{42} BALLAD FOR A FRIEND
{43} POOR BOY BLUES

Published lyrics: Writings and Drawings; Lyrics *1985;* Lyrics *2004.
Both recorded for Leeds Music, New York, January 1962.*

In *Chronicles,* Dylan gives his own account of the circumstances surrounding the six songs he recorded for music
publisher Leeds Music, applying the usual modicum of
veracity, liberally sprinkled with disingenuous salt. As he
writes in this memoir:

> I didn't have many songs, ' I was making up some composi-
> tions on the spot, rearranging verses to old blues ballads,
> adding an original line here or there, anything that came
> into my mind – slapping a title on it. . . . I rattled off lines
> and verses based on the stuff I knew. . . . [I'd] start out with
> something, some kind of line written in stone and then
> turn it with another line – make it add up to something
> else than it originally did.

It may be a fair description of *Love and Theft,* but not of the
Leeds Music demos. Half the songs he demoed were drawn
from his fall 1961 set, while just a single song, 'Standing on
the Highway,' can be applied to the above description.

They may not have been made up 'on the spot,' but of the
four* Leeds Music demos not part of his 1961 repertoire, just

---

* Seven songs were recorded for Leeds Music, with an eighth ('He one would be recorded at second-album sessions in April, which does rather suggest he hardly lived with the songs he gave to Levy's little company. Yet there is some gold in them thar hills. 'Ballad for a Friend' and 'Poor Boy Blues' both demonstrate a heightened craftsmanship, even while Dylan consciously reverted to that most restrictive of templates – the twelve-bar blues. Neither song is symptomatic of someone who 'rattled off lines and verses based on stuff I knew,' a description that *does* fit the songs left at the MacKenzies the summer before.

On 'Ballad for a Friend,' perhaps for the first time, every line is weighed in the balance. The story builds incrementally, offset by the kind of accomplished bottleneck Dylan was now threatening to make a personal trademark. Its tragic conclusion reveals that this former friend has been found dead on a Utah road. Originally called 'Reminiscence Blues,' the references to 'watching trains roll through the town' and days spent among 'lakes and streams and mines so free' suggest that a real nostalgia for the North Country has been fuelled by his recent trip home. Though we know of no 'friend' found dead on a Utah road, shortly after Dylan left Hibbing his lifelong friend, Larry Kegan, had an accident in Florida that left him permanently wheelchair-bound. According to Dylan's mother, 'This was a real tragedy in Bobby's life.'

'Poor Boy Blues' is another three-line whiff of the blues. Dylan is learning to rely on the listener's imagination to fill in the gaps, each of the nine verses ending with the narrator querying, 'Can't you hear me cryin', Hm, hm, hm.' What has

Was a Friend of Mine') lodged from a session-tape at Columbia. Those seven songs were as follows: 'Ballad for a Friend,' 'Hard Times in New York Town,' 'Man on the Street,' 'Poor Boy Blues,' 'Rambling Willie,' 'Standing on the Highway,' and 'Talking Bear Mountain Picnic Massacre Blues.'

reduced the po' boy to tears is never elucidated, but there is no doubting Dylan's commitment to the song, or the blues. If this represents rattling 'off lines and verses based on the stuff I knew,' it was a necessary part of the ongoing reinvention of Robert Zimmerman.

Over a six-month period, he would become as comfortable with the blues' own concordance of commonplaces and conventions as he was already with its folk counterpart. For now, he wanted to make the blues the focal point of the second album – hence its working title, *Bob Dylan's Blues* (*before* he had a song of the same name). As he began to try on assorted blues personae for size, one figure loomed as large as Guthrie had in the folk-troubadour realm: the late, great Robert Johnson.

Note: The transcript of 'Ballad for a Friend' used in the 1965 songbook *Bob Dylan Himself* and all subsequent collections of lyrics has the final line as 'Listenin' to them church bells tone.' Dylan mumbles the last word – probably because, although tone does rhyme with moan, the word should surely be toll, à la 'Barbara Allen,' that stalwart of his 1962 repertoire.

{44} DEATH OF ROBERT JOHNSON

{45} STANDING ON THE HIGHWAY

#45 – Published lyric: Writings and Drawings; Lyrics *1985;* Lyrics *2004.*
Recorded for Leeds Music, New York, January 1962.

The last song recorded that January afternoon at the Leeds offices also qualifies as Dylan's 'Song to Robert.' 'Standing on the Highway' was a homage that relied heavily on the dead man's *modus operandi*. Dylan had been introduced to his latest hero by producer John Hammond. Robert Johnson provided the last piece in a mosaic of folk and blues that would serve as a perennial backdrop to all Dylan would build, brick by lyrical brick. Everything he had been writing in the lead-up to the November 1961 sessions became straws in the wind, as he was swept up by a new enthusiasm. The Dylan of *Chronicles* again defies any true chronicler to call him a liar when recounting his introduction to *King of the Delta Blues Singers*:

> John Hammond put a contract down in front of me – the standard one they gave to any new artist. . . . Before leaving that day, he'd [also] given me a couple of records that were not yet available. . . . [One] was called *King of the Delta Blues* by a singer named Robert Johnson. . . . Hammond said I should listen to it, that this guy could 'whip anybody.' . . . From the first note the vibrations from the loudspeaker made my hair stand up. . . . I immediately differentiated between him and anyone else I had ever heard. The songs weren't customary blues songs. They were perfected pieces – each song contained four or five verses, every couplet inter-twined with the next but in no obvious way. They were so utterly fluid. . . . If I hadn't heard the Robert Johnson record when I did, there probably would have been hundreds of lines of mine that would have been shut down.

One would love to buy into Dylan's account, which manages to convey Johnson's impact with a vivid immediacy. He is clearly suggesting he heard Johnson in September 1961, when he first talked turkey with Hammond. But the absence of even the slightest hint of Johnson's influence at the Carnegie Recital Hall gig, the November sessions, or on the Minneapolis Hotel Tape raises a big question mark about the timing of his epiphany – though not its impact.

Given the way the influence of Johnson became omni-present by the turn of the year, the end of the *Bob Dylan* sessions is a much more likely date for when Hammond gave Dylan his first 'promo' LP. On February 1, 1962, the wonder boy informed Izzy Young he was writing a song about the death of Robert Johnson, a demise shrouded in more mystery than Christ's. He probably begged Hammond for more details about the man, but even the esteemed producer knew only the myth – and the few records. Dylan immediately latched onto the legend via Frank Drigg's sleeve notes. Yet it is unclear whether he ever completed the song. It does not appear on any known recording that winter.

By the time he mentioned it, Dylan had already written 'Standing on the Highway,' a self-conscious attempt to rework Johnson's 'Crossroad Blues.' Emulating Johnson did not come as easily as emulating Woody. He could play a fine burst of bottleneck, as the December 1961 Hotel Tape avers, but he was no Johnson. And never would be. When performing 'Standing on the Highway' on a February radio show with Cynthia Gooding he comes across, rather, as the sorcerer's apprentice.

Another key difference between the fledgling folksinger and the mythic persona of Johnson is that the young Dylan who was 'Standing on the Highway' was *not* awaiting the devil or planning to exchange his soul for the unearthly gift with which Johnson was not so much blessed as damned. Underneath he was still Guthrie's man, prone to imagining he'd 'been hittin'' some hard travelin' too.' As he asserted in 'My Life in a Stolen Moment,' 'I made my own depression / rode freight trains for kicks, got beat up for laughs.' There he was, wholly steeped in the *romance* of suffering, continuing to play the poor boy crying down the phone, nine hundred miles from home.

At this tender age, the idea of suffering for his art held great allure. The reality proved less appealing. As for living the blues, Dylan confessed to Nat Hentoff in 1965: 'I just drifted round. I've been up a lot of times . . . with no places to go and it's been very early in the morning and it never fazed me.

It was never like, here I am stuck on the highway, bumming down the railroad line, hell and I feel sad.' But just hearing Johnson made him feel connected to something still buried in his songwriting soul. Hence that revelatory comment to Cameron Crowe: 'Robert Johnson, for me . . . is a deep reality, someone who's telling me where he's been, that I haven't, and what it's like there – somebody whose life I can *feel*.'

Commensurate feelings would come, but only with the white heat of experience. When they did he would mine them to the core. For now, he was obliged to confine himself to an inferior rewrite of 'Crossroads' and leave it at that. Within months, entire verses from Johnson's concise canon were popping up in Dylan's set. Meanwhile Dylan gave his arrangement of 'Man of Constant Sorrow,' scheduled to be published by his erstwhile music publisher, its own Johnsonesque finale: 'It's a hard, hard road to travel, when you can't be satisfied / I've got a rope that's hanging o'er me, and the devil's at my side.' Now *that* is a case of Dylan 're-arranging verses to old blues ballads'!

{46} RAMBLIN' GAMBLIN' WILLIE

Published lyric: Writings and Drawings; Lyrics *1985;* Lyrics *2004.*
Known studio recordings: Leeds Music, New York, January 1962; Studio A, NY, April 24, 1962 – 4 takes [FR Mk.1] [TBS – tk.4].

Robert Johnson was hardly the only romantic figure to loom large in the young Dylan's psyche. He felt all his heroes should fit one of two criteria: an early death or, in Guthrie's – and later Rimbaud's – case, a prolonged disintegration that left one creatively dead. Along with Hank Williams, Lead Belly, James Dean, and Johnny Ace, Johnson lived in a mythopoeic past of Dylan's own making, where he could be relied on to remain till summoned at will. Dylan now cast around for song characters who could inhabit much the same mythological plain.

'Ramblin' Gamblin' Willie' was Dylan's first crack at writing an outlaw blues along similar lines to Guthrie's 'Pretty Boy Floyd' or 'Jesse James,' themselves modelled on the ponderous morality tales-in-verse printed by the British broadside press in the eighteenth and nineteenth centuries. Dylan certainly loved his outlaws. As he opines in *Chronicles*, 'Pretty Boy Floyd . . . stirs up an adventurous spirit. Even his name has something to say . . . yet he's the stuff of real flesh and blood.'

There was another real-life figure that gave Dylan the kind of framework he needed – the Irish highwayman, Willie Brennan. Immortalized in a number of English nineteenth-century broadsides, 'Brennan on the Moor' was a figure nightly invoked by those Irish rabble-rousers and Village drinking buddies, the Clancy Brothers. (In fact the song seems to have been far better known in England than in Ireland, its tune being a variant of 'The Painful Plough.') Dylan later told Derek Bailey for his TV documentary on the Clancys: 'All the legendary people they used to sing about . . . it was as if they'd just existed yesterday . . . . I would think of Brennan on the Moor the same way as I would think of Jesse James, you know. They just became very real to me.'

'Ramblin' Gamblin' Willie' aims to invoke the same 'adventurous spirit' as Brennan. He is a rambler and a gambler, the uncle Dylan hoped he'd had. (He liked to tell people he had an uncle who was a gambler in Vegas. And he did have an uncle living in Vegas, Vernon Stone, but there is no evidence he was a career gambler.) Willie is cast as an American Robin Hood, someone who likes to 'spread his money far and wide, to help the sick and poor.' There is no question that Dylan sought to idealize such men. He admitted as much to Dave Herman, twenty years later: 'I grew up admiring those type of heroes, Robin Hood, Jesse

James . . . the person who always kicked against the oppression and had high moral standards. I don't know if these people I write about have high moral standards, I don't know if Robin Hood did, but you always assumed they did.'

'Ramblin' Gamblin' Willie' also gave Dylan an excuse to play the 'dead man's hand.' Back in October 1961 he had told Izzy Young, 'Dead man's hand and Aces and Eights – believe in them. Believe in cards. Plays a lot of cards. It's time to cash in when you get Aces and Eights.' And by December he had added the following verse to Big Joe Williams's 'Baby Please Don't Go': 'Lookin' down at two cards. . . . One looks like it's the eight of diamonds / The other looks like it is the ace of spades.' The following month the same verse was transposed to 'Standing on the Highway,' before being introduced to signal Willie's death. On being gunned down, the gambler drops his cards, displaying this 'dead man's hand,' an early manifestation of an enduring belief in the forces of fate. The song became one of just two songs demo-ed for Leeds that Dylan then recorded for his second album. Indeed, up until the recall of that album's initial pressing, it was destined to appear on *Freewheelin'* (the full story of the original *Freewheelin'* and the substitution of four tracks by new recordings can be found in *Behind The Shades – Take Two*).

{47} TALKIN' JOHN BIRCH SOCIETY BLUES

Published lyric: Broadside #1; Writings and Drawings; Lyrics *1985*; Lyrics *2004*.
Known studio recordings: Studio A, NY, April 24, 1962 – 3 takes *[FR Mk.1]*.
First known performance: Carnegie Hall Hootenanny, New York, September 22, 1962.

The most significant song Dylan wrote in January 1962 would prove to be 'Talkin' John Birch,' simply because of its appearance in the first issue of a mimeographed magazine produced in New York by Gil Turner and 'Sis' Cunningham, concentrating on 'topical songs.' The goal of *Broadside* was to create the same kind of political ferment in folk circles that they fondly remembered from the forties. At the time, it was a goal the impressionable Minnesotan shared.

Written in the now-familiar talkin' blues idiom, the song picked on a tangible target, the John Birch Society, a right-wing organization that had supported McCarthy's modern-day witch hunt. The John Birchers were an easy target for potshots from a progressive pen, and Dylan didn't spare them, suggesting at one point, 'We all agree with Hitler's views / Though he killed six million Jews.' Fifteen months later this couplet would get the song yanked from his second album and get him yanked from the *Ed Sullivan Show*. That, though, was still a lifetime away. *Broadside* had no such concerns, and gave the song pride of place in its premier issue.

Dylan, however, did not live with the song long. It does not appear on any of the club tapes from 1962. But when the song was censored by the producer of the *Ed Sullivan Show* in May 1963, it became a one-song cause célèbre in folk circles, confirming the capricious nature of corporate America. Dylan thus felt obliged to champion the song in concert. For the next eighteen months it generated whoops of recognition. These latter-day variants tarred the censors with the same brush as 'the rest of the Birchnuts.' The verses also got a little slicker. The version Dylan gave Izzy Young to mimeograph in May 1963, as part of a protest of the banning of the song, concentrated more on the humour of a one-man 'commie' witch hunt and less on the organization, greatly improving at least that aspect:

> I looked high an' low, under the rug
> Looked in the ol' bathtub
> Looked in the cracks an' the radiator

Even inside the refrigerator.
You can't tell nowadays . . .

But the song was already a relic, and Dylan knew he'd gotta travel on.

{48} THE DEATH OF EMMETT TILL

Published lyric: Broadside #16; Writings and Drawings;
Lyrics *1985;*
Lyrics *2004.*
*First known performance: Cynthia Gooding's Folksingers Choice,
New York, February 11, 1962.*
*Known studio recordings: Studio A, NY 24/4/62 – 1 take;
Broadside session, June 1962 [BR].*

For the next eighteen months Dylan proved ever willing to cater to *Broadside's* ongoing demands for new songs in a 'topical vein,' the mimeographed zine receiving the first opportunity to publish such memorable Dylan originals as 'Blowin' in the Wind,' 'Masters of War,' and 'Ballad of Hollis Brown.' After he left the genre far behind, Dylan would go so far as to claim that he 'never wanted to write topical songs . . . [but] in the Village there was a little publication called *Broadside*, and with a topical song you could get in there. I wasn't getting far with the things I was doing . . . [and] *Broadside* gave me a start,' an outlandish distortion of the true position.

Yes, Dylan hitched his wagon to *Broadside* for a while, donating some eighteen hot-off-the-press songs in as many months. But it was never – as he later claimed – mere opportunism. It is hard to imagine "Sis" Cunningham having a greater effect on the man than his girlfriend at the time, Suze. And it was her stamp of approval he sought night and day. As he told Robert Shelton on a bone-weary flight to nowhere in March 1966: '[Suze]'ll tell you how many nights I stayed up and wrote songs and showed them to her and asked her, "Is this right?" Because I knew her father and mother were associated with unions and she was into this equality-freedom thing long before I was. I checked the songs out with her.'

'Emmett Till,' published by and subsequently recorded for *Broadside*, was the first such song from this protest pen. At the time that Dylan wrote his account of the murder of Emmett Till, he considered it the most important song he had ever written. After he talked about it to Izzy Young on February 1, 1962, the folklorist wrote down a shorthand account of their conversation for his journal: 'Wrote a song the other night – "Ballad of Emmett Till." After I wrote it someone said another song was written but not like it. I wrote it for CORE – I'm playing it February 23. I think it's the best thing I've ever written. Only song I play with a capo. Stole the melody from Len Chandler – a song he wrote about a Colorado bus driver.'

Two years later to the day, Dylan dismissed the song in scathing terms, calling it 'a bullshit song' and questioning his own motivation for writing it in the first place. In the hiatus between *Times . . .* and *Another Side*, no longer content to let Suze check songs out, he began to distance himself from the broadside ballads he'd written when words of righteous concern teemed out of him ('My Back Pages' was but a couple of months away):

I used to write bullshit songs. I went through a phase of writing bullshit songs about two and a half years ago. . . . I made this second record, then people wanted me to sing songs I wrote. I used to write songs, like I'd say, 'Yeah, what's bad, pick out something bad, like segregation, O.K., here we go' and I'd pick one of the thousand million little points I can pick and explode it, some of them which I didn't know about. I wrote a song about Emmett Till, which in all honesty was a bullshit song . . . but when I wrote it, it wasn't a bullshit song to me. But I realize now that my reasons and motives behind it were phony, I didn't have to write it; I was bothered by many other things that I pretended I wasn't bothered by, in order to write this song about Emmett Till, a person I never even knew. . . . . It was quick at hand, and knowing that people knew who Emmett Till was, I wrote the song.

'Emmett Till' delighted his highly impressionable lass, who was a part-time volunteer at the Campaign of Racial Equality (CORE) and had put his name down for their February 23 benefit. It was an ideal place to present another new Dylan, who was now responding to the call from 'people [who] wanted me to sing songs I wrote.' He later told Scott Cohen, 'I started writing because things were changing all the time and a certain song needed to be written. I started writing them because I wanted to sing them. . . . I stumbled into it, really.'

He didn't stumble for long. The new songs gave him a renewed sense of purpose, pouring out of him in the aftermath of 'Emmett Till.' As Suze recalls, 'He was very fast about his writing.' Such polemics certainly weren't cut from the same cloth as the songs penned the previous year. And he knew it. When he aired 'Emmett Till' for the first time on Cynthia Gooding's radio show, he informed his host, 'I don't claim to call [my songs] folk songs. I just call them contemporary songs. You know, there's a lot of people paint . . . if they've got something that they wanna say. . . . Well, I just write a song. It's the same thing.' The songs of a new Depression, it seemed, were gone for good.

Yet the events portrayed in this new ballad hardly qualified as *contemporary*. Notorious, yes; contemporary, no. Emmett Till had been murdered back in August 1955, ostensibly for whistling at a white woman. Two white men were later charged with his murder but were acquitted by an all-white jury. They subsequently owned up to the deed but could not be tried again under the 'double jeopardy' rule. So when Dylan refers in his song to the two brothers that 'confessed that they had killed poor Emmett Till . . . to stop the United States of yelling for a trial,' he shows himself to be hopelessly confused about the facts of the case (a pattern he would repeat on two more Southern murder ballads: 'Only a Pawn in Their Game' and 'The Lonesome Death of Hattie Carroll').

A long feature in the January 24, 1956, issue of *Look* magazine by William Bradford Huie told the story from the murderers' point of view, suggesting that Till actually touched the white woman, who was the wife and sister-in-law of the accused; that they only intended to frighten the boy; that he had ample opportunity to escape; and that it was his continuing insolence and repeated claims to have had white girlfriends that finally drove the brothers to silence him for good. Such motivations were simply disregarded by a Dylan bent on his own verbal execution. The couplet, 'They said that they had a reason / I disremember what' – the only line in the song in which the narrator addresses the listener directly – is an open admission that the facts of the case held zero interest for this zealot. This is a pattern Dylan was to repeat a number of times, while holding those interested in such 'detail' to ridicule. For the next eighteen months he would prefer 'lies that life is black and white,' even if the result was a 'bullshit song.'

{49} BALLAD OF DONALD WHITE

Published lyric: Sing Out! *October 1962;* Writings and Drawings; Lyrics *1985;* Lyrics *2004.*
First known performance: Cynthia Gooding's apartment, March 1962.
Known studio recordings: Broadside session, June 1962 [BR].

Having decided to address head-on the notion of selecting 'one of the thousand million little points I can pick and explod[ing] it,' Dylan waited barely a fortnight before exploding another. 'The Ballad of Donald White' again appropriated its tune and rudimentary template from a 'traditional' predecessor, in this case 'The Ballad of Peter Amberly,' a nineteenth-century ballad about the death of a Prince Edward Island lumberman. Penned by John Calhoun around 1880, the evocative 'Peter Amberly' had been covered by the likes of Paul Clayton and Sandy Ives. It was also part of Bonnie Dobson's repertoire circa February 1962, as she was making her Gerde's Folk City debut. Both Dylan and Gil Turner were there on opening night, and when the latter heard Dylan perform 'Donald White' later the same month, he knew right away where he had last heard that familiar refrain.

The story of Donald White was a lot more topical than Emmett Till's, having been inspired by a TV programme Dylan watched at his Fourth Street apartment with girlfriend Suze and their friend Sue Zuckerman. The show in question – a programme about crime and capital punishment called 'A Volcano Named White' – was broadcast on February 12. The twenty-four-year-old Donald White (who was, appropriately, black) was filmed on Death Row talking about how his cries for help were ignored until he finally went and killed someone, and now he was waiting to be executed. According to Zuckerman, 'Bobby just got up at some point and he went off in the corner and started to write. He just started to write, while the show was still on, and the next thing I knew he had this song written.'

Yet Dylan did not play the song to Izzy Young until March 14. I suspect Zuckerman overstates the case, and that it took him a while to get the song's lyrics – told in the first person, like 'Dope Fiend Robber' – sufficiently sanctimonious for his new set of friends. He told Gil Turner the song's seed had been planted some time earlier: 'I'd seen Donald White's name in a Seattle paper in about 1959. It said he was a killer. The next time I saw him was on a television set. . . . He murdered someone 'cause he couldn't find no room in life. Now they killed him 'cause he couldn't find no room in life. . . . When are some people gonna wake up and see that sometimes people aren't really their enemies, but their victims?' Though the song stayed in his set for a few months and was recorded for a *Broadside* radio show in June, Dylan didn't even *attempt* to foist it on Columbia. He knew he could do better.

{50} LET ME DIE IN MY FOOTSTEPS

Published lyric: Broadside #3; Writings and Drawings; Lyrics *1985;* Lyrics *2004.*

Known studio recordings: Studio A, NY, April 25, 1962 – 1 take [FR Mk.1] [TBS – tk.1].

First known performance: Finjan Club, Montreal, July 2, 1962.

Most Dylan chroniclers would probably designate 'Blowin' in the Wind,' written in April, as his first major composition. I would argue he reached his first real writing plateau a month before. In March 1962 he finally got a handle on what he wanted to say about 'the bomb,' composing the majestic 'Let Me Die in My Footsteps,' a.k.a. 'I Will Not Go Down Under the Ground.' At the time, he claimed it was an idea he had carried around in his head for quite some time, informing Izzy Young that he had originally 'wanted to write a song about 1½ years ago on fall-out shelters, to tune of "So Long, It's Been Good To Know You."' The now-lost 'Strange Rain' may have been another attempt at a 'bomb' song, but it took a little longer for Dylan to find the right way to proclaim the importance of 'learning to live, 'stead of learning to die.'

Though 'Let Me Die in My Footsteps' would also end up discarded – remaining officially unreleased (though widely bootlegged) until 1991 – Dylan knew it represented a real breakthrough. Forty-two years after its last performance, he described it in his memoir as 'a slightly ironic song . . . based [around] an old Roy Acuff ballad . . . [It] was inspired by the fall-out shelter craze that had blossomed out of the Cold War. . . . When I began performing [it], I didn't even say I wrote it. I just slipped it on somewhere, said it was a Weavers song.'

Actually, he was no longer remotely coy about the songs he was writing. On the verge of his majority, and a new-found maturity, he was especially proud of this one. Not only did he perform it for Izzy Young on March 19, but he also knew it would be perfect fodder for the magazine that Turner and Cunningham were struggling to keep going. It duly appeared in issue #3 under the title, 'I Will Not Go Down Underground.' The following month he cut the song at Columbia in a single take – usually a good sign – and set about assigning it pride of place on the album to come. In the fall, he talked about its composition at great length to sleeve-note scribe Nat Hentoff, again affirming that it was an idea he had carried around for some time:

['Let Me Die in My Footsteps'] has been on my mind for about two years. . . . I was going through some town . . . and they were making this bomb shelter right outside of town. . . . I was there for about an hour, just looking at them build and I guess I just wrote the song in my head back then, but I carried it with me for two years until I finally wrote it down. As I watched them building [the shelter], it struck me sort of funny that they would concentrate so much on digging a hole underground when there were so many other things they should do in life. If nothing else, they could look at the sky, and walk around and live a little bit instead of doing this immoral thing. I guess that . . . you can lead a lot of people by the hand. They don't even really know what they're scared of. I'd like to say that here is one song that I am really glad I made a record of. I don't consider anything that I write political. But . . . this is one song that people won't have to look at me or even listen closely or even like me, to understand.

Yet by December 1962, when he tried to tape it for his new music publisher, Witmark Music, he couldn't even make it through the whole song, stopping after a couple of verses and calling it 'a drag . . . I've sung it so many times.' The first flush of enthusiasm had evidently faded. Unsurprisingly, it became one of the songs pulled from the recalled version of *Freewheelin'* the following April.

{51} TALKIN' FOLKLORE CENTER

Published lyrics: Bob Dylan in His Own Words *(Omnibus Press, 1978);* Words Fill My Head.

First known performance: Gerde's Folk City, New York, April 1962.

Throughout the winter of 1962 Dylan made a regular habit of stopping by Izzy Young's Folklore Center to play the owner his latest bout of inspiration. During one such visit, on March 19, after hearing 'Let Me Die in My Footsteps,' Young convinced the boy wonder to pen a talkin' blues celebrating this inestimable Village institution. The result – which he signed on the original manuscript, 'Bob Dylan '62 of Gallup, Phillipsburg, Navasota Springs, Sioux Falls and Duluth' – was printed up and sold as the Center's very own broadside.

Though this was one talkin' blues intended for the printing press, rather than as a performance piece, Dylan integrated a chunk of it into a live performance of 'Talkin' New York' at Gerde's in April. Indeed the lyrics are in many ways an extension of that earlier talkin' blues, describing how he first found the Folklore Center: 'On MacDougal Street I saw a cubby hole / I went in to get out of the cold / Found out after I entered / The place was called the Folklore Center.' The kind of thing that Dylan could write in a coffee break, it was a therapeutic diversion from the real stuff . . .

{52} BLOWIN' IN THE WIND

Published lyrics: Broadside #6; Writings and Drawings; Lyrics 1985; Lyrics 2004.
First known performance: Gerde's Folk City, New York, April 1962.
Known studio recordings: Studio A, NY, July 9, 1962 – 3 takes [FR – tk.1]; Studio B, NY, June 30, 1970.

> Q: Where was Dylan's political strand lost?
> John Hammond: I think it was lost with 'Blowin' in the Wind,' and money, and being with Grossman. . . . He made Dylan a businessman. – *Fusion*, 1969

Dylan's third Gerde's residency, but first as a headliner, in April 1962, included the introduction of a song that would change his world – nay, *the* world – fusing much of what he'd been reaching for in his foundation year. At the time he wrote 'Blowin' in the Wind,' sometime during the second week in April, he was still considered by his contemporaries (and his record label) a performer first and a songwriter a distant second. Not surprisingly he was visibly excited by the experience of writing something that set folks thinking. Gil Turner recalls how Dylan 'came flying into Folk City where I was singing, [saying], "Gil, I got a new song I just finished. Wanna hear it?"'

The moment had such resonance that Dylan used it in his own 1977 film, *Renaldo and Clara*, where a brightly lit David Blue (*né* Cohen) relates the evening in question as he remembers it: '[After] Bob wrote "Blowin' in the Wind," he came over to Gerde's Folk City and played it for Gil Turner, who was scheduled to play that night. Turner thought it was incredible. Bob wrote the words and music down on a sheet of paper, and when Turner went on stage he taped the paper up on the microphone and played the song. Everybody was stunned. As far as I know that was the first time that song was ever played to an audience.' The songwriter had announced himself.

On those few occasions when he has ignored his own dictum – and looked back – Dylan has made it clear that 'Blowin' in the Wind' was one song that came very quickly. Conversing with Hilburn in 2004, he claimed he 'wrote "Blowin' in the Wind" in ten minutes, just put words to an old spiritual. . . . That's the folk music tradition. You use what's handed down.' Forty years earlier, talking to *Gargoyle*, he was only marginally more modest, claiming he 'wrote [it] in twenty minutes . . . in the Black Pussycat, down on MacDougal Street. I just wrote it just like that.'

As with all things Dylan, the truth is not so simple. Yes, he wrote the song most hurriedly. But on that first occasion – and for a couple of weeks more – the song had just two verses, the first and the third. Indeed, it was like this when he performed it at a (taped) Gerde's performance in mid-April, which he prefaced with the statement, 'This here ain't a protest song or anything like that, 'cause I don't write protest songs. . . . I'm just writing it as something to be said, for somebody, by somebody.'

Why so defensive all of a sudden? One can only presume that the song was already being misinterpreted and misrepresented, in roughly equal measures, within *days* of its composition. For the first time the young Dylan was having to provide himself with some artistic elbow room. At the same time, he remained positively effusive about the song and its theme/s to Gil Turner, the man who actually performed it first. When his friend was preparing a *Sing Out!* profile (and cover story) that summer, Dylan genuinely tried to explain what inspired him to write it:

> There ain't too much I can say about this song except that the answer is blowing in the wind. It ain't in no book or movie or TV show or discussion group. Man, it's in the wind – and it's blowing in the wind. Too many of these hip people are telling me where the answer is but oh I won't believe that. I still say it's in the wind and just like a restless piece of paper it's got to come down some time. . . . But the only trouble is that no one picks up the answer when it comes down so not too many people get to see and know it . . . and then it flies away again. . . . I still say that some of the biggest criminals are those that turn their heads away when they see wrong and know it's wrong. I'm only 21 years old and I know that there's been too many wars. . . . You people over 21 should know better . . . 'cause after all, you're older and smarter.

Though he had already debuted it, he didn't feel he had reached that finishing end. An extra verse, written by early May, was presumably composed after two days at Studio A (on April 24–5), given that he did not even attempt a single studio take of the song that would make his name (and make Albert Grossman rich). It was to the likes of 'Ramblin' Gamblin' Willie,' 'Talkin' John Birch,' 'Emmett Till,' and 'Let Me Die in My Footsteps' that he turned his mind when John Hammond rolled tape.

Unfortunately, whatever inspirational zone Dylan found at the Black Pussycat earlier in April had now deserted him. All the portentous talk about the song's meaning seems to have had a detrimental effect on the boy writer, convincing him to give folk the surface-level profundity they sought, devising a trio of platitudes regarding the number of times one must look up in order to see the sky, the number of ears required to 'hear people cry,' and finally how many deaths it takes to get a rhyme for *sky* and *cry*. For an inspirational lyricist like Dylan, this was an important lesson – one reiterated in later years, notably to *Rolling Stone*'s nervous young editor Jann Wenner: 'I try to write the song when it comes. I try to get it all . . . 'cause if you don't get it all, you're not gonna get it.'

He wasn't even sure where this new verse went, initially placing it last – which was how it appeared in *Broadside* #6 at the end of May. But Dylan quickly realized it lacked the power the other two held and moved it mid-song, where it could do the least harm. The handwritten version of the song included in *The Bob Dylan Scrapbook* – probably from the Cunningham archive – has a long, looping arrow moving the verse to its final resting place (this manuscript, a copy of the finished song in Dylan's handwriting, was written at least a month after the song's original composition, making it a lot less interesting than a fragment that he dated and signed April 12, quite possibly its composition date).

For now, Dylan didn't seem to know what to do with the song, save record it for his label, which he did across three takes in July. If he really didn't want the song to be considered a topical song, then giving it to *Broadside* wasn't the wisest decision (it also allowed a student named Lorre Wyatt to learn the song early enough to claim to friends he wrote it and sold it to Dylan – a lie *Newsweek* dredged up in an infamous October 1963 'hatchet' piece). He soon tired of trying to explain this 'feeling' without a name. Yes, it could be interpreted any which way, but at its nub was a sense that any purpose and/or answer would remain ever out of reach.

As he told one Canadian journalist at the time, 'I'm not politically inclined. My talent isn't in that area; it's just to play music. As it is, it falls into areas where people are politically motivated. . . . "Blowin' in the Wind" was just a feeling I felt because I felt that way.' Sixteen years later, when the pan-dimensional beings in Douglas Adams's *Hitchhiker's Guide to the Galaxy* had to concoct the ultimate question, they actually came up with, 'How many roads must a man walk down?'

Only later did Dylan come to view 'Blowin' in the Wind' to 'Every Grain of Sand' as an eighteen-year journey from yearning to redemption. As such it is entirely fitting that the song sprang from a spiritual, as he informed Marc Rowland in 1978, a matter of months before Christ entered his life: '"Blowin' in the Wind" has always been a spiritual. I took it off a song . . . called "No More Auction Block." . . . "Blowin' in the Wind" follows the same feeling. . . . I just did it on my acoustical guitar when I recorded it – which didn't really make it sound spiritual – but the feeling, the idea . . . that's where it was coming from.'

What prompted him to talk in these terms was a grandiose new arrangement of the song he was performing nightly. When he worked up this big-band version for the very first time at the January 1978 Rundown rehearsals – though only after a particularly painful reggae version was thankfully abandoned – he turned to the girls and said, 'Like a church choir.' It stayed this way through 1981, at which point Dylan gave the first verse over to the girl singers entirely.

It is not mere happenstance that prompted Dylan to adopt the antislavery song 'No More Auction Block' (a.k.a. 'Many Thousand Gone') as his template for 'Blowin' in the Wind.' The original song, composed by runaway slaves who fled to Nova Scotia in the early nineteenth century – after Britain had abolished slavery in all its colonies – was passed on to Negro Union soldiers during the Civil War. The traditional song drives home its point without hectoring its audience; it simply juxtaposes new-found freedoms – 'No more driver's lash for me . . . No more mistress' call' – with a powerful lament for the 'many thousand gone,' i.e., those who died in slavery.

'Blowin' in the Wind' expresses a similar disquiet with the order of things, but on a grander canvas. Unfortunately, when the Peter, Paul, and Mary version rose to the top of the charts in the summer of 1963, it began to tear apart its author's cozy world. Dylan soon began to be pestered by those who thought that anyone asking such questions had answers. Having previously performed the still-unreleased song at the Town Hall show in April 1963 – where it barely drew a smattering of recognition – six months later, now at Carnegie Hall, he felt obliged to preface the performance with a long, anti-intellectual monologue, dissecting the first verse of the song line by line, then asking a hypothetical teacher perplexed by the song's meaning if he understands each line as it stands. The teacher replied that he understood each line, just not the whole song. Dylan then informed the audience, 'And this man has a degree!'

Unsure how he should respond to those who saw confusion in the song's oblique message, Dylan stopped talking about the song, and then stopped playing it altogether. Gone by his next New York showpiece, he only returned to it in 1971, responding to a personal request from George Harrison by playing it at the two concerts for Bangladesh. But he remained reluctant to invest it with any of himself. It took until June 28, 1984, playing to many thousand rabid Spaniards at a show in Barcelona, for him to finally understand the universality of its appeal. As the Iberians began to sing along with him word for word, a galvanized Dylan rose to the occasion, delivering the remainder of the song with the passion of a complete unknown, introducing it to those twenty hardy souls at Gerde's for the very first time.

{53} **CORRINA, CORRINA**

{54} **HONEY, JUST ALLOW ME ONE MORE CHANCE**

#53–4 – Published lyrics: Writings and Drawings; Lyrics *1985;* Lyrics *2004.*

First known performance: Gerde's Folk City, New York, April 1962.

#55 – Published lyrics: Bob Dylan Himself *songbook.*

First known performance: Cynthia Gooding's apartment, April 1962.

#53 – Known studio recordings: Studio A, NY, April 24, 1962 – 2 takes; October 26, 1962 – 7 takes [FR – tk.6].

#54 – Known studio recordings: Studio A, NY, July 9, 1962 – 1 take [FR – tk.1].

#55 – Known studio recordings: Studio A, NY, April 25, 1962 – 3 takes; November 1, 1962 – 2 takes [FR Mk.1].

While starting to transcend Guthrie's influence on songs like 'Let Me Die in My Footsteps' and 'Blowin' in the Wind,' Dylan was still content to pay his dues when it came to the blues. Save when he immersed himself in those caffeine-fueled writing sessions in the bars and coffee houses, it was to the blues greats that he liked to defer. Along with Robert Johnson, who continued to shape his universe, he now embraced the likes of Leroy Carr, Skip James, Big Joe Williams (with whom he recorded that March), Lonnie Johnson, and Henry Thomas, willing himself to become their heir apparent.

Of these mostly mythical figures, only Williams and Lonnie Johnson were able to make their influence felt in person. It may well have been Williams who had shown him the blistering bottleneck arrangement of 'Baby Please Don't Go' with which he wowed his Minnesota friends the previous December (but which he failed to rekindle for Columbia four months later). And according to Dylan, in both *Biograph* and *Chronicles,* Lonnie Johnson had an equally profound effect: 'He greatly influenced me. You can hear it in that first record – I mean "Corrina, Corrina."'

The pair chanced to meet at Gerde's, where they were both working in September 1961. Johnson, booked at the club for a fortnight-long residency immediately preceding Dylan's second residency, was a highly accomplished jazz-blues guitarist who had been making records since 1925, scoring his biggest hit with the standard 'Tomorrow Night' (respectfully covered by Dylan on 1992's *Good As I Been to You*). Yet it was not so much the sound he got from a twelve-string acoustic as that loping 12/8 metre that Dylan seems to have applied to his own version of 'Corrina, Corrina.'

As to his source for the song itself, the traditional 'Corrina' had been recorded by the Mississippi Sheiks' Bo Carter as early as 1926 (Dylan's lifelong fascination with the Sheiks probably began when Big Joe Williams introduced him to 'Sitting on Top of the World' in the winter of 1962). 'Corrina' also appears in Alan Lomax's *Folk Songs of North America* (1960), a tome Dylan had been steadily working his way through since finding a copy at the MacKenzies' in the spring of 1961.* Also recorded at the same April 1962 Columbia session was his version of 'Milk Cow Blues,' with one verse from 'Good Morning Blues,' the entry before 'Corrina' in Lomax's vast compendium.

Lomax himself described 'Corrina' as 'a tender little blues with a touch of jazz and a flavour of hillbilly . . . [which] has been so often resung by white and negroes in the south that it is now impossible to say on which side of the Jim Crow line it was born.' In Dylan's hands it crossed the line again, befitting its status as one of the more successful 'Bob Dylan blues.' Lyrically, the influence of the *other* Johnson drips from every line. The second verse as recorded ('I

---

* Among the MacKenzie papers are a list of numbers, in Dylan's hand, which turn out to be references to specific songs in Lomax's *Folk Songs of North America*, so we can be sure Dylan was referring to this book on a regular basis even then.

got a bird that whistles . . .') has been lifted whole from 'Stones in My Passway,' while in its earliest incarnation, at Gerde's in April, Dylan also appropriated lines and verses from 'Hellhound on My Trail,' 'Me and the Devil Blues,' and '32.20 Blues,' making it a one-song tribute to this king without a crown.

'Rocks and Gravel' was another quasi-traditional 'original' debuted at that Gerde's residency, as Dylan was preparing for make-or-break sessions at Columbia. Recorded in acoustic and electric incarnations for *Freewheelin'*, it remained part of Dylan's set for the remainder of the year, before being copyrighted to him in February 1963. It appeared in numerous early songbooks (but not *Writings and Drawings*). Like 'Corrina, Corrina,' it demonstrated that Dylan could take a traditional blues – in this case 'Solid Road,' another song collected by the Lomaxes – and tie together a fleet of floating verses with enough wit to make it his own. Though he would subsequently transpose the most famous verse in 'Rocks and Gravel' to 'It Takes a Lot to Laugh,' it was never one of his own, 'originating' in Leroy Carr's 'Alabama Woman Blues':

> Don't the clouds look lonesome across the deep blue sea,
> Don't my gal look good when she's coming after me.

In the months to come, presumably in response to Grossman's importunities, Dylan became less and less coy about copyrighting songs he had merely tweaked. Yet on the one song in which he created something almost entirely his own, he gave co-credit to its originator, Henry Thomas – at least initially.* 'Honey Won't You Allow Me One More Chance' may have formed the basis for Dylan's 'Honey Just

---

* Though 'Honey Just Allow Me One More Chance' was credited to Dylan-Thomas on the original LP, the lyrics in *Writings and Drawings* (and both editions of *Lyrics*) are attributed to Dylan alone.

Allow Me One More Chance,' but it is only the refrain that Dylan purloined from Thomas's 1927 original. As Todd Harvey has written, 'Dylan wrote, for the most part, new text . . . increased Thomas's tempo and added his own guitar accompaniment, placing harmonica solos between verses.' Quite a change.

Even among Dylan's Village buddies, few would have known Henry Thomas's original or his work, save for his memorable contribution ('Fishing Blues') to Harry Smith's bootleg boxed set, the *Anthology of American Folk Music*. 'Honey Won't You Allow Me One More Chance' – originally issued on an ultra-rare Vocalion 78 – was not reissued until 1961, and then only on a limited-edition LP, *Henry Thomas Sings the Texas Blues*. Perhaps the sheer obscurity of Thomas's work prompted Dylan to co-credit him on *Freewheelin'*. After all, the long dead Texas singer was not about to come knocking for his cut of any royalties.

Although Dylan did not get around to recording Thomas's song until July, it featured in the same April Gerde's set as 'Corrina, Corrina.' And like the latter, it was clearly a song he was working out in performance. In April he was looking for 'someone who will understand.' By July she was 'a worried woman / [who] needs a worried man.' The song continued to serve as light relief in concert into 1963 (and maybe 1964, if it was played at the Royal Festival Hall), only to be unexpectedly revised and re-recorded at a joint session with George Harrison in May 1970, while Dylan was running through all the Henry Thomas songs he knew.

{56} QUIT YOUR LOWDOWN WAYS

First known performance: Finjan Club, Montreal, July 2, 1962.

{57} BABE, I'M IN THE MOOD FOR YOU

{58} DOWN THE HIGHWAY

#56–9 – Published lyrics: Writings and Drawings; Lyrics *1985;* Lyrics *2004.*

#56–9 – Known studio recordings: Studio A, NY, July 9, 1962.

#56 – 1 take [TBS – tk.1]; #57 – 4 takes [BIO – tk.3]; #58 – 1 take [FR – tk.1]; #59 – 3 takes [FR – tk.1].

'Quit Your Lowdown Ways' demonstrates the increasing sophistication with which Dylan was concocting his own stew from the melting pot of tradition. On the face of it, it is little more than a clever reworking of bluesman Kokomo Arnold's 'Milk Cow Blues' ('You can read out your Bible / You can fall down on your knees / Pretty mama and pray to the Lord / Ain't gonna do you no good' is a direct lift), a song he had recorded back in April, in the vein of Robert Johnson's remake. In fact, Dylan took the underlying idea from a Negro spiritual, 'Your Low Down Ways' ('God's goin' to get you 'bout your lowdown ways'), crossing it with Arnold, Johnson, and even a bit of Elvis. Finally he takes a whiff of Blind Willie Johnson's 'You're Gonna Need Somebody on Your Bond,' adding an exuberant performance that succeeds in making the song his own.

'Babe, I'm in the Mood for You' is an early example of a Dylan come-on song. He will make a number of forays into similar territory with the likes of 'I Don't Believe You,' 'If You Gotta Go, Go Now,' 'Love Is Just a Four-Letter Word,' 'Lay, Lady, Lay,' and 'Rita Mae.' It is a slightly frenzied performance, distilling a number of verbal come-ons down to a two-minute-something song that captures the knee-pumping hyperactivity of the man. In the *Biograph* notes Dylan suggests it was 'probably influenced by Jesse Fuller . . . more 'n' likely my version of his thing.' If so it was Fuller's style, not a specific song, he was emulating, also adding elements of the incendiary version of 'Baby, Please Don't Go' he was performing at the time. In fact, in a letter written to absent muse Suze in the same month he recorded it, he says the song 'is for you but I don't mention your name.'

'Down the Highway' is a real oddity. This one he tells Suze she is 'in' (along with another now-lost song 'about that statue we saw in Washington of Tom Jefferson'). It would survive every vagary of the convoluted process by which Dylan eventually arrived at his second album, though there is no record of him ever performing the song live (unlike songs 53–7) or returning to the song at demo sessions or informal jams during the six months he spent awaiting the return of the lover who'd taken his heart in a suitcase. Perhaps it made the album *because* it was addressed to this lady, who returned to his side just in time to shoot the album cover.

For the second time Dylan was attempting to write some-thing as archetypal as 'Crossroads Blues.' But while 'Down the Highway' is superior to 'Standing on the Highway,' Robert Johnson it is not. Not only did Dylan not live with the song in performance, he barely dallied with it in the studio, executing the album version in a single take. The next song written to his long-distance lover is of an entirely different calibre. And a whole lot more personal.

{60} TOMORROW IS A LONG TIME

Published lyrics: Writings and Drawings; Lyrics *1985;* Lyrics *2004.*
First known performance: [Tony Glover's, Minneapolis, August 11, 1962]. Town Hall, NY, April 12, 1963 [MGH].
Known studio recordings: Witmark demo, November 1962.

The starting point within tradition for 'Tomorrow Is a Long Time – which Dylan shared with his Minnesota friends at an informal jam session at Tony Glover's home in August 1962, when it was little more than a raw idea – proves to be the starting point for pretty much *all* Anglo-American folk music. 'Westron wind,' a fifteenth-century relic from oral tradition, comprises just an aching melody and four lines, yet nonetheless manages to encompass a whole world of pain:

> O westron wynde when wyll thow blow
> The smalle rayne downe can rayne
> Cryst yf my love wer in my armys
> and I yn my bed agayne.

Dylan redrafts lines 3–4 as 'Only if she was lying by me / Then I'd lie in my bed once again' and takes it from there. For the heartbroken lad from Hibbing, a world of 'endless highways' and 'crooked trails' separates him and his true love. And so, while heading down the highway to his North Country home to escape the bed they had shared and the haunted memories it brought, he began to write this song. The August recording by Tony Glover – which Dylan prefaces by saying, 'My girl, she's in Europe right now. She sailed on a boat over there. She'll be back September 1, and till she's back, I'll never go home' – is just the bare bones of the song, conveying little save the feeling Dylan is hoping to translate. Those feelings he communicated to Suze in letter form – 'It's just that I'm hating time – I'm trying to . . . bend it and twist it with gritting teeth and burning eyes – I hate it I love you,' – but not with anything like the despair in his voice the day he played this song to his old friends.

Perhaps if she had been privy to this recording, Suze might indeed have returned around Labor Day as she had planned. Instead, she phoned to inform him that she had decided to stay on in Italy to work on her art. He had no choice but to return to his Fourth Street apartment, where he finished this song of inconsolable loss. At this point he turned up at the Van Ronks' Village apartment, knowing that Terri and Dave would not turn him away, or stop him from playing the same song over and over again. As Terri told Scaduto, 'He used to play . . . the one about him wishing he could lie next to her again *all the time*.' (my italics)

As the September deadline passed, he began to play around town again, reworking heartbreaking ballads like 'Barbara Allen' and bruised blues about capricious females like 'Kind Hearted Woman.' But 'Tomorrow Is a Long Time' was left for moments of quiet reflection. He even overlooked the song when imposing his blues persona on Columbia tape at several sessions in November and December. And it is almost an afterthought when he agrees to demo it for his music publisher, Witmark. Yet as soon as he began the song, the emotion he'd been bottling up for months came flooding out, Dylan proceeding to deliver the single most powerful performance on the entire set of Witmark demos.

Upon the return of Suze the following January, one might have expected Dylan to drop the song entirely. But he performed a surprise version on Skip Weshner's radio show some time that winter, and then made it a part of the Town Hall showpiece in April. There had apparently been a row between the reconciled lovers beforehand, so he could have been trying to contritely convey how lost he'd been without her. One wonders if Suze was actually hearing the song for the very first time. The fact that Dylan included this version on a second collection of greatest hits in 1971 suggests some personal significance to the performance.

Yet he still refrained from capturing the song's quixotic essence in the confines of Studio A, even when he was obliged to tape more selections for *Freewheelin'* the week after the showpiece. By August, when he started work on his third album, the song had been quietly forgotten. By him. But that magnetic Witmark recording would result in the song being covered by the likes of Ian and Sylvia, Harry Belafonte, and Odetta in the next eighteen months, even as

Dylan was dismissing the song during a long interview in Toronto in early February 1964:

> I've only written one song, to my mind, that I don't believe in, one song that puts me uptight and gets me embarrassed when I hear it. . . . There are just a few lines in it that aren't really true. . . . I'm only speaking of one verse in the song, and the song is 'If Today Were Not a Crooked Highway.' It's a beautiful song, the only verse I can't make in it is the last verse that goes: 'There's beauty in the silver singing river / There's beauty in the rainbow in the skies / But of these nothing else can match / The beauty I remember in my true love's eyes.' It's pillow-soft, it's not me. . . . I don't think that way, that way has been spoken for a million times. . . . The second verse is my words, and the first verse is my words.

Such sustained analysis of his own work is a rare bird indeed, though one would have to say he is spot-on. The lyrics he quotes *are* 'pillow-soft,' and as such the antithesis of everything he'd written to date. However heartfelt those first two verses may be, the song, like 'Blowin' in the Wind' before it, struggles to resolve itself; which is perhaps why it was ultimately passed over in favour of the more acerbic 'Don't Think Twice, It's Alright.'

Thankfully, that magical publishing demo and the early cover versions above ensured the song would live on, ultimately inspiring some of the greatest performers of the rock era – Sandy Denny, Rod Stewart, and Elvis Presley – to tackle its tender underside. By the time Elvis cut the song in just two takes for 1966's *Spinout*, Dylan was caught up in a different kind of storm. But when *Rolling Stone* editor Jann Wenner inquired, in 1969, as to his favourite cover of one of his songs, he singled out Elvis's version of this.

And whatever his misgivings about that third verse,

Dylan never rewrote it. Even when he finally got around to recording the song properly, cutting a Presley-esque rendition at the June 1970 *New Morning* sessions. In the end, he again decided not to include the track on the released album – perhaps because it suggested that he lacked enough songs to make a wholly new album. But the song was never far from his mind, and when it came time to compile another greatest hits collection the following summer, he chose that in-the-moment rendition to the Town Hall throng, placing it alongside 'When I Paint My Masterpiece.'

Nor was this the last such demonstration of a songwriter more sensitive than soft. The song he dismissed as 'pillow-soft' in 1964 retained a firm hold on the man's psyche, appearing when he was most troubled by 'witchy women,' as in 1978 when it made its electric debut; and in 1987, when a lovely piano-guitar arrangement was a nightly highlight of the European tour. Rare Never Ending Tour incarnations have generally reverted to an acoustic guise – once, spellbindingly, as a request at a 1990 show in Toronto. He replied, 'It sure is. Awfully long,' and began to revisit some thirty-year-old feelings in song.

Note: The second line of the demo, 'If tonight I could finally stand tall,' is omitted from all subsequent performances. The published lyrics are not taken from the demo but from the version performed at Town Hall and released on *Greatest Hits Vol. II*.

{61} AIN'T GONNA GRIEVE

Published lyrics: Broadside #11–12; Writings and Drawings; Lyrics 1985; Lyrics 2004.

Known studio recording/s: Witmark demo, August 1963.

{62} LONG AGO, FAR AWAY

Published lyrics: Writings and Drawings; Lyrics 1985; Lyrics 2004.

First known performance: [Tony Glover's, Minneapolis, August 11, 1962].

Known studio recordings: Witmark demo, November 1962.

Though Dylan had been drawing another kind of inspiration from spiritual fare since his college days in Minneapolis – when he adapted 'Sinner Man' and 'Every Time I Feel the Spirit' – it took until 1997 for him to articulate what he generally found there in an interview: 'I find the religiosity and philosophy in the music. I don't find it anywhere else. Songs like "Let Me Rest on a Peaceful Mountain" or "I Saw the Light" – that's my religion. . . . The songs are my lexicon. I believe the songs.'

After performing fire 'n' brimstone renditions of 'Gospel Plow' and 'Wade in the Water' in December 1961, he temporarily halted his exploration of the genre. But 'Quit Your Lowdown Ways' got him back in the mood, though, and 'Ain't Gonna Grieve,' composed during the same summer, was the first time he turned a spiritual into an out-and-out civil rights anthem, the chorus of Dylan's song being a revivalist revamp of 'Ain't Gonna Grieve My Lord No More.' Rather than outlining the many ways 'you can't get to heaven,' as the original did, Dylan exhorts everyone 'brown and blue and white and black' to 'raise the roof until the house falls in' – an early demonstration of the way he transposed revolution from songs of redemption. 'Ain't Gonna Grieve' would appear in *Broadside* 11–12, for which it was almost certainly written, before being demo-ed for Witmark. But it was never earmarked for Columbia.

'Long Ago, Far Away' also sees him questioning modern humanity's moral compass. Like 'Blowin' in the Wind,' it hangs upon a rhetorical question. After listing some atrocious things that happened 'long ago, far away,' he wonders aloud whether 'things like that . . . happen nowadays.' Dylan also demonstrates an early fascination with Christ, talking of a man who 'preached brotherhood / Oh, what might be the cost?' His answer: 'They hung him on a cross.' For now, though, He would remain in Dylan's mind 'some dead man who had a bunch of good ideas, and was nailed to a tree.'

Note: The version of 'Ain't Gonna Grieve' published in *Broadside* in August 1962 and excerpted in *Sing Out!* in October contains a fifth verse, which is absent from the version later printed in *Writings and Drawings*, as follows:

> There's a time to plant and a time to plow
> Time to stand and a time to bow
> There's a time to grieve, but that ain't now
> I ain't gonna grieve no more.

{63} LONG TIME GONE

Published lyrics: Writings and Drawings; Lyrics 1985; Lyrics 2004.
First known performance: [*Tony Glover's, Minneapolis, August 11, 1962*].
Known studio recordings: Witmark demo, November 1962.

Of a slightly higher calibre than most other songs demo-ed for Witmark, 'Long Time Gone' suffered a similar fate – dispensed by Dylan to the dark halls of song-publishing even as he was recording the likes of 'Mixed Up Confusion' and 'Whatcha Gonna Do' for his record label. There is something both affecting and affected about a twenty-one-year-old almost celebrating his own devil-may-care approach to death and decay:

> You can have your youth, it'll rot before your eyes
> You can have your beauty, it's only skin deep and it lies
> Just give to me a tombstone with it clearly marked upon
> I'm a long time coming and I'll be a long time gone.

'Long Time Gone' is the song of a man who yearns to see the world through world-weary eyes, like the bluesmen he so admired. Something of a minor gem.

{64} TALKIN' HYPOCRITE

First known performance: [Tony Glover's, Minneapolis, August 11, 1962].

'Talkin Hypocrite' continues to be something of a mystery. We are reliant on a single description of the song from that unreliable chronicler, Robert Shelton, Tony Glover having been more successful sitting on his last two Dylan home tapes (August 1962 and July 1963) than his first two (May and December 1961). According to Shelton the song asks, 'What kind of a hippo is a hypocrite?' which does rather suggest that this was another talkin' blues Dylan conceived as a passing whim, while on the way to something better.

{65} GATES OF HATE
{66} THAT CALIFORNIA SIDE

Both songs have survived only on paper and each only as a single verse, but they appear to date from the summer of 1962.
#65 published in Sing Out! *Oct./Nov. 1962.*
#66 published in Isis *#28.*

Here are two more lost songs written within weeks of a WBAI radio interview with Pete Seeger, in which Dylan claimed he wrote songs before breakfast. 'Gates of Hate' is mentioned (and quoted) in Gil Turner's *Sing Out!* profile, whereas 'That California Side' was written on a scrap of paper – the other side of a shop receipt dated June 22, 1962. 'That California Side' contrasts the joys of California with the East Coast, a subject he would tackle again on 'California' (cut at the first *Bringing It* . . . session in January 1965 and frequently bootlegged). Dylan's repeated crossings-out suggest a general dissatisfaction with where the song is going, and it probably died there and then, as he sat in a cafe scribbling to his heart's content.

On the other hand, 'Gates of Hate' probably *was* finished, though all that is known of it derives from Gil Turner's *Sing*

Out! feature. According to Turner the song was about John Henry Faulk, who was then married to folksinger Hedy West. On June 28, 1962, Faulk had been awarded $3.5 million in damages in a libel suit against AWARE, a 'clearance' service that vetted people in the entertainment industry for any left-wing inclinations or Communist affiliations. The chorus of the song, quoted in Turner's piece, suggests Dylan was closing in on 'Masters of War':

> Go down, go down you gates of hate,
> You gates that keep men in chains,
> Go down and die the lowest death,
> And never rise again.

It also suggests a likely source for any tune, Ewan MacColl's 'Go Down You Murderers' – a favourite as far back as his student days in St. Paul.

{67} A HARD RAIN'S A-GONNA FALL

Published lyrics: Sing Out! *December 1962;* Writings and Drawings; Lyrics *1985;* Lyrics *2004.*
First known performance: Carnegie Hall, New York, September 22, 1962.
Known studio recordings: Studio A, NY, December 6, 1962 – 1 take [FR – tk.1].

I wrote it at the time of the Cuban crisis [*sic*]. I was in Bleecker Street in New York. We just hung around at night – people sat around wondering if it was the end, and so did I. Would one o'clock the next day ever come? . . . It was a song of desperation. What could we do? Could we control men on the verge of wiping us out? The words came fast, very fast. It was a song of terror. Line after line after line, trying to capture the feeling of nothingness. – Bob Dylan, 1965

My seemingly original observation, made back in 1991, that Dylan clearly wrote this song *before* the so-called Cuban Missile Crisis – adopted uncredited by certain American writers – has now become common enough knowledge for Dylan to observe in a recent interview: 'Someone pointed out it was written before the missile crisis, but it doesn't really matter where a song comes from. It just matters where it takes you.' And this from a man who spends most of his *Theme Hour* radio show reciting the history of songs, and singers, he is about to play.

As he knows rather well, it matters a great deal 'where a song comes from'; especially when the song *seemingly* comes from nowhere. Because nothing in Dylan's canon leads up to this example of wild mercury poetry. It is so unexpected that it takes its author another eighteen months before he mines the same rich vein of poetry again. The main question arising is, Where had Dylan been hiding all this *erudition*? With 'Hard Rain' he abandoned any pretence that he was just a worried man with a worried mind and grabbed hold of a word that has haunted him ever since – 'poet.' Given that he here imagines the fate of such a man is to die 'in the gutter,' he was probably right to shy away from the word.

We have Dylan's biographical word – given shortly before he revisited 'Hard Rain' at 1971's Concert for Bangladesh – that he wrote 'Hard Rain' 'at the bottom of the Village Gate, in Chip Monck's place. It was his apartment, a real cruddy basement apartment but it had wall-to-wall carpeting and the carpeting even ran up the walls.' He has been flatly contradicted by Tom Paxton, who informed Robbie Woliver that 'there was a hide-out room above The Gaslight where we could hang out. Once Dylan was banging out this long poem on Wavy Gravy's typewriter. He showed me the poem and I asked, "Is this a song?" He said, "No, it's a poem." I said, "All this work and you're not going to add a melody?"'

In a 1993 interview, Wavy confirmed the essential reliability of Paxton's account: 'Dylan wrote the words to "A Hard Rain's A Gonna Fall" on my typewriter. A lot of Bob's early stuff would start with him singing and strumming upstairs [in my room] at the Gaslight, then running downstairs and doing it on stage.' Incredible as it may seem, Paxton also appears to be sound in asserting that the song began life as a *poem* on the page. Talking to *Melody Maker*'s Max Jones in May 1964 – sufficiently close to its composition to not be shrouded by the myth – Dylan suggested that 'Hard Rain' was not the first or the last time he adopted such a technique: 'I've written a lot of things with no structure. . . . I wrote the words of ['Hard Rain'] on a piece of paper. But there was just no tune that really fit to it.'

Another of Dylan's friends, John Cohen, told him in 1968 that the first time he read the lyrics, he couldn't see how it *could* be sung. According to this dialogue:

John Cohen: I had just come back from Kentucky and you showed me 'Hard Rain,' at Gerde's or upstairs from the Gaslight. . . .

Bob Dylan: I believe at the time you were wondering how it fit into music. How I was going to sing it.

John Cohen: That was my initial reaction. . . . The question I asked you on seeing this stream of words was, if you were going to write things like that, then why do you need Woody Guthrie? How about Rimbaud?

The only other known instance of something similar was when Dylan read out the lyrics to 'Isis' – which he'd just completed with songwriter Jacques Levy's help – at the Other End one night in July 1975. And yet the whole structure of 'Hard Rain,' as has often been observed, is clearly based on a very specific song, Child Ballad #12, 'Lord Randall,' in which a lord returning home finds he has been poisoned by a lover/ stepmother/witch (take your pick). As he is asked where he's been, what he ate, and the like, it becomes clear that he is done for, though generally for reasons left unexplained.

The same balladic convention – the pregnant question succeeded by a cascade of unhelpful responses – served other hoary ballads, like 'Edward' and 'The Cruel Brother.' In each instance, after some terrible crime is revealed (generally incest or patricide), the son tells his mother what he is going to do now – usually leave and never return. Though this is exactly what Dylan does at the end of 'Hard Rain,' it is not a feature of 'Lord Randall,' unless it has somehow comingled with 'The Cruel Brother.' And, as Harvey points out, 'It would be consistent with Dylan's [early] compositional process that he [borrowed] melodically as well as lyrically' from 'Lord Randall.' But in this instance he does not.

Dylan was now drawing on an entire *language* of song. As he told *Gargoyle* magazine less than eighteen months later, 'From folksongs, I learned the *language* [my italics] . . . by singing them and knowing them and remembering them. . . . You have to use [folk music] to learn about you, and whatever you want to do. English ballads, Scottish ballads, I see them in images . . . it goes deeper than just myself singing it.'

The sturdy, balladic framework here allows Dylan to encapsulate all he wants to say using the broadest of canvases, even if the imagery of 'Hard Rain' more closely resembles a *ballade* Dante might have written than any anonymous 'knitter i' the sun.' Even its ostensible song structure cannot hold him. The five verses are irregular in length and number of line breaks (totaling five, seven, eight/ nine, six, and twelve respectively). The third verse soon lost one of its better lines – 'I heard the sound of one person who cried he was human' – in order to provide an element of structural consistency.

The rapt way audiences hung on every word of this audacious work also taught Dylan that a song need not be short to hold people's attention. And, as he reveals in *Chronicles*, the epic ballads had shown him the way: 'A lot of the songs I was singing were indeed long . . . at least lyrically. "Tom Joad" had at least sixteen verses, "Barbara Allen" about twenty. "Fair Ellender," "Lord Lovell," "Little Mattie Groves" and others had numerous verses. . . . I had broken myself of the habit of thinking in short song cycles and began reading longer and longer poems. . . . I began cramming my brain with all kinds of deep poems.'

And, boy, does it show in 'Hard Rain.' Here was a song that needed every one of its seven minutes to tell its unrelenting tale, even if Dylan took at least one former standard-bearer by surprise when he chose a multiartist bill at Carnegie Hall on September 22 to debut it. As Pete Seeger recalls, 'Once again they had too many people on the program and I had to announce to all the singers, "Folks, you're gonna be limited to three songs. No more. 'Cause we each have ten minutes apiece." . . . Bob raised his hand and said, "What am I supposed to do? One of my songs is ten minutes long."'

What separates 'Hard Rain' from the likes of 'Barbara Allen' – performed in the same Gaslight set as the new epic within a fortnight of Carnegie Hall – 'Lord Thomas and Fair Ellender,' 'Lord Lovell,' and 'Little Musgrave,' which he *never* performed, is the relentless rivulet of images, pouring down on one another in a stream so unending that in the final verse he cannot stop himself from breaking the very bounds of song form itself in order to 'tell it and think it and speak it and breathe it' like it is. Such a freewheelin' verse structure was not something he acquired from either Woody Guthrie or Robert Johnson. It smacked more of Ginsberg's *Howl* or the speed-rapping of Kerouac – and it transformed Dylan into a folk modernist. As he told Cohen in 1968 during their discussion of this epochal composition:

The language which [the Beats] were writing, you could read off the paper, and somehow it would begin some kind of tune in your mind. . . . You could see it was possible to do . . . something different than what Woody and people like Aunt Molly Jackson and Jim Garland did. The subject matter of all their songs wasn't really accurate for me. . . . When that subject matter wasn't there anymore for me, the only thing that was there was the style. [And] the idea of this type of song which you can live with in some kind of way, which you don't feel embarrassed twenty minutes after you've sung it.

Though the world crisis that precipitated it soon passed away, he had discovered he could tap into a general need for songs of desperation and fear. That fear was as personal as it was universal. As he told Shelton in 1966, 'I was actually most afraid of death in those first years around New York . . . because I still hadn't written what I wanted to. I had written "Blowin' in the Wind," but I wasn't satisfied with that.' Now, afraid he would only to get to write one more song, he decided he had better summarize his unique world-view. The feeling he was reaching for was later conveyed to Studs Terkel during an April 1963 radio show appearance:

[When] I wrote ['Hard Rain'] – every line in that is really another song. . . . I wrote that when I didn't know how many other songs I could write. That was during October of last year and I remember sitting up all night with some people, some place, and I wanted to get the most down that I knew about into one song as I possibly could. . . . It's not atomic rain, it's just a hard rain. It's not the fall-out rain. It isn't that at all. I just mean some sort of end that's just gotta happen. . . . In the last verse, when I say 'When the pellets of poison are flooding the waters', I mean all the lies that people get told on their radios and [in] their newspapers.

His comment to Terkel was just the start of Dylan disassociating the song from its *specific* apocalyptic backdrop, giving it a wider relevance not mired in some little spat between JFK and Khrushchev. When he gave it a full-bodied electric rearrangement in 1980, as part of a set teeming with righteous millennial fury, it reacquired that apocalyptic intent, one fully imbued with the spirit of St. John the Divine. By then Dylan was convinced that 'hard rain' did not mean *hard* rain. Or even strange rain. It meant something genuinely apocalyptic: Judgement Day. And, as he told writer and actor Antoine de Caunes in 1984, when the song again reverted to its acoustic self, he felt like it had already started to fall.

Continuing to mean new things to its author and audience, it retained its acoustic identity, save for a special series of concerts in Nara City, Japan, in May 1994, when Dylan was accompanied by the Tokyo New Philharmonic Orchestra, and the song acquired a symphonic sweep worthy of its nebulous narrative. Needless to say, Sony saw fit to bury this majestic arrangement on the European-only CD single, 'Dignity.'

{68} BALLAD OF HOLLIS BROWN

Published lyrics: Broadside #21; Writings and Drawings; Lyrics 1985; Lyrics 2004.

First known performance: Carnegie Hall, New York, September 22, 1962.

Known studio recordings: Studio A, NY, November 14, 1962 – 1 take; August 6, 1963 – 4 takes; August 7, 1963 – 1 take [TIMES – tk.1].

'The Rise and Fall of Hollis Brown' – as it was originally called – sees Dylan reiterating the 'hard times come again no more' genre that Guthrie had previously made his own. About a poor man who has run out of options and can't see beyond the well at the bottom of his 'garden' – down which he proceeds to fling his seven children and wife – 'Hollis Brown' even shares the same relentlessness as 'Hard Rain.'

Dylan set his tale to the tune of another ill-starred murder ballad. 'Pretty Polly,' which related the murder of Polly by a capricious lover, was a song he'd featured in his early New York set and on the Minneapolis Party Tape. In all likelihood, he was directly influenced by the version recorded by B. F. Shelton at the 1927 Bristol sessions, on which Shelton accompanied himself with a driving banjo.

'Hollis Brown' was darker still. When Dylan recorded it for *Freewheelin'* in November, offset by Bruce Langhorne's electric guitar, it belaboured Brown's suffering with a graphic verse about the gangrene eating away at the man: 'There's bedbugs on your babies, and there's chinches on your wife, [x2] / Gangrene snuck in your side, it's cutting you like a knife.' This verse was subsequently cut, perhaps because it implied that Brown was already dying, making the murder of his family an essentially selfish act.

Dylan wanted to retain this sense of a man driven to an unspeakable crime by the indifference of the world. Even in death the Browns are destined to remain just 'seven more people.' Though the song was not short-listed for *Freewheelin'*, it stayed a part of Dylan's live set, appearing at the Town Hall in April (where he introduced it as 'a true story') and constituting one of the three songs performed on his TV debut, on the special *Folk Songs and More Folk Songs* in May, when its melody had a counterpoint provided by a banjo, in the style of B. F. Shelton.

In early August, still exercising a hold on Dylan's imagination, it was given two tryouts for what was now his third album. The one recorded on August 6 failed to frame it right. A single take the following day did the trick, making it one of just two songs that Dylan recorded for consecutive albums prior to the mid-eighties. It also survived a general cull of protest songs in 1964, featuring in Dylan's so-called BBC Broadcast in June 1965, his last all-acoustic set for a long, long time.

Twenty years on, it would be given another airing at the global charity-fest Live Aid, where it was a discordant adjunct to Dylan's speech about the plight of American farmers. However, it took till the Never Ending Tour for a full resurrection to live duties, in both electric and acoustic guises, most notably in June 1989, when G. E. Smith's electric guitar accompaniment at a show in Den Haag drove the song relentlessly forward, conveying the inevitability of the outcome as compulsively as the old words.

{69} JOHN BROWN

Published lyrics: Broadside #22; Writings and Drawings; Lyrics 1985; Lyrics 2004.
First known performance: Gaslight Café, New York, early October 1962.
Known studio recordings: Broadside session, New York, February 1963 [BB].

'John Brown,' another protest song Dylan couldn't be bothered to record for Columbia, has been restored to favour in recent years. Any blame for this state of affairs should be directed at the fulsome frame (for worms) of Jerry Garcia. The song was first exhumed in 1987 at the request of the guitarist for a disastrous series of shows with the Grateful Dead. In keeping with the majority of songs in these sets, Dylan could barely remember the order of the verses, let alone the point the song was trying to make (though in fairness, on this one, he stumbled over the words at the *Broadside* session, as well as at the Town Hall in 1963). Unfortunately a narrative with a moral, such as 'John Brown,' stands or falls on its delivery.

Given his difficulties with the Dead, few expected the attention with which Dylan dished out the song with the Heartbreakers barely three months later. Indeed, it seems to have become one of Dylan's favourite early songs, given the gusto with which he has continued to perform it in the past decade and a half. It even got a Sony release, on 1995's *Unplugged*. And yet, in its day, it never warranted a Columbia CO number, though it had been written shortly before four *Freewheelin'* sessions in late fall. When he did get around to recording a rendition, within the woolly walls of *Broadside* in winter 1963, he struggled to remember how it went. Yet he allowed this rather imperfect rendition to appear on the *Broadside Ballads* LP (for which he adopted the alias Blind Boy Grunt to bypass his contractual obligations to Columbia).

As to the song's source, it has been suggested that an Irish street ballad, 'Mrs. McGrath' – recently given a 'hey diddle diddle' arrangement by Bruce Springsteen on *The Seeger Sessions* – probably provided Dylan with the idea. And there is at least one couplet in the street ballad that confirms a direct association. When the returning soldier appears before his mother, Mrs. McGrath, minus both his legs, she asks him if he was drunk or blind, because he's left 'two fine legs behind.' The son replies:

> Oh I wasn't drunk and I wasn't blind
> But I left my two fine legs behind
> For a cannonball on the fifth of May
> Took my two fine legs from my knees away.

In 'John Brown,' the line 'a cannonball blew my eyes away' is a clear allusion to the Irish original. But Dylan has now got the hang of this rewriting lark, and the description Brown gives of his experiences to his mother packs a greater punch than 'Mrs. McGrath,' as does his discovery that 'when my enemy

came close / I could see that his face looked just like mine.'
'John Brown' also sets up the dramatic denouement from the
outset, detailing just how proud Mrs. Brown was when her
son 'went off to war / to fight on a foreign shore,' whereas
'Mrs. McGrath' passes quickly from the boy's recruitment to
his return, battered and bruised. Dylan has begun to let such
songs speak for themselves. So, whereas Mrs. McGrath rails
at everyone from the King of Spain to 'Don John' for her son's
fate, in 'John Brown' the returning soldier simply 'drops his
medals down into her hands' and leaves it at that.

{70} DON'T THINK TWICE, IT'S ALL RIGHT

Published lyrics: Broadside *#20;* Writings and Drawings;
Lyrics *1985;* Lyrics *2004.*
First known performance: Gaslight Café, New York, early October 1962.
Known studio recordings: Studio A, NY, November 14, 1962 – 1
take [FR – tk.1]; Studio B, May 1, 1970.

Dylan's studio recording of 'Don't Think Twice, It's All
Right' represents one of the most perfect fusions of tune,
lyric, vocal, and musical performance in the man's forty-five
years as a recording artist. And he achieved it all in a single
take. As perfect in its own, concise way as more ostentatious
classics from more mature albums, 'Don't Think Twice' also
stands as one of his more contentious works. The song owes
interrelated debts to Paul Clayton and Bruce Langhorne (for
its tune and accompaniment, respectively), neither readily
acknowledged at the time. Only when those pesky biographers began picking at Bob's biographical bones did a
suspicion grow that this sublime song should perhaps have
credits that read, 'Dylan, arr. Clayton-Langhorne.'

The tune is unquestionably another traditional melody
appropriated by that most casual of credit-givers. But it is more
than that. Like the version of 'House of the Rising Sun' he
included on his debut LP, it utilizes a unique arrangement that

a close friend had already adopted as his own. And this time the arrangement in question had already appeared on disc, and was incontrovertibly the source of Dylan's melody (and some of the song's *nuance*).

Paul Clayton, a friend and sidekick, had spent his teenage years as a fastidious field collector, part of a team of students from the University of Virginia under the tutelage of Professor A. K. Davis. It was on one of his scouting missions that Clayton came upon 'Who's Gonna Buy You Ribbons (When I'm Gone),' a bastardized variant drawn from the 'Who's Gonna Shoe Your Horse' family of songs. In 1960 he recorded a syrupy version on *Home-Made Songs and Ballads*. Yet beneath the strong strings it is clearly the template for Dylan's tune, though it would take Dylan twenty-five years to own up to the debt, via *Biograph* note-taker Cameron Crowe.

Though the tune was a real winner, it presented another intractable problem to the man – it was not an easy piece to play for a guitarist who rarely fingerpicked. One listen to the Witmark version – also fingerpicked – explains why. The rhythm veers all over the place. Whenever he has played the song live – even at the Gaslight, a matter of days before the official recording – Dylan flatpicked the melody. But played this way, it is notably less effective. And Dylan knew it.

On the day he recorded it for Columbia, 'he' apparently managed both an effortless fingerpicked accompaniment and a word-perfect vocal in a single take. Also in attendance at that session was Bruce Langhorne, the masterful guitarist who would subsequently play those effortless, picked leads on the *Bringing It* version of 'Mr Tambourine Man.' And according to Langhorne, it is his playing on the *Freewheelin'* version of 'Don't Think Twice.' Dylan's (presumably less accomplished) guitar part was probably wiped – though it could still be on the multitrack. I suspect it might resemble what one hears on the Witmark version.

At least the lyrics are all Dylan – the Dylan who would later turn, turn, turn on old friends with songs like 'Ballad in Plain D,' 'It's All Over Now, Baby Blue,' 'Like a Rolling Stone,' and 'Positively Fourth Street.' This time he wields his wordplay at his muse and dream lover for deserting him. Tired of awaiting her return, he writes what he later described in the *Freewheelin'* notes as 'not a love song. It's a statement that maybe you can say to make yourself feel better. It's as if you were talking to yourself.'

Probably a direct response to the phone call from Suze, informing him that she would not be coming back around Labor Day as originally planned, 'Don't Think Twice' does a (deliberately) lousy job of disguising the very real hurt underlying those verbal put-downs – a Dylan trademark since his student days. (When Gretel Hoffman told him she'd married his best friend, Dave Whitaker, he apparently span off down the street with the immortal one-liner, 'Call me when you get divorced.') For the first time the 'verbal bayonet' comes out in song, where he could be sure to hit the target. He tells her, 'Goodbye is too good a word, babe / So I'll just say fare thee well,' only to reveal himself in the verbal aside, 'I gave her my heart but she wanted my soul.' Even the title is designed to pierce to the quick. Unfortunately for its author, his target remained three thousand miles away, enjoying her freedom from a rather possessive man.

{71} MIXED-UP CONFUSION

Published lyrics: Writings and Drawings; Lyrics 1985; Lyrics 2004.
Known studio recordings: Studio A, NY, October 26, 1962 – 5 takes; November 1, 1962 – 6 takes; November 14 – 5 takes [45] [BIO].

'Mixed-Up Confusion,' surely the oddest song Dylan recorded with John Hammond, provides a fleeting glimpse of the rock & roller who renounced the music of his youth after hearing Odetta in 1959, trading in his electric guitar for an acoustic Martin. Thankfully for a burgeoning career, nothing was revealed. The single – issued at the turn of the year – disappeared without a trace, becoming the man's first serious collectible (it was so unsuccessful that 'stock' copies are rarer than 'promos'). Dylan was still embarrassed by it in 1985, claiming in the *Biograph* notes that the song was his producer's idea. It was not. Hammond did not stint from naming the true culprit in a 1969 *Fusion* interview: 'Grossman's first idea was to combine Dylan with a Dixie band.' (It's more honky-tonk than Dixieland, but we are *definitely* talking about the same song).

The young apprentice, who had previously gone to great lengths to hide his rock & roll past, went along with his manager. But when Cynthia Gooding began to mention his rockier roots on her radio show the previous February, Dylan quickly changed the subject. Only close friends were allowed to know about his rock & roll apostasy. In the fullness of time, Dylan was able to use this vinyl oddity as evidence that he was always a rocker. It even enjoyed a second life as a Dutch-only single, post-'Rolling Stone' – and at least the Europeans put out the right version. The full effect was lost when an alternate version, verging on folka- billy, was used for two multivolume anthologies in 1978 and 1985, *Masterpieces* and *Biograph*. Mixed-up confusion, indeed.

{72} I'D HATE TO BE YOU ON THAT DREADFUL DAY

Published lyrics: Writings and Drawings; Lyrics 1985; Lyrics 2004.
Known studio recordings: Broadside session, November 1962 [BR].

'Dreadful Day' is a dry run for 'When the Ship Comes In,' which sails through the mist ten months later. Another song of vengeful judgement, it predicts a purgatory of pain for those not willing to hasten the Great Day Coming, when- ever it may be. Fans and critics in 1979 – when Dylan had an actual timetable, courtesy of Hal *Late Great Planet Earth*

Lindsey – cited the song as evidence that even the young bard had it in him to become a Bible-thumping zealot. And unlike the earlier 'I Hear a Train A-Rolling,' this one he recorded.

Even as a twenty-one-year-old lapsed Jew, he seemed to believe in an actual Judgement Day, an essential part of Christian eschatology, but not of mainstream Judaism. On 'Dreadful Day,' though the target for God's (and Dylan's) wrath is not specified, there is a strong implication he is a rich man ('You're gonna have to walk naked / Can't ride in no car'). Warming up for the bilious Pirate Jenny, he has taken a leaf from 'Dives and Lazarus,' a sixteenth-century English ballad he would have known via more modern variants. Dives, a rich man who refuses to feed the hungry Lazarus, causes the latter to envisage his fate on 'that dreadful day' (though the phrase itself probably derives from the Carter Family's rendition of 'The Day of Wrath,' which opens, 'The day of wrath, that dreadful day . . .').

{73} PATHS OF VICTORY

Published lyrics: Broadside #17; Writings and Drawings; Lyrics 1985; Lyrics 2004.

Known studio recordings: Broadside session, New York, November 1962; Studio A, NY, August 12, 1963 – 1 take [TBS – tk.1].

Whereas 'Dreadful Day' targets the black hearted, 'Paths of Victory' flips the coin, vouchsafing victory for those movers and shakers willing to share the author's righteous zealotry. As with the contemporary 'Ain't Gonna Grieve,' Dylan does little to disguise the gospel source of 'Paths of Victory.' It is less than a skip from 'Palms of Victory, crowns of Glory / Palms of Victory I shall wear' to 'Trails of troubles, roads of battles / Paths of Victory I shall walk.' 'Palms of Victory,' a traditional hymn, was collected by the likes of Vance Randolph in the Ozarks (and we know that Dylan had access to Harry Weber's copy of Randolph's four-volume collection), though Dylan probably drew from a less traditional source: the June 1936 recording made by the Carter Family (under the title 'The Wayworn Traveler').

Though Dylan allowed the song to appear in a December 1962 *Broadside*, he had not quite finished the lyrics. At this stage it seemed to have acquired a couple of discarded images from 'Tomorrow Is a Long Time': 'I walked along the highway / I walked along the track. . . . I went out to the valley / I turned my head up high / I saw the silver lining / That was hangin' in the sky.' By August 1963, when one might have expected the song to have already slipped from his crowded mind, Dylan had the song how he wanted it, cutting it for the *Times . . .* album. It would not make the short list, though, perhaps because he ended up reusing the 'original' Carter Family melody on the altogether more poetic 'When the Ship Comes In.'

{74} TRAIN A-TRAVELIN'

Published lyrics: Broadside *#23;* Writings and Drawings; Lyrics 1985; Lyrics 2004.

Known studio recordings: Broadside session, New York, November 1962 [BR].

Still in a vengeful mood, and perhaps feeling like 'I Hear a Train A-Rolling' was one of those ideas whose time had arrived, Dylan test-ran this more apocalyptic variant at a November 1962 home session, seemingly for *Broadside's* use. On 'Train A-Travelin',' Dylan envisages another slow train 'with a firebox of hatred and a furnace full of fears.' Once again he personifies the forces of evil – a curiously Christian concept – preempting 'Sympathy for the Devil' by a good five years as he suggests, 'You've heard my voice a-singin' and you know my name.' Performed in prototype for the Cunningham tape recorder, Dylan added another three verses before its publication in late March 1963, accompanied by a Suze Rotolo drawing of this trainload of fools, carrying placards proclaiming 'Support War,' 'KKK,' and the like. By then, he had much better songs in his locker. He was just no longer sure that *Broadside* was where they should end up.

{75} WALKIN' DOWN THE LINE

Published lyrics: Writings and Drawings; Lyrics *1985;* Lyrics *2004.*
Known studio recordings: Broadside session, New York, November 1962; Witmark demo, New York, March 1963 [TBS].

The narrator of 'Walkin' Down the Line' can no longer see the silver lining in the sky, oppressed as he is by a 'heavy-headed gal,' and frustrated by all the money that 'flows / through the holes in the pockets of my clothes.' When he does 'see the morning light,' it is only because he has had another sleepless night – *à la* 'Tomorrow Is a Long Time.' Yet the song has a jaunty melody and an upbeat delivery, which belies its troubled message, making it more of a partner-in-rhyme for 'Paths of Victory' than 'Dreadful Day.' Another song he was content to give away, 'Walkin' Down the Line' came back to haunt him in June 1987, when at least one member of the Dead expressed a yen for it. He even ran it down at tour rehearsals, though that was as far as it got. But the song continued to have its fans, and in 1991 it appeared on *The Bootleg Series* in its Witmark guise (no Columbia take being available), presumably because it struck a chord with compiler Jeff Rosen.

{76} CUBAN MISSILE CRISIS

Published lyrics: Words Fill My Head.
Known studio recordings: Broadside session, New York, November 1962.

As late as 1965, Dylan was still claiming that he wrote 'Hard Rain' at the time of the Cuban Missile Crisis: 'We just hung around at night- people sat around wondering if it was the end, and so did I.' Actually it is this innocuous three-verse ditty that depicts 'the fearful night [when] we thought the world would end.' If the crisis passed soon enough, so did this cursory by-product.

{77} YE PLAYBOYS and PLAYGIRLS

Published lyrics: Broadside #18; Writings and Drawings; Lyrics 1985; Lyrics 2004.

Known studio recordings: Broadside *session, New York, November 1962.*

First known performance: Newport Folk Festival, July 27, 1963 [NB].

Being one of those souls who liked hanging out at the *Broadside* offices – a.k.a. Gil Turner's apartment – Pete Seeger was among the first to hear this simple little rallying cry, which Dylan recorded for *Broadside* at the end of an eventful year. And this one evidently lodged in Seeger's memory, because in the summer of 1963 he convinced Dylan to reprise the song at a Newport workshop. By then, the acolyte had better material with which to exhort the festival goers – as the recent Newport DVD demonstrates – but he still made a brave fist of this checklist for countless broadside ballads, past and present: fall-out shelters ('Let Me Die in My Footsteps'), Jim Crow ('Only a Pawn in Their Game'), lynch mobs ('Emmett Till'), 'insane tongues of war talk' ('Masters of War'), and 'red baiters and race haters' ('With God on Our Side').

Note: The song's belated appearance on the 1964 *An Evening at Newport* LP seems to have convinced Dylan that the song belongs with the *Another Side* songs in *Writings and Drawings*, not with the 'early songs.' This position has remained unchallenged in subsequent editions of *Lyrics*. Dylan also omitted a verse or two – 'Your cold prison walls / Can't change my mind. . . .' and 'Your free-talking money-makers / Can't get me down. . . .' being two of the targets deleted (or more likely forgotten) by the time he appeared at the Newport workshop.

Published lyrics: Broadside #17; Writings and Drawings;
Lyrics 1985; Lyrics 2004.

*First known performance: Broadside session, New York,
November 1962.*

*Known studio recordings: Studio A, NY, December 6, 1962 – 1 take
[FR – tk.1].*

There are some songs written *to order,* i.e., take a theme and
explode it, and those that are written *to order.* 'Oxford Town'
appears to belong to the latter category, being the product
of an informal competition set by editors 'Sis and Gordon' in
Broadside #14, to get someone to write 'a song about one of the
most important events of this year – the enrollment of [black
student] James Meredith in the University of Mississippi. . . .
The least tribute we could pay him would be a good lasting
song in his honor.' The first response to their plea came from
a young Phil Ochs, recently arrived in town, whose 'Ballad of
Oxford, Mississippi' appeared in the following issue. In #16, five
more nominees wrote the kind of tripe that had been giving
broadsides a bad name for four hundred years. Finally, in issue
#17 – appearing on stands in early December – Dylan showed
everyone how it was done, giving the magazine 'Oxford Town'
(the title of a quite different traditional song).

In five four-line verses he showed the gulf that was daily
growing between him and his so-called peers in the topical-
song field. While the others sank beneath a mire of platitudes,
Dylan came up with an amulet of structural sophistication.
Using all the 'leaping' but little of the lingering generally
found in olde worlde precursors, Dylan found another use for
that verbal bayonet: to make a polemical point – 'He come in
the door, he couldn't get in / All because of the color of his
skin,' a clear reference to Meredith's courageous attempts to
gain admission to the University of Mississippi.

By astutely placing the narrator at the centre of the *contretemps*

131

that initially greeted Meredith – 'Me and my gal, my gal's son / We got met with a tear gas bomb' – he makes it difficult for the listener to place him- or herself at any emotional distance from the seismic events occurring down South. And yet he never mentions Meredith or the university by name, enabling the song to live on long after the actual incident has become a footnote to academic treatises. As he told Studs Terkel the following April, 'It deals with the Meredith case, but then again it doesn't. . . . I wrote that when that happened, and I could have written that yesterday. It's still the same. "Why doesn't some-body investigate soon," that's a verse in the song.'

The studio take, recorded when the song was wholly fresh and vital – and *Broadside* #17 was rolling off the presses – has so much power and immediacy that, when Dylan nailed it in one go, his producer exclaimed at song's end, 'Don't tell me that's all.' It is. It would be another twenty-eight years before he allowed the song another live airing, but it was a momentous one: an almost word-perfect performance at the University of Mississippi in October 1990, for which he received a standing ovation from black *and* white attendees alike.

{79} I SHALL BE FREE

Published lyrics: Writings and Drawings; Lyrics *1985*; Lyrics *2004 [recorded version:* Words Fill My Head].

Known studio recordings: Studio A, NY, December 6, 1962 – 5 takes [FR – tk.2]; Broadside session, New York, December 1962; Witmark demo, April 1963.

During conversations with the *Dallas Morning News'* Pete Oppel in October 1978, Dylan went to great pains to empha-size the diversity of material brought to his early acoustic albums: 'If you check those [early] albums out carefully, you'll see there's more on those albums than just the spokes-man's role or the generation role. On all those albums there were some songs on there that had nothing to do with being a spokesman for anybody but myself.' 'I Shall Be Free' is just such a song, and a clear indicator that he was already thinking of an upbeat way to end that difficult second album.

It was, after all, recorded at what he envisaged would be the final session, on December 6, 1962. The decision to end the album with this variant of a talkin' blues was probably intended to show how rooted his music remained in the forms that served him well before he ever dreamed of becoming the songwriter now daringly displayed. He still liked to leave 'em laughing. Dylan's association with the kind of talkin' blues on which he had built much of his early reputation underlines the whole song. Indeed, the structure of 'I Shall Be Free' is copped from a 1944 song, 'We Shall Be Free,' recorded by Woody, 'Cisco and Sonny and Lead Belly, too' – though its main lyrical debts are to Lead Belly's rambunctious 'Take a Whiff on Me' and the traditional 'Talkin' Blues.'

'Take a Whiff on Me' had already provided Dylan with a couplet for 'Honey Just Allow Me One More Chance' ('I'm a-walkin' down the road with my hat in my hand / Lookin' for a woman who needs a worried man'). It now provided further grist. Lines like 'I got a woman six feet tall / Sleepin' in the kitchen with her feet in the hall' gave Dylan the necessary licence to get more wacky (*his* woman actually 'works herself blind'). And from 'Talkin' Blues' he appropriates not just occasional lines but its whole licentious leer; witness its final verse:

> Ain't no use me workin' so hard,
> I got a gal in the rich folks' yard.
> They kill a chicken, she sends me the head.
> She thinks I'm workin', I'm a-layin' up in bed,
> Just dreamin' about her, having a good time,
> Two other women.

Dylan's rewrite of this verse – which also takes something from Hank Williams's 'My Bucket's Got a Hole in It' – survives to the recorded take. In his original, six-verse typescript, though, it contains yet more of its paradigm:

> There ain't no use in me working so hard,
> I got me a woman who works in the yard,
> Rakes the leaves up to her neck,
> Every week she sends me a check.
> She's a humdinger. . . .

That typescript also contains a coupla rhymes that were bound to go – notably an admission that 'sometimes I might get high / Walk like a duck, buzz like a fly' – but Dylan had more. Its six verses are embellished by a further *five* on the *Freewheelin'* take, suggesting that the second half of the song was largely an act of spontaneous creation (all seven verses on the *Broadside* version he recorded in December are different from the typescript, but he stumbles over the performance, as if he can't quite remember how it goes, suggesting that it probably postdates the Columbia session).

The 'I Shall Be Free' on *Freewheelin'* was actually a first complete take (along with another eight songs on the LP!). Yet he wasn't sure he'd quite got it out of his system, and made three more attempts before admitting he'd got it right the first time around. At some point he decided to use the song to renounce one aspect of his previous persona, the first verse ending with him tossing that trademark hat on the fire:

> I was standing on the corner, just waiting around,
> The prices were up and the temperature was down,
> Cost too much to freeze outside,
> So now I sit by my fireside.
> Burning telephone books, burning newspaper clippings,
> Huckleberry Finn hats.

By the end of the session, though, he reverts to starting with, 'I took me a woman . . .' (which is how it is on the LP).* Throughout Dylan sounds like he is enjoying himself. He also sounds at least half a lifetime away from telling an interviewer, 'I lose my inspiration in the studio real easy, and it's very difficult for me to think that I'm going to eclipse anything I've ever done before. I get bored easily, and my mission, which starts out wide, becomes very dim after a few failed takes.' On December 6, 1962, there would be very 'few failed takes.' Having a ball, he lets wordplay be his guide.

Nor would this be the last time he felt a need to update the template, re-recording the song for Witmark the following spring, adding a verse about going to Reno on a horse 'to get a divorce.' On the face of it, he appeared to give it another makeover in 1973 for the benefit of readers of *Writings and Drawings*. The version included in the first collected lyrics even has a touch of the basement tapes, with couplets that would not have seemed out of place on 'Tiny Montgomery' or 'Yea! Heavy and a Bottle of Bread':

> She took off her wheel, took off her bell,
> Took off her wig, said, 'How do I smell?' . . .
> Well, I got a woman sleeps on a cot,
> She yells and hollers and squeals a lot. . . .
> Oh, there ain't no use in me workin' so heavy,
> I got a woman who works on the levee.

Except that – guess what – those first two couplets appear, clear as type, in Dylan's original six-verse typescript, as do his

---

* The session-tape for December 6, 1962 is in circulation, having been initially misplaced by Columbia, marked, 'Audition Folksinger.' Some audition! As such, we have five versions of 'I Shall Be Free,' of which takes two and five are complete. The second take, recorded after a single false start, is the one that appears on *Freewheelin'*.

rhymes of 'honeymooner / crooner / spoon feeder' and 'folk singer / dead ringer,' also preserved in *Writings and Drawings*. Only the third couplet quoted above appears to have been a latter-day tweak. So it would seem Dylan held onto a notebook or two, doing a lot more editorial work on that edition of lyrics than he ever did on its successors.

{80} KINGSPORT TOWN

Published lyrics: Words Fill My Head.
Known studio recordings: Studio A, NY, November 14, 1962 – 1 take [TBS – tk.1].

When 'Kingsport Town' entered general circulation in the late eighties, it seemed like a real throwback. Its use of folk commonplaces – and inclusion alongside a first-album outtake – suggested an early composition. Yet its delivery bore the hallmark of a songwriter who was some way down the road to the fully realized 'Seven Curses' and 'Percy's Song,' both written the following year. In fact Dylan appears to be purposely demonstrating how sophisticated his grasp of traditional templates is becoming.

Though he self-consciously builds the song around the 'Who's Gonna Shoe Your Pretty Little Feet?' motif, a balladic construct that dates back to at least the eighteenth century – where it first appeared in the Scottish 'Lass of Loch Royal' ballad series – the story Dylan tells is neither the one used by Woody and Cisco on 'Who's Gonna Shoe Your Pretty Little Feet?' nor the so-called 'Storms Are on the Ocean' variant, favoured by the likes of Doc Watson, the Carter Family, and Jean Ritchie, familiar as he would have been with both of these.

If anything 'Kingsport Town' is a 'letter home' song, drawn from the same lineage as 'I Was Young When I Left Home.' In this instance he is writing to 'the gal I'm a-thinkin' of' (two months before 'Boots of Spanish Leather') – she of the Memphis lips, dark eyes, coal-black hair, and sandy-coloured skin (quite how this translates into an 'African-American woman,' as Harvey suggests, I know not). In the song the narrator has been driven from old Kingsport Town because of an illicit affair, probably with the high sherriff's daughter, and is left wondering who will be taking care of his babe when he's 'out in the wind.' 'Kingsport Town' remains a fascinating ragbag of ideas that Dylan has yet to formalize into a style he can really call his own (which in no way explains – or excuses – its absence from the latest edition of *Lyrics*).

{81} HERO BLUES

Published lyrics: Writings and Drawings; Lyrics *1985*; Lyrics *2004*.
Known studio recordings: Studio A, NY, December 6, 1962 – 4 takes; August 12, 1963 – 3 takes.
First known performance: Town Hall, New York, April 12, 1963.

Having spent much of 1962 compiling a veritable New Wobblies' Songbook for the Cause, Dylan got around to writing another of his 'feel better' songs, this time castigating 'the gal I got' because 'she wants me to be a hero / So she can tell all her friends.' Another of his funny-ha-ha songs, 'Hero Blues' takes great delight in ridiculing a girl who 'reads too many books / she got new movies inside her head.' In the end, the singer suspects she won't be satisfied until he winds up dead – at which point she can 'stand and shout hero / All over my lonesome grave,' a delightfully Dylanesque exaggeration.

Though hardly a major composition, Dylan remained quite attached to it. The song survived in his set until Town Hall in April and was even attempted honky-tonk style at the *Times They Are A-Changin'* sessions in August. Indeed, even after acetates were cut for the sequenced album, 'Hero Blues' was scheduled for the side-one, track-four slot. Only at the last minute did good sense prevail, and it was ousted by 'One Too Many Mornings,' Dylan recognizing that the sentiments underlying 'Hero Blues' could be further refined.

In May 1964 he decided to rewrite the song in an alto-gether more sarcastic, biting vein. The author of 'It Ain't Me, Babe' started thinking that even dying for 'her' might not be enough. As for 'Hero Blues,' it made a most unexpected comeback in January 1974 as opening song for the first two shows on Dylan's 'returning hero' tour. Though the new set of words is not entirely audible on either tape, references to heading 'out on the highway / As fast as I can go' and having 'one foot on the highway / The other in the grave' suggest he was hoping audiences had come to see a song-and-dance man, not a hero of the old school. After all, it had never been his 'duty to remake the world at large.'

{82} WHATCHA GONNA DO?

Published lyrics: Writings and Drawings; Lyrics 1985; Lyrics 2004.
Known studio recordings: Studio A, NY, November 14, 1962; December 6, 1962 – 1 take.

At the penultimate *Freewheelin'* session, Dylan made one last attempt to cut the kind of blues he had originally intended to make the crux of this 'make or break' album, demon-strating how the ghost of Robert Johnson was still rattling at his windowpane. Conceiving of a conversation with the Johnson of 'Me and the Devil Blues,' Dylan asks what plans he has 'when the Devil calls your name' and whether he is prepared to meet his Maker – a full seventeen years before 'Are You Ready?' Already preparing for 'that dreadful day,' he wants to know of this other sinner man: 'What're you gonna do when you can't play God no more?' Next album around, he would be quoting directly from the Bible, raining judge-ment down on his elders as the times began to change at his command.

1963

{ The Freewheelin' Bob Dylan; The Times They Are A-Changin' }

Dylan began 1963 where he had left off at year's end, writing up a storm of songs combining derivative melodies with stunningly original lyrics and execution. Indeed he would still be drawing on the many song ideas acquired in a matter of weeks in England through the spring of 1963, when the likes of 'Liverpool Gal' and 'With God on Our Side' were composed. It would take till the end of October – when he wrote the third-album finale, 'Restless Farewell' – for the lyrical musing to abate. As far as we know, it was the last song he wrote until 1964.

Among the thirty-two songs from ten more months in Inspiration's fiery furnace would be a quartet of songs that complete his second album, the ten that would make up his third, and another double album's worth of songs debuted in concert but discarded, including songs of balladic brilliance ('Seven Curses,' 'Eternal Circle,' 'Lay Down Your Weary Tune,' and 'Percy's Song'). But by October 31, when Dylan recorded 'Restless Farewell,' the first phase of his career had drawn to a close. When he emerged again in the new year, he had put away all protesty things . . .

Published lyric: Broadside *#20;* Writings and Drawings;
Lyrics *1985;* Lyrics *2004.*

*First known performance: Gil Turner's home, New York, January
21, 1963.*

*Known studio recordings: Columbia Studio A, NY, April 23,
1963 – 3 takes [FR – tk.3].*

There may be some dispute regarding the date of composition for 'Masters of War,' but there can be none about the
actual source of the tune. That source was assuredly folksinger
Jean Ritchie's 'Nottamun Town,' a traditional English folk
song now thought to constitute part of the mummers' plays
performed for the common people on holidays during the
middle ages. The song itself has perhaps the most surreal set
of lyrics found in traditional song, an incongruous compound
that, one must suppose, held a meaning for the folk that is now
lost to the ages ('Met the King and the Queen and a company
more, a-riding behind and a-marching before / Came a stark-
naked drummer a-beating a drum, with his heels in his bosom
come marching along'). That the song spoke to Dylan is clear.
As he told Nora Ephron in 1965, '"Nottamun Town," that's
like a herd of ghosts passing through on the way to Tangiers.
"Lord Edward" [*sic*], "Barbara Allen," they're [all] full of myth.'

And yet the original song, with its magnetic modal
melody, had almost dropped from the face of tradition when
collected by England's dean of field collecting, Cecil Sharp, in
his travels through the Appalachian Mountains in 1917. His
primary source? Jean Ritchie's great aunt, Una. Apparently
brought to America by her great-great-grandfather Crockett,
the song was duly recorded by Jean on her self-titled 1960
album. Ritchie also returned the song to its ancestral home
when she toured Britain, where it took root among revivalists, being recorded by both Davey Graham and Bert Jansch
on key folk-revival collections, albeit post-Dylan.

As such, everyone in those circles, either side of the pond, knew it was one of Jean's. As Martin Carthy says, 'I remember [Bob] singing it and me thinking, "Oh, that's 'Nottamun Town.' He would have learnt that from Jean Ritchie. That's Jean Ritchie's song."' It is simply inconceivable that Dylan would not have already known Ritchie's own rendition, given his deep knowledge of immediate predecessors, the number of times he has name-checked Ritchie, and the song's position as one of the standards of the folk revival (the idea that he took it from the singer Jackie Washington, a recent claimant, is patently absurd).

Unlike many a fellow folkie – even those whose unique arrangement of a traditional song had been appropriated by the young Dylan – Ritchie went after the young tyke and his music publisher for using 'her' tune. According to her, a settlement was made, though due credit was still not forthcoming. Ritchie responded in kind, writing in the preface of her 1965 songbook, 'Because of recent developments in the field of folk music, I have found it necessary to copyright many of the Ritchie family songs.' Gee, I wonder, what can she mean?

Of course, it is possible Dylan felt prompted to reuse the tune because he heard a revivalist singing Ritchie's arrangement. British folksinger Bob Davenport has claimed he played the song when Dylan was in the audience in London that January, reminding him of the tune. On the other hand, the more credible Martin Carthy insists Dylan played the song the first time he saw him play, in December 'at the Troubadour. . . . He'd written [it] already.' Well, if Carthy is right, he was certainly performing it for the first time, and almost certainly the day he wrote it, because he *definitely* wrote it in London. As an uncirculating recording of a version he played to folklorist Alan Lomax, on his return to New York, proves. On that rare reel, he prefaces the song with the kind of open, honest explanation of its inspiration that he will never make again:

> I wrote it in London . . . about all them people over there in England – they don't like Kennedy too much. I remember when the papers came out, I was at this rehearsal place out in Putney and I kept seeing in the papers every day, [them] putting down MacMillan, [saying] Kennedy's gonna screw him, on these missiles. . . . They got headlines in the papers, underneath MacMillan's face, saying, 'Don't mistrust me, don't mistrust me, how can you treat a poor maiden so?'

The song certainly appears to be another one that came quickly – and largely complete. An early typescript of the song in the notebook he kept at the time contains just two couplets different from its April 1963 recording. The first, 'You're like the dirty rotten water / that runs down my drain,' he improves by exchanging 'dirty rotten water' for the kind one can 'see through.' The second, 'For all of your money / You ain't worth a hole in the ground' has also been changed *in crayon* to the vastly superior, 'All the money you made / Will never buy back your soul.' No question, the same man who'd written 'I'd Hate to Be You on That Dreadful Day' now instructed *Freewheelin'* sleeve-note writer Nat Hentoff: '["Masters of War"] is a sort of striking out, a reaction to the last straw, a feeling of what can you do?'

Dylan may well have been prompted to vent these 'feeling[s] of what can you do' after first responding to a request at the end of 1962 from folklorist Izzy Young for a contribution to an anthology of anti-bomb literature. Dylan gave him a forty-line poem, 'Go 'Way Bomb,' that shares the same kind of tone that spills over into 'Masters of War':

I hate you cause you make my life seem like nothin at all
I hate you cause yer name's lost it's [*sic*] meanin an you can fool
   anybody now
I hate you cause yer man made and man owned an man handled
An' you might be missmade and miss-owned an miss handled
   an even miss used.

At the time of its composition, Dylan thought he had already completed his second album. But when *Freewheelin'* was recalled in April – purportedly because it included the potentially libelous 'Talkin' John Birch' – he decided to add 'Masters of War,' demonstrating a keen awareness of how his grasp of the protest-song genre had come on in leaps and bounds in the past year. The pace at which he was moving probably surprised even him. As he said in 1984, 'If I wrote a song like ["Masters of War"] now I wouldn't feel I'd have to write another one for two weeks. . . . The old records I used to make, by the time they came out I wouldn't even want them released because I was already so far beyond them.'

'Masters of War' would make its concert debut at the legendary Town Hall show in April 1963. Over the next eighteen months, it would become one of those songs with which he was most identified. And yet within five years he was suggesting it was simply another song he'd written to order: '[Masters of War] was an easy thing to do. There were thousands and thousands of people just wanting that song, so I wrote it up. . . . I no longer have the capacity to feed this force which is needing all these songs. . . . My insight has turned into something else.'

It took another decade before he felt the need to 'feed this force' again, 'Masters of War' finally being restored to live favour at Hollywood shows in June 1978 in a heavy-metal guise. It received much praise for its new arrangement in the European press that summer. Indeed, it retained this sledgehammer-cracking-a-nut guise through 1991, when he performed the song at Radio City Music Hall prior to receiving a Grammy Lifetime Achievement Award. Having informed the blustering Joe Queenan that he played this particular song that evening because the Gulf 'war [was] going on and all that,' he later flatly contradicted himself, asserting that the song has 'got nothing to do with being anti-war. It has more to do with the military industrial complex that Eisenhower was talking about,' which is what he had told Lomax.

The song finally returned to base in February 1994, when Dylan unveiled its first acoustic rendition in thirty years at a concert in Hiroshima, the most apposite place to reintroduce such a compelling sentiment. As gripping in its own way as the 'Hard Rain' he performed at Nara City three months later, the acoustic 'Masters of War' was retained for the remainder of the year, a reminder to the tens of thousands at the shows and the millions who tuned into Woodstock '94 that 'the military industrial complex' could yet bring down a hard rain.

{84} GIRL FROM THE NORTH COUNTRY

Published lyrics: Writings and Drawings; Lyrics 1985; Lyrics 2004.
First known performance: Oscar Brand's World of Folk Music, March 1963.
Known studio recordings: Studio A, NY, April 23, 1963 – 6 takes [FR – tk.2].

Bob went away to . . . Italy and in the time he was away . . . he wrote 'Girl from the North Country,' 'cause he came back and he said, 'I've got a song to play you.' It was at the Troubadour, and he started to play, and he had that little guitar thing that I play in 'Scarborough Fair.' He was singing the song and he went into this figure and he just burst out

laughing . . . and he wouldn't do the rest of it. He went all
red. – Martin Carthy, *Isis* #83

Never one to disabuse claimants to muse status, Dylan
has refused to lay to rest the eternal question of whom he
had in mind when he wrote 'Girl from the North Country.'
The most insistent claimant, high school sweetheart Echo
Helstrom, laid it on thick for journalist Toby Thompson
when he was writing his sophomoric book about the young
Dylan, *Positively Main Street*. Yet Echo is surprisingly absent
from the long litany of girls who broke the boy's heart in
a poem he wrote back in 1960. He did, however, introduce
'Girl from the North Country' at a 1978 L.A. Forum
performance by saying, 'First girl I ever loved is here in the
house tonight. I wrote a song about her, though she left me
a long time ago for an older man.' Echo *was* apparently there
that night.

However, Echo was not in the audience two nights earlier
in Oakland, when Dylan described 'Girl . . .' as 'a song about
a girl who left me to be a movie star'; or the following night,
when he admitted he 'never came to see her, but she's here
tonight, so I'll play this.' Presumably, *these* dedications were
for Bonnie Beecher, his Minneapolis girlfriend, who had
settled in Oakland with Hugh 'Wavy Gravy' Romney and
was the 'actress girl who kneed me in the guts,' as so vividly
described in 'My Life in a Stolen Moment,' an autobiographical poem written within four months of 'Girl from the
North Country.' (Just to muddy the waters a little, it would
appear that both Echo and Bonnie attempted to become
actresses. The one reference to Beecher in *Chronicles* refers to
a meeting in Hawaii in April 1966, while she was working on
a John Wayne film.) Dylan, meanwhile, continued to introduce 'Girl from the North Country' at those fall shows with a
reference to the 'first girl that ever broke my heart [and] left

me for an older man. I wrote [her] this song and still wish her well.' However, after L.A., he stopped claiming she was in the audience.

Critic Robert Shelton was always of the opinion that Bonnie was the 'true' girl from the North Country. Of other potential candidates, Gretel Hoffman, who 'left' Dylan to marry his best friend, the older Dave Whitaker, is another gal for whom Dylan professed to carry a torch. Judy Rubin, another home-state Jewess singled out in poems written in 1960 and 1963, evidently got under his skin, though the one biographer to tackle her, Bob Spitz, found a lady who never took Dylan as a serious suitor. When asked point-blank by a Minneapolis journalist in 1986 if Echo Helstrom was *the* North Country girl, Dylan ducked and dived, finally suggesting, 'Well, she's *a* North Country girl through and through.'

There is one gal the song *is definitely* about, by proxy, and that is Suze. 'Girl . . .' is as much of a requiem to his 'lost' true love as that 'first' love; establishing another pattern Dylan would repeat throughout his career, generally with magnificent results. On *Blood on the Tracks*, at the end of another great love affair, an earlier such experience is recalled in 'Simple Twist of Fate.' 'In the Summertime,' on *Shot of Love*, also seems to refer more to an earlier summer spent on the farm in Minnesota than any recent relationship with a 'God-fearing woman.'

Less contentious is Dylan's source for the tune to 'Girl from the North Country' – and this one he acknowledged. It derives directly from English folksinger Martin Carthy's arrangement of 'Scarborough Fair' (also known as 'Whittingham Fair'), a rationalized variant of the supernatural ballad, 'The Elfin Knight.' As Dylan told Kurt Loder, 'I learned a lot of stuff from Martin [Carthy]. "Girl from the North Country" is based on a song I heard him sing – that

"Scarborough Fair" song, which I guess Paul Simon just took the whole thing.' Simon made the song famous, and in the process broke the code all folk revivalists were expected to abide by. Whereas Dylan simply took the tune – with Carthy's blessing.

Dylan even puts in a pun on the title of the tune he has stolen, sending his traveller to the 'north country fair'(adjective), rather than the 'county fair' (noun). Though he told Scaduto he wrote 'Girl . . .' down by the banks of Italy, it was apparently another idea he had been carrying around. As he told *Boston Broadside* later the same year: 'I had the idea for that song for a long time, but it just wasn't the right time for it to be written. When the right time finally did come, the song was in my mind and it was ready.'

What finally sent him into 'reminiscence blues' mode again was surely the unprecedented weather he had encountered in England. Just as when he first came to New York, he arrived in London as the worst winter in living memory set in. Airports were closed, train services were suspended, and the country all but ground to a halt. As a house guest to the Carthys one evening, he had joined in chopping up a piano for firewood in a desperate attempt to stay warm. No wonder he felt inspired to muse upon 'the north country fair / where the winds hit heavy on the borderline'!

{85} BOOTS OF SPANISH LEATHER

Published lyrics: Writings and Drawings; Lyrics 1985; Lyrics 2004.
First known performance: Town Hall, New York, April 12, 1963.
Known studio recordings: Studio A, NY, August 6, 1963 – 1 take;
August 7, 1963 – 1 take [TIMES – tk.1].

When Dylan first flew to London in mid-December 1962 – to appear in a BBC production of a new TV play called *Madhouse on Castle Street* – at the back of his mind he apparently had a half-formed notion he might track down his elusive girlfriend Suze at her Italian refuge in Perugia. Though Suze was scheduled to sail home at the exact same time Dylan landed in London, she *had* already changed her plans once, back in September. The result had been, in Mikki Isaacson's words, 'Bobby . . . running around the Village looking lost and skinnier, a real mess. When he talked about Suze, he'd always say, "I don't think she's ever coming back."'

That nagging and, this time around, unfounded feeling provided the germ of an idea which would grow into 'Boots of Spanish Leather,' a song Dylan told Scaduto he wrote in Italy when there in January 1963: 'Suze had gone back to the States, and that's when I worked up the melodies of "Boots of Spanish Leather" and "Girl from the North Country."'

In fact, by the time he arrived in Italy, Suze was back home in New York. As Suze writes in her memoir, 'Our letters had crossed in the mail.' We know that Dylan now *knew* Suze was not in Italy because the lady in question recently auctioned a postcard Dylan sent her *from* Italy that January, addressed to 'Sue Rotolo c/o Bob Dylan, 161 W. 4th Street.' The card – posted the day Dylan returned to London (the tenth) – is remarkably upbeat if it was written the same week he composed the maudlin 'Boots of Spanish Leather,' displaying plenty of flashes of that characteristic off-beat humour: 'Gotta go, gotta [*sic*] meeting with the Pope about all the colored people coming over here. Amore, Bob.'

It was that 'amore' that inspired Dylan to write about the dark days when he thought she ain't 'ever coming back.' The verbal jousting (originally between a virgin and the devil) that constitutes the conceptual core of 'Scarborough Fair' again gave Dylan a format. But whereas 'Girl from the North Country' is a lyrical lament, pure and simple, 'Boots of Spanish Leather' is an old-world ballad from someone whose grasp of traditional modes was coming on in leaps and bounds. The first six verses represent a conversation between two lovers, one of whom is set to sail the seas and has asked the other what kind of token they might want. The other insists it is unnecessary, professing undying love. After half-a-dozen verses lingering on the lovers' parting, the narrator leaps to the devastating denouement, demonstrating real mastery of so-called 'leaping and lingering.'

The tone shifts 180 degrees in a single ominous couplet: 'I got a letter on a lonesome day / It was from her ship a-sailin' . . .' Having led the listener to expect a 'Dear John' letter, Dylan leaves the convention behind and digs instead into his own memory banks: 'She says I don't know when I'll be coming back again / It depends on how I'm a-feelin'.' Bereft, the narrator bids her a fond farewell with the subtlest of references to the hurt she's engendered, instructing her to 'take heed of the western wind,' the same wind which had blown through 'Tomorrow Is a Long Time.'

Dylan later described 'Boots of Spanish Leather' to a Carnegie Hall audience as a 'when you can't get what you want, you have to settle for less kinda-song.' In the last couplet, with his love now forsaken, he finally asks for that token – 'Spanish boots of Spanish leather.' It is a request commonly held to refer to 'Gypsy Davey,' but the reference there has no bearing on this song. And 'Shoes of Spanish Leather' is also the title of an English nursery rhyme. And here the list of trinkets desired by a lady has a meaning commensurate with Dylan's:

> My shoes are made of Spanish [leather]
> my stockings are made of silk
> My petticoats of calico
> and that's as white as milk.
>
> *Refrain*:
> Here we go round and round
> Till our frocks touch the ground.

Assuming this *is* Dylan's point of reference, it must be something he heard or read about on his trip to London. The rhyme has no known provenance in America. 'Boots of Spanish Leather' was a song he kept close to his chest for a couple of months more. He is not known to have performed it before April's Town Hall performance and did not record it 'properly' until the first third-album session in August. Perhaps he thought it unwise to highlight melodic similarities to that other song penned in Perugia, which he *was* anxious to debut. 'Boots of Spanish Leather,' though, has continued to be a song he can surrender to in performance, whether in Prague or Perugia.

{86} BOB DYLAN'S DREAM

Published lyrics: Writings and Drawings; Lyrics *1985;* Lyrics *2004.*
First known performance: 'The Banjo Tape,' Gerde's Folk City, February 8, 1963.
Known studio recordings: Studio A, NY, April 23, 1963 – 2 takes [FR – tk.2].

> We would have some sessions out at my sister's house. She and Bob and I would travel out there. Later, when I heard the song 'Bob Dylan's Dream,' I couldn't help but think that some of the sessions we had at my sister's house were part of that 'Dream.' . . . We used to love to play and sing. – John Bucklen to Robert Shelton, *Isis* #98.

The nostalgia Dylan was feeling for the North Country, five thousand miles away but still blasted by winter winds, was expressed in another song whose melody he appropriated from Carthy that January. Again he does not confine his debt to the traditional tune. He takes the whole 'dreamed a dream' section from the song Carthy obligingly shared with him – which, though it has an alternate title, 'The Sailor's

Dream,' is better known as 'Lady Franklin's Lament.' In Lady Franklin's case, she 'had a dream, which I thought was true / Concerning Franklin and his bold crew.' Her lament was written not by the lady concerned, but from the vantage point of the distraught wife hoping a search expedition might yet find her husband, Sir John Franklin, the Arctic explorer who had gone missing in 1845 while searching for a Northwest Passage. In 1859 a stone cairn on King William Island dashed Lady Franklin's hopes. This broadside ballad presumably dates from the interim.

Dylan now drew on traditional-sounding imagery with such sophistication that his variant of Lady Franklin's plea – 'Ten thousand pounds would I freely give / To learn that my husband still did live' – is seamlessly stitched onto a moralizing coda usually found in derivatives of 'Love Has Brought Me to Despair' (Laws P25): 'I wish, I wish, I wish in vain / that I was single again.' Together they comprise one of Dylan's most evocative final verses – which originally read, 'I wish, I wish, I wish in vain / that I could sit simply in that room again / Ten thousand dollars at the drop of a dime / I'd give gladly if my life could be like that time.'

By the time Dylan was playing it to Gil Turner at an after-hours session at Gerde's, barely a fortnight after returning 'home,' he had changed that final rhyme to the superior 'drop of a hat / . . . could be like that.' He also turned 'played many a joyful tune' into 'spent many an afternoon,' and that was that.

'Bob Dylan's Dream,' which formed part of the Town Hall showcase and a revamped *Freewheelin'*, was a way of reflecting on the friends he had left behind in his youthful zest to leave Hibbing. A nostalgia for more innocent times was already colouring his view of these modern times. In the early nineties, at his lowest ebb since perhaps 1966, he revived 'Bob Dylan's Dream' in concert and the sense of a deep yearning was palpable. Later still, he told the *Times*: '[Minnesota] was a very itinerant place – no interstate highways yet, just country roads everywhere. There was an innocence about it all, and I don't recall anything bad ever happening. That was the Fifties, the last period of time I remember as being idyllic.' It was this exact idyll he wistfully recalls in 'Bob Dylan's Dream.'

Note: As Todd Harvey points out, Dylan was surely already conversant with 'Lady Franklin's Lament' when he came to England, it having been recorded by his good friend, Paul Clayton, on the 1957 album, *Whaling and Sailing Songs: From the Days of Moby Dick*. But he is closer to Carthy's arrangement – found on his second Topic album.

{87} FAREWELL

Published lyrics: Broadside #24; Writings and Drawings; Lyrics *1985*; Lyrics *2004*.

Known studio recordings: Broadside session, New York, January 19, 1963; Studio A, NY, August 6, 1963 – 4 takes.

One might reasonably presume that Dylan's adaptation of 'The Leaving of Liverpool' – from which he took the lilting melody and fare-thee-well theme for 'Farewell' – was another product of his trip to its island home. After all the song was played to Village friends less than a week after he returned from London. Indeed, over the next couple of months he rarely passed up an opportunity to pull out this 'moving on' lament, recording it for both *Broadside* and Witmark, where it was copyrighted under three separate titles (including 'Farewell Pamilina,' fourteen months before 'Farewell Angelina'). Though not a part of the Town Hall showcase, he opened with it on Studs Terkel's radio show a fortnight later, and he attempted it at the first *Times* session in August, rather than another song with a Liverpool connection, 'Liverpool Gal.'

Given its lowly status among collectors, one wonders why the song had this hold on its author. Perhaps it was simply its lilting tune, which in its original guise was a staple of the Clancy Brothers' live set. Liam Clancy seems in no doubt that *they* were Dylan's source, putting him in good company with the likes of Paul Clayton and Jean Ritchie.

Fellow Clancy Brother Pat, though, made an altogether more extraordinary claim in a 1984 interview with Patrick Humphries: 'There was a little folk club here in London, down in the basement [presumably the Troubadour]. . . . Anyway, Albert Grossman paid somebody and gave them a tape-recorder, and every folk-singer that went up there was taped, and Bob Dylan got all those tapes.'

Quite why Grossman would go to such lengths when Dylan had ample opportunity to hear similar fare in the Village, Pat fails to reveal. However, the Minnesotan could well have heard the song 'in London, down in the basement' – just like 'Lady Franklin' and 'Nottamun Town,' two songs he also knew from the Village. The generally reliable Carthy recently suggested Dylan heard Louis Killen sing it in England, and it was Killen's rendition of 'The Leaving of Liverpool' that set these wheels in motion, though the end product stopped somewhere short of official status.

{88} TALKIN' DEVIL

Published lyrics: Words Fill My Head.
Known studio recordings: Broadside session, New York, January 19, 1963 [BB].

It would be easy enough to dismiss this two-verse rant as an unimportant fragment in Dylan's canon (its exclusion from every edition of *Lyrics* suggests as much). Yet 'Talkin' Devil' appears to demonstrate a belief in the *literal* existence of the devil sixteen years before its author read Hal Lindsey's *Satan Is Alive and Well on Planet Earth*. Dylan even introduces the song by saying, 'This is all about what the Devil is. Some people say that there is no Devil. . . .'

In January 1963 it would appear that his demon was the devil of the delta, who enticed Skip James to do dark deeds and came to Robert Johnson's door and said, 'I believe it's time to go.' If so, his horned self doubled as a member of the KKK, hiding his head under a 'snow white hood,' while busy learning 'to kill, with his face well hid.' Personified in 'Talkin' Devil,' he is anyone who 'wants you to hate, wants you to fear.'

{89} ALL OVER YOU

Published lyrics: Writings and Drawings; Lyrics *1985;* Lyrics *2004.*
First known performance: 'The Banjo Tape,' Gerde's Folk City, February 8, 1963.
Known studio recordings: Witmark demo, New York, Winter 1963.

'All Over You' – or as it perhaps should be known, 'If I Had to Do It All Over Again (Baby, I'd Do It All Over You)' – demonstrates that Dylan's interest in American roots music embraced everything from bluegrass to ragtime. A substitute of sorts for the 'talkin' blues,' which were beginning to sour on his pen, 'All Over You' was another way for Dylan to demonstrate his lyrical wit. Here he shows an early penchant for Old Testament allusions, referring to the time when David 'picked up his pebbles' and to Sampson's predicament 'after he went blind.' And for all its light-hearted tone, he has rarely bettered his description of the kind of heartbreak recently experienced:

> Well, you cut me like a jigsaw puzzle,
> You made me a walkin' wreck,
> Then you pushed my heart through my backbone,
> Then you knocked off my head from my neck.

{90} GOING BACK TO ROME

First known performance: 'The Banjo Tape,' Gerde's Folk City, February 8, 1963.

A seemingly improvised piece of nonsense Dylan put down for posterity during a fairly loose after-hours session at Gerde's in early February, 'Goin' Back to Rome' decisively demonstrates that the man never forgets a good rhyme. Who'd have thought anyone would rhyme 'see 'em' with 'Coliseum' not once, but twice! Yet there it is again, on 1971's 'When I Paint My Masterpiece.'

{91} BOUND TO LOSE

Known studio recordings: Witmark demo, New York, winter 1963.

All that is now extant from this 'lost' song is the chorus, which Dylan laid down on tape during one of his Witmark 'pop-in' sessions. In this denuded form, it bears all the hallmarks of another 'walking down the road of hope' song, à la 'Paths of Victory' and 'Walkin' Down the Line.' Suspecting that 'bound to lose, bound to win, bound to walking the road again' did not constitute a song, Dylan told engineer Ivan Augenblink that he had a bunch of verses to go with said chorus, which he said he would give him in due course. One must presume he changed his mind or, like as not, just forgot. Either way, the song was never copyrighted, remaining an afterthought on one more disorganized Witmark reel.

{92} ONLY A HOBO

Published lyrics: Broadside #22; Writings and Drawings; Lyrics 1985; Lyrics 2004.

First known performance: Broadside session, New York, February 1963 [BB].

Known studio recordings: Studio A, NY, August 12, 1963 – 2 takes [TBS – tk.2]; September 24, 1971 – 5 takes.

Ever on the lookout for a traditional template to tweak, Dylan decided to tackle the 'Only a . . .' family of songs shortly after returning to New York. Leaving the likes of

'Only a Cowboy' and 'Only a Brakeman' well alone, Dylan took his notion from the well-known 'Only a Miner,' specifically the variant of this native ballad 'composed' by activist Aunt Molly Jackson in the thirties. The chorus of 'Poor Miner's Farewell' – as she liked to call it – runs thus:

> Only a miner, killed under the ground,
> Only a miner, and one more is found,
> Killed by some accident, there's no one can tell,
> Your mining's all over, poor miner, farewell.

The one time Jackson came up in recorded conversation, it was on the 1984 'Dylan on Dylan' Westwood One radio show, when Dylan bemoaned those rigid folkies who 'didn't want to hear it if you couldn't play the song exactly the way that Aunt Molly Jackson played it. I just kind of blazed my way through all that.' It is curious that Dylan should cite Jackson as an examplar of 'pure' tradition. Jackson herself played *very* free with those traditional songs she adapted to the Cause. As a union organizer of fierce and fixed opinions, her primary concern was *never* the preservation of tradition.

It could be that Dylan did not take this song firsthand from Jackson's version, but from John Greenway's 1961 Folkways recording (prefaced by an Aunt Molly interview). There are at least two other influences at work on 'Only a Hobo' as well. The more intriguing is the 1939 country 'classic,' 'Tramp on the Street' (a song that had already left its mark on the early Dylan song 'Man on the Street'), of which 'Only a Hobo' is just a better-written version, even down to its culmination, which is still 'to lie in the gutter and to die with no name.'

'Tramp on the Street' – a variant of 'Only a Tramp' – was a staple of Hank Williams's forties radio repertoire, and though Hank's version was not released in Williams's lifetime, there is a good chance Dylan heard Williams's version on the *On*

Stage Vol. 2 LP, which was released at the turn of the year, around the time Dylan composed 'Only a Hobo.' Or he could just as easily have been listening to the version on Ramblin' Jack Elliott's 1961 album. 'Tramp on the Street' references the ballad of 'Dives and Lazarus,' a possible template for 'I'd Hate to Be You on That Dreadful Day' as well:

> Only a tramp was Lazarus that begged
> He who laid down at the rich man's gate
> He begged for the crumbs from the rich man to eat
> He was only a tramp, found dead on the street.

But the greatest melodic debt 'Only a Hobo' has is to Sara Carter's 'Railroading on the Great Divide,' performed by Dylan at Gerde's in September 1961. Despite a couple of half-hearted studio takes during the first batch of *The Times . . .* sessions, it was left to *Broadside* (in tandem with Folkways) to release 'Only a Hobo' on the *Broadside Ballads* LP in the summer of 1963. It languished in relative obscurity until 1970, when it was memorably revived by Rod Stewart on his second solo album, *Gasoline Alley*. The following year, possibly reminded of the song by Rod's rasping re-working, Dylan re-recorded it for *Greatest Hits Vol. II*. However, the version he cut with musician Happy Traum didn't work out, and it became one more song done and gone.

{93} RAMBLIN' DOWN THRU THE WORLD

First known performance: 'Gerde's Folk City' Hootenanny, winter 1963.

If it wasn't for the recent emergence of a low-quality audience tape from what sounds like an impromptu three-song hootenanny set in early 1963, one would continue to think this single-verse 'come all ye' call was written especially for the Town Hall show in April. Perhaps the 'hoot' was a dry run for Town Hall. Much like 'Tell Me, Momma' in 1966,

'Ramblin Down Thru the World' was probably intended to serve as an introduction to the persona Dylan presented on this occasion, and as such fulfilled its (limited) purpose.

{94} WALLS OF RED WING

Published lyrics: Writings and Drawings; Lyrics *1985;* Lyrics *2004.*
First known performance: 'Gerde's Folk City' Hootenanny, winter 1963.
Known studio recordings: Studio A, NY, April 23, 1963 – 3 takes;
August 7, 1963 – 1 take [TBS – tk.1].

On the face of it, 'Walls of Red Wing' is an innocuous *Times*-era protest song Dylan performed for more than a year, but never released. However, it has recently invoked speculation regarding a possible autobiographical dimension. Red Wing was a reform school in Minnesota, just forty miles southeast of Minneapolis. As such, one is bound to wonder whether Dylan knew any one-time inmates. Or whether he was drawing on time spent at a 'country-club reform-school' in Pennsylvania in the late fifties (see *Behind the Shades Take Two,* p. 28). Dylan's disappearance from the face of the earth for much of the summer of 1959, plus the fact that he (in *Chronicles*) and his parents (in conversation with biographer Robert Shelton in 1968) construct wildly improbable chronologies to explain a prolonged absence from Hibbing, lends credence to the suggestion that he had been a naughty boy.

In 2006 such speculation was fanned by one Larry Haugen, who self-published a book called *Red Wing, a Year and a Day,* in which he claims Dylan was an inmate at the same time as him, not in the summer of 1959 but the previous year (Haugen says Bobby was there 'no more than a month'). According to Haugen, it was possible to be sent to Red Wing for such inconsequential infractions as truancy – though presumably not for breaking the high school piano's foot pedal. Photos of Dylan at Camp Herzl in Wisconsin that summer cast doubt on Haugen's dates.

An unpublished poem dating from early 1963 – contemporaneous with 'Walls of Red Wing' – was recently auctioned from Suze Rotolo's personal archive. It deals with someone who has been sent to jail and there 'met . . . ramblin college students / runnin high school hoboes,' both of which Dylan had been. The narrator ends up 'talkin to myself in a strange cell.' As the auction catalogue states, 'Whether or not the poem . . . has any autobiographical significance, its message reflects common themes in Dylan's early work: . . . [particularly] the different treatment meted out by the law to the rich and poor.' In 'Red Wing,' Dylan again suggests the line between ending up a lawyer or a deadbeat could be a thin one.

As with 'Girl from the North Country' and 'Boots of Spanish Leather,' Dylan seemed to write two separate sets of lyrics to this tune that winter. As Todd Harvey points out, 'The first three phrases of "Only a Hobo" and "Walls of Red Wing" match, and the fourth phrase of [the latter] corresponds to the final phrase in the [former's] chorus.' A more direct source, however, is a Scottish bothy ballad (bothy ballads are songs of manual labourers), specifically Ewan MacColl's rendition of the ballad, 'The Road and the Miles to Dundee,' released on his 1961 Folkways LP, *Bothy Ballads of Scotland*. Dylan was not averse to learning from those with whom he'd crossed swords back in December, and though MacColl was famously furious at him for playing his own songs at the strictly 'trad.' Singer's Club, run by him and wife Peggy Seeger, Dylan was a fan.

Given the maudlin Scottish melody to which he grafted this possibly autobiographical song, one might have expected Dylan to put more emotion into its few performances. Perhaps he was still uncomfortable writing about that time and place. On his next North Country song ('North Country Blues'), he would need a sex change to put it across. Meanwhile, the arbitrary nature of justice continued to colour a whole set of songs in the ensuing months ('Seven Curses,' 'The Lonesome Death of Hattie Carroll,' and 'Percy's Song' all being written before summer was done). The last documented performance of 'Walls of Red Wing' would be at London's Festival Hall in May 1964, where a few folk probably recognized the tune, if not the song's already stale sentiments.

{95} BOB DYLAN'S NEW ORLEANS RAG

Published lyrics: Writings and Drawings; Lyrics *1985;* Lyrics *2004.*
First known performance: Town Hall, April 12, 1963.
Known studio recordings: Studio A, NY, August 6, 1963 – 1 take; August 7, 1963 – 3 takes; October 24, 1963 – 4 takes.

In 2004 Robert Hilburn, that reliable chronicler, got Dylan to talk about a Village friend – surely Dave Van Ronk – giving him a book of François Villon poems in 1963. In it he was delighted to discover 'Villon talking about visiting a prostitute, and I [thought I] would turn it around. I won't visit a prostitute, I'll talk about rescuing a prostitute . . . turning stuff on its head, like "vice is salvation and virtue will lead to ruin."'

'New Orleans Rag' (presumably set in this town as a nod to 'House of the Rising Sun') is the only original song from these 'younger days' that addresses the oldest profession. It is slightly surprising that prostitution does not loom large in the Dylan lexicon, given his infatuation with the symbolists and fellow lowlifes. 'Goin' to Acapulco,' with which 'New Orleans Rag' shares a euphemistic way of talking about 'working women,' is the only other 'brothel song' that springs to mind, though 'Simple Twist of Fate' – in its draft form – implies a one-night stand with a lady of the night back in 1962.

Needless to say, the participant in 'New Orleans Rag' does not save the lady in one-oh-three from a life of sin. Indeed, he is so intimidated by the dissolute look of her recent customers as they depart that he doesn't even enter the premises. Rather, he '[runs] a bloody mile.' Though tried out on guitar first, the October studio recording is set to a pounding piano accompaniment, and fits the song's manic quality better.

{96} YOU'VE BEEN HIDING TOO LONG

{97} DUSTY OLD FAIRGROUNDS

Published lyric: Telegraph #5; Lyrics 1985; Lyrics 2004.

{98} WHO KILLED DAVEY MOORE?

Published lyric: Broadside #29; Writings and Drawings; Lyrics 1985; Lyrics 2004.

All songs, first known performance: Town Hall, New York, April 12, 1963 (#98 – Carnegie Hall, October 26, 1963 [TBS]).

One of the extraordinary things about Dylan's Town Hall performance is the number of songs he debuted there and then and never performed again or even recorded in the studio. 'You've Been Hiding Too Long,' 'Ramblin' Down Thru the World,' and 'Dusty Old Fairgrounds' all suffered such a fate. Even the perennially popular 'Who Killed Davey Moore?' he refrained from recording in the studio.

Quite why Dylan never recorded 'Davey Moore' in Studio A has never been adequately explained (he even copyrighted it from the live recording). Questioned by Elliott Mintz about the song on its first official appearance, in 1991, Dylan seemed at a loss to explain its absence from the canon: '["Who Killed Davey Moore?"] was done at the same time as the "Hattie Carroll" song. . . . Those two songs kinda went together . . . One got left off the record for some reason. . . . To me these songs were never about blame. They were more about justice.' Actually 'Hattie Carroll' was written six months later, after he had begun to question the purpose of such 'fact-based' topical balladry. However, the maid's death occurred only a few weeks *before* Moore's – hence, perhaps, the association in Dylan's mind.

The boxing bout that claimed the life of Davey Moore occurred on March 22, 1963, in Los Angeles – a contest for the featherweight championship of the world between current titleholder Davey Moore and the Cuban 'Sugar' Ramos. In the bloody contest, Ramos finally knocked Moore out in the tenth round. Moore subsequently lapsed into a coma and died three days later. So Dylan was not hanging about, performing it less than three weeks later, even though he hadn't quite worked up the tune.

The Town Hall performance relies heavily on the audience going along with the song's premise – that no-one will accept the blame for what happened. Set to the fabled nursery rhyme 'Who Killed Cock Robin?' it showed how such fables could be turned into contemporary songs (and vice versa – the sixteenth-century 'Froggy Went A-Courtin,' covered by Dylan in 1992, is believed by some to be a coded commentary on Elizabethan court politics). As for topicality, it confirmed that Dylan was still keeping his lyric notebook next to a copy of the morning newspaper.

Altogether more disposable is 'You've Been Hiding Too Long,' another two-verse talkin' blues that, like 'Talkin' Devil,' sails well wide of its target. Because this little song has as its punch line, 'Let the world see what a hypocrite you are,' there may be a relationship with 'Talkin' Hypocrite,' the song he played to Tony Glover in August 1962. If so, a song rhyming 'patriotism' with 'boy in prison' had survived eight extraordinarily creative months. At the Town Hall its primary purpose seems to be as a prelude to the altogether weightier 'With God on Our Side.' That Dylan continued to harbour hard feelings about 'hypocrites' (marked down for damnation as early as September 1961's 'I Hear a Train A-Rolling') was revealed in 1980, when he rapped about the origins of the word:

A long time ago they used to have those Greek plays. . . . Back
then, they had actors too, but they called them hypocrites.
There'd be like a play with thirty people in it, but actually
there'd be only four. They'd all just wear masks. . . . There's
a lot of hypocrites [now]; they're talking, using Jesus's name,
but . . . they're still dealing with the world.

'Dusty Old Fairgrounds,' probably a last-minute whim,
complimented another outlandish account of his youth
already included as part of the night's programme, 'My Life
in a Stolen Minute' (only later would that last word become
'Moment'). The carnival that travelled from dusty fairground to dusty fairground had loomed large in some rather
tall tales he had spun to the likes of Izzy Young, Cynthia
Gooding, Robert Shelton, and Billy James, all 'on the record,'
during that first year in New York, so such a salute had been
a long time coming.

Note: 'Dusty Old Fairgrounds' was one of the few omissions
from *Writings and Drawings*. It was added to the published
canon with the 1985 edition of *Lyrics*, having been recorded
in the interim by Blue Ash for their 1973 album, *No More, No
Less*.

{99} SEVEN CURSES

Published lyrics: Writings and Drawings; Lyrics *1985;* Lyrics *2004.*
First known performance: Town Hall, April 12, 1963.
Known studio recordings: Studio A, NY, August 6, 1963 – 3 takes
[TBS – tk.3].

The recent emergence of the Town Hall performance
of 'Seven Curses' necessitates a reassignment of the song
to the spring, not the summer, of 1963, and begs the question, Why was this masterful song not one of those Dylan
attempted at a session, eleven days later, intended to reshape
Freewheelin' at the last minute? Surviving in the live set until

October, 'Seven Curses' is one of a trio of quasi-traditional original songs which refined to a quintessence the balladic conventions he had been purloining/emulating, and were performed for the Carnegie Hall crowd, only to be omitted from the album he was finishing up.

Whereas songs like 'Bob Dylan's Dream' and 'Kingsport Town' self-consciously lean on the Anglo-American folk tradition, 'Seven Curses' takes a more Eastern route. Dylan here adapts a Central European folk legend – concerning a judge who seduces a young girl by promising to save her father/brother from the noose, only to break his word – making it heartbreakingly real to a new audience. The stream of tradition from which Dylan here drew certainly took its winding way to reach him. By the time Dylan began singing 'Seven Curses,' Judy Collins was also singing a rather similar song called 'Anathea.'

Credited to Neil Roth and Lydia Wood, 'Anathea' was Collins's adaptation of a poem she had been given by Roth when she was in Paris a few years ealier. Collins's song reiterated the exact same Hungarian legend. If a Mr. Roth conceived of such a poem, it was a few centuries back, and he was really a Hungarian Jew called Rothstein. The song was collected at least three times by classical composer Béla Bartók in the early 1920s when he was at work on his seminal study, *The Hungarian Folk Song (1924)*. And though it has been suggested that the song was first translated into English by the postwar English folklorist A. L. Lloyd, there was an English translation of Bartók's work as far back as 1931.

Dylan was knowledgeable enough to know that the story was not Roth's. Indeed, he seems to have had some knowledge of its Eastern European source. Judy Collins, in a 1996 e-mail interview with Manfred Helfert regarding the two songs, confirms that 'the "Seven Curses" are related to "Anathea." [But] there are old themes, world themes, centuries old dramas that get worked out in the creative process by artist after artist. . . . I see what Dylan has always done is to connect with this inner, subterranean river of the sub-conscious.' So, no hard feelings here. Nor should there be.

The ballad has a number of names in its original tongue, though 'Feher Anna' comes closest to its Anglo-American equivalent. In 'Feher Anna,' Anna's brother Laszlo is in prison for stealing a horse (or six), so she races to the prison with 'a bushel of gold pieces' only to be told by the judge, 'I do not want a bushel of gold pieces, I only want a night with you.' In the original the brother predicts that the judge will use her and betray him, whereas in 'Seven Curses' the father pleads with his daughter not to sleep with the judge for more moral reasons: 'My skin will surely crawl / If he touches you at all.' I tend to prefer the brother's more understandable suspicions, though Dylan's portrayal of the father unquestionably displays its own psychological power. At the end of 'Feher Anna,' the curses are delivered directly to the judge, and there are thirteen of them:

> Hearken Judge, Judge Horvat,
> May your horse stumble on his feet.
> May your horse stumble on his feet,
> And you be thrown to the ground.
> May thirteen cartloads of straw
> Rot away in your bed!
> May you for thirteen years
> Lie upon it in cruel illness!
> May thirteen doctors work
> At dressing your wounds,
> Thirteen shelves of drugs
> Be emptied on your account!
> Indeed, Judge, I wish you well!
> May your washing-water turn to blood,
> Your towel spit flames,
> And God never bless you!

In making it seven curses, Dylan demonstrates that he already knew about the power the number seven held in Anglo-American folklore, evincing a knowledge of the well-known 'Cruel Mother' (which has recently been covered by singer-songwriter Richard Thompson as 'Bonny Saint Johnston'), in which the lady is told by the spirits of the children she murdered that she will spend seven years in hell serving one penance, then seven more serving another, ad infinitum. Having gotten the idea for the song, and a few lines, from the 'Feher Anna' antecedent, Dylan comes up with his 'own' tune, a variant on the 'Tomorrow Is a Long Time' template.

{100} WITH GOD ON OUR SIDE

Published lyrics: Broadside *#27*; Writings and Drawings; Lyrics *1985*; Lyrics *2004*.

First known performance: Town Hall, New York, April 12, 1963.
Known studio recordings: Studio A, NY, August 6, 1963 – 5 takes; August 7, 1963 – 1 take [TIMES – tk.1].

By the time Dylan arrived in London in December 1962, he knew that Guthrie was hardly the only modern balladeer to have found a way to mint a new currency from old 'penny dreadfuls.' He had perhaps not yet realized just how immersed Britain was in its very own 'folk revival,' which had both a popular (skiffle) and a political (socialist) dimension. And the British breed of broadside bards were slightly ahead of their American East Coast cousins in the contemporary songs they were crafting.

Ewan MacColl, with whom Dylan tangled on his winter travels, had songs like 'Dirty Old Town' and 'Go Down You Murderers,' a big favourite of Dylan's, while Irish playwright Dominic Behan had composed a tuneful tirade against the kind of patriotism propagated by the IRA as a recruitment tool. The song in question, 'The Patriot Game,' was set to a well-known traditional tune called 'The Nightingale.' Written in 1957, after young IRA member Fergal O'Hanlon was shot in an attack on Dungannon Barracks, 'The Patriot Game' used a familiar format to berate those who played their part in the patriot game:

> Come all you young rebels and list while I sing,
> For love of one's land is a terrible thing.
> It banishes fear with the speed of a flame,
> And makes us all part of the patriot game.

Powerful stuff, especially for a young Dylan who had found little competition among New York's topical-song merchants. Apparently, he first heard Behan's diatribe sung by fellow folksinger Nigel Denver at the Troubadour in the Old Brompton Road and afterwards interrogated another folksinger, Jim McLean, about it. MacLean says, 'In those days Dylan was a young man eager for new material, and I remember discussing the merits of the song, especially Behan's use of the word "patriot," which agreed with Doctor Johnson's belief that "patriotism is the last refuge of the scoundrel."'

Though it would take Dylan another twenty years to find a direct use for Johnson's aphorism (in 'Sweetheart Like You'), he began writing a lyric that encapsulated the eminent doctor's dictum, directed at an American audience. Unconvinced that Behan had tapped into the universality of the sentiment, he seized upon a motto emblazoned on every dollar bill, 'In God We Trust.' He would later suggest to journalist Margaret Steen that he felt such songs were somewhat forced in their diction, because he imposed line after line to drive home his point: 'Before [*Another Side*] . . . every song had to have a specific point behind it, a person, a thing; I would squeeze a shapeless concept into this artificial shape, like "With God On Our Side." . . . This thing I wanted to say, I had to jam into a very timed, rigid, stylized pattern.'

In the process Dylan sparked another controversy concerning the scale of any debt owed to Behan, and this time it was crystal clear that his precursor was unhappy with such a brazen act of appropriation. A quarter of a century later, Behan was still steaming. When journalist Robin Denselow referred to Dylan's condemnation of bootlegging in a 1985 review of *Biograph*, Behan let readers of *The Guardian* know just what he thought of Dylan the pirate: 'Bob should know [all] about such piracy. Let me give you an instance: my song "The Patriot Game" . . . Dylan's "God on Our Side" takes my music lock, stock and barrel, and very nearly the words. . . . The song is a complete parody of "The Patriot Game."'

Behan promptly brought the wrath of the Dylan-listening, *Guardian*-reading demographic down upon his head, as letter writers galore pointed out it was hardly 'his' tune. Behan now became disingenuous, stating, 'I made a recording of "The Nightingale" sometime in the sixties for Major Minor Records and I sang it to the tune of "The Patriot Game."' In fact 'The Nightingale' had been sung to that tune by Jo Stafford as far back as 1948, nine years before Behan wrote his song; a point made by, among others, Liam Clancy.

Perhaps Dylan was already aware of Behan's ire. During a July 1963 workshop performance at Newport (now on DVD), he claimed that he'd learned the 'The Patriot Game' from the Clancys and that he'd heard Liam sing it 'two years ago.' Though Dylan is probably exaggerating, the Clancys *did* issue their own version of 'The Patriot Game' in 1963. So maybe the Troubadour was not the first place Dylan heard 'The Patriot Game' (or 'Nottamun Town' or 'Lady Franklin'). As for the tune, when 'The Patriot Game' was published in *Sing Out!* the following year, it clearly stated, 'music adapted from traditional airs.'

Behan's assertion that Dylan's song is 'a complete parody of "The Patriot Game,"' is also patent nonsense. Yes, the songs share a similar concern. However, Behan is preaching to the converted with his references to the likes of James Connolly and de Valera – martyrs to the Irish cause of 'freedom' – while Dylan picks grander struggles, like two world wars, as the backdrop to a song that universalizes its subject matter. He also shows a sharper eye for the absurdities underlying the patriots' position. In an era of reds under the bed, he both lectures and lampoons. When he says in verse six, 'I've learned to hate Russians / all through my whole life,' no-one knew at the time that here was a boy who grew up sharing a home with at least one grandparent who had emigrated from Odessa at the turn of the century. As he would write in *Chronicles*, 'These were the same Russians that my uncles had fought alongside only a few years earlier. Now they had become monsters who were coming to slit our throats and incinerate us.'

At the time of its composition, he found himself obliged to explain the tenor of the song to his father (both of whose parents were Russian). Misled by the title into thinking it was a patriotic song, Abraham was set right by his son. As he told Robert Shelton, shortly before his own death in 1968: 'When I heard about this song – "With God On Our Side" . . . I mentioned it to Bob. He said, "Dad, it's not the kind of song you think it is." Because I hadn't seen the words yet. I said, "The title infers that it is a beautiful song," and he said, "No, it's kind of a sarcastic song."'

'A sarcastic song' it may have been, but Dylan insists he was trying not to sermonize. As he told British journalist John Preston at the time of *Chronicles*, 'Some people seemed to think that listening to songs should be like listening to dull sermons. I didn't want my songs to be anything like that.' Unfortunately, 'With God on Our Side' crossed the line, laying the ground for yet more judgemental songs to come.

Not surprisingly, *Broadside*'s Sis Cunningham, *Sing Out!*'s Irwin Silber, and a besotted Joan Baez all loved the song and insisted on publishing or performing it. Dylan was less convinced and soon decided to vent his sarcasm on shadier targets. Prior to the song becoming a surprise radio hit after being recorded by The Neville Brothers for their 1988 *Yellow Moon* album, he had performed it exactly twice in twenty-five years: once at a 1975 Rolling Thunder show in Providence (maybe as a request from some old Newportees) and then during a joint Dylan/Baez set at Peace Sunday in June 1982. Yet for a brief time in the fall of 1988, he began performing the song again, incorporating the sophomoric extra verse the Nevilles themselves had written about Vietnam.

As for any moral debt he had to 'The Patriot Game,' Dylan would doubtless argue that both he and Behan were drawing from the 'folk idiom' – and the (long out of copyright) collected works of Samuel Johnson. Dylan, though, probably now wishes one *could* copyright an idea, since he would now be entitled to a share of the untold millions earned by Tim Rice and Andrew Lloyd Webber from *Jesus Christ Superstar*, a rock opera that began life because Rice decided to write a libretto that would answer the question Dylan posed at the end of 'With God On Our Side' – 'whether Judas Iscariot / Had God on his side.'

{101} TALKIN' WORLD WAR III BLUES

Published lyrics: Writings and Drawings; Lyrics 1985; Lyrics 2004.
Known studio recordings: Studio A, NY, April 23, 1963 [FR].
First known performance: The Bear, Chicago, April 25, 1963.

When Dylan returned to Columbia in late April 1963, it appears to have been with one specific idea in mind – to update the album he thought he'd completed the previous

December, incorporating winter 1963 songs at the expense of the winter 1962 songs. Out went the once highly regarded 'Let Me Die in My Footsteps,' 'Ramblin' Gamblin' Willie,' and 'Rocks and Gravel,' all songs cut the previous April, to be replaced by 'Masters of War,' 'Bob Dylan's Dream,' and 'Girl from the North Country,' all penned during the previous three months.

Also part of the cull – indeed the purported reason for *Freewheelin'*s recall – was the earliest original composition scheduled for the album, 'Talkin' John Birch Paranoid Blues.' The reason for its exclusion? A potential libel suit that necessitated a new set of sleeve notes, a new album sequence, and the recalling of promotional copies and a few stock copies of the original version (now worth at least five figures).

The legend does not quite tally with the fact that these 'replacement songs' were recorded in the studio a good three weeks before the aborted Ed Sullivan show appearance, which allegedly triggered the album's recall. Evidently Columbia expressed their concerns *before* the (cancelled) TV appearance and instructed Dylan – via attorney Clive Davis – to come up with an alternative. The fact that Dylan chose to replace 'Talkin' John Birch' with another talkin' blues, newly penned, strongly suggests that the decision had already been made by April 24 – when he made these new recordings.

As one would expect, the song with which Dylan replaced the former talkin' blues was funnier, more topical, and altogether more relevant to the world of 1963. And yet, according to Scaduto, 'Talkin' World War III Blues' 'was nothing more than a partially worked out idea in Dylan's mind when he went into the studio.' There is probably something to this. We have plenty of evidence of Dylan's capacity for improvising around a central lyrical idea. And he doesn't seem to have had the song at hand twelve days earlier, when he unveiled almost his entire repertoire at Town Hall (including 'Talkin' New York'). Unlike the wildly unfunny 'Talkin' Devil,' 'You've Been Hiding Too Long,' 'Masters of War,' and 'Train A-Travelin',' this spontaneous display of antibomb rhetoric allowed Dylan to convey a life after the bomb that is more *Beyond the Fringe* than *Omega Man*.

The talkin' blues had become so innate to Dylan's art form that he captured the song in the studio in a single full take (after four false starts). And what a deliriously sardonic tour de force this *Freewheelin'* performance is. Here in microcosmic (as opposed to capsule) form is the cerebral seed of every surreal flight of fancy he will embark on post-acid (his first 'trip' was still a year away, to the day). Rather than murdering the singer for coming up with such a post-apocalyptic scenario, the doctor in 'TWWIII Blues' has a simpler solution: 'Nurse, get your pad, this boy's insane.' It doesn't stop the singer spending eight verses traversing this eery landscape. He even manages to slip a dig at red-baiters past the Columbia lawyers:

> I seen a man, I said, 'Howdy friend, I guess there's just us two.'
> He screamed a bit and away he flew. Thought I was a Communist.

{102} LIVERPOOL GAL

Published lyrics: In His Own Words 2.

Nothing was known of this intriguing song until the late eighties, when it appeared in manuscript form as part of the so-called Margolis and Moss papers. Given that the majority of these papers, mostly typescripts of poems and an unfinished play, date from the fall of 1963, it was presumed that the song also came from this period, when Dylan was taking a break from songwriting. It subsequently came out that the song featured on the last of the Tony Glover 'home tapes,' recorded the previous July on another of Dylan's trips home, putting its composition back to a period when the ink still poured out of his pen. It probably dates from a trip to Woodstock in May, a time when according to Suze, 'songs . . . were coming out of him rapid fire.' (There is a Woodstock connection to all of the Margolis and Moss material.)

Though the July tape remains solely in Glover's possession, the inclusion of the song on a tape of originals played to impress old friends and one curmudgeonly critic (Paul Nelson) barely three weeks before he began work on his third album makes it all the more surprising that he made no attempt to record the song for Columbia. Nor did he copyright it with Witmark, the company for which he continued to cut demos. Maybe the song was already old hat and was played for a specific reason (and person) that July evening.

Nelson, who had just given Dylan's second album a lukewarm review in *Little Sandy Review #27*, was giving the songwriter a hard time about the topical songs he was then writing, so this performance could have been a palliative to Nelson's bruised sensibilities; what with him being steeped in the genuinely traditional. Nelson would definitely have recognized the template to which Dylan set his tale, 'When First Unto This Country,' a stalwart of many a revivalist repertoire, and a song Dylan performed in both electric and acoustic guises at the start of the Never Ending Tour in 1989 and 1991.

Originally about the son of a poor immigrant, Dylan inverts the folk song's vantage point, making the singer a traveller who'd gone to 'London town' but cannot help 'thinkin' about / the land I left back home.' This depiction of someone who 'walked the streets so silently' and 'did not know no one' may well reflect his own feeling on arriving in the great city, the previous December. The verse where he describes the winter weather also has the ring of authentic experience: 'I gazed all up at her window, where the stormy snowflakes blowed / I put my hands deep in my pockets, and I walked on down the road.'

One ineluctable question the song raises is whether there really was a 'Liverpool gal / who lived in London town,' with whom the singer spent the night, only to feel the following morning, 'Of her love I know not much.' Its belated, solitary appearance suggests a song that gestated for some time. And its appearance among papers assembled after the completion of *Times* . . . presumably means it was a song he had not quite resolved to forget. At least he ended up saving the idea for 'I Don't Believe You.'

{103} ONLY A PAWN IN THEIR GAME

Published lyrics: Broadside *#33*; Writings and Drawings; Lyrics *1985*; Lyrics *2004*.

First known performance: Greenwood Rally, Mississippi July 6, 1963 [DLB].

Known studio recordings: Studio A, NY, August 6, 1963 – 6 takes; August 7, 1963 – 1 take [TIMES – tk.1].

Medgar Evers was a field secretary for the NAACP (National Association for the Advancement of Colored People) in Mississippi. He was therefore both a prominent and an easy target for racist agitators. And by the summer of 1963, tensions had risen to an all-time high. Even locals, though, were stunned when Evers was gunned down outside his own home in Jackson on June 12. The reaction, from both a primed media and an angry mob, resulted in localized rioting. The local police had no problem arresting twenty-seven (mostly black) rioters, but when they arrested a white suspect for the murder, he was immediately released.

With said tensions (and concomitant political pressure) still mounting, the one and only suspect, Byron de la Beckwith, was finally indicted for the shooting a fortnight later. By then, one must presume, Dylan had already written this response-in-song, which appears to take its immediate inspiration from a quote supplied by NAACP executive secretary Roy Wilkins for the June 16 edition of the *New York Times*. According to Wilkins, it was the 'Southern political system' that had put the murderer 'behind that rifle.' Wilkins thus provided Dylan with an evocative couplet and a core theme:

> A bullet from the back of a bush took Medgar Evers blood
> A finger fired the trigger to his name . . .
> But he can't be blamed
> He's only a pawn in their game.

In keeping with the topical rivalry Dylan now enjoyed with certain Village peers, the race was on to provide the first expression of outrage for the *Broadside presses*. Once more, Dylan let others fire the first retaliatory volleys. It was poetaster Phil Ochs who again offered his 'Ballad of Medgar Evers' to Cunningham's magazine, taking great delight in portraying the killer as a cowardly bigot:

> The killer waited by his home hidden by the night
> As Evers stepped out from his car into the rifle sight
> He slowly squeezed the trigger, the bullet left his side
> It struck the heart of every man as Evers fell and died.

Like Dylan, Ochs offered no name for the killer. Indeed, initial reports of the murder were careful not to name Beckwith as the likely culprit. Yet by the time Dylan debuted the song in Mississippi on July 6, Beckwith had been charged with the crime. Unfortunately for Dylan's thesis, de la Beckwith – as his name implies – was hardly someone who came 'from the poverty shacks.' In fact he paid the $10,000 bail set in cash. Nor did he feel any need to 'hide 'neath the

[KKK] hood.' A high-ranking official in the Ku Klux Klan, he made no secret of his views or affiliation. Nor, it appears, did he need to. Such was the groundswell of support for the man and his views that when he ran for lieutenant governor of Mississippi, four years after being charged with Evers's murder, he still polled some 34,000 votes.

By then he had been subjected to two trials, both of which failed to reach a verdict. Eventually the charges were dropped (though he was never formally acquitted). These high-profile trials – which made it plain that the man was a bigot, but no pawn – failed to convince Dylan to quietly let the song go. He would still be performing it in October 1964 – fifteen months after its debut at a voter registration rally in Greenwood, Mississippi (a performance memorably inserted into *Don't Look Back* at the last minute).

Throughout the summer of 1963 Dylan used the song to validate his credentials as a civil rights activist still willing to activate his pen for the cause. He performed it passionately at the Newport Folk Festival; a CBS Sales Convention in San Juan, where its performance apparently instigated a mass walkout by the southern reps; and to half a million strong at the Washington Civil Rights March in late August. Its most select audience, though, was Tony Glover and friends, back home in Minnesota just eleven days after the Mississippi rally. And despite its tenuous thesis, Dylan's song received very little opprobrium, save from Paul Nelson, who boldly challenged his motives for writing such a song in the first place:

After [*Freewheelin'*] we had this debate. . . . It went on and on. [The *Little Sandy Review*] were sort of the anti topical song people, not because we disagreed with it politically but just because we thought it was such shitty art, y'know. These songs were like fish in the barrel stuff. I didn't like the Phil Ochs songs much. . . . It's like patting yourself on the back music, it just seemed so obvious and not particularly well done. And Dylan was arguing, 'No, no, this is really where it's at.' But he also made the point that the easiest way to get published if you wrote your own songs was to write topical songs 'cause *Broadside* wouldn't publish if you didn't, and you had a tough time getting in *Sing Out!*

Dylan thought 'Only a Pawn in Their Game' provided the lyrical ammunition necessary to shoot down Nelson's argument, playing it twice that night – as if Nelson just hadn't quite got it first time around. A few days later, he continued putting his side of the argument in an open letter 'For Dave Glover,' intended for the Newport Folk Festival programme at the month's end. In this free-verse poem he claimed he 'don['t] worry no more bout the covered up lies an twisted truths in front a my eyes / . . . [or] bout the no-talent criticizers an know-nothin philosophizers.' Nelson, it appears, had got under his skin.

Even after the courts failed to prosecute de la Beckwith successfully for his crime, Dylan continued to argue that the song succeeded in its aim. He informed *Melody Maker*'s Max Jones the following May that the assassin was 'sheltered' by a deep-rooted ignorance: 'If someone gets killed, who's to say who fired the gun? And why? He fired just because he was uptight. Everybody reacts to what he knows, to what he's been taught and has come in contact with. He's been taught there's only one way; he's been sheltered. He's gonna get uptight about it when he sees something different. We have to ask why these people have sheltered him and taught him this. They have reasons too.'

Later that day Dylan performed 'Only a Pawn in Their Game' to a sell-out crowd unconversant with the facts of the case, at his first London concert. Just a couple of weeks later he sent his best in a letter to 'good critic paul,' at the same time that he began disavowing songs that pretended 'life is black and white.' The days of 'Only a Pawn in Their Game' were numbered. But the outrage was not entirely forgotten.

In 1991 Byron de la Beckwith found out he was to be retried for the murder of Evers, after Evers's body was exhumed 'amid allegations of tampering with evidence and jurors.' In the interim, he somehow managed to get himself arrested for having a trunk full of dynamite, finally receiving the life sentence he so richly deserved. And yet, even on his deathbed, confessing to the murder, he remained unrepentant. As for Dylan's prediction that he would be buried in an unmarked grave, Beckwith was given a hero's funeral attended by thousands of rednecks. Indeed, according to *Judas!* editor Andrew Muir, 'a number of websites . . . still hail him as a hero and martyr.'

{104} ETERNAL CIRCLE

Published lyrics: Writings and Drawings; Lyrics *1985;* Lyrics *2004.*
Known studio recordings: Studio A, NY, August 7, 1963 – 4 takes; August 12 – 4 takes; October 24 – 4 takes [TBS].
First known performance: [Community Theater, Berkeley, February 22, 1964] Royal Festival Hall, London May 17, 1964.

To more attentive attendees at London's Royal Festival Hall, the likes of 'Eternal Circle' and 'Mr. Tambourine Man' would have suggested Dylan was intending to celebrate the power of song on his next album. Imagine their disappointment when that LP appeared minus such songs, giving the world 'Motorpsycho Nitemare' and 'I Shall Be Free #10' instead. In fact, 'Eternal Circle' took twenty-seven years to see the light of official day. Yet as the first song of its type to enter Dylan's repertoire, it was that all-important springboard for 'Lay Down Your Weary Tune' three months later, and the even more mystical 'Mr. Tambourine Man' a further four months down the line. It was another song he was anxious to play that July night at Glover's, a demonstration of the range of his songwriting.

A song about Song, 'Eternal Circle' shows a structural sophistication absent from his contemporary displays of tub-thumping topicality. In it the singer ostensibly describes the experience of singing a song, all the while wondering about its effect on one audience member, who 'called with her eyes / to the tune I's a-playin'.' The 'circle' in the title is clearly the circle of song, Dylan beginning with, 'I sang the song slowly,' and ending with, 'I began the next song.' Poet James Reeves called it *The Everlasting Circle* (1960) in his second anthology of English folk songs.

Adding resonance, Dylan copped aspects of the melody from 'Song to Woody,' albeit radically rearranged. He even attempted to fingerpick the melody, but this approach was abandoned after a single session, all subsequent attempts at the song being flatpicked. After the two attempts to capture the song at August 1963 sessions, he returned to it at the penultimate *Times* session on October 24 (though it did not feature at Carnegie Hall two days later). The fact that he persevered with the song into 1964, it being performed at Berkeley in February and London in May, suggested that he still envisaged completing this circle one fine day. Only with the composition of 'Mr. Tambourine Man,' another lyric that fixates on the song process itself, does it appear that the fate of 'Eternal Circle' was sealed. It would devolve to the bootleggers to champion this forgotten gem. Rock band McGuinness Flint also exhumed the song for their 1972 LP of unreleased Dylan songs, *Lo & Behold*, which opens and closes with it.

{105} NORTH COUNTRY BLUES

Published lyrics: Writings and Drawings; Lyrics *1985*; Lyrics *2004*.
First known performance: Ballad Workshop, Newport Folk Festival, July 26, 1963 [OSOTM].
Known studio recordings: Studio A, NY, August 6, 1963 – 4 takes [TIMES – tk.4].

Given that 'North Country Blues' was *not* one of the songs Dylan sang to Glover and friends on July 17, 1963 – and yet he had the whole thing by the time he was playing a Newport ballad workshop nine days later – we can probably assume he wrote the song in the interim. Once again, a trip home seemingly inculcated him with nostalgia for his 'younger days,' when 'the red iron pits ran plenty.' The sight of his hometown gripped by irreversible decline, as it would have been by 1963, set off a whole set of memories, good and bad, prompting one of his most effective ballads.

When Dylan wrote 'North Country Blues,' very little was known about the troubled troubadour's Midwest background. He continued to pepper the truth with tales of hard times spent 'ramblin' down thru the world.' Initially, he failed to own up to any autobiographical dimension to the song, hiding behind the female persona, a wife of a miner. His introduction to the song on its live debut at Newport merely stated that it was about 'iron-ore mines and an iron-ore town.' At Carnegie Hall in October, he was no less coy: 'I'm sure you all know about the coal-mining countries, down in Virginia. This is a song that comes from the ore countries.'

But in the hallowed hall that night were a pair of proud parents who knew exactly of what their son sang, and which experiences he might be drawing on. Beattie and Abe had flown in to confirm for themselves that their son could sell out the most prestigious venue in New York. But even they were probably unprepared for this unrelenting account of a life in the North Country, written as if by a widow affected by all the economic travails the region suffered. And on some level, he was performing this ballad largely for them (as he would deliver 'I Believe in You' to his mother and brother at the final Minneapolis show in 1992).

Evidently Dylan had been storing away a number of formative experiences from his youth, and a trip home was all that was needed to trigger them. Perhaps the most profound one lodged in his memory was the time his father took him to see the town where this Abraham had been born. Except it was no longer there. As Mr. Zimmerman recalled in 1968, 'I was born in a town twelve miles out of Hibbing called Stevenson Location, named after a man who went there to mine. . . . There is no more town there. It is an abandoned mine and the houses are all gone. It is just weeds and forest now. It is due west from here. We took Bobby up there once to show him the house, and there was no house. It was just a dead end.' One can imagine the impact such an experience had on his deeply impressionable son.

The song conveys that desolation in undiluted form. It is a ballad *and* a blues. 'North Country Blues' would also be the last time he could hide behind the smokescreen of a carefully constructed, apocryphal 'life in a stolen moment.' A couple of days after the Carnegie performance, Dylan was brought down with a bump and his cover blown when Andrea Svedburg ran her *Newsweek* expose of the man's North Country roots: 'He shrouds his past in contradictions, but he is the elder son of a Hibbing, Minn. appliance dealer named Abe Zimmerman and, as Bobby Zimmerman, he attended Hibbing High School, then briefly the University of Minnesota.'

From here on he would have to talk about home in interviews, while disguising its influence in song. However, he never forgot what impelled him to write such a mother's lament – even though he was one of the sons who was now beyond her command. As he told Nat Hentoff from the vortex of a later media storm: 'Hibbing, Minnesota was just not the right place for me to stay and live. There really was nothing there. The only thing you could do there was to be a miner, and even that kind of thing was getting less and less . . . . The mines were just dying, that's all; but that's not their fault. Everybody about my age left there. . . . It didn't take any great amount of thinking or individual genius. . . . So leaving wasn't hard at all. It would have been much harder to stay.' As for 'North Country Blues' itself, it was resurrected just once, at a benefit for Friends of Chile in April 1974, when it was sung by a man who, like John Thomas the miner, 'smelled heavy from drinking.'

{106} GYPSY LOU

Published lyrics: Writings and Drawings; Lyrics *1985;* Lyrics *2004.*
Known studio recordings: Witmark demo, August 1963.

Copyrighted from a demo recording made circa September 1963, this is surely somewhat older than its copyright suggests. (Its companion piece, 'Whatcha Gonna Do?' was almost a year old.) Dylan clearly thought so, because he included it with 'Early songs' (i.e., 1961–2 compositions) in *Writings and Drawings.* The lyrics certainly conjure up that more derivative phase of his songwriting, reusing lines from the collective blues lexicon like 'she's a ramblin' woman with a ramblin' mind' with little of his later facility. The list of locations, à la 'Dusty Old Fairgrounds,' does equally little to retain its grip on the listener's attention. One doubts the song detained its author long.

{107} TROUBLED AND I DON'T KNOW WHY

Published lyrics: The Telegraph *#1;* Words Fill My Head.
First known performance: Forest Hills, NY, August 17, 1963 [RLC].

Two months before Svedburg gave him a reason to be troubled, Dylan wrote his first song to reflect a discontent *not* brought on by romantic distress. As girlfriend Suze Rotolo once said, 'Dylan seems to lack that sort of simple hope.' 'Troubled and I Don't Know Why' is a minor song about a couple of major Dylan bugbears: the pressures of modern living (generally) and the burden of expectation (person-ally). Though this places it in the same part of the canon as songs like 'It's Alright Ma,' 'Idiot Wind,' and 'Most of the Time,' it is an innocuous aperitif to such fulsome fare. The song targets soon-familiar Dylan concerns, like the tabloid papers ('it rolled in the door / and bounced on the floor / Said things ain't going so well') and the television ('it roared and it boomed / And it bounced around the room / And it didn't say nothin' at all'). But this time it is strictly for laughs.

Dylan was merely letting off steam, as suggested by the song's solitary appearance on a short tour with Joan Baez in August. He was saving his real wrath for the likes of 'When the Ship Comes In,' written days later. The lady's warbling on the only extant recording, from Forest Hills, provides the usual falsetto echo. It also ensured that the song was finally given an official release, on a 1993 Joan Baez retrospective box-set titled *Rare, Live & Classic*, which credits words and music to her erstwhile paramour.

The tune, though, is a straight copy of that perennial, 'What Did the Deep Sea Say?' – a song previously covered by the likes of the Carter Family and Bill Monroe. We know the melody was on Dylan's mind because it was the one song he played to Glover and friends for light relief on that fraught July evening in Minneapolis. It evidently remained one of his favourites, too, because ten years later he used it again, on another so-called original, 'Peco's Blues,' an instrumental originally intended for the soundtrack to *Pat Garrett and Billy the Kid*.

{108} WHEN THE SHIP COMES IN

Published lyrics: Writings and Drawings; Lyrics 1985; Lyrics 2004.
First known performance: Washington Civil Rights March,
August 28, 1963.
Known studio recordings: Studio A, NY, October 23, 1963 – 4
takes [TIMES – tk.4].

If we believe the Dylan who wrote *Chronicles*, he had been trying to write his own version of Kurt Weill's 'Pirate Jenny' (from *The Threepenny Opera*) for some time when he composed 'When the Ship Comes In.' Introduced to Bertolt Brecht and cowriter Weill by girlfriend Suze – who was helping out on a production of *Brecht on Brecht* in the early months of 1963 (it opened at the Sheridan Square Playhouse in April) – he claims to have penned a song that was a cross between Brecht and a murder ballad:

> Totally influenced by 'Pirate Jenny,' though staying far away from its ideological heart, I . . . took a story out of the *Police Gazette*, a tawdry incident about a hooker in Cleveland, a minister's daughter called Snow White, who killed one of her customers in a grotesque and ugly way. I started with that using the [Brecht-Weill] song as a prototype and piled lines on . . . and used the first two lines of the 'Frankie & Albert' ballad as the chorus . . . but the song didn't come off.

Whether or not this song ever existed, Dylan placed its composition improbably early (in the winter of 1962). Nor is it the only song he claims was inspired by the Brechtian ballad. In the *Biograph* notes, he states, '"the set pattern" to "The Lonesome Death of Hattie Carroll" also derives from "Pirate Jenny."' Todd Harvey concurs, suggesting that they share 'structural, melodic and lyric connections.' But any melodic connection can only be accidental, Hattie's tune having an altogether more ancient antecedent.

It takes the merest of introductions to Weill's black-hearted song to recognize a rather more direct parallel within Dylan's canon. It is a song he composed in August 1963 – a month before he wrote his other maid's song – when the influence of Brecht was at its most profound. And we have firsthand testimony as to the immediate circumstances that inspired this song. It comes from Joan Baez, with whom he was touring when the song welled up inside:

> You know when he wrote 'When the Ship Comes In'? That was amazing, the history of that little song. We were driving around the East Coast, we were out in the boondocks some-where, and I had a concert to give. I don't even know whether he was singing with me at that point, but he and I were driving together and we stopped. I said, 'Run in and see if this is the right place,' so he went in and came out and said, 'Hey, there's no reservation here.' I said, 'You sure?' and I went in and they said, 'Hello, Miss Baez, we've been waiting for you.' And I said, 'Hold it a minute. I want an extra room please.' And then Bobby walked in, and he was all innocent and looking shitty as hell and I said, 'Give this gentleman a room.' And they said, 'Oh certainly,' but they wouldn't talk to him. He had said, 'Does Joan Baez have a room here?' and they had said, 'No.' And he went out. So then he went to his room and wrote 'When The Ship Comes In' . . . took him exactly one evening to write it, he was so pissed [off]. . . . I couldn't believe it, to get back at those idiots so fast.

'Pirate Jenny' is the song of a downtrodden maid who dreams of the uppance-to-come when a black ship shall descend on the men she has to serve daily. After the vengeful crew has destroyed the town, they give her the opportu-nity to decide the fate of those she waited on, and she duly commands their destruction:

> And a ship with eight sails and with fifty great cannon
> Sails into the quay,
> When folk ask: now just who has to die?
> You will hear me say at that point: All of them!
> And when their heads fall, I'll say, 'Whoopee!'

In other words, this is another Judgement Day song, a celebratory 'I'd Hate to Be You on That Dreadful Day' – or rather, 'I Can't Wait to See You on That Dreadful Day.' The symbolic 'ship' in Dylan's 'When the Ship Comes In' – which will reappear in two equally seminal compositions twenty years later ('Caribbean Wind' and 'Jokerman') – is part of the same fleet as Jenny's pirate ship, sailing especially close in a verse like:

Oh the foes will rise
With the sleep still in their eyes
And they'll jerk from their beds and think they're dreamin'
But they'll pinch themselves and squeal
And know that it's for real,
The hour when the ship comes in.

By August 1963 Dylan had become too good a songwriter to simply vent his spleen on 'those idiots' who thought him too scruffy to frequent their establishment. In his poetic sight are all neo-phobes, indeed any shadowy figure trying to apply brakes to the forward motion of history – the masters of war, the playboys and playgirls, the talkin' devils. His inner eye was also on that great day, later in the month, when he would be sharing a rickety stage with Martin Luther King Jr. and his bandwagon of brothers at the Washington Civil Rights March, where he would be called upon to rally the troops with the lyrical equivalent of 'I Have a Dream.'

Sure enough, he performed 'When the Ship Comes In' with great gusto on this historic occasion, all the while doing his best to keep Joannie well away from the mike (a news telecast of this memorable moment surfaced recently and is available on assorted bootleg DVDs). He raised the song even higher at Carnegie Hall eight weeks later, three nights after cutting the album take, introducing it with an opaque allusion to the story of David and Goliath, suggesting there were modern Goliaths who were 'crueller,' but would also be slain. He was alluding to the song's final verse, an apocalyptic prediction that would not be out of place on 1979's *Slow Train Coming*: 'Like Pharaoh's tribe, they'll be drownded[!] in the tide / And like Goliath, they'll be conquered.'

'When the Ship Comes In' follows a familiar pattern in Dylan's songwriting. An idea's long gestation – in this case basing a song around 'Pirate Jenny' – combines with the rapid-fire trigger of inspiration, enabling a song to spew forth with electric ease. Talking about the song to *SongTalk*'s Paul Zollo twenty-eight years after the fact, Dylan admitted, 'That's not [a case of] sitting down and writing a song. Those kind of songs, they just come out.' And are then forgotten. 'When the Ship Comes In' has been performed only once since 1963, at Live Aid in 1985, where the underlying message – 'judge not lest ye be judged' – sailed over almost two billion heads.

{109} THE TIMES THEY ARE A-CHANGIN'

Published lyrics: Broadside #39; Writings and Drawings; Lyrics 1985; Lyrics 2004.
Known studio recordings: Witmark demo, October 1963 [TBS]; Studio A, NY, October 23, 1963 – 7 takes [L+T ver.1 – tk.1]; October 24 – 1 take [TIMES].
First known performance: Carnegie Hall, NY, October 26, 1963 [LACH].

> Anybody that's got a message is going to learn from experience that they can't put it into a song. I mean, it's not going to come out the same message. After one or two of these unsuccessful attempts, one realises that his resultant message – which is not even the same message he thought up and began with – he's now got to stick to it. – Dylan to Nat Hentoff, October 1965

'When the Ship Comes In' may *feel* like an Old Testament prophet railing at his foes, but it does not rely on any direct biblical parallels – unlike its immediate successor and sister song, 'The Times They Are A-Changin'.' Penned barely a couple of weeks later, it was altogether more self-conscious, even paraphrasing a line from the gospel according to Matthew ('The many that are first will be last, and the last first'). Though the lesser work, it threatened to be an anthem for the ages – or at least until Dylan decided to allow its message to be appropriated by a Canadian merchant bank for one of their TV ads in the nineties.

Where 'The Times . . .' differs from 'When the Ship Comes In' is in its declamatory tone, established with that famous opening couplet, 'Come gather 'round people / wherever you roam.' Using a commonplace of the folk idiom dating back to medieval times – 'the come all ye . . .' *incipit* – he has not come to entertain but to berate. Like a lay preacher, Dylan lays into those whom he has asked to gather 'round, informing them that they are in danger of drowning in the tide just foretold on 'When the Ship Comes In.'

One can't help but think he might be singing, in part, to the stoic throng at the Washington March who, on the basis of the film footage, remained wholly unmoved by that song's stark warning. 'The Times . . .,' written in the immediate aftermath of that auspicious day, qualifies as a summation of things left unsaid. And yet in conversation with *Melody Maker*'s Ray Coleman eighteen months later – when 'The Times . . .' was *still* riding high in the UK singles chart – Dylan insisted a different epiphany sparked the song:

I was on 42nd street. People were moving. There was a bitterness about at that time. People were getting the wrong idea. It was nothing to do with age or parents. . . . This is what it was [about], maybe – a bitterness towards authority – the type of person who sticks his nose down and doesn't take you seriously, but expects YOU to take HIM seriously. . . . I wanted to say . . . that if you have something that you don't want to lose, and people threaten you, you are not really free. . . . I don't know if the song is true, but the feeling's true. . . . It's nothing to do with a political party or religion.

This remains Dylan's longest and most lucid 'explanation' of the feeling for which he was reaching when writing such an overt anthem. But it is directly contradicted by the testimony of a close friend who stumbled on the typescript of the song just after Dylan completed it. Tony Glover was in town to play on a 'supergroup session' of young blues players at the instigation of Elektra Records (*The Blues Project* being the end product).

As he later told Marcus Whitman, Glover called at Dylan's Fourth Street apartment, perhaps just to say hello, but probably to ask if he'd like to play at the session/s (which he did, under the alias Bob Landy). Glover says he saw the typed lyrics lying on Dylan's table. Picking up the paper, he read one of the more quotable lines – 'Come senators, congressmen, please heed the call.' Turning to Dylan he said, 'What is this shit, man?' (a line unconsciously echoed by critic Greil Marcus in his *Rolling Stone* review of *Self Portrait*). Dylan simply shrugged his shoulders and said, 'Well, you know, it seems to be what the people like to hear.'

Describing an occasion barely six weeks after that evening with Paul Nelson, when Nelson dismissed the entire protest-song genre, Dylan may have felt a need to get all defensive with Glover about the kind of topical song he still felt compelled to write. But that's not what he would say in the years after he scratched the song from his repertoire (1965–74). At such times he simply suggested that all those early topical songs were 'written in the New York atmosphere. I'd never have written any of them – or sung them the way I did – if I hadn't been sitting around listening to performers in New York cafes and the talk in all the dingy parlors. . . . I suppose there was some ambition in what I did. But I tried to make the songs genuine.' It is of 'Times . . .' de facto that he is speaking.

Having laid some kind of gauntlet down to his elders, 'The Times . . .' would come in for a lot of stick in the immediate aftermath of its release, affirming as it did Dylan's role as 'spokesman for a generation' – just as its author sought to break free of that burdensome moniker. Middle-aged journalists, in particular, wanted to know if he was preaching revolution when he sang lines like, 'Your sons and your daughters are beyond your command.' Dylan now began to backpedal somewhat, telling one Midwesterner, 'Maybe those were the only words I could find to separate aliveness from deadness. It has nothing to do with age.' When that didn't work, he claimed the lyrics contained several layers of meaning not readily apparent on cursory examination: 'I can't really say that adults don't understand young people any more than you can say big fishes don't understand little fishes. I didn't mean ["Times . . ."] as a statement. . . . It's a feeling, just a feeling.'

That inchoate feeling, bound up with a new order he felt was just around the corner, dissipated with the dawn of a particularly fateful Friday. As of the third weekend in November – with the song less than a month in the can, and still two months away from a Columbia release – he ceased to recognize the song's relevance in a world that no longer contained its most potent symbol of change, president John F. Kennedy. He told Scaduto:

> [The day after Kennedy was shot] I had a concert upstate, in Ithaca or Buffalo. There was a really down feeling in the air. I had to go on the stage, I couldn't cancel. I went to the

hall and to my amazement the hall was filled. . . . The song I was opening with was 'The Times They Are A-Changin'.' . . . That song was just too much for the day after the assassination. But I had to sing it, my whole concert takes off from there. . . . I had no understanding of anything. Something had just gone haywire in the country and they were applauding that song. And I couldn't understand why they were clapping or why I wrote that song, even.

But Dylan was now tied to the song, for better or for worse. As he says, his whole show at the time was predicated around opening with this song (and closing with 'When the Ship Comes In'). These circle songs, reflecting his latest persona, were inseparable for a while. Both were demo-ed at a single session for Witmark in September (on piano, for a change). Both were also recorded at the first of three sessions in late October designed to complete his second album of 1963.

Yet 'Times . . .' was hardly the first call to arms written by the young evangelist. Its most obvious predecessor, 'Paths of Victory,' possibly provided the basis for its tune, another derivative from the 'Palms of Victory' family of tunes. (Another candidate previously suggested in print is 'Farewell to the Creek,' a pipe tune adapted by Hamish Henderson for his own 'Banks o' Sicily,' which itself may be a variant of this hymnal source.) Dylan proves typically unhelpful in the *Biograph* liner notes, suggesting that the song was influenced 'by the Irish and Scottish ballads,' a statement akin to suggesting Shakespeare's sonnets were influenced by Sidney.

After being dropped from the live set in spring 1965, it would take Dylan another twenty years to provide interviewer Charles Kaiser with his most pithy explanation of what generated 'The Times They Are A-Changin'': 'I wanted to write a big song in a simple way.' By then, it was fully restored to the repertoire in its most apocalyptic guise. In

1978 a revamped electric arrangement with electric violin and wailing girls had injected life back into the old chestnut. At the same time, he responded to a question about the song's meaning by complaining, 'I get tired of having to explain my songs. I got tired of that years ago. Take a line that you read someplace, or something you see that means something to you. I mean, everybody sees something different. . . . I know what it means to me and I know what it meant to me when I was writing it – where the inspiration came from.'

Even pre-Svedburg, he was tired of being continually misrepresented in print. Nor did he ever change his mind about the validity of that second verse about critics 'who prophesize with your pen,' telling interviewer Matt Damsker fifteen years later, 'These critics . . . unless they're educated in that type of music, or have lived where that artist has lived, [or] felt what that artist has felt, then they really have no right to criticize in a negative way anything which they themselves don't quite understand.'

If he hoped a song like 'The Times . . .' might get sympathetic folk off his back, he would be sorely disabused. The editors of *The Little Sandy Review*, who *were* amply 'educated in that type of music,' opined on its release that the song 'seems to exist merely as a sop for the parent-defying teenage ego.' Nor were they the only critics to focus on this single aspect of the lyrics, or suggest that it was the whole message. For Dylan the criticism served as an important lesson. Future declamations on society's ills would be a whole lot more kaleidoscopic and harder to define.

{110} PERCY'S SONG

Published lyrics: Writings and Drawings; Lyrics *1985*; Lyrics *2004*.
Known studio recordings: Studio A, NY, October 23, 1963 – 1 take; October 24, 1963 – 3 takes [BIO].
First known performance: Carnegie Hall, NY, October 26, 1963.

By October 1963 the royalties must have started rolling in from the many traditional tunes to which Dylan had attached his own words. And inevitably, he was starting to get grief from the green-eyed for the casual way he appropriated the arrangements of fellow folkies, almost all of whom were struggling to make ends meet – unlike Grossman's protégé.

Before the end of the year, Dylan would devote one of the 'outlined epitaphs' included with his third album to a confession: 'I am a thief of thoughts. . . . I have built an rebuilt / upon what is waitin.' Before this he had gone to great pains, in his introduction of 'Percy's Song' at his Carnegie Hall show, to attribute the melody and arrangement to his old friend, Paul Clayton. In the *Biograph* notes, he also admits, '"Don't Think Twice" was a riff that Paul had. And so was "Percy's Song." . . . A song like "Percy's Song," you'd just assume another character's point of view. I did a few like that.'

As just one more inheritor of the folk process, Clayton had no actual claim on this variant of the ancient ballad 'The Two Sisters,' which had first been collected by a lady called Mrs. Buchanan from a reverend in Pageton, West Virginia, in 1937. But it was Clayton who highlighted the song's convoluted melodic history during a ballad workshop at the 1963 Newport Folk Festival on July 27, at which he had played three variants of 'The Two Sisters,' concluding with a four-verse fragment, 'The Wind and the Rain,' originally collected by Fletcher Collins in Fancy Gap, Virginia.

Todd Harvey suggests that this is where Dylan first heard the song. He presumably means the latter, not the former. 'The Two Sisters' was one of the earliest traditional ballads Dylan ever learned, performing it for Karen Moynihan's tape recorder in May 1960. In the original ballad, one sister, jealous of the other, flings her into a rushing river. Swept downstream, the drowned girl's body is pulled out by a miller/carpenter, who proceeds to make a harp from her bones and strings from her hair. The harp is then carried by a minstrel to the sister's wedding, but when the harpist attempts to play, 'the only tune the harp would play' is the story of the two sisters, during which the murderer is duly named and shamed.

The version Dylan sang for Moynihan (née Wallace) is the one usually found in American tradition – 'There was an old lady lived by the sea-shore' – a rationalized variant from England that made the miller who pulled the drowned girl from the river put on trial for her murder. The whole fantastical finale has been dropped as too incredible even for your average folksinger. Any residue of that original element remains extremely rare in American tradition, but it is there in 'The Wind and the Rain.' And we know Dylan did attend the same Newport workshop as Clayton, hosted by Jean Ritchie (he wisely did not play 'Masters of War,' which he reserved for the following day's topical song workshop). 'The Wind and the Rain,' as originally collected, was slightly longer than the version Clayton played:

> Two little girls in a boat one day,
> *Oh the wind and the rain* (refrain)
> Two little girls in a boat one day,
> *Crying, of the wind and the rain.* (refrain)
>
> They floated down on the old mill dam, &c.
> Charles Miller came out with his long hook and line, &c.
> He hooked her out by the long yellow hair, &c.
> He made fiddle strings of her long yellow hair, &c.
> He made fiddle screws of her long finger bones, &c.
> And the only tune the fiddle would play, &c.

The composition of 'Percy's Song' appears to date from a few weeks after Newport, Dylan further rationalizing this hopelessly corrupt variant of the ancient story. He does, however, retain most of its original power, as he suggests that 'The only tune my guitar would play / Was "Oh the Cruel Rain and the Wind."' But this time the instrument plays the song because the narrator has failed to get justice, not as a means of getting justice.

'Percy's Song' tells the tale of a friend who has been sentenced to ninety-nine years in Joliet Prison for 'manslaughter / in the highest of degree,' after he is held responsible for a car crash in which four people have died. The singer confronts the judge in person and pleas for mercy, but the judge is as unforgiving as the one in 'Seven Curses' and the singer is left 'with no other choice / except for to go.' The ballad, thanks to two internal refrains – 'turn, turn, turn again' and 'turn, turn, turn to the rain and the wind' – maintains the air of inevitability throughout (and the Carnegie performance is almost nine minutes long).

Paul Cable, in his *Unreleased Recordings*, suggests it is the length of 'Percy's Song' that might have been responsible for its omission from Dylan's third album. Yet the song was recorded twice in the studio in late October and played live at the Carnegie showcase, which all points to a song he was planning to include. But in the end he simply had too much material for one album to contain. This left it to electric folk band Fairport Convention to give the song some retrospective recognition, courtesy of their marvellous 1969 recording, which was made just weeks before their own roadie, Harvey Bramham, fell asleep at the wheel and crashed the band's van, killing their drummer and Richard Thompson's girlfriend. He served just six months for *his* deed.

Published lyrics: Broadside #43; Writings and Drawings; Lyrics 1985; Lyrics 2004.

Known studio recordings: Studio A, NY, October 23, 1963 – 4 takes [TIMES – tk.4].

First known performance: Carnegie Hall, NY, October 26, 1963.

> By all accounts, [Jesse] James was a bloodthirsty killer who was anything but the Robin Hood sung about in the song. But [the balladmaker] has the last word and he spins it around. – *Chronicles*

While events soon taught Dylan to steer clear of message songs like 'The Times They Are A-Changin'', his next composition would (temporarily) close the lid on the topical song genre he had made his own in just eighteen months. Like 'When the Ship Comes In,' 'The Lonesome Death of Hattie Carroll' was a subject he'd been thinking about since the spring. But when the song finally demanded that he write it, in early October, it came fast. Dylan associating the song with 'Who Killed Davey Moore?,' composed in early April, suggests he had been brooding about Hattie Carroll's demise since the first topical song about the lady's death appeared in his favourite bedtime read, *Broadside*, in March. 'The Ballad of Hattie Carroll,' nine verses of doggerel from song-writer and poet Don West, displays the usual disregard for any facts at odds with his polemic:

> The big man pounded on the table
> She hardly heard what he did say
> When Hattie went to get his order
> He took his cane and flailed away.

West's ballad barely registered with the prince of protest, but the article the *Broadside* editors reproduced beneath it, from a local Baltimore paper, clearly caught his eye. Its headline was stark and unambiguous: 'Rich Brute Slays Negro Mother of Ten.' Gordon Friesen, coeditor of *Broadside*, later claimed he would sometimes point out potential subject matter to Dylan. This may have been one such instance. The article by Roy H. Wood, from a February feature (Carroll died on February 9), painted a picture of unbridled brutality:

Mrs Hattie Carroll, 51, Negro waitress at the Emerson Hotel, died last week as the result of a brutal beating by a wealthy socialite during the exclusive Spinsters' Ball at that hotel. Mrs Carroll, mother of ten children, was the deacon of the Gillis Memorial Church. She died in the hospital where she had been taken after being felled from blows inflicted by William Devereux Zantzinger, 24, owner of a 600-acre tobacco farm. . . . Zantzinger's father is a member of the state planning commission in Maryland. Others of his relatives in the Devereux family are prominent in politics here. The judge who released Zantzinger on bond has already permitted his attorney to claim that Mrs Carroll died indirectly as a result of the attack rather than directly. There is speculation here that attempts will be made to get Zantzinger off with a slap of the wrist.

Reading this article made Dylan's blood boil with so much righteous fury that six months later he got around to lashing out at those parties 'who philosophize disgrace,' wrapping his personal philosophy in a parable about the murder of a 'negro mother of ten [*sic*].' A month before he actually wrote Hattie's song, William Zantzinger (the *t* in his name about to become one of the more celebrated consonants dropped in a Dylan lyric) had been sentenced to six months for involuntary manslaughter.

One thing is certain – Dylan hadn't spent the intervening months researching the case or even keeping abreast of developments. Every so-called fact he presents in the initial three verses of his ballad stems from Wood's February article. Unfortunately for the cause of truth, Wood got just about every important fact wrong. Had the events of the night of February 8 really been as Wood portrayed them, Zantzinger would have more than warranted Dylan's disdain. But Wood was the kind of journalist wont to criticize first and establish facts second – and the only journalist who ever suggested that Carroll died 'as the result of a brutal beating' from Zantzinger.

Dylan had no problem buying into the brutishness of Wood's account, unequivocally portraying Hattie as 'killed by a blow / lay slain by a cane.' Actually Carroll died of a massive coronary after suffering for many years from elevated blood pressure and a serious weight problem. Her heart attack *may* have been induced by some verbal bullying from a drunk Maryland farmer named Billy and a single 'tap' on the shoulder with a hollow carnival cane. But even that tap may have never happened. Key witnesses in court claimed the cane had been snapped in four by another guest before Zantzinger began calling Carroll names for being tardy with an order of drinks.

In fact, while Carroll was taken to the hospital suffering from a heart attack, Zantzinger was hauled off by the police and charged with being drunk and disorderly and resisting arrest. Only when Carroll subsequently died were the charges ramped up to murder in the second degree. Such an outlandish charge was always going to be unsustainable, though, and it was reduced to involuntary manslaughter during the trial. Hence the 'modest' sentence. Carroll was never 'felled from blows,' making Dylan's opening couplet a million-dollar libel case waiting to happen:

William Zantzinger killed poor Hattie Carroll, [no, he didn't]
With a cane [nope] that he twirled round his diamond ring
    finger [no diamond ring].

Though that suit didn't transpire, Dylan didn't learn his lesson. When he wrote 'Hurricane' twelve years later, he again got important material facts in the case wrong, and this time he *was* sued. Already responsible for two Southern murder ballads featuring material falsehoods – 'Emmett Till' and 'Only a Pawn in Their Game' – Dylan bought into Wood's account wholesale, extracting every detail inserted into the song from that original article: the size of Zantzinger's farm, the 'high office relations in the politics of Maryland' (largely a figment of Wood's imagination), and even the number of children Hattie had (which was nine, not ten). On such shaky foundations, he constructed a scenario to fit a preconceived point of view rather more brilliantly than the prosecution did.

There is no evidence that Zantzinger 'reacted to his deed with a shrug of his shoulders / And swear words and sneering.' Any bout of swearing came when he was arrested for being drunk (and seems to have come mainly from his wife). How could there be any account of his reaction to Carroll's death, since he had already been released from jail when the news arrived? Only later did he (voluntarily) give himself up to the authorities. And Dylan's portrait of Carroll as someone who 'carried the dishes and took out the garbage' is no less condescending than his portrayal of Zantzinger.

By the time he came to write 'Hattie Carroll' in October, he surely must have begun to realize that he'd got certain salient facts wrong in the earlier 'Only a Pawn in Their Game.' And the debate with Nelson should have given him cause to pause before trying to shoot another big fish in the *Broadside* barrel. By snapping the truth into little pieces, he proved himself a masterful poet but a lousy historian. As he recently admitted in *Chronicles*, 'Protest songs are difficult to write without making them come off as preachy and one-dimensional.' Here's hoping Nelson had a wry smile on his face when he read this.

Now if the song *had* been written in a blaze of fury back in February, or even during the month-long June trial – when the local papers were full of headlines like 'Barmaid at Society Ball Dies Following Caning,' leading to the trial being moved from Baltimore to Hagerstown – it would be a lot easier to give Dylan the benefit of the doubt. For a while it really did seem as if Zantzinger was the devil incarnate. And the prosecution did its best to stoke such prejudices, portraying Zantzinger in their closing argument as 'playing the lord of the manor, presiding over the old plantation.' Gradually, though, the facts began to colour the pure black portrait drawn by papers like the *Baltimore Sun*. The actual evidence clearly demonstrated that Zantzinger had no murderous intent, having merely been a belligerent drunk caught up in a tragedy he could not have foreseen even in the sober light of day.

Convicted of manslaughter at the end of June, Zantzinger's sentence was deferred until August so that he could bring in his tobacco crop (thus saving many jobs on Zantzinger's farm). When the sentence was finally delivered, the day of the Civil Rights March in Washington, Judge McLaughlin had no need to pound his gavel as he delivered his verdict – six months in jail and a five hundred–dollar fine – along with his measured legal opinion: 'Here is an unfortunate set of circumstances. If the deceased had been a well person, we would not have heard anything about it. We don't feel Mr. Zantzinger is an animal type. Our problem is to . . . [establish] the type of punishment Mr. Zantzinger should have.'

By the time of the verdict, even the *New York Times* had

toned down the tenor of its coverage. The headline in its August 29 edition – which Dylan presumably saw – read simply: 'Farmer Sentenced in Barmaid's Death.' And still Dylan did not turn the story into song. Only after he travelled to California at the end of September, to stay at the Carmel home of Joan Baez, did he decide to make the tale his own. Both Joan Baez and another house guest at the time, her brother-in-law Richard Fariña, confirmed that he wrote the song there – which means that Dylan either retained a photographic recollection of Wood's article from *Broadside* or he referred to Baez's copy of the March issue when writing the song.

Presumably it was being in the company of Baez that prompted Dylan to set the tale to the tune of Child Ballad 173, 'Mary Hamilton,' a song Baez had already filleted on her 1960 album. In *Chronicles* Dylan claims he used to do the song himself and that he 'could make [it] drop into place like she did, but in a different way.' There is no evidence it *ever* featured in his set, but even if it did, by this juncture he was telling friends, 'I can't sing "John Johannah" cause it's his story an his people's story /[I gotta sing "With God on Our Side" cause it's my story and my people's.' Back in January he had even questioned why Baez continued to sing songs about sixteenth-century Scottish court intrigues, telling her brother-in-law, 'she's still singing "Mary Hamilton" . . . where's that at?'

In this instance, though, 'Mary Hamilton' served as a rather appropriate choice. The ballad in question, based on the murder of a child conceived by a maid (and a French apothecary) at the court of Mary, Queen of Scots, in 1563, was a thin tissue of lies designed to implicate the queen's husband, Lord Darnley ('the highest Stuart of them all'), in the child's murder. The song may well have been instrumental in influencing Mary to pass an act, shortly afterwards, making the dissemination of scurrilous ballads punishable by death.

In this libel, the guilty party becomes one of Mary's ladies-in-waiting, the 'four Maries' as they were commonly known. Yet the common form of the ballad only manages to name two of the four correctly and was probably originally called 'Mary Mild.' There never was a historical Mary Hamilton (at least not in Mary's time; there was a Scottish lady-in-waiting at Peter the Great's court in 1718 named Mary Hambleton, who was executed for a similar crime, which may be how this name attached itself to the earlier incident). Much like Dylan, the original, anonymous balladeer wasn't interested in the facts, only in implicating 'the lord of the manor' in the deed.

Aspiring to make his ballad convincing enough to evoke 'the only, true valid death you can feel today,' Dylan missed just one trick. He failed to use what were reportedly the last words of Mrs. Carroll. Having slumped against the bar, after Zantzinger's battery of abuse, Hattie apparently slurred the memorable sentence, 'That man has upset me so, I feel deathly ill' – words that could have sprung straight from some sixteenth-century ballad. But Dylan was too fixated on the moral to let the real story seep in.

He almost admitted as much to TV host Steve Allen in February 1964. Making his national TV debut on Allen's popular show, he chose 'Hattie Carroll' as the statement he wished to make to the nation. When Allen tackled him about the song's source, Dylan replied, 'I took [it] out of a newspaper. It's a true story. [But] I changed the reporter's view – I used it . . . for something that I wanted to say . . . . and turned it that way.' Allen earnestly asked Dylan to elaborate further. The increasingly uncomfortable singer asked to be allowed to let the song speak for itself.

He duly delivered such a compelling performance that viewers couldn't help but be convinced of the singer's civil rights credentials. And though on the verge of detaching himself from the topical song genre, 'Hattie Carroll' stayed a favourite of Dylan's – the one topical song he was (justifiably) proud of on a technical level, it being a remarkable synthesis of words, tune, performance, and philosophy. But when it came to the underlying story, Dylan never sought out the truth. Asked about the song by critic Robert Hilburn in the last couple of years, he was still claiming, 'I just let the story tell itself. Who wouldn't be offended by some guy beating an old woman to death and just getting a slap on the wrist?' And who wouldn't.

{112} LAY DOWN YOUR WEARY TUNE

Published lyrics: Writings and Drawings; Lyrics *1985;* Lyrics *2004.*
Known studio recordings: Studio A, NY, October 24, 1963 – 1 take
[BIO – tk.1].
First known performance: [Hollywood Bowl, LA, October 12,
1963] Carnegie Hall, NY, October 26, 1963 [LACH].

'The Lonesome Death of Hattie Carroll' was not the only song written during Dylan's stay at Carmel through the first fortnight in October. 'Lay Down Your Weary Tune' was also written on the same visit, probably a couple of days prior to Baez's October 12 show at the Hollywood Bowl, at which he insisted on debuting the song (though I think we can probably take Baez's claim that 'he had just written "Lay Down Your Weary Tune," it was forty-five minutes long,' with a truckload of salt).

We actually have Richard Fariña's recollection of the circumstances of its composition, given to Robert Shelton in 1966, shortly before Fariña's fatal motorcycle crash: 'I recall in Carmel was where he wrote "Hattie Carroll" – at Joan's house . . . [and] that he had written "Lay Down Your Weary Tune" [there]. One evening, we were out surfing with a surf-board and he rode the motorcycle back and wrote that tune. I remember that because she was on her way to do a concert at the Hollywood Bowl and he was very keen that she should sing it with him. But she was unsure of the song and the words and didn't want to do it yet.'

Evidently, when he wasn't swimming and surfing (or nearly drowning, if we are to believe a concert rap he gave in November 1980), Dylan immersed himself in the Scottish ballads of which he and Baez shared a mutual appreciation, working his way through Joan's personal record collection. It could even be Jeannie Robertson's deathless rendition of 'Mary Hamilton,' not Baez's, that prompted him to appropriate its melody for 'Hattie Carroll.'

In the notes accompanying *Biograph*, Dylan suggests that 'Lay Down Your Weary Tune' also came about because 'I had heard a Scottish ballad on an old 78 record that I was trying to really capture the feeling of, that was haunting me. I couldn't get it out of my head. There were no lyrics or anything. It was just a melody. . . . I wanted lyrics that would feel the same way.' Well, all ballads have lyrics, but precious few are short enough to fit on a ten-inch 78-rpm record.

Predictably Dylan's remark led to some dispute regarding the song he was recollecting. Harvey suggested 'The Water Is Wide,' but that is hardly a song Dylan would have needed to hear in such an arcane fashion – a trip to any Anglo-American folk club would suffice. On the other hand, the seventeenth-century Scottish lyric, 'Waly, Waly' – of which 'The Water Is Wide' is a modern Anglo-Irish derivative – provides an almost perfect combination of sentiment and melody, though it is less well known in folk circles (first published in 1725 by Allan Ramsay, sans tune, it has been anthologized a lot but rarely covered).

Unlike the title of his 1997 collection, Dylan's source would not have been Ramsay here. But it could well be Robertson again, a singer he almost name-checks in *Chronicles* (as Jeannie Robinson), and generally regarded as *the* great Scots traditional ballad singer of the postwar era. Which is not only a fair description of the wee old lass but the title of the 1959 Topic album where Dylan could have found 'I Wish, I Wish' – or, as it was called by Topic, 'What a Voice' – a variant of the song Ramsay anthologized that retained its ancient air. (It also features some lines Dylan had already appropriated: 'I wish, I wish, I wish in vain / I wish I was a maid again.') Robertson's rendition has no instrumentation save Jeannie's piercing voice, but the tune is certainly a haunting one, and Dylan knew a good ballad tune when he heard one.

The song would be transformed by Dylan into a ringing rhapsody of rhythm and rhyme – partly by putting the song in a major key and partly by speeding up its dirgelike tempo, but largely through the sheer forcefulness of his singing. The live version performed a couple of days after its studio rendition is even more of a tour de force, Dylan never faltering with his diction or delivery.

And yet the song was destined to be forgotten before his guitar strings ceased to hum. A perfect album closer, it was superseded by 'Restless Farewell.' Dylan's desire to nail *Newsweek* to the mast of his black ship took precedent over what was clearly the superior composition – even though 'Lay Down Your Weary Tune' was *brand-new* and had been recorded in a single take, usually factors which would have worked in its favour. It would be some time before Dylan rekindled such pantheistic patterns again, perhaps because he had to wait another four months before he got to enjoy the preternatural power of Carmel's vistas again. By then, he was already thinking on 'Mr. Tambourine Man.'

{113} ONE TOO MANY MORNINGS

Published lyrics: Writings and Drawings; Lyrics 1985; Lyrics 2004.
Known studio recordings: Studio A, NY, October 24, 1963 – 6 takes

[TIMES – tk.6]; Studio A, Nashville, February 17, 1969 – 11 takes; February 18, 1969 – 2 takes; Studio B, NY, May 1, 1970 – 1 take.
First known performance: BBC Studios, London, June 1, 1965.

One can imagine how well Suze took the news, doubtless delivered as Dylan stood at 'the crossroads of my door-step,' that her supposed live-in boyfriend was heading off to California to spend a couple of weeks with a woman who could shatter glass with her voice. In fact, this announce-ment would result in Suze deciding to move out on her man and in with her 'parasite sister.' Dylan's conflicted loyalties, held in check for most of the nine months since Suze came back, now produced a song that was almost the exact reverse of 'Don't Think Twice,' with him now the one who is 'one too many mornings / and a thousand miles behind.'

Dylan might well have composed this particular restless farewell while sunning himself out West. If so, it was a song he kept close to his chest, not performing it at Carnegie Hall and not even including it on the initial test-pressing for *The Times They Are A-Changin'* LP. Even after the breakup sign-posted in this song got its decree absolute, the following March, the song enjoyed none of the favour its predecessor continued to enjoy. Only belatedly did Dylan come to realize what a concise classic he almost discarded. All those conflicted feelings, offset by an uncertain future, make this song an epitome of romantic restraint – a trait he only rarely emulated in the songs written in the following six months.

The song ultimately benefited from two of the man's best electric arrangements, on the highly charged 1966 and 1976 tours. On the latter tour it also acquired a brand-new coda that suggested faults on both sides: 'You've no right to be here / And I've no right to stay / Until we're both one too many mornings / And a thousand miles away.' Its inclusion in the set, at a time when Dylan had reached much the same point in his relationship with wife Sara as he'd reached with

Suze in October 1963, suggests its return to favour was no coincidence. Subsequent performances, which have tended to be (semi-)acoustic, suggest it is a song Dylan can plug his inspired self into at will, as anyone who caught performances at New York's Beacon Theatre in October 1990, or at the second Supper Club show in 1993, can readily testify.

{114} RESTLESS FAREWELL

Published lyrics: Writings and Drawings; Lyrics 1985; Lyrics 2004.
Known studio recordings: Studio A, NY, October 31, 1963 – 9 takes [TIMES – tk.9].
First known performance: Quest Show, Toronto, February 1, 1964.

> About twenty years ago I'd do interviews. You'd be honest with that person. Then you'd see the article and it would all be changed around. . . . You really felt like you were suckered or something. – Dylan at a Sydney press conference, February 1986

On either October 23 or 24, 1963, Columbia publicist Billy James arranged for Dylan to meet a *Newsweek* reporter named Andrea Svedburg, who had been sniffing around, sensing a story in the way that the Bar Mitzvah boy from Minnesota had reinvented himself as the prince of protest. Dylan quickly 'clocked' Svedburg's agenda, grew irate, and stormed off into the night. Svedburg still posted her story, which appeared in the following week's edition, hitting the stands on or around October 29 (Svedburg mentions Dylan's parents attending the Carnegie Hall show, so the story was probably not posted until the twenty-seventh).

Dylan's response was fast, furious, and unsparing – a song initially called 'Bob Dylan's Restless Epitaph' but released as 'Restless Farewell.' It marked the end of Bob Dylan's separation from Robert Zimmerman. He booked a studio the following afternoon. He was going to record the song while still fuming. And record it he did, though his unfamiliarity with the words and an uncertain hold on the melody meant it took nine takes to nail it. He finally felt he had the album closer he'd been hunting for all along (and writing the album closer last would become another pattern within the man's quixotic quilt).

Given the extraordinary speed with which Dylan conceived, wrote, and recorded the song, it is no great surprise that the typescript he tapped out (hurriedly, hence typos like 'the dark doe die' for 'the dark does die'), varies in only minor details from the take he released. In the second verse, he sacrifices sense on the recording for the sake of an internal rhyme, changing, 'But t remain as friends yuh need the time / t make amends and stay behind' into something a lot more convoluted: 'But to remain as friends and make amends / You need the time and stay behind.'

The clearest expression of Dylan's anger in the typescript comes not with an actual word change but in the fact that its final line ends with a 'DAMN!' – capitalized and exclaimed – even though this is one piece of writing he is not planning to show to 'unknowin' eyes.' Also, at the top of the page is a couplet that does not appear in the song but acts as a commentary on it: 'The time cant be found t fit / all the things that i want t do.' Perhaps he thought the song should have a spoken introduction, à la 'Bob Dylan's Blues.' Or maybe this was just a note to himself. Either way, the song proper begins with the singer disowning all wealth and property:

> Of all the money in my whole life i did spend
> Be it mine right or wrongfully
> I let it slip gladly t the hands of my friends
> T tie up the time most forcefully.

It had been a while since Dylan had overtly 'adapted' *both* content and structure from his ostensible tune-source, but he was a man in a hurry. And 'Restless Farewell' couldn't help but be a self-conscious attempt to update the old Irish drinking song, 'The Parting Glass'* (this time surely acquired from the Clancys, whose own rendition had just been released on *In Person at Carnegie Hall*). The generic nature of its original leave-taking occupies just three verses, of which these are first and last:

> Of all the money e'er I had, I spent it in good company;
> And all the harm I've ever done, alas was done to none but me;
> And all I've done for want of wit, to memory now I can't
>   recall,
> So fill me to the parting glass, goodnight and joy be with
>   you all . . .
>
> If I had money enough to spend and leisure time to sit awhile,
> There is a fair maid in this town who sorely has my heart
>   beguiled.
> Her rosy cheeks and ruby lips, I own she has my heart in thrall,
> So fill me to the parting glass, goodnight and joy be with
>   you all.

Dylan, on the other hand, needs a full five verses to confess his sins, redeem himself, and 'head on down the road.' 'Restless Farewell' may well share the same pretence (of a carefree soul) as 'The Parting Glass.' But, whereas the original's final couplet shows just how heartbroken our Irish traveller is, Dylan pulls back from revealing himself, even though the original title has made it clear that this is one

---

* 'The Parting Glass' is itself probably an updated version of a well-known Scottish drinking song, collected (and rewritten) by Robert Burns in the eighteenth century, 'Here's to Thy Health.'

instance where narrator and writer are one and the same. Instead, we get the litany of familiar regrets, such as having acquired money 'wrongfully,' remorse for 'every girl that ever i hurt,' and an inability to 'remain as friends' with those he has left behind. Only in the final verse do we find out what triggered such self-analysis. When that moment finally comes, he blasts Andrea and her ilk to kingdom come:

> Oh a false clock tries t tick out my time
> T disgrace distract and t bother me
> And the dirt of gossip blows into my face
> And the dust of rumors covers me.

It is a memorable declaration of independence from 'unknowin eyes,' signalling a desire to write only 'for myself' from this point forwards. Never again would he knowingly expose himself to anyone looking to bury him in a 'dust of rumors.' As he told critic Robert Hilburn twenty years later, 'It was right to be vague [in those early interviews] because they were trying to dig a hole for you. . . . You had to respond in a way that wouldn't hurt you.' His guard was now up. As for 'Restless Farewell,' it served its purpose the minute he got it out of his system.

Thankfully, the song did enjoy an unexpected resurrection three decades later at the request of a most unlikely fellow singer, Frank Sinatra. As far as Ol' Blue Eyes was concerned, it had always been one of his favourite Dylan songs, and he personally asked the songwriter to perform it at his eightieth-birthday bash at the Shrine Auditorium in L.A. in 1995. Dylan agreed, giving it a stately semi-acoustic arrangement, and transforming the song's whole meaning by the simple act of performing it for someone else who did it 'his way.' When the fifty-something singer bade 'farewell in the night,' it was the dark night of the soul he was singing about.

That November night the pertinence of the performance was not lost on singer *or* recipient. Dylan would play the song just one more time – the following spring, after hearing the sad news that the king of crooners had died.

1964

{ Another Side of Bob Dylan }

A troubled year, professionally and personally, resulted in some of Dylan's most important songs, even if quality control remained an issue. After writing a couple of songs in February that opened up a whole new approach to songwriting – 'Chimes of Freedom' and 'Mr. Tambourine Man' – he was distracted by a traumatic (and irreconcilable) breakup with girlfriend Suze. As a result he poured his feelings into songs of heartbreak ('Mama You Been on My Mind'), paranoia ('Ballad in Plain D'), and a yearning for lost intimacy ('To Ramona'). Only after he had got these 'kinds of songs' out of his system did he return to those 'chains of flashing images,' writing the unexpectedly pastoral 'Gates of Eden' and the utterly urban 'It's Alright, Ma (I'm Only Bleeding)' at summer's end, debuting them at his fall 1964 shows, when the ghost of electricity crackled in the air . . .

{115} GUESS I'M DOING FINE

Published lyrics: Writings and Drawings; Lyrics 1985; Lyrics 2004.
Known studio recordings: Witmark demo, January 1964.

'Guess I'm Doing Fine,' a slight but not insignificant song in the canon, has no obvious folk source, melodically or structurally, and its real 'inspiration' is probably not traditional. But it does resemble Hank Williams's 'Everything's Okay,' a jokey ditty based on a well-known comedy routine that relies on understating the various hardships piling on top of one another for Uncle Bill, who manages at the end of every catastrophe/verse to suggest that, all things considered, everything's OK.

Any significance rests with its expression of an ongoing dissatisfaction couched in a begrudging *joie de vivre*, as well as its unique position as neither one of those songs Dylan bid a restless farewell to, nor the new kind of song heralded by major compositions come February. A second cousin to 'Restless Farewell,' it relies on its punch line at each verse's end – 'Hey, hey, so I guess I'm doin' fine' – to command sympathy from the listener. There is the usual litany of things he never had – 'much money,' 'armies / to jump at my command' – or once had, but lost (that increasingly mythical childhood). He even lifts a line – 'my road might be rocky' – from an earlier, more succesful attempt to count his blessings: 'Paths of Victory.'

Though its one recording (a Witmark demo) postdates *The Times . . .* sessions by a couple of months, when it came time to compile *Writings and Drawings*, Dylan put 'Guess I'm Doing Fine' with the third-album songs. If it can be placed in a definable period, it is from a time when he occasionally tried too hard. As he told Nat Hentoff, when about to record his fourth album: 'From now on, I want to write from inside me, and to do that I'm going to have to get back to writing like I used to when I was ten – having everything come out naturally.'

Published lyrics: Writings and Drawings; Lyrics *1985;* Lyrics *2004;* The Bob Dylan Scrapbook *[manuscript].*

First known performance: [Denver Civic Auditorium, February 15, 1964] Newport Folk Festival, July 26, 1964 [NDH].

Known studio recordings: Studio A, NY, June 9, 1964 – 7 takes [AS – tk.7].

Just about the only genuinely revealing lyric draft included in *The Bob Dylan Scrapbook* (2004), an ill-conceived 'companion' coffee-table volume published in tandem with *No Direction Home,* was 'Chimes of Freedom,' written on both sides of some headed paper from The Waldorf-Astoria Hotel, 80–88 Charles St., Toronto. This fascinating document, initially written in pencil with additions in pen, directly refutes the account of the song's composition given in Scaduto's biography, derived from Pete Karman's notes, made during a February 1964 road trip Dylan and friends took from New York to Berkeley, via New Orleans. According to Scaduto/Karman, 'As Victor [Maimudes] drove away from Hazard, Dylan climbed into the back of his station wagon, put the portable typewriter on his lap, and began to write. Later, [Peter] Karman got a look at the page: "Chimes of Freedom" was the title, a poem that would later become a song.'

This couldn't have been the moment he began 'Chimes of Freedom.' Dylan was in Toronto at the end of January doing interviews and preparing to film his contribution to CBC's *Quest* TV series on February 1. While there he evidently started 'Chimes.' Even if he was still working on the song during said road trip – and the two additional verses and various amendments added in pen to the draft *could* have been written 'on the road' – he clearly did not *write* the song at a 'portable typewriter.' Typescripts of songs from 1963–4 are invariably 'clean' copies culled from handwritten drafts like the one for 'Chimes of Freedom.'

The so-called Margolis and Moss manuscripts – composed in the weeks leading up to this road trip – comprise only free-form poems, outlined epitaphs and others, plus the odd play. But there are no song drafts.* Among these attempts at being a poet is one representing a genesis of sorts for 'Chimes of Freedom.' Dating from the fall – specifically the immediate aftermath of the assassination of John F. Kennedy – the poem shows that Dylan was as traumatized as most folk by this catastrophic intervention from an assassin's bullet (or three). The poem in question is just six lines. It reads: 'the colors of friday were dull / as cathedral bells were gently burnin' / strikin for the gentle / strikin for the kind / strikin for the crippled ones / an strikin for the blind.' The Friday in question, in the context of the other poems surrounding it, is unquestionably November 22, the day JFK got caught in a Texas shooting gallery.

Of equal significance is Dylan's reference to the 'cathedral bells,' which suggests he already planned to utilize the image of tolling church bells to herald Kennedy's death (as they once foretold the death of Barbara Allen, in one of Dylan's favourite Child ballads). The storm becomes both a physical manifestation of 'the chimes of freedom flashing' and a metaphor for the storm surrounding the death of a president – a trick he could have copped from *King Lear*. Or not. Dylan denies that the assassination triggered his pen, telling Scaduto, 'If I was more sensitive about [JFK's death] than anyone else, I would have written a song about it. . . . The whole thing about my reactions to the assassination is overplayed.' Pages and pages of poems on the subject in the Margolis and Moss manuscripts belie this assertion.

---

* The Margolis and Moss manuscripts contain three songs, two in typescript ('I'll Keep It With Mine' and 'Phantom Engineer') and one in manuscript ('Liverpool Gal'), but none of these date from the same period as the various poems and play that make up the bulk of the collection, i.e. the fall of 1963 or the winter of 1964.

By the beginning of February, when Dylan had completed the first, four-verse draft of 'Chimes of Freedom,' he had integrated all the important elements from that six-line fragment. But the cripples and the blind had been replaced by 'guardians an protectors of the mind,' lessening any comparison between JFK and another martyr from long ago and far away. Everything coalesces around two lovers finding shelter from a storm in the doorway of a church/cathedral, where they 'see the chimes of freedom flashing.'

There is a possibility that Dylan consciously drew the title from a 1948 song he may have heard: Tom Glazer's 'Because All Men Are Brothers.' Its second verse reads:

My brothers are all others, forever hand in hand,
Where chimes the bell of freedom, there is my native land.
My brothers' fears are my fears, yellow, white or brown,
My brothers' tears are my tears, the whole world around.

But it is just as likely that Dylan independently struck on the phrase and liked how it sounded. 'The bells of freedom' was already a phrase in common use, having been the title of a patriotic standard in the thirties. And it is quite clear that Dylan had begun to transcend those right-on sources he had previously relied on for parts of his philosophy. 'Chimes of Freedom' represents an entirely new kind of song, its litany of life's losers resembling the work of the Beats. Perhaps it was no coincidence he had first met Allen Ginsberg five weeks earlier. By the following year, in conversation with a friend, he was self-consciously distancing himself from those earlier albums: 'The [Guthrie] influence has all been on the first, second, third record. The fourth one, it was kinda wearing off a little bit.'

Determined to signpost this significant, daring shift with a typically ambitious statement, Dylan sought something with the scale and sweep of 'A Hard Rain's A-Gonna Fall.' Even after he pencilled in those first four verses, Dylan had already written '5.,' indicating a song not yet done. Sure enough, he returned to it with pen in hand, the final two verses spilling across both sides of the sheet, the lines jumping around the page as inspiration struck.

A line like 'The twisted sidewalk's mist was lifting' ultimately resolves into something more satisfactory: 'As the splattered mist was slowly lifting.' Likewise, though initially unable to improve on the opening line of verse four – 'In the wild cathedral nite the rain beat out its tales' – he brackets the latter phrase in pen, knowing it needs to be replaced, which it is by the mnemonically memorable 'the rain unravelled tales.'

Another line would plague the man long after the song was supposedly finished. In the draft, he envisages the chimes striking 'for the poet an the painter who reflect their given time.' And though he leaves the line unchanged on the page, by the time it was recorded in June, the poet and the painter are 'far behind their rightful time.' Still not right. Unveiling the song at the Newport Folk Festival in late July, he changed this line again, deciding that such an artist 'lights up his rightful time.' Better. Dylan, though, had not finished with it. When he came to *Writings and Drawings*, nine years after last performing the song, he could not resist tinkering, coming up with the worst of the lot: 'An the unpawned painter behind beyond his rightful time.' Ghastly. (And resolutely unchanged in subsequent editions of *Lyrics*.)

But perhaps the most curious discarded line in the Toronto manuscript is written upside down, in pen, and is not something that obviously pertains to the song. It reads, 'You just can't satisfy everybody.' (Dylan provided a corollary to this on the dedication page to *Writings and Drawings*: 'If I can't please everybody / I might as well not please nobody at all.'

He subsequently qualified this by writing in one journalist's copy of the book, 'DO NOT TAKE THIS STATEMENT AT WHITEFACE VALUE – IT MIGHT GO LIKE THIS, "If I can't please everybody, I only might as well please myself."') But it does pertain, expressing dissatisfaction with the audience accrued to date, a feeling expressed the same day he probably penned this sentiment to a Toronto journalist: 'If the kids say I speak for them, that's beautiful but I haven't reached the masses one little bit. . . . I don't want to be known as a folk singer.' 'Chimes of Freedom' was a clear attempt to reach a wider constituency than the one for 'Restless Farewell.' Three months earlier he claimed it was only for himself and his friends that he sang his stories. Now it was 'for every hung-up person in the whole wide universe.'

By the time he pulled his portable typewriter out of the back of his station wagon and began typing up a clean copy – his usual *modus operandi* when a lyric needed no more than cosmetic changes – he had a song he felt he could sing to his old constituency. When he arrived in Denver on February 15, four days after visiting New Orleans, he decided to debut the song at that night's Civic Auditorium concert. For the next few months, 'Chimes of Freedom' would constitute the centrepiece of live performances and, as of June 9, his fourth album, *Another Side of Bob Dylan*.

Oddly enough, though, when it came time to record it in the studio, Dylan couldn't get the song straight in his head, stumbling through six false starts before getting the entire song, and largely right. Given that 'Chimes of Freedom' was one of just three songs recorded that evening which he had previously played live – and the only one he had performed more than once – he was either trying too hard, or was already starting to feel disconnected from a song that, just four months earlier, provided a new summit to his songwriting. The straining-at-the-edge performance at Newport in late July – now available on DVD – sees him forcing the words out. By the time he performed his autumnal New York showcase at the Philharmonic Hall, the 'Chimes of Freedom' had ceased to ring. It would be twenty-three years before they pealed again.

When they did ring anew, it was as a duet with Roger McGuinn – who had already 'rogered' the song on the Byrds' debut LP, shearing it of two of its better verses (the third and fourth). Yet an even more incongruous setting awaited the former anthem. In January 1993 Dylan rushed through the song, at Bill Clinton's presidential inauguration. I find it hard to believe the born-again Bob thought Clinton had the mark of Kennedy on him. The fifty-one-year-old Dylan certainly evinced precious little connection to these words of hope, written when the 'cathedral bells were gently burnin.'

{117} MR. TAMBOURINE MAN

Published lyrics: Writings and Drawings; Lyrics *1985;* Lyrics *2004.*
First known performance: Royal Festival Hall, London, May 17, 1964.
Known studio recordings: Studio A, NY, June 9, 1964 – 2 takes
[NDH – tk.2]; January 15, 1965 – 6 takes [BIABH – tk.6].

> That is all we did in those days. Writing in the back seat of
> cars and writing songs on street corners or on porch swings.
> Seeking out the explosive areas of life. – Bob Dylan, 1977

One of 'the explosive areas of life' that Dylan was interested in exploring on the February 1964 road trip was the New Orleans Mardi Gras. Which is why he and his excitable entourage arrived in Louisiana on February 10 – to hopefully catch some shut-eye before revelries began the following day and into (i.e., through) the night. The Dylan who spent the night of the eleventh as a largely anonymous party-goer, alternating between 'weed' and wine, felt this constituted a necessary part of the systematic derangement of all senses that French symbolist Arthur Rimbaud had so eloquently endorsed a hundred years earlier, and which Dylan had now adopted as a *cri de coeur*.

Not surprisingly, he began to wax lyrical as the night wore on, informing Pete Karman, 'Rimbaud's where it's at. That's the kind of stuff that means something. That's the kind of writing I'm gonna do.' All the while he dismissed notions of freedom only recently addressed in song: 'No one's free. Even the birds are chained to the sky.' It was a line that imprinted itself on Dylan's mind long enough to become the final one of a song he was three months away from writing.

If 'Ballad in Plain D' was first formulated in that moment, an evening spent wandering 'the ancient empty streets' also provided ignition for a song that reduced to rubble the last vestiges of traditional song structures in Dylan's constructs, reassembling them as pure poetry-in-song. The finished 'Mr. Tambourine Man' would transcend even 'A Hard Rain's A-Gonna Fall' as a poetic statement. It even dared to draw comparisons with Rimbaud's own 'magic swirlin' ship,' 'Le Bateau Ivre,' which Arthur had described at one point as 'a little lost boat in swirling debris,' leaving the poet 'heartsick at dawn.'

For now, down in N'Orleans, in the 'jingle jangle morning,' Dylan experienced just the faintest flicker of what he was reaching for, not so much a poem as a sound – those 'vague traces of skippin' reels of rhyme' that would prove so mercurial. In 1977 he spoke to journalist Ron Rosenbaum of such moments: 'Music filters out to me in the crack of dawn . . . . You get a little spacey when you've been up all night, so you don't really have the power to form it. But that's the sound I'm trying to get across.' In November 1965, when he felt he had figured it out, he told critic Joseph Haas, 'I can hear the sound of what I want to say.'

By his own admission – in the *Biograph* notes – he 'wrote *some* [my italics] of the song in New Orleans.' Just that. 'Mr. Tambourine Man' did not come with the same alacrity as those chimerical 'Chimes of Freedom.' Dylan was probably wary of rushing to finish the song, sensing he was venturing far into that unknown region. As he told critic Max Jones in May 1964, '[The songs] come up and stay in my mind . . . sometimes a long time. I just write them out when the right time comes.' The same still held true forty years on, when he informed journalist Robert Hilburn, 'Songs don't just come to me. They'll usually brew for a while, and you'll learn that it's important to keep the pieces until they are completely formed and glued together.'

Since it tore at the borderline between poetry and song, 'Mr. Tambourine Man' needed a great deal of attention, lest such a sensual set of images should fail to form one cohesive whole. The song as initially penned 'on the road' probably lacked its chorus. The young Dylan had generally not been inclined to abide by such pop conventions – burdens, yes, choruses, no. However, a particular image now lodged in Dylan's head, helping to crystalize the Pied Piper figure who inhabits the song without making an actual appearance (like the later Johanna and her visions).

The specific Tambourine Man he had in mind was Bruce Langhorne, the magnificent multi-instrumentalist who would usher in Dylan's electric era with some spellbinding guitar playing on *Bringing It All Back Home* (notably on 'Mr. Tambourine Man' itself). Dylan told Cameron Crowe that his abiding image of Langhorne, whom he knew well from the Village streets, was of him carrying 'this gigantic tambourine. . . . It was as big as a wagon wheel.' Langhorne produced said tambourine when I interviewed him in 2000, confirming that he liked to brandish it whenever he strode those not-so-silent streets:

I used to play this giant Turkish tambourine. It was about [4"] deep, and it was very light and it had a sheepskin head and it had jingle bells around the edge – just one layer of bells all the way around. You play it with fingers on your left hand. I bought it 'cause I liked the sound. Hanza El Deen showed me how to play it. . . . I used to play it all the time, I used to carry it around with me and pluck it out and play it anytime. It had a bass tone, and it had an edge tone and it had jingles.

Maddeningly, there is no obvious way of extracting an exact date for the completion of this defining composition. It does seem to have been in New York. Suze Rotolo, in her memoir, suggests it was 'written about a lonely night Bob had spent wandering the streets after the two of us had quarreled,' but provides no concrete evidence that allows us to be sure that this is really her recollection (her reference to Langhorne as 'Bob's vision for the Tambourine Man' suggests she is relying on the very biographers she castigates earlier in her chronicle).

According to the *New York Post*'s Al Aronowitz – not always the most reliable chronicler – it was written at his house: 'He stayed up all night listening to music and had it the next morning. He threw out all his reject slips in the garbage. I picked them up and put them in a file.' Which he then lost. However, his memory once served Al well, and this was a period when the two were close. I'd suggest the song was completed shortly after the bitter breakup with Suze, probably some time in mid-to-late March, which would explain why Dylan would be haunting his friend's house, the then-usual post-breakup pattern.

At this juncture Dylan was not shy of playing his latest song to those he wanted to impress. And he knew right away how good this one was. Judy Collins got to hear the song

222

firsthand (she also claimed it was written at her home), as did Patty Elliott, the former wife of Ramblin' Jack Elliott, who probably heard it in the company of Albert Grossman's wife-to-be, Sally, and a friend of Sally's whom Dylan seemed rather stuck on, Sara Lowndes. Patty was so impressed with the song that she memorized it and sang it to her ex-husband before Dylan had even recorded it.

Dylan also supposedly played it to singer-songwriter Eric Von Schmidt when visiting him in Sarasota Springs, Florida, that spring; though it is hard to see where he could have found the time. In fact, Von Schmidt later insisted Dylan never visited him there. Altogether more likely is that the Bostonian folksinger heard the song at his own home in Massachusetts when Dylan was touring New England in mid-to-late April. An undated tape of a Dylan / Von Schmidt home session does exist and features the song. So Dylan did play it to Von Schmidt *somewhere* that spring.

An April recording date would make it the earliest known performance. It would also confirm that he finished the song before experiencing LSD, which he apparently first took at the end of that road trip (*sic*). The song's subsequent adoption by more hedonistic advocates as a 'drug song' clearly annoyed Dylan, driving him to tell *Musician*'s Bill Flanagan, 'I'm not going to write a fantasy song. Even a song like "Mr. Tambourine Man" really isn't a fantasy. There's substance to the dream. . . . You have to have seen something or have heard something for you to dream it.'

The songwriter stayed in the grip of this particular dream. Even as late as May he couldn't wait to blow old friends away with his extraordinary new song. Almost as soon as he landed in London on May 9, he was on the phone to Martin Carthy. As Carthy recalls, 'He came around. And he sang . . . "Mr. Tambourine Man" and it was [like], "Where [the hell] is this man going?"' The rest of London's folk fraternity wouldn't have to wait much longer to hear the song. On the afternoon of Sunday, May 17, he debuted it at the Royal Festival Hall.

The recording of that night's performance ranks high in the pantheon of great Dylan live performances. He takes the song at a measured pace, phrasing every syllable with military precision, but it is the unerring 'tonal breath control' he exercises on a set of lyrics he has never before sung in public that takes one's breath away. A single harmonica break before the final verse is the only respite from a riveting vocal. The spontaneous applause confirms the power of the song, convincing Dylan he has another winner.

According to Dylan, he even produced a sister song. As he told friend John Cohen, 'I tried to write another "Mr. Tambourine Man." It's the only song I tried to write "another one."' (There is no obvious candidate, so one must assume the song was hastily discarded.) And yet when he got around to recording his fourth album three weeks after its live debut, 'Tambourine Man' did not make the final cut. He later claimed it was precisely because it was special: 'I was just a kid [when I wrote "Blowin in the Wind"]. I didn't know anything about anything at that point. I just wrote that, and that wasn't it really. "Mr. Tambourine Man" . . . I was very close to that song. I kept it off my third [sic] album just because I felt too close to it.'

Actually, he simply failed to deliver the performance needed. And he knew it. As he disarmingly admitted to Robert Shelton in March 1966, when the album's failure no longer smarted: 'What I was trying to do on my fourth album . . . well, I was just too out of it, man, to come across with what I was trying to do. It was all done too fast.' Not only did he make a perfectly serious attempt to record the song at the *Another Side* session, he made the peculiar decision to let Ramblin' Jack Elliott duet on the chorus. Surprise, surprise, it didn't work. He also fatally delayed cutting the song until the session was well under way, along with his consumption of Beaujolais.

After struggling to realize 'Chimes of Freedom,' he gave himself the briefest of breathers, tossing off the throwaway 'Motorpsycho Nitemare,' before attempting to capture his most complex vision to date. Though he got through the whole song after a single false start, he blew a line in the final verse, tripping over the adjective applicable to 'leaves,' singing 'haunted leaves,' then realizing that the next line is 'haunted, frightened trees.' (The adjective he had sung at the Festival Hall was 'hidden.' By Newport, six weeks later, it would be 'frozen.') But this single slip was not the real problem with his performance (at least two other songs on *Another Side* used inserts to mask mistakes). It *drags*. At least he had the wit to recognize that releasing 'Mr. Tambourine Man' in anything less than its realized state would fully warrant being hung as a thief.

The delay in the song's appearance ultimately worked in its favour. This was, in part, because an acetate copy of the *Another Side* outtake found its way into the hands of Jim Dickson, who was trying to put together a band that would be a West Coast hybrid of the Beatles and the New Lost City Ramblers. By the time the Jet Set went from demo to record deal, they were in flight as the Byrds, and at their first session for Columbia, they cut a pop-confection single-length version of 'Mr. Tambourine Man' that would give the songwriter his first number one, both sides of the pond.

For Dylan, though, 'Mr. Tambourine Man' remained an acoustic song, pure and complex. It would take until the final show of the 'comeback' tour in 1974 for him to attempt his own electric version, and until the final show of his 1980 residency at the Warfield for Dylan *and* a guesting McGuinn to produce an amalgam of the two strains. After 1981 – when he came up with the one electric arrangement that actually worked – the song again reverted to its acoustic self, retaining such a hold on Dylan that he continued to discover previously unfathomed depths. Indeed performances given on the spring 1995 European tour saw Dylan nightly forsaking his guitar to stand at the microphone with only a mouth harp to help him, and the song came frighteningly close to its spring of '64 self.

{118} I DON'T BELIEVE YOU (SHE ACTS LIKE WE NEVER HAVE MET)

Published lyrics: Writings and Drawings; Lyrics *1985;* Lyrics *2004.*
Known studio recordings: Studio A, NY, June 9, 1964 – 5 takes [AS – tk.5]; Studio B, NY, May 1, 1970 – 1 take.
First known performance: Philadelphia Town Hall, October 10, 1964.

Songs from the spring of 1964 are the last ones for a decade in which a reasonably complete set of song drafts – both typed and handwritten – allows us to construct a credible chronology to their composition. Almost all of the songs that make up Dylan's fourth album exist in such a form, probably because the bulk of the album was written in Europe in the last two weeks of May, and therefore these materials were kept together, unlike previous collections written at random moments in assorted coffee shops. It was the first time Dylan escaped New York to write an album's worth of songs, even if he went to great pains to point out that 'it was still an American album.'

Any songs written in the months preceding the irrevocable wrench from Suze disappeared, save for 'Chimes of Freedom' and 'Mr. Tambourine Man,' neither of which form part of the *Another Side* manuscripts. Three other songs exist only as typescripts, i.e., 'final' drafts of finished songs: 'I Don't Believe You,' 'Motorpsycho Nitemare,' and 'Spanish Harlem Incident.' These probably postdate Dylan's ejection from the Rotolos' apartment for the final time, in mid-March, but predate his overnight flight to London on May 8.

A well-crafted song, 'I Don't Believe You' relates an uncommon occurrence: a woman sleeping with the prince of protest, then spurning him in the morning (we know he slept with at least one obliging gal on his February jaunt, despite having someone on each coast awaiting him). One presumes our traumatized narrator has conflated a one-night stand with the exit of his 'dream lover,' who has just left his life for good, making this something of a dry run for 'Simple Twist of Fate.'

Though the typescript of 'I Don't Believe You' is faithful to its finished form, it is not given the name by which it shall become known. 'She Acts Like We Never Have Met,' like a handful of other Dylan subtitles ('Tales of Yankee Power' and 'Has Anybody Seen My Love?' to name but two), has always been the song's name in Dylan's mind. Indeed, it still bore this title in 1984, when it appeared on a set-list for the European tour (though it went unperformed). Dylan also continued to rate the song highly himself, giving it magnetic makeovers in concert in 1965–6, 1975, 1978, 1981, and episodically on the Never Ending Tour, while sometimes struggling to fully recall the order of verses – as in 1964, when he famously forgot the first verse at a New York showcase, or in 1981, when an impromptu one-off performance in London stuttered to a premature conclusion.

{119} SPANISH HARLEM INCIDENT

Published lyrics: Writings and Drawings; Lyrics *1985;* Lyrics *2004.*
Known studio recordings: Studio A, NY, June 9, 1964 – 5 takes
[AS – tk.5].
First known performance: Philharmonic Hall, NY, October 31, 1964 [L64].

Untitled in its typed draft, 'Spanish Harlem Incident' strongly suggests that the spurned songwriter had reverted to type, playing the field, home and away – as with 'I Don't

Believe You' and 'It Ain't Me, Babe.' Irrespective of whether there ever was a 'gypsy gal' who, like Gypsy Davey, could 'cast the glamour' over others, Dylan's depiction of this female fortune-teller smacks of wish fulfillment in the aftermath of a breakup with the person he'd once called 'the true fortune-teller of his soul.' There is no verbal suggestion that this spellbinding lady is doing anything but reading the narrator's fortune. Still, he allows himself to fall hopelessly under her spell.

Finding himself in her thrall, he experiences an unfamiliar and thrilling sensation ('come an make my / pale face fit into place (ah please)'). The finished song slightly blurs such neediness. Its first two verses, as typed, conclude by asking whether her palm-reading skills foretell a future together: 'let me know babe about my fortune / hidin down along my palms.' On record this becomes, 'let me know babe, my hands're askin / if it's you my lifeline's traced.' In the final verse, he starts to wonder whether he is being suckered: 'By your wildcat charms I'm swindled.' Modified in the studio, this line becomes a more picaresque representation of his precarious state: 'On the cliffs of your wildcat charms I'm riding.' At song's end, in draft form, he makes one last plea, 'I gotta know babe, will I be touchin you / So I can know if I'm really real.' The song's single documented live performance would take place sixty blocks south of 'the hands of Harlem,' on All Hallow's Eve, 1964.

{120} MOTORPSYCHO NITEMARE

Published lyrics: Writings and Drawings; Lyrics 1985; Lyrics 2004.
Known studio recordings: Studio A, NY, June 9, 1964 – 4 takes [AS – tk.4].

Had Dylan (and producer Tom Wilson) exercised a little due thought before compiling *Another Side*, they would surely have nixed this nugget of fool's gold. But CBS was breathing down their necks. The singer won't feel he has to be this funny-ha-ha again until *Love and Theft*. Juxtaposing the folk-loric myth of the farmer's daughter with an off-kilter remake of Alfred Hitchcock's 1960 movie *Psycho*, Dylan starts with a premise that has real potential, but almost all of its humour falls flat. Dylan's vocal manages to make him sound like an overexcited schoolboy, a common problem on this album. At least he shows himself to be a proper film buff, name-checking Fellini's *La Dolce Vita*, a film released at almost the same time as *Psycho* (featuring, in a cameo role, the beguiling lady Dylan met in Paris that May). Unlike these two classics of modern cinema, though, Dylan's audio account was never destined to become one for the ages.

{121} IT AIN'T ME BABE

Published lyrics: Writings and Drawings; Lyrics 1985; Lyrics 2004.
First known performance: [Royal Festival Hall, London, May 17, 1964]. Newport Folk Festival, July 24, 1964 [LAN].
Known studio recordings: Studio A, NY, June 9, 1964 – 2 takes [AS – tk.2]; Studio B, NY, May 1, 1970.

Of the ten *Another Side* songs for which Dylan's hand-written lyrics definitely exist, six are on headed stationery, à la 'Chimes of Freedom.' The other five appear on Mayfair Hotel notepaper, suggesting that they were either started while he was in London, from May 9 to 18, or he had yet to exhaust his stationery supply as he travelled across mainland Europe, after his spellbinding Festival Hall performance. The Mayfair Hotel, off Piccadilly, would be Dylan's chosen resting place in both 1964 and 1966. Of the songs penned on their emblematic paper, the one we can be sure Dylan 'completed' during the week in London is 'It Ain't Me, Babe,' since it constituted part of the Festival Hall set.

That performance, which was recorded by Pye Records for Columbia, has not circulated, so we have to rely on author Richard Mabey's description of it in *The Pop Process*, with its 'soaring "No, no, no" chorus-line . . . [which] deliciously parodies the Beatles' "yeah, yeah, yeah"' (on 'She Loves You'). Bob and the Beatles were already forming a mutual fan club, though their first, fragrant meeting was still three months away. George Harrison's purchase of Dylan's second album in Paris the previous February was the start of a lifelong obsession. Dylan was at the same time driving through Colorado, hearing nonstop Beatles on AM radio stations and concluding, 'In my head the Beatles were it. . . . I started thinking it was so far out that I couldn't deal with it – eight in the top ten. It seemed to me a definite line was being drawn.'

What we don't know about the song's live debut was whether 'It Ain't Me Babe' was *four* verses long, the complete draft of the song containing an extra verse, which was later scrapped:

> Your talking turns me off, babe.
> It seems you're trying out of fear,
> [*Your terms are time behind*]
> And you're looking too hard for what's not here.
> You say you're looking for someone
> That's been in your dreams, you say,
> To terrify your enemies
> An scare your foes away,
> Someone to even up your scores.
> But it ain't me babe . . .

The rest of the song was almost identical to its *Another Side* self (save for a slight tongue-twister in verse one, 't hold open for you each an every door,' which managed to lose three little words). Yet Dylan must have worked on the song long and hard between bouts of socializing. An early draft of the first verse, also on Mayfair paper – and included in *The Bob Dylan Scrapbook* – suggests it was the phrase 'it ain't me, babe / it ain't me you're looking for' that sparked the song, making this an exception for a man who once informed *Musician* editor Bill Flanagan, 'Most of the time the words and melody come at the same time, usually with the first line.'

The 'no, no, no' certainly came later, perhaps as he gradually realized the sheer scale of Beatlemania in Britain. At this early stage it is the singer who is looking to leave, informing the 'babe' at verse's end, 'I got t be going.' Initially the song portrays a woman who wants someone 't protect you from all sadness . . . one you can count on not t leave,' more closely resembling the figure in 'To Ramona.' Whereas in the final 'It Ain't Me Babe,' her version of a picture-perfect romantic hero has been stripped bare.

Having started with the refrain, Dylan only later went back to the starting point. When the first line does appear, the song spins around. Now it is *she* who must be going, and *he* who is on the balcony, telling her to leave – a hundred and eighty degrees removed from his own situation with Suze. That opening, enjoining her to 'Go way from my window,' is another traditional allusion. As he well knew, it was the opening line (and title) of a modern reworking of a sixteenth-century lyric (Dylan used to sing 'Go 'Way From My Window' in St. Paul). Once he had this line, he knew he could reinforce its message with each successive verse, the recalcitrant ex-lover refusing to take a number of hints as the narrator tells her to 'Step lightly from the ledge, babe,' and finally to 'go melt back into the nite, babe' (that 'babe' becomes more insistent as the verses multiply).

Yet Dylan does not utilize the lovely tune to 'Go 'Way from My Window,' preferring to develop Martin Carthy's 'Scarborough Fair' template for a third time, refining it to fit the eight-line stanzas à la 'Boots of Spanish Leather.' In fact, so close are the arrangements that on one occasion, in September 1993,* Dylan started performing 'Boots of Spanish Leather' – which he'd already played at the show! – realized his error, and reverted to 'It Ain't Me Babe,' as intended.

Oddly enough, this devastating antiromance song struck a chord with Joan Baez – though she would be told to 'go 'way from my window' soon enough – and so, whenever the opportunity arose for a Dylan/Baez duet, she insisted on letting her soprano cut the lyric to pieces. Dylan finally reclaimed the song for himself in September 1965 when the Hawks gave it the full electroshock treatment (an attempt to now reclaim it from the Turtles, who'd also desecrated this sacrilegious lullaby). Save for a faux-reggae arrangement ten years on – one of the absolute highlights of the *Renaldo and Clara* film – the song has usually relied on the sparsest of acoustic accompaniments in live performance, often serving as a set closer, which tempts one to suggest it addresses the audience – specifically that element that wants the man to stay the same. That ain't him.

{122} DENISE DENISE

Published lyrics: Writings and Drawings; Lyrics 1985; Lyrics 2004.
Known studio recordings: Studio A, NY, June 9, 1964 – 1 take.

I think we can safely assume that there was no 'literal' Denise for whom the singer was pining. Rather, Dylan is intentionally lampooning the title of a Top Ten single for Randy and the Rainbows the previous August (which, after a sex change, would become an even bigger smash for Blondie). In Dylan's hands 'Denise Denise' is not so much playing hard to get as hard to comprehend. The baffled suitor fires off a

---

* The performance in question, preserved as a soundboard tape, was at Wolftrap, Vienna, Va., on September 8, 1993, when Dylan also played 'Series of Dreams' live for the first time.

string of questions before realizing, in the final verse, that he is talking to himself: 'I'm looking deep in your eyes, babe / But all I can see is myself.'

Dylan seems to have finished the song to his satisfaction while still in London. He wrote out all five verses with the usual crossed-out lines and rewrites (though not on hotel notepaper), and then subsequently wrote out a clean version – along with an equally 'fair' copy of 'Mama, You Been on My Mind' – on Mayfair paper. He then signed both songs (as if signing off on the songs?). However, the 'Denise Denise' he wrote out is quite different from the one he recorded (and rejected) at the June 9 Columbia session. Verses two and three read thus:

> Are you some kind of genius or just playin cat an rat [x2]
> I know you're laughin, but what're you laughin at?

> With your eyebrows raised, babe, your mouth is pointin
>   down [x2]
> If you show me what you mean, babe, I swear you won't
>   have t make a sound.

The first and last verses, though – which are required to bear the brunt of the song's *raison d'être* – survive intact to the studio, though Dylan can't resist making one of those inexplicable changes to a lyric prior to its inclusion in *Writings and Drawings*, replacing the perfectly serviceable, 'Denise, Denise, are you for sale or just on the shelf?' with the impenetrable, 'Denise, Denise, you're concealed here on the shelf.' Either way, one suspects the song was always destined to serve as a warm-up exercise in both its hotel and studio settings.

{123} MAMA, YOU BEEN ON MY MIND

Published lyrics: Writings and Drawings; Lyrics *1985;* Lyrics *2004.*
Known studio recordings: Studio A, NY, June 9, 1964 – 1 take [TBS].
First known performance: Forest Hills, NY, August 8, 1964.

In compiling *Times . . .* Dylan knew he had a surfeit of strong songs. The same cannot be said of its successor, an album with more filler than any other pre-accident collection. Which makes it more than a little perverse that Dylan should decide not to include this superb love song, the best of a three-song suite directly addressing the situation with Suze: 'Mama, You Been on My Mind,' 'Ballad in Plain D,' and 'To Ramona.' These three would occupy much of his songwriting energies in Europe, encapsulating the three phases of this intense breakup: recognition of a great loss, a lashing out at everyone (himself included), and, lastly, rueful resignation.

Dylan's decision not to include this pivotal piece on *Another Side*, the ambiguous nature of some of his lyrical rewrites, and the fact that he ultimately donated the song to Joan Baez – who presumably only got to hear it in late July, on venturing east for Newport – all served to diminish what should have been an elevated position among the man's breakup songs. It could also have acted as a necessary antidote to the coeval 'Ballad in Plain D.' Demonstrably, he always rated the song, performing it in 1974 *and* 1975, when it was known to fans only via Baez or bootlegs. Yet despite singing the song with Baez in 1964–5 and then in 1975, Dylan seemed to forget the song's composition history, telling a radio audience in 1991 that it 'was one of the California songs, Big Sur songs. There was a batch of them. . . . [Baez] drove me once from the airport to her house and that song might have been written during that trip in the back seat of her car.' Not unless he had been keeping some Mayfair stationery in reserve!

There are at least two drafts on Mayfair-headed note-paper, one containing three largely complete verses plus two more sketched out, the other being a clean, signed set. And though he made no claim on 'Mama, You Been on My Mind' at the time, it is surely the song he had in mind (boom, boom) when he told Nat Hentoff, a week after the *Another Side* session: 'When I'm uptight and it's raining outside and nobody's around and somebody is a long way from me – and with someone else besides – I can't sing "Ain't Got No Use for Your Red Apple Juice." . . . I have to make a new song out of what I know and out of what I'm feeling.'

'Mama, You Been on My Mind' in many ways mirrors 'Girl from the North Country,' another song written in Europe when the 'Suze situation' seemed hopeless. However, that song both was and wasn't about Suze, whereas there is no such doubt concerning 'Mama, You Been on My Mind.' In its original state, he even insists in verse two that he is 'not pleading for lost love I can't get,' an overt admission that this relationship is *kaput*. And in the penultimate verse – subsequently cut – 'she' seems to be refusing to take his long-distance call:

> Please understand you need not answer t my call,
> The world is too big for me t be that small,
> I am not putting any pressure on you t come back t me at all
> [But] mama you been on my mind.

A remorseful Dylan ultimately decided he'd rather not stand quite so 'naked under unknowin' eyes,' changing this verse dramatically by the time he wrote out a fair copy. Here he informs her, 'I'm not calling for you t go / I'm just whispering t myself, tho which me's talking I don't know,' a lovely couplet, but one he can't leave well alone. Eventually it sinks into the same mixed-up confusion as its author, '. . . pretendin', not that I don't know / that mama you been on my mind.'

After this final rewrite, he recorded it at the June 9 session in a single, sublime take, as the penultimate song of this long, dark night. But then he decided to let Baez do what she wanted with it. At least Baez, to her credit, pushed Dylan to reembrace the song. They shared a terrific country-rock rendition on the first leg of the Rolling Thunder tour, when they had almost learned to duet with each other. And, after its inclusion on 1991's *The Bootleg Series*, Dylan rediscovered its proper setting, as a gentle acoustic song of wistful regret, proving the truth of something he said to interviewer Lynne Allen back in 1978: 'I never leave the songs behind. I might leave the arrangements and the mood behind, but the songs, I never leave them behind.'

{124} BALLAD IN PLAIN D

Published lyrics: Writings and Drawings; Lyrics *1985;* Lyrics *2004.*
Known studio recordings: Studio A, NY, June 9, 1964 – 4 takes [AS – tk.4+insert].
First known performance: [Ann Arbor, MI, July 1964].

> I look back at that particular one and say, of all the songs I've written, maybe I could have left that alone. . . . It overtook my mind so I wrote it. Maybe I shouldn't have used that. I had other songs at the time. – Bob Dylan, 1985

Though described at the time by author David Horowitz as 'not really a song at all . . . only the raw material for a song,' 'Ballad in Plain D' seems to be one composition that 'enjoyed' an awfully long gestation. Dylan had quoted the last line of the song ('Are birds free from the chains of the skyway?') to Pete Karman at that year's New Orleans Mardi

Gras on February 11. He had also extemporized upon its theme to Suze over dinner at Emilio's that winter, 'all fired up about the concept of freedom.'

On the other hand, its most embarrassing line, 'for her parasite sister I had no respect' – aimed foursquare at Suze Rotolo's sister, Carla – postdates his visit to Berlin the last week in May, appearing on a page headed by the statement, 'I went in t east berlin.' It appears to be one of those songs mentioned to Max Jones a fortnight earlier, that 'come up and stay in my mind . . . a long time. I just write them out when the right time comes.'

Between these stolen moments lies one mad March evening, when Dylan and his girlfriend had the last of several, increasingly heated rows about his possessiveness and philandering, during which Carla interceded on her sister's behalf, thus exposing herself to the man's verbal bayonet and personal enmity. When folk guitarist Barry Kornfeld, in the company of Paul Clayton, arrived at the apartment, he found 'Carla practically foaming at the mouth, Dylan practically foaming at the mouth, and Suze sitting in bed, literally in shock. Suze had just sort of tuned out. Bob and Carla were still going at it – they were both totally incoherent.'

By then Carla knew all about the way Dylan could distort the truth. As she later said, 'He could look at you and pick out a weakness and suddenly grab it and use it on you. Which is what he did with everybody. He'd find their vulnerable spots and just demolish them. At that time he was very vicious to everybody. . . . It was just devastating, the way he could twist somebody's words back on themselves and make them feel he was right and they were wrong.' 'Ballad in Plain D' applied the technique in song, attempting to 'twist somebody's words back on themselves' in a medium where he was supreme.

But he had yet to demonstrate that his undoubted dexterity when demolishing someone verbally could be transferred to a lyric. 'Like a Rolling Stone' was more than a year away. Also, fatally, he had allowed himself precious little emotional distance. Still endlessly reliving the breakup in his mind, even thousands of miles away, he had forgotten, 'Revenge is a dish best served cold.' There is nothing level-headed about Dylan's depiction of events in 'Plain D.' The emotion of that evening was still red-raw when he wrote out the first line ('I once loved a girl, her skin it was bronze') and the last verse ('My friends from the prison, they ask unto me . . .') on Mayfair notepaper.

There is only one other verse on this sheet, detailing how he 'took her away / from the mother and sister, tho' close did they stay,' but it points out where the song is going. He also had a tune, and this time it *was* the one that generally accompanied his opening sentiment. 'I once loved a girl' is not only a folk commonplace but also one of tradition's most familiar song types. 'Once I Had a Sweetheart' (a.k.a. 'The Forsaken Lover') provided the template for 'a new song out of what I know and out of what I'm feeling.' Along with its opening phrase and tune, he planned to adapt the closing-verse riddle that featured in at least one traditional variant:

> My friends, my friends, they say unto me,
> How many strawberries grow in the salt sea?
> And I answer them, with a tear in my e'e,
> How many ships sail in the forest?

For once he failed to match the original's grasp of grief. 'Are birds free from the chains of the skyway?' hardly conveys the same sense of despair as this highly tractable floating verse – even though Dylan had been carrying his little riddle around for months, probably for as long as the idea of remaking 'Once I Had a Sweetheart' held sway. One suspects he had been seeking solace in such songs in the days that lay between. And there was no shortage of them known to this one-man song-bank.

If 'Plain D' had stayed as a short lyric, it could well have made another 'Girl from the North Country.' It certainly benefits from a gorgeous tune and a surprisingly warm vocal on the album. But as soon as Dylan got to the Greek village of Vernilya at the end of May and started to 'group' the material he planned to record on his return, he seems to have decided this personal tragedy warranted an epic ballad, and thus began raking over the coals of an affair while both ends were still burning.

Even here, though, cut off from the world, Dylan continued to allow his mind to wander. On each of the double-sided sheets where he worked painstakingly on 'Plain D' can be found verses for the absurd 'I Shall Be Free #10.' One can't imagine two more different songs, yet it would appear that this 'bipolar' approach to songwriting – heartbreak and irony entwining like the red rose and the briar – was a technique adopted throughout his European jaunt. 'Mama, You Been on My Mind' shares a sheet with 'Denise Denise.' 'To Ramona' and 'All I Really Want to Do' appear on the same back page.

Less typical of other 'Vernilya drafts' was Dylan's decision to type out lines for 'Plain D,' though a fair copy remained a long way off. These he liberally embellished with handwritten alterations and additions, still an unusual approach for Dylan, though it would become the norm by the time of *Blonde on Blonde*. In this case he made three attempts to develop 'Of two daughters, she was the young' into something more traditional sounding, akin to the common opening for 'The Twa Sisters': 'There lived twa sisters in a bower / The youngest o them, O she was a flower.'

Some of the lines he comes up with smack of the confession box. The lines, 't protect her from hurt / I thought to keep her from my reckless wild escapades,' comprise a particularly original way of saying, 'Hey, it was OK for me to party, but not you'; 'we grew up at each other / in the most awful way,' is another way of saying Suze was pissed off at Dylan's cavorting, knowing full well he no longer had to work at the art of seduction. But he continues to reserve most of his deep reservoir of recriminations for 'her paracite sister' and 'her possessin mother,' both of whom 'overlooked her creative instincts . . . completely.'

It took thirteen cathartic verses to get all of this out of his system, without Dylan ever transcending his material. 'Plain D' remains an exercise in painful autobiography best worked out in therapy, not on the page. Ten years later, he did not make the same mistake. Yet he probably retained a sneaking fondness for the song. Though he never played it live after July 1964, he chose to incorporate it into his 1977 celluloid experiment, *Renaldo and Clara*, sung by Gordon Lightfoot in a Toronto hotel room on the Rolling Thunder tour, and the song was rehearsed at Rundown Studios in January 1978, prior to a world tour dubbed the Alimony Tour by crueller critics.

{125} BLACK CROW BLUES

Published lyrics: Writings and Drawings; Lyrics 1985; Lyrics 2004.
Known studio recordings: Studio A, NY, June 9, 1964 – 3 takes [AS – tk.3].

Aside from the five songs (# 121–5) he sketched out at the Mayfair – or on its notepaper – Dylan started at least three other songs he then abandoned. Certainly none of them made it to the one studio session or subsequent performance. One of these, concerning something he spied 'one foggy morning / upon the phantom ship,' never got beyond its unrealized opening verse. Another, 'Oh Babe, I'll Let You Be You,' presumably provided the basis for a slightly less condescending song, 'All I Really Want to Do.' Yet another only ever amounted to a handful of stray lines and a single verse about a 'fearless cop' whose 'life is leased . . . t the system of evil.' The prince of protest had not entirely abandoned griping about the status quo.

On the reverse side of the last of these, Dylan started another song that seems to peter out after just two-and-a-half verses. Another Bob Dylan blues, it leaves little doubt as to the source of his blues: *her* absence. In fact, this song had already petered out once before. On another sheet we find not only draft verses for 'I Shall Be Free #10' (the one about Cassius Clay) and 'All I Really Want to Do' ('i don't want t battle you / or shatter you / rat on you . . . i don't want t advertize you / mesmerize you / analyze you') but also two stabs at an opening verse to this twelve-bar blues, starting with 'In the wee wee hours, on the edge of the morning . . .' and ending up as 'pretending with[out] a doubt / that my long lost lover's gonna meet me an tell me what it's all about.' 'Black Crow Blues' had begun its journey.

It was probably just a day or two later when he returned to the Mayfair writing desk, took another sheet from his depleted supply of stationery, and took up where he left off, 'wishing my long lost lover'd whisper from nowhere / an tell me what it's all about.' A second verse draws on the lines, 'my wrist was empty / but my nerves were tickin',' originally found in the 'wee wee hours' draft. After all the bravado of 'It Ain't Me Babe,' the starting point for a third verse, 'you can come back t me sometime daytime anytime you want,' gives the game away, but the draft ends there.

Dylan persevered. At some point, he finished the third verse and a further two, the final one of which invokes a painter 'far beyond his rightful time' to express a concomitant romantic anguish. Van Gogh expressed his by cutting off an ear, then representing his distress pictorially in a painting of 'black crows in the meadow' (the original working title, 'Weird Consumption,' perhaps alludes to another nineteenth-century artist known for his romantic anguish). One Mayfair fragment Dylan got around to finishing, 'Black Crow Blues' at least provided a welcome example of his syncopated piano playing on record. Which is where it was laid to rest.

{126} I SHALL BE FREE #10

Published lyrics: Writings and Drawings; Lyrics *1985;* Lyrics *2004.*
Known studio recordings: Studio A, NY, June 9, 1964 – 4 takes
[AS – tk.4+insert].

As with its numberless predecessor, 'I Shall Be Free #10' appears to have been composed in stages, as the whim took him, with verses two to five (of twelve) appearing among the *Another Side* papers (three of these verses appear on the same sheets as a draft of 'Ballad in Plain D'). There are also two unfinished, indeed unrecorded, verses – one about wanting to live life 'as a blond' and visiting East Berlin, the other admitting his unsuitability for a variety of public roles:

> now malcolm x is on my trail
> robert welch wants t throw me in jail
> bishop sheen says i got no belief
> rabbi greenbaum says I'm a thief.

We can assume from all this that Dylan continued to add verses right up to the day of the session (and probably during it). He does seem somewhat unfamiliar with some of his own jokes on the recorded version, blowing the song completely when he gets to the woman who's so mean she sticks him with buckshot when he's nude. Producer Tom Wilson suggests he sing the rest of the song as an insert, but Dylan asks if he can start again. An argument ensues.

Wilson gets his way, as the pressure of cutting an entire album in a night begins to tell on Dylan. He records the insert, but leaves out two of the verses and has to record it again. It hardly seems worth the effort, especially since the second time around, Dylan fluffs the little instrumental squiggle on the final verse, which is meant to be 'something I learned over in England.' It was presumably intended to have them rolling in the isles.

{127} TO RAMONA

Published lyrics: Writings and Drawings; Lyrics 1985; Lyrics 2004.
Known studio recordings: Studio A, NY, June 9, 1964 – 1 take [AS].
First known performance: Newport Folk Festival, July 26, 1964.

On a collection that lurches from peak to trough, 'To Ramona' provides a necessarily impressive conclusion to side one. A song of resignation composed after getting 'Plain D' out of his system, 'Ramona' remains an occasional concert treat to the present day. Again the idea for the song seems to be one he stored away for his European travels. Though the song had been worked on initially in London, it was not completed until Dylan had removed himself from further distractions, save for the nubile Nico and the tavernas of Greece. Alongside 'some other kinds of song,' he began to type out a clean copy, only for dissatisfaction to set in, prompting him to wield his pen again.

In London town the first identifiable element in the song appeared on the back of the sheet where Dylan first outlined that epitaph to a dead relationship, 'Ballad in Plain D,' suggesting that without 'Plain D,' there might be no 'Ramona.' Just two lines penned on the reverse of 'Plain D' suggest the healing process has begun: 'your cracked country lips will soon [blank] / tho they will twist it, don't resist it.' Allowing his mind to wander again, he proceeded with ribald rhymes that may or may not have been intended for 'I Shall Be Free #10' (one of which is 'the pin boy cried / you're on another side'!). On another pristine sheet, beneath the returning phantom ship, Dylan scribbled three more lines. This time they come with a name:

Ramona, you ask me t tell you about
You speak about rocks in the road an you ask what they [be]
An you capture any moment enough for me t say.

On another sheet, where a skeletal outline of what shall be 'All I Really Want to Do' has begun to form, Dylan finally began counselling Ramona 'in line.' Though still just jotted-down phrases circling around a central idea, recognizable elements are in place – the city versus the country; rejecting the opinions of others who just want 'to hype you and type you'; the difficulty of staying true to oneself in a political world ('acceptance means nothing / as you're bound t find out some time'). Some of these wild thoughts survived the writing process intact, like 'the flowers of the city.' Some would take shape during the process ('you'll only be defeated if you go back t the south'). Some were simply sidelined ('your body's your own, babe'), as he built around a series of internal rhymes ('breath like,' 'death like').

By the time Dylan reached the taverna/s, he had all five verses – and presumably that gorgeous tune (which I strongly suspect has some little-known traditional Mexican ante-cedent, given that Waylon Jennings used the *exact* same tune the following year for 'Anita, You're Dreaming,' without any kind of co-credit). He was still shy a couple of lines – 'as to be next t the strength of your skin' and 'there's no one to beat cept the thoughts of yourself as you stand' being added in pen. But only the second half of verse five now needs a major fix, as its original form tripped over itself:

Your sorrow is stemmin from forces an friends that define
of hypin you typin (leadin needin you to know they're alive)

Dylan's use of that bracket again suggests dissatisfaction. Sure enough, at the bottom of the page come two attempts at an improvement. First there is, 'just to add talk t their time,' and then, 'making you feel like you have t be just like them.' Got it. As the song *and* the process near their finishing end, the singer achieves an empathy with Ramona's predicament, 'torn between remainin' and returnin' back t the south.' When it came time to cut the song in Studio A, it was realized in another flowing first take.

Quite whom the singer is trying to mollify (and/or seduce) remains pure guesswork. One possibility must be Sara Lowndes, who became close to Dylan in the aftermath of his breakup with Suze. She could be said to have 'cracked country lips,' being a Delaware girl, and her bronzed skin and dusky features may have suggested Spanish ancestry – and the Mediterranean goddess status the name 'Ramona' implies. 'Ramona' could even be a feminine alter ego. He was certainly spending a lot of his time having 'to deal with the dyin.' And as he observed in 1978, 'I've been to the city, and I can't avoid that. So it does enter into my music – but the backbone of it comes from the country.'

{128} ALL I REALLY WANT TO DO

Published lyrics: Writings and Drawings; Lyrics *1985*; Lyrics *2004 [1978 version:* Words Fill My Head.].
Known studio recordings: Studio A, NY, June 9, 1964 – 1 take [AS].
First known performance: Newport Folk Festival, July 26, 1964.

At a time when Dylan was dishing out advice in song left, right, and centre, 'All I Really Want to Do' was his only real attempt at garnishing it with a little levity. The song's constant triple-rhymes allow him to have some fun with the scenarios he has thought up. Even in its first draft – still not sure whether the song's refrain should be, 'All I wanna do is just be friends with [you],' or the inferior, 'I don't want t be your best friend' – he is insisting, 'I don't want t marry you / nor carry you / nor bury you.' Nor does he 'want t rob you blind / [or] steal your mind.' The man is all heart.

But its bam-bam-bam rhyme scheme also tied him down. By the time he wrote out a finished lyric, on the same page as a fair copy of 'My Back Pages,' the lines were exactly as he recorded them in a single take at the June 9 session. Written to make him *and* his audience feel better, the song kicks off an album intended to signify a change in direction. A quite different statement to his last album opener, 'All I Really Want to Do' announces a set of songs written to get things off his chest.

Dylan later claimed he didn't want his fourth album to be called *Another Side*: 'I thought it was just too corny and I just felt trouble coming when they titled it that.' In fact, the album's title appears among the album papers (twice); while 'All I Really Want to Do' is just as much of a statement as its predecessor, disowning a mantle he had barely assumed. Only with the album's failure – critical *and* commercial – did he start to cover his tracks, claiming to one supporter in the press, 'the songs are insanely honest. . . . i needed t write them. . . . if i wasn't so bloody famous, I'd look for rocks to kick down the street.'

And as a statement song, 'All I Really Want to Do' was a regular feature of the sets to come, though early live performances have an unfortunate tendency to sound not so much ebullient as hopped-up on helium. It would take Dylan until 1978 to find the appropriate vocal tone to go with such an outlandish rhyme scheme, but when he did, it was with a devil-may-care attitude to someone else's melody. The sing-along rendition played at the end of most shows on the year-long world tour took Paul Simon's '59th Street Bridge Song' as its preferred accompaniment. Nor did Dylan feel tied to the original lyrics, hamming it up in true Vegas fashion on verses like:

> I ain't lookin to make you fry,
> See you fly or watch you die . . .
> And I don't want to drag you down,
> Chain you down or be your clown.

{129} I'LL KEEP IT WITH MINE

Published lyrics: Writings and Drawings; Lyrics *1985;* Lyrics *2004.*
Known studio recordings: Witmark demo, June 1964; Studio A, NY, January 13, 1965 – 1 take [BIO]; January 14, 1965, Evening; January 27, 1966 – 1 take [TBS]; February 15, 1966 – 10 takes.

Having left at least two classic creations off *Times . . .* – the beginning of a career-long trend – Dylan continued the practice on *Another Side.* Despite its Suze-centric subject matter, he donated 'Mama, You Been on My Mind' to Baez, who probably enjoyed singing about his heartbreak over her main rival; while 'I'll Keep It with Mine' was written for, and apparently about, his travelling companion from Paris to Vernilya. Nico, Christa Päffgen's adopted name, was introduced to Dylan by the French folksinger Hugues Aufray. An aspiring actress who had been obliged to take up modelling to make ends meet, Nico had a young son who was the apple of her eye. As with Sally G's friend Sara and her daughter Maria, the young Dylan seemed to find it easier to relate to the woman/child package than just the woman.

Dylan's undoubted attraction to the imperious ice maiden cannot come as any great surprise (the Nordic blonde as statuesque Suze surrogate, discuss). Yet allowing her to accompany him all the way down to Greece when he had an album to write suggests he yearned for some female

247

companionship. Their time together does not seem to have resulted in any great meeting of minds. As Nico later observed, 'He did not treat me very seriously, but at least he was interested in my story. . . . As I was from Berlin, he asked me if I knew the playwright Brecht. . . . For a man who was preaching about politics he did not know his history too well. . . . We went . . . to Greece for a short time . . . and he wrote me a song about me and my little baby.'

And what an exquisite song it is. Author Paul Cable once described 'I'll Keep It with Mine' as 'possibly the best thing he had written up to that point . . . [while] the lyrics form the least patronizing way I have yet heard of saying, "I'm older than you – therefore I know better."' In just three verses, bound to a three-line refrain, Dylan manages to encapsulate so much of what he had been hoping to say in the trio of songs to Suze. In her case, though, he hadn't got beyond his tangled feelings long enough to whisper words like, 'If I can save you any time / Come on, give it to me / I'll keep it with mine.'

Having apparently offered Nico the song on an 'exclusive' basis, he refrained from releasing it on either *Another Side* or *Bringing It All Back Home*. Indeed, on June 9, Dylan elected not to record the song at all, even though his fourth album needed just such a song. When he later claimed, 'I never even recorded "I'll Keep It with Mine,"' an odd statement given that it accompanied the official release of a January 1965 studio outtake, he perhaps meant he did not record it *at the time*. For though he eventually made some three attempts to record the song 'officially,' these came *after* Nico blew her chance to turn pop diva.

So when Nico called on him at the Savoy Hotel the following spring, it was still hers to do with as she wished. Instead, Nico wanted to talk about recording 'Mr. Tambourine Man,' not 'I'll Keep It with Mine,' before proceeding to cut two songs suggested by *Stoned* impresario Andrew Loog Oldham ('I'm Not Saying' b/w 'The Last Mile'). Hence why her first single sank like a stone. And Dylan hadn't forgotten the song, which he had 'demo-ed' at least twice – once as a demo for his music publisher and once as a piano 'demo' for the fifth album. (There was also an aborted semi-electric *Bringing It . . .* version, the tape of which has been 'lost,' perhaps because the whole session was a disaster.) He demonstrated that he still remembered it well by pounding out the full tune on a stand-up piano backstage at the Albert Hall (included in the recent *Dylan 65 Revisited* documentary).

When Nico hightailed it to New York in September 1965, she again sought Dylan out. Dylan, though, was no longer the little boy lost she had met eighteen months earlier, and preferred to stand back as she attached herself to another trendy pop coterie, the one that centred around painter Andy Warhol. By the second week in January 1966, she would be rehearsing with a four-piece called the Velvet Underground. Much to the chagrin of Lou Reed and John Cale, she insisted they work up an arrangement of 'I'll Keep It with Mine' – which they did (a January 1966 rehearsal tape of it exists). But lacking the necessary business sense and already overburdened with gigantic egos, they refused to record it for their debut album.

At the same time, Dylan seemed to be struggling to come up with a sufficient supply of songs worthy enough to succeed the groundbreaking *Highway 61 Revisited*, and so, during a lull in a session he set up to record his next single, Dylan and his backing band (the Hawks) broke into a cursory rendition of 'I'll Keep It with Mine' (subsequently issued on *The Bootleg Series*). Reminded of the song's undoubted quality, and with another set of sessions booked for February in Nashville, Dylan let the southern session musicians work through ten instrumental takes of the song at Columbia's Music Row studio (perhaps as a stand-by song, in case he failed to come up with the goods). But he held back from recording a vocal, and that is the last we hear of the song from the songwriter himself.

At least it is *if* we discount a certain unidentified song he sang to another 'moon chick,' Rosemary Gerrette. The Australian lady witnessed an all-night hotel session in Sydney in late April 1966, while Dylan awaited a flight to Copenhagen. Gerrette's account of the evening includes Dylan playing one melody which he claimed, 'I'll never have it published [or] recorded. I wrote it for this way-out moon chick. We just sat on the floor on these mattresses . . . and like for two hours I spoke to her with my guitar. And she under-stood. . . . This isn't quite like I played it, because it meant something to me at the time. But now it doesn't.' Presuming she heard something other than a lost 1966 song, then Nico might be a credible candidate for 'this way-out moon chick,' and 'I'll Keep It with Mine' a good candidate for the song he played.

Nico did ultimately release the song the following year, while Dylan was recuperating upstate, making it an essential part of her arresting debut long-player, *Chelsea Girl*, produced by the man who recorded Dylan's most perfect rendition back in January 1965, Tom Wilson. With its belated release, it quickly gained acceptance as a real classic by Dylan fans and a good song for other artists to cover. The following year, Fairport Convention made almost as good a version of it as Nico had, releasing their more harmonic rendition on *What We Did on Our Holidays*. And while Dylan would go on to write his fair share of compassionate classics, Nico would go on to produce some of the most avant-garde and challenging material in the rock idiom. But then she learned her trade from New York's finest.

Published lyrics: Writings and Drawings; Lyrics 1985; Lyrics 2004.
Known studio recordings: Studio A, NY, June 9, 1964 – 2 takes [AS – tk.2].
First known performance: Mountain View, CA, June 11, 1988.

> I wrote the fourth record in Greece. . . . There was a change
> there . . . but the records before that, I used to know what I
> wanted to say before I used to write the song . . . and [in the
> end] I couldn't write like it anymore. It was just too easy,
> and it wasn't really 'right.' – Bob Dylan, San Francisco press
> conference, December 3, 1965

One can't be 100 percent sure, but it would appear that 'My Back Pages' – the working title of which was 'Ancient Memories' – was the last *Another Side* song written. It was certainly the last song recorded, completed after a single false start at the end of a *very* long night. Among the loose-leaf pages of song drafts, it exists only as a final draft, albeit one that underwent a couple of crucial changes in the days leading up to that all-night recording session. It also seems to reflect what was on his mind that week, if his statement to Nat Hentoff as he arrived at the recording session qualifies as spontaneous: 'There aren't any finger-pointing songs [here]. . . . Now a lot of people are doing finger-pointing songs. You know – pointing to all the things that are wrong. Me, I don't want to write for people anymore. You know – be a spokesman.'

'My Back Pages' is the song he wrote to make this new vantage point plain. The most dramatic change he made between Vernilya and Studio A was to alter the refrain that ends each verse. In the fair copy, Dylan tips his hat to one of his favourite traditional songs, that seventeenth-century Scottish elegy, 'Young but Daily Growin.' At this stage he intends to sing, 'Ah, but that's when I was older, I'm growin'' younger now,' a reference to his expressed desire to write like he used to when he was ten.

The change to '. . . I'm younger than that now' is part of a general tightening up of the whole song. In verse two, rather than the tongue-twisting 'uncondemnable,' he makes the line less of a mouthful, if more obtuse – with 'Unthought of, though, somehow.' Likewise, 'those who insanely teach' has become 'the mongrel dogs who teach,' while the terms clearly defined in the song are no longer 'right an wrong,' but 'good an bad.' Such changes were made to facilitate singing, not to clarify. One suspects he may have still been uncomfortable with the song's convoluted rhymes and wordplay, given that he didn't sing it for the longest time. He later claimed that he sometimes 'get[s] the rhymes first and . . . then [I] see if [I] can make it make sense in another kind of way.' Yet he does not cite 'My Back Pages' as an occasion when he failed to 'make sense' at all. Yes, the song is a presentiment of future greatness, but it is still a flat-footed failure from a man who wanted to sprint when he could still only jog.

As such, it is astonishing that well-respected man and editor of *Poetry Review*, Peter Forbes, should select 'My Back Pages' as one of just two Dylan lyrics for his anthology of twentieth-century poetry, *Scanning the Century*. Here is a song that merely reinforces the suspicion voiced by inferior poets that Dylan does not dally long on the meanings of words. On 'My Back Pages,' he teeters on the edge of gibberish with constructs like 'confusion boats.' A number of lines are clumsily executed or simply superfluous. 'Unthought of, though, somehow' is the Dylanesque equivalent of 'And I tell you no lie' in traditional ballads, a line put there to get from one thought to another without blowing the stanzaic pattern. Dylan has admitted that 'there are [some] songs in which I made up a whole verse just to get to another verse.' This is one such song.

Once Dylan entered the altogether more kaleidoscopic world that lay behind the gates of Eden, 'My Back Pages' was rendered redundant. As he told Margaret Steen at the height of his midsixties fecundity, 'My Back Pages' was a song written 'in my New York phase, or at least, I was just coming out of it. I was still keeping the things that are really *really* real out of my songs, for fear they'd be misunderstood.' 'My Back Pages' still brought enough criticism raining down on the man. The mongrel dogs weren't amused and tried to bark him down.

Thankfully, the Byrds came to his aid, emphasizing the song's strong melody and not its half-baked words. Indeed, when Dylan decided that he was finally experienced enough to sing the song live, in 1988, it was to the Byrds' template that he turned. Having made its live debut with a rousing G. E. Smith arrangement, stripped of some of its more risible lines, it subsequently passed through a wealth of electric and quasi-acoustic arrangements as Dylan grew to appreciate more of his own back pages.

{131} GATES OF EDEN

Published lyrics: Writings and Drawings; Lyrics *1985;* Lyrics *2004; [draft:* The Bob Dylan Scrapbook].

First known performance: Philharmonic Hall, NY, October 31, 1964 [L64].

Known studio recordings: Studio A, NY, January 15, 1965 – 1 take [BIABH]; Studio B, NY, May 1, 1970.

Dylan told Nat Hentoff, the week after the *Another Side* session, 'I've been getting freer in the songs I write, but I still feel confined. That's why I write a lot of poetry.' Stretching at the very bounds of song itself, he could sense the line between poetry and song starting to dissolve. As his page-bound poems became little more than speed-screeds, the songs became so much more, lateral *and* linear, literary yet lyrical. The all-important 'Gates of Eden' appears to have been composed at the same time as he was tapping out a number of rambling, nonrhymin', *vers libre* poems for the jacket of his fourth album, circa late June/July 1964.

Given that a complete draft resides among the *Another Side* papers, 'Gates of Eden' presumably predates 'It's Alright, Ma,' even though its live debut came later. With it Dylan finally ventured beyond the 'haunted, frightened trees . . . far from the twisted reach of crazy sorrow.' Sidelining songs about Suze, he willingly embraced that intensely creative nexus in which he may 'not really know exactly what [a song] is all about, but I do know the minutes and the layers of what it's all about,' a sentiment he voiced the following year.

Perhaps the prosaic process by which he tapped out every crazy thought that came to him that summer, hoping to deliver a literary masterpiece of speed-writing – and perhaps trump Richard Fariña's *Been Down So Long It Looks Like Up to Me* – played its part in attuning his hand to a chemically enhanced mind's eye. However, this 'naturalistic' approach to composition wasn't adopted for 'Gates of Eden' or 'It's Alright, Ma,' two songs far beyond their rightful time.

The frustratingly clean draft for 'Gates of Eden' gives the briefest glimpse of the writing process, suggesting that the song came with the dawn, and with a great deal more ease than either 'Mr. Tambourine Man' or 'Chimes of Freedom.' Eight of the nine verses are wholly realized. Just two verses change before the song arrives at its final form. In verse six, 'All men are kings inside the gates of Eden' becomes 'There are no kings . . .'; while in the eighth he ultimately prefers, 'And there are no trials inside the Gates of Eden,' rather than the foreboding, 'There's nowhere t hide inside the gates of Eden' – a presentiment, perhaps, of the later dystopia, 'Desolation Row.'

Just the final verse requires completion, comprising two lines, both brimming with ideas. 'At dawn my lover comes t me / an tells me of her dreams,' is one train of thought he completes easily enough. However, the suggestion that 'there are no words, but these t tell no truths,' needs unravelling. Eventually he arrives at, 'There are no words but these to tell what's true / And there are no truths outside the Gates of Eden,' a couplet that suggests time spent with the *I Ching* had not been wasted.

Though the song seems to have been written in time for his annual Newport appearance/s, the last week in July, he kept it back until his next New York showcase, on Halloween. On a night when he was struggling to focus on that sure vision of his, 'Gates of Eden' is *the* stand-out performance. He also effortlessly unravelled the song in the studio the following January, recording it in a single take, while continuing to make it an exemplar of his new creed in live performance, when he nightly stirred the melting pot.

It would take the introduction of the *Blonde on Blonde* songs in the winter of 1966 for Dylan to feel he had moved beyond this particular 'kingdom of Experience.' After which it would take him another twenty-two years to return to this Eden – perfunctory acoustic versions in 1974 and 1978 notwithstanding. Only at the start of the Never Ending Tour, partnering an equally electric 'My Back Pages' with an arrangement of heart-stopping intensity, would 'Gates of Eden' come back into its own. Disappointingly, this dramatic reinterpretation was dropped after just a handful of performances. Thankfully, in the spring of 1995, it returned to join 'Mr. Tambourine Man' and 'It's All Over Now, Baby Blue' in laser-precise acoustic sets that acted as a crash course in the compositional quantum leap achieved three decades prior.

{132} IT'S ALRIGHT, MA (I'M ONLY BLEEDING)

Published lyrics: Writings and Drawings; Lyrics 1985; Lyrics 2004.
First known performance: Philadelphia Town Hall, October 10, 1964.
Known studio recordings: Studio A, NY, January 15, 1965 – 2
takes [BIABH – tk.2].

> What I did to break away was to take simple folk changes
> and put new imagery and attitude to them, use catchphrases
> and metaphor combined with a new set of ordinances that
> evolved into something different[,] that had not been heard
> before. [Irwin] Silber scolded me in his letter [in *Sing Out!*]
> for doing this, as if he alone . . . had the keys to the real
> world. I knew what I was doing, though, and wasn't going
> to take a step back or retreat for anybody. – Bob Dylan,
> *Chronicles* (2004)

If there is a single song that defines this 'new set of ordi-
nances,' it is 'It's Alright, Ma.' Written in Woodstock, where
Dylan had retired for the summer, it is one of those songs
over which the author felt he exercised very little conscious
will. In recent interviews he has repeatedly singled out
this song as the kind of breakthrough mysterious even to
him: '"Darkness at the break of noon / Shadows even the
silver spoon / The hand-made blade, the child's balloon . . ."
There's a magic to that, and it's not Siegfried and Roy kinda
magic. It's a different kind of penetrating magic. And I did it
at one time. . . . I did it once, and I can do other things now.
But I can't do that.'

His own amazement undoubtedly explains why the song
has never left the man's live set for any sustained period, even
if its performance is a travesty these days. Back in November
1980, finally accepting he needed to reintroduce some old
songs after a year of gruelling Godliness, it even led Dylan
back to a place former fans feared he had left for good. In

conversation with Robert Hilburn, he picked this song out as one of those that still meant a lot to him: 'I don't think I could sit down now and write "It's Alright Ma" again. I wouldn't even know where to begin, but I can still sing it.' And sing it he did, usually at night's end.

Once again he was 'outside society,' commenting on its foibles and follies. As he had been back in 1964, when for the first time he was no longer content to 'pick one of the thousand million little points I can pick and explode it.' Dylan now had the whole of America's way of life in his sights. As he informed Hentoff at the time, 'There's only one way to change things, and that's to cut yourself off from all the chains.' 'It's Alright, Ma' is the sound of a chain saw revving. Herein, he forensically dissects every societal ill to which, two years earlier, he'd devoted entire albums of songs. Like 'Hard Rain,' which comprises a line from every song he ever hoped to write, 'It's Alright, Ma' is a manifesto of all the protest songs he swore off writing ever again.

By song's end he has confronted all three of the great taboos: religion, sex, and politics, putting more quotable lines into a single song than anyone before or since. No longer thinking he could change anyone but himself, he *was* at last prepared to let his 'thought-dreams . . . be seen,' at the exact moment when his worldview was becoming a whole lot darker, and the shadow of nihilism came creeping in his room. On 'It's Alright, Ma' there is an air of futility absent from earlier songs, even the apocalyptic ones. It seems he had finally got around to reading Sartre and Kierkegaard, for here is the first evidence of an existential strain that suffuses much of what he would write in the coming year. This was Dylan's 'life, and [his] life only' – the song's original subtitle, an existential statement if ever there was one.

Like 'Mr. Tambourine Man,' 'It's Alright, Ma' was an idea he was prepared to linger over – and, with the imminent release of a stopgap fourth LP, he had time. And like that other break-through, 'A Hard Rain's A-Gonna Fall,' the waterfall of images cascades down so quickly that one almost misses the intricacy of the rhyme scheme – five interlinked sets of triple-rhyming verses broken into six- and seven-line stanzas in *Writings and Drawings*, but clearly all six lines rhyme thus: AAAAAB CCCCCB DDDDDB, while a three-line refrain also rhymes AAB, as Dylan dared to be both poet and song-and-dance man.

Even on 1978's *Street-Legal* – which generally features his most ambitious rhyme schemes – Dylan never again displayed such daring. As he told journalist Jon Pareles in 1997, 'The alliteration in ["It's Alright Ma"] just blows me away.' Unsurprisingly, the song occasionally sacrifices linear logic in its desire to maintain rhyme-upon-rhyme-upon-rhyme, while Dylan still has to use his voice to make 'phony,' 'lonely,' and 'show me' alliterative, an effect he tried to mask in print. Thus, in the second *Writings and Drawings* verse, a strict end-rhyme reprint should read:

> From the fool's gold mouthpiece the hollow horn
> Plays wasted words, proves to warn
> That he not busy being born
> Is busy dying.

Whereas it has been set more logically, less effectively, as:

> From the fool's gold mouthpiece
> The hollow horn plays wasted words,
> Proves to warn
> That he not busy being born
> Is busy dying.

Dylan felt a real sense of accomplishment when finishing his most complex song to date (and with an original tune as compelling as any culled to date). What his house guests at the time – Joan Baez, her sister, Mimi, and Mimi's husband Richard Fariña – thought has not been documented. He was now moving too fast for even these hip folk, determined to put distance between him and the Irwin Silbers of this world. Silber's open letter, cited by Dylan in *Chronicles*, was published in the October/November 1964 issue of *Sing Out!* (which came out in September). 'It's Alright, Ma' may not have been Dylan's *direct* response to Silber's accusation – that his 'new songs seem to be all inner-directed now, inner-probing, self-conscious' – but it definitely demonstrates a singer-songwriter who ain't marching to *Sing Out!*'s tune no more.

{133} IF YOU GOTTA GO, GO NOW

Published lyrics: Writings and Drawings; Lyrics 1985; Lyrics 2004.
First known performance: Philharmonic Hall, NY, October 31, 1964 [L64].
Known studio recordings: Studio A, NY, January 13, 1965 – 1 take;
January 15, 1965 – 4 takes [45 + overdubs] [TBS w/out overdubs];
Levy's Recording Studio, London May 12, 1965.

Were I obliged to wager on a date when Dylan penned this early pop-song parody, I'd plump for some time shortly after August 28, 1964, and his auspicious first meeting with the Fab Four at the Delmonico Hotel (though its inclusion in the *Another Side* section in *Writings and Drawings* suggests Dylan thinks it came earlier – whatever its actual recording dates). Dylan was smart enough to feel the wind of change the Beatles blew in on, and some part of him wanted to be part of the same mighty storm. But he wasn't sure his current crop of fans would wear it. Hence a song like 'If You Gotta Go, Go Now,' which flexes those buried pop sensibilities in a song that itself pastiches the still-ephemeral genre.

After spending much of the previous season entertaining audiences with this compendium of innuendo, Dylan considered making 'If You Gotta Go, Go Now' his entrée into the world of pop singles – after seeing the success the Animals were enjoying with a form of 'folk-rock.' By the end of January he had recorded the song in a folk-rock guise, at the last of the *Bringing It All Back Home* sessions (having recorded it acoustic at the first one), only to then record a bluesier version in London shortly after his May 1965 English tour.

He had somehow found out about John Mayall's Bluesbreakers, Britain's premier blues makers – probably from the Animals' Alan Price or another member of the English pop pantheon who crowded his suite at the Savoy throughout his stay. And so a session was set up for May 12 to record this song. As further evidence of some serious intent underlying the exercise, Dylan's producer, Tom Wilson, was flown over to supervise proceedings.

Unfortunately the session was something of a bust, producing no usable take of 'If You Gotta Go, Go Now.' But Wilson hadn't given up on getting a releasable cut, and while Dylan jetted off to Europe with his new paramour, he returned to New York and, at a session on May 21, over-dubbed a couple of unspecified musicians onto the *Bringing It* . . . version – possibly at the same time that he did something similar to Simon and Garfunkel's 'The Sound of Silence' – creating a composite version that he hoped Dylan might OK for single release.

By the time Dylan heard the results, though, he'd already come up with a grander way to make his grandstand entrance into the pop charts: 'Like a Rolling Stone.' 'If You Gotta Go, Go Now' would still find its way into the charts, though. The acoustic version Dylan performed at a session for the BBC on June 1 – almost his last pass at the song – was made into an acetate by his music publisher and forwarded on to Manfred Mann, who promptly cut their own folk-rock version, replete with Britbeat harmonies. Mann's mannered rendition promptly gave Dylan a Top Ten version, just not the one he'd originally intended.

{134} FAREWELL ANGELINA
{135} LOVE IS JUST A FOUR-LETTER WORD

Published lyrics: Writings and Drawings; Lyrics 1985; Lyrics 2004 *[complete version of #135:* In His Own Words, *vol. 2].*
Known studio recordings [#134]: Studio A, NY, January 13, 1965 – 1 take [TBS].

One can't help but consider these two songs of a piece, and not just because they were both first released (and for decades, only available) by Joan Baez. They both seem to be songs Baez heard in the immediate aftermath of creation, and in the case of the former, at least, a song Dylan donated to her because he no longer needed it himself. As such, one must suppose *both* songs were penned in late November 1964, when Dylan was again hovering around Big Sur, playing shows in the Bay Area and beyond.

'Farewell Angelina' does date from this visit, as confirmed by its appearance on a January 1965 recording session and its subsequent inclusion as the title track to Baez's own semi-electric 1965 LP – with Dylan's musical director, Bruce Langhorne, all over it. Again Dylan seems to have spent his time in Carmel rifling through Baez's collection of Scottish ballads, leaning on another Scotch standard for Angelina's mournful tune. 'Farewell Angelina' borrowed elements of 'Farewell to Tarwathie,' a song about leaving Scotland for Greenland hoping 'to find riches in hunting the whale,' first collected in 1857. (A possible source may again be Ewan MacColl, who included the song in his 1960 collection, *The Singing Island*.)

However, rather than trying to console the one he plans to leave behind, Dylan is telling Angelina it is time to go, even though she cannot see the portents ('the sky is on fire . . . is trembling . . . is folding . . . is changing color . . . is erupting'). One of those songs that acts almost as a glossary on a single line from 'It's Alright, Ma' – 'He not busy being born is busy dying' – 'Farewell Angelina' contained an additional verse when Dylan recorded it, making that connection clearer still:

> The camouflaged parrot, he flutters from fear
> When something he doesn't know about, suddenly appears
> What cannot be imitated perfect, must die
> Farewell Angelina,
> The sky is flooding over, and I must go where its dry.

It may be that Dylan added this verse post-Carmel, but it seems more likely that Baez exercised some editorial control and clipped 'the camouflaged parrot' from her version. She was right to do so. It adds only atmosphere to what is, in either form, a classic 'mid-period' Dylan composition. As I have suggested elsewhere, it was probably only because he duly wrote an even better song along similar lines ('It's All Over Now, Baby Blue') that he set Angelina aside, leaving fans to think he never even recorded such a well-constructed song. (Though it appeared on a list of material in the CBS vault compiled in the early seventies, it was under the working title given it at the session, 'Alcatraz to the Ninth Power,' the true identity of which remained unknown for a quarter of a century.)

In the case of 'Love Is Just a Four-Letter Word,' there is more doubt concerning its composition date, simply because the first we hear of the song is in May 1965, when Baez insisted on serenading its composer with it in his Savoy suite. Dylan seemed slightly annoyed to be reminded of it, exclaiming, 'You still remember that goddamned song?!' – which does rather suggest he already considered it an old (and best-forgotten) song. This makes it unlikely that it was composed in March, when the pair was last together, touring the East Coast. November seems the safer bet.

As to why the song was not attempted at any of the *Bringing It . . .* sessions, Dylan's assertion (to camera) that he never finished it fits the evidence. Baez retorted that he finished the song 'eight different ways,' before magnanimously offering to record it if he'd finish it properly. He did not take up her offer, but she recorded it anyway, albeit not until 1968. When she did disinter it, she sang a final verse that, though clearly Dylan's, may not have been the one he had in mind. It is omitted from *Writings and Drawings*, perhaps because he meant it when he said he'd never finished the song; and though the opening couplet remains a classic, this conclusion on the wall does rather peter out:

Strange it is to be beside you, many years the tables turned
You'd probably not believe me if I told you all I'd learned
And it is very, very weird indeed
To hear words like 'forever,' 'please,'
Those ships sail through my mind, I cannot cheat
It's like lookin' in the teacher's face complete
I can say nothing to you but repeat what I heard,
That love is just a four-letter word.

According to Joannie, Dylan had a different kind of ending originally in mind, one that he abandoned when she made fun of his tendency to make out at song's end: 'He'd just written it all out on paper, and he said, "Hey, can ya dig this?" I read it off, he hadn't finished the last verse yet. He said, "Bet ya can't guess what's gonna happen," and I said, "Sure I can, you're gonna go back to the girl's house and fuck her." And he said, "You bitch, how'd you figure that out?" And I said, "'Cause that's what you always do."'

I would be hard pressed to name even a handful of songs that end this way, but Baez's snotty remark probably ensured the song stopped short of completion. Further evidence that the song never quite transcended its unfinished state comes in one of the rarer songbooks of the period, published to accompany the release of *Don't Look Back*. This oddity contains a selection of items from the soundtrack, including 'Four-Letter Word,' which has a sheet of music with hand-written lyrics scrawled across it that one would have a hard time matching with the version in the film. They include a quite different third verse:

> I went on my way unnoticed in the winter driving rain,
> In and out of lifetimes unmentioned of my name,
> Searching for my double. Looking for
> Complete admiration to the core,
> Tho' I tried and failed in finding anymore,
> I prob'ly . . . I prob'ly thought 'There's nothing more
> Absurd than that love is just a four-letter word.'

The song remains one of Dylan's more worthy 'lost' (i.e., unrecorded) compositions. Sadly there is no solid evidence he *ever* recorded it in any form. (Though according to one Internet source, I apparently have a demo of it. Mmm, wonder which box I keep that in?)

1965

{ Bringing It All Back Home;
Highway 61 Revisited }

The year Dylan rewrote the book – and I don't mean Tarantula
(which he never tampered with after finishing it in early spring).
Superlatives fail and comparisons disappear in a blizzard of inspi-
ration. The Dylan of 1965 was making the most direct, powerful,
and artistically important song-statements of the twentieth
century. At the absolute epicentre of popular culture for an eighteen-
month period when he, and he alone, was in the unknown region,
he returned with regular bulletins of prophetic perspicacity. The
thirty songs recorded in those twelve months, even in stark isola-
tion, would make him the single most important singer-songwriter
of the postwar era. Going from 'Love Minus Zero' to 'Visions of
Johanna' in eleven months, Dylan was travelling at the artistic
equivalent of the speed of light.

Between these twin beacons he would find time to create the first
true 'rock' single, 'Like a Rolling Stone.' And on its live debut, he
irrevocably rendered those divisions that still dominated popular
song redundant. The Newport Folk Festival slammed the door on

the past just in time. Dylan recorded his template for a modern music of the mind the following week and called it Highway 61 Revisited. *What he had not realized was how far he still had to go before journey's end.*

{136} SUBTERRANEAN HOMESICK BLUES

Published lyrics: Writings and Drawings; Lyrics *1985;* Lyrics *2004 [typewritten draft:* Writings and Drawings; Lyrics *1985]*
First known performance: Concord Pavilion, June 7, 1988.
Known studio recordings: Studio A, NY, January 13, 1965 – 1 take [TBS]; January 14, 1965, afternoon – 3 takes [BIABH – tk.3]; January 14, 1965, evening.

Between the end of November 1964 and the second week in January 1965, Dylan wrote the bulk of his fifth album, *Bringing It All Back Home.* Save for 'Gates of Eden,' 'It's Alright, Ma,' and, lest we forget, the almost ancient 'Mr. Tambourine Man,' there is no evidence he had much else ready when setting out for the West Coast that month to undertake another successful set of shows. And yet by the first session of the year, six weeks later, he had nine spanking-new songs to record (as well as 'If You Gotta Go, Go Now' and 'I'll Keep It with Mine,' two songs of an earlier vintage).

Of the eleven songs cut that first January day, 'Subterranean Homesick Blues' is the only one seen in draft form, appearing complete with coffee-mug stains in *Writings and Drawings* and the 1985 edition of *Lyrics* – though it has been mysteriously removed from the latest *Lyrics*, replaced by a single typed verse of 'To Ramona.' (Good one, Geoff!) It is a fascinating document for any number of reasons, the primary one being that it is entirely typed (save for one line: 'to walk on your tip toes').

Line breaks are indicated by a slash [/]. Evidently any line between his new songs and the rhetorical letters that punctuate the book of prose-poems he had almost completed was becoming rather blurred. Dylan admitted as much at the time: 'The words [to "SHB"] are rather squeezed together. You could call it an unconscious poem set to music.' In its draft state, he was not even sure what part of it might serve as the chorus and/or refrain (it would appear there were two main candidates: 'careful if they tail you / they only wanna nail you,' and, 'don't be bashful / check where the wind blows / rain flows').

Missing entirely is its memorable opening: 'johnny's in the basement / mixing up the medicine / I'm on the pavement / thinking 'bout the government.' Instead, 'daddy's in the dimestore / getting ten cent medicine.' But it is there for take one, day one, bringing it all back at Studio A. This is the version on *The Bootleg Series* – which hardly sounds like a 'demo,' as has been suggested, even if Witmark initially used this acoustic version for transcription purposes (cf. the original *Bringing It . . .* songbook). Even acoustic, one hardly notices how Dylan has found a way to rhyme *medicine* (or *medicent*) with *basement*, *pavement*, and *government*.

'Subterranean Homesick Blues' may have started as an acoustic rap-poem only to be made electric. According to Dylan, at the time, 'It [just] didn't sound right on guitar. I [also] tried it on piano, harpsichord, harmonica, pipe organ, kazoo. But it fit right in with the band.' Well, I can't speak for those other instruments, but the acoustic-guitar version recorded on January 13 sounds just fine. However, he had simply grown tired of the lack of dynamics in his music. As he said, looking back in 1977, 'I couldn't go on being the lone folkie out there, strumming "Blowin' in the Wind" for three hours every night. I hear my songs as part of the music, the musical background.' No question, 'Subterranean Homesick Blues' acquired a kick like a mule when Dylan returned to it the following afternoon, band in tow.

Dylan had also abandoned, seemingly for good, the

process that had served him well on *Freewheelin'* and *Times . . .*, recording new songs in fits and starts and pruning an album's worth from the resulting harvest. As of now he began recording an album in a block of sessions, relying on being fleet of foot and inspiration, trusting producer Tom Wilson to find the right alchemical mix of musos to come to his aid.

And yet initially, at these hastily assembled sessions, Dylan was not sure of the right setting for a number of songs he planned to record – electric or acoustic. As such, some songs he recorded acoustic *and* electric, some resolutely acoustic. Just one was conceived only in an electric guise ('Maggie's Farm'). Some combination of the two appears to have always been his intention, so one must assume that the all-acoustic session on the thirteenth was his way of hedging his bets.

'Subterranean Homesick Blues' was *electric* all the way down to its obvious R & B roots. No traditional ballad provided this song with its underlying infrastructure. Acoustic or electric, it had been taken at quite a different clip from any folk ballad – or, indeed, the southern boogie Chuck Berry utilized when devising the template on April 16, 1956. And Dylan would be the last to deny Berry's overt influence. As he told Hilburn recently, this first foray into folk-rock was 'from Chuck Berry, a bit of "Too Much Monkey Business," and some of the scat songs of the forties.'

A close examination of the original Berry lyrics suggests 'Subterranean Homesick Blues' took a scintilla more than 'a bit' of Berry's teen anthem. Dylan even changed one typed line, 'Says he's got a bad bill,' to, 'Says he's got a bad cough,' in order to blur one particular debt found in verse one of the Berry original: 'Runnin to and fro, hard workin' at the mill / Never fail in the mail, yeah, come a rotten bill!' Likewise, it is hardly a leap from, 'Same thing every day, gettin up, goin to school / No need for me to complain, my objections over-ruled,' to, 'Twenty years of schoolin / And they put you on the day shift' – great slogan that it assuredly is.

Nor was 'Subterranean Homesick Blues' the first time (that year) Dylan dipped into the work of rock & roll's original poet for a musical starting point. Check out the opening riff to Berry's 1960 recording of Big Maceo Merriweather's 'Worried Life Blues' and think, 'I Don't Believe You.' It used to go like that, and now it goes like *this*! Berry might even have approved. After all, he had not been averse to a little borrowing of source material himself. His breakthrough 45, 'Maybellene,' had been a thinly veiled reworking of Bob Wills's 1938 recording of 'Ida Red.'

'Subterranean Homesick Blues' served an important purpose. As side one, track one, it was another of those statements of intent. The 'ex rock & roll forbidden fruit picker' was back! He even fucks with the folkies a little by starting up with a little acoustic guitar strum before somebody tips a table's worth of cROCKery on top of him. As windups go, it's a good 'un. When he was accused of just having a laugh (as he is by at least one brave Liverpool gal in *Don't Look Back*), he made it crystal clear that he saw this as the way ahead, telling *Melody Maker*'s Ray Coleman, '[It's] NOT a put-on, like somebody said. Nobody is going to push me into writing rock & roll songs.' But he *would* be pushed into making a promotional video for the song, not only going along with the wheeze, but adding some ancillary advice in sign language – like 'Dig Yourself!' and 'Watch It.'

Despite being a tad premature in inventing the 'promo' pop video (and rap music into the bargain), 'Subterranean Homesick Blues' gave Dylan his first Top Forty U.S. hit. But he hardly felt like replicating its amphetamine rush in concert, and the song was left on record only. Imagine the surprise, then, in 1988, when his forty-seven-year-old vocal cords opened *every* show with a rousing rockabilly arrangement of the song. As for Berry's original template, it has continued to serve many a 'forbidden fruit picker,' notably Elvis Costello ('Pump It Up') and R.E.M. ('It's the End of the World').

{137} CALIFORNIA
{138} OUTLAW BLUES

Published lyrics: Writings and Drawings; Lyrics *1985;* Lyrics *2004.*
#137 – *Known studio recordings: Studio A, NY, January 13, 1965 – 1 take.*
#138 – *Known studio recordings: Studio A, NY, January 13, 1965 – 2 takes; January 14, 1965, afternoon – 3 takes [BIABH – tk.3].*

Leaving aside the throwaway nature of a song like 'Outlaw Blues' on an album of bona fide pearls, its relationship with another light-hearted piece of 'improv' recorded for *Bringing It All Back Home* provides a valuable insight into the way Dylan built up 'a rhythm of unpoetic distortion' – as he put it in the album sleeve notes – from building blocks of words and sounds. Ever since the inclusion of the oft-bootlegged 'California' in 1973's *Writings and Drawings*, where it is identified as 'an early version of "Outlaw Blues,"' the assumption has always been that 'California' was simply superseded by a superior version.

Not so. The emergence in 2005 of the January 13 acoustic demo of 'Outlaw Blues' – as a downloadable single on the official Dylan Web site – ended years of confusion about the identity of certain 'mis-labelled' songs on this particular session tape; while laying to rest, once and for all, the notion that these two songs were ever interchangeable. On this solo prototype of 'Outlaw Blues,' recorded the same evening as 'California,' but listed on the session sheet as 'Barb Wire,' Dylan sings a previously undocumented fourth verse:

> Well, I paid fifteen cents,
> I did not care if I was right or wrong, [x2]
> Then I saddled up a nightmare
> And I rode her all night long.

Meanwhile, as the final take on another marathon evening in Studio A, Dylan cut another humorous little blues at the piano, listed simply as 'Tune X,' the fourth and final verse of which he sang as:

> Well, I got my dark sunglasses,
> I got for good luck my black tooth. [x2]
> Don't ask me nothin' about nothin',
> I just might tell you the truth.

The song in question proves to be 'California' (as the timings on the studio log confirm). The following afternoon, when Dylan (with Wilson's help) brought a band to lend a hand, he re-recorded 'Outlaw Blues' with a lethal dose of electricity. By then he had decided to dump 'California,' save for its final verse, which he transposed to 'Outlaw Blues.' It was a wise decision. With this switcheroo, he swiftly got the take he wanted. He also unwittingly bequeathed the world forty years of arguments over the exact status of 'California.'

{139} LOVE MINUS ZERO / NO LIMIT

Published lyrics: Writings and Drawings; Lyrics 1985; Lyrics 2004.
Known studio recordings: Studio A, NY, January 13, 1965 – 3 takes; January 14, 1965, afternoon – 3 takes [BIABH – tk.3]; January 14, 1965, evening.
First known performance: Santa Monica Civic Auditorium, March 27, 1965.

By January 1965 Dylan was no longer content to let the song's refrain equate to its title. Rather, as he claimed to

Ray Coleman the following May, 'The lead for the listener will lie in the title of the song.' Presumably, listing 'Farewell Angelina' as 'Alcatraz to the Ninth Power' told us it was one of his mathematical songs. And not the only one. The session sheet for January 13, 1965, suggests money and mathematics had begun to preoccupy the wealthy young man, with songs logged as 'Dime Store,' 'Bank Account Blues,' and 'Worse Than Money' (or 'Love Minus Zero,' 'I'll Keep It with Mine,' and 'She Belongs to Me' – as they are generally known).

Of these, 'Dime Store' is the most prosaic, since there is a dime store (and a bus station) in the song in question. In fact, 'Love Minus Zero' became the only song released with a more cryptic title than the one on the log sheet. The original label to the album remains the only place where that song title appears correctly:

$$\text{LOVE} \quad \frac{\text{MINUS ZERO}}{\text{NO LIMIT}}$$

When Dylan began to talk about writing 'mathematical songs' at a number of year-end press conferences, he wasn't joking – even if it was useful as an act of obfuscation. He could have called this song 'Sara,' but he wanted to save that one. Sara Lowndes was the woman he now depicted in song as 'true, like ice, like fire,' as he confirmed to Robert Shelton the following March, saying he knew 'just two holy people. Allen Ginsberg is one. The other . . . I just want to call "this person named Sara." What I mean by "holy" is crossing all the boundaries of time and usefulness.'

If the young songwriter still displayed a tendency to see all women as Earth Mothers, Madonnas, or whores (or to use more Gravesian terminology – lover, mother, or hag), the woman in this song combines the first two. Ten years later Sara would complain that, after all this talk about Goddesses and Madonnas, she should end up playing a whore in her husband's celluloid vision, *Renaldo and Clara*. By then she had perhaps stopped 'crossing all the boundaries of time and usefulness.'

On the evidence of this song, her Zen-like detachment – commented on by everyone who knew her – was catching. For here Dylan begins to speak in irreconcilable opposites: she 'speaks like silence,' all the while managing to be 'like ice' *and* 'like fire.' Most memorably of all, 'She knows there's no success like failure / And that failure's no success at all.' John Keats, a poet Dylan grew to greatly admire, had a term for such mental balancing acts – 'negative capability' – a notion he defined as 'when man is capable of being in uncertainties, Mysteries, doubts without any irritable reaching after fact & reason.'

Dylan actually offered to explain the above couplet to a (doubtless attractive) lady journalist later in 1965, in terms she might understand: 'When you've tried to write this story about me, if you're any good you'll feel you've failed. But when you've tried and failed, and tried and failed – then you'll have something.' Which is as close as he came to explicating what would drive him towards that palace of wisdom over the next eighteen months. From the other side of the divide (1977 to be precise), he would define failure differently: 'You fail only when you let death creep in and take over a part of your life that should be alive.'

'Love Minus Zero' seems to be one of those songs he is still proud he wrote. Ultra-keen to perform it live, he has made it an acoustic evergreen from this point forwards, save for its one incarnation with the not-so-magic flute on the 1978 World Tour. When he entered Studio A in January 1965, though, he still wasn't sure how he wanted it to sound. Hence the two acoustic versions recorded on the thirteenth, when it was one of two songs remade at the end of the session.

Both remakes – 'Love Minus Zero' and 'She Belongs to Me' – appear to have been serious contenders for the album; until, that is, he got an understated, on-the-money band version the following afternoon.

{140} SHE BELONGS TO ME

Published lyrics: Writings and Drawings; Lyrics 1985; Lyrics 2004.
Known studio recordings: Studio A, NY, January 13, 1965 – 2 takes [NDH – tk.2]; January 14, 1965, afternoon – 2 takes [BIABH – tk.2]; January 14, 1965, evening.
First known performance: Santa Monica Civic Auditorium, March 27, 1965.

> The songs I was writing last year, songs like 'Ballad in Plain D,' they were what I call one-dimensional songs, but my new songs I'm trying to make more three-dimensional, you know. There's more symbolism. They're written on more than one level. – Bob Dylan, April 1965.

One cannot discount the possibility that 'She Belongs to Me' and 'Love Minus Zero' derived their inspiration from two entirely different dames (after all, while falling ever more under Sara's spell, the man still invited Baez to come up and see him sometime). But it would be entirely in keeping with this new-found duality if each song was an equal and opposite depiction of the same 'gypsy gal' (as per 'Abandoned Love' and 'Sara,' both recorded at the same 1975 session – with the lady in question in attendance).

Each certainly received due diligence and a real attention to detail at the January sessions. After acoustic remakes on the thirteenth, they acquired instrumental embellishment the following day, as Dylan attempted to record them with a full band. He then got rid of most embellishments when, in the evening, he laid the songs down with just guitars and bass. On the released album – where the songs are separated from each other by a single female farmer – the performances reflect each other lyrically, vocally, and instrumentally.

The words, though, tell entirely different tales. On 'Love Minus Zero,' his 'love' comes to him at song's end 'like some raven / at my window with a broken wing,' whereas the artistic alter ego who belongs to him (actually vice versa) continues to demand that he should 'bow down to her on Sunday' and 'salute her when her birthday comes.' This altogether more capricious lady would introduce proceedings on every night of the 1966 world tour, the singer's devotion expressed in a series of soaring harmonica breaks. After this, though, it became an altogether rarer incursion into other nightly rituals. Finally, in 1992, it became a soft-shoe shuffle. In the meantime 'She' spawned many a daughter, as Dylan's attraction to 'witchy women' continued unchecked.

{141} IT'S ALL OVER NOW, BABY BLUE

Published lyrics: Writings and Drawings; Lyrics 1985; Lyrics 2004.
Known studio recordings: Studio A, NY, January 13, 1965 – 1 take [NDH]; January 14, 1965, evening; January 15, 1965 – 1 take [BIABH].
First known performance: Les Crane Show, NY, February 17, 1965.

After *Another Side* fell flat, Dylan abandoned recording entire albums in a single session. But he was still confident enough to cut the entire second side of *BIABH* in a single afternoon – January 15, 1965. And as he told a Nashville journalist in 1978, 'I used to do [a] song live before you ever made a record, so it would evolve.' Which was assuredly the case with 'It's Alright, Ma,' 'Gates of Eden,' and 'Mr. Tambourine Man,' all recorded the same January afternoon. But 'It's All Over Now, Baby Blue' was an exception that became the rule. An equally exemplary song, it was one he'd 'taken into the studio before I was too familiar with [it].'

Still unsure how to give 'It's All Over Now, Baby Blue'

the best possible opportunity to 'evolve into something else,' Dylan recorded it acoustically (on the thirteenth), in a semi-electric guise (on the evening of the fourteenth), and finally, in a single superlative take the afternoon of the fifteenth, completing his most wordy album to date. Whatever possible deficiencies 'It's All Over Now, Baby Blue' suffered as a result of Dylan delaying its live debut until the LP was completed, it has proven one of those rare midsixties works that could flit lightly from acoustic to electric and back again.

At the same time, it established a new way to say farewell to someone who was once a close friend but now on another wavelength. This would become something of a forte in the coming eighteen months. Its admonitory tone would even start to become a little wearing by the time of 'Can You Please Crawl Out Your Window?' and 'One of Us Must Know.' But, for now, he still wanted to let the subject down gently but firmly, personally springing for a box of metaphorical matches.

Inevitably, because of its intensely personal tone, the song has been seen in an autobiographical light, and a number of names have been put forward as Angelina's kid brother. 'Blue' has even been taken as a pun on David Blue's (né Cohen) adopted name. However, the most persistent candidate for these words of wisdom has been Paul Clayton. Clayton has generally been portrayed as just another faded folkie who stood too close to the man's flame – a gross over-simplification. And Dylan failed to fully set the story straight even when he came to write *Chronicles*, though he treated Clayton generously, both in terms of space assigned and in evident affection for the man.

The old friends had parted company at the crossroads of Dylan's electric apostasy, not because Clayton disliked Dylan's new direction, but because Clayton's amphetamine abuse had made him impossible to be around, a warning

Dylan chose not to heed himself. Hence, perhaps, why Dylan still finds it a song to which he can relate. As for Clayton, he did not stick around long enough to recognize the quality of the advice Dylan was dispensing. Indeed, barely had Dylan begun the first leg of his 1966 world tour when the news came through that he had killed himself. Already part of the nightly ritual, 'Baby Blue' was now pushed to ever greater levels of intensity, as Dylan skirted his own, individual precipice.

{142} BOB DYLAN'S 115TH DREAM

Published lyrics: Writings and Drawings; Lyrics 1985; Lyrics 2004.
Known studio recordings: Studio A, NY, January 13, 1965 – 2 takes; January 14, 1965, afternoon – 2 takes [BIABH – tks.1+2]; January 14, 1965, evening.
First known performance: Tower Theatre, Philadelphia, October 13, 1988.

When Dylan told journalist Jules Siegel in April 1966, 'I see things that other people don't see. . . . They laugh,' he could have been talking about '115th Dream.' Of course in the case of '115th Dream,' he meant for them to laugh. He had, after all, produced in under six minutes a *1066 and All That* version of American history that takes a baseball bat to literature, history, and religion. As kaleidoscopic as 'Mr. Tambourine Man,' as off-beat as 'Talkin' World War III Blues,' as anarchic as 'I Shall Be Free,' the song begins with the narrator on a version of the *Mayflower* that doubles as Herman Melville's whaling ship, and ends with him getting the hell out of there just as Columbus sails into the bay. Between such totemic occurrences, he truncates the early history of his homeland into one withering sentence: 'Let's set up a fort / And start buying the place with beads.' As for those Puritans, he demolishes them in a single vignette:

Well, I rapped upon a house with the U.S. flag upon display
I said, 'Could you help me out, I got some friends down the
way.'
The man says, 'Get out of here, I'll tear you limb from limb.'
I said, 'You know they refused Jesus too,' He said, 'You're
not Him.'

Hard on the Cuban heels of 'Outlaw Blues' and 'On the
Road Again,' 'Bob Dylan's 115th Dream' leaves them laughing
before they flip the record over (as we used to do) to an altogether more existential side. He even leaves a little joke at his
own expense etched in vinyl. Providing an insight into the
entirely new experience of working with a band, he keeps the
falsest of false starts, the first take on the afternoon of the fourteenth, which collapses when nobody joins in on cue.

Dylan and his band were quick learners, though, as '115th
Dream' duly demonstrates. They nail the song on the very
next take, even at the fair ol' clip they take it (it still takes
them a half-minute more than it took Dylan on his own,
the previous evening). When Dylan resurrected the song,
at his eldest son's behest, just before a week-long New York
residency in October 1988, such sureness is long gone. At
Radio City the song became something of a drag, perhaps reinforcing the truism that those who do not learn from
history are destined to repeat its mistakes.

{143} ON THE ROAD AGAIN

Published lyrics: Writings and Drawings; Lyrics *1985;* Lyrics *2004.*
Known studio recordings: Studio A, NY, January 13, 1965;
January 14, 1965, afternoon – 4 takes; January 15, 1965 – 13 takes
[BIABH – tk.13].

Sandwiched between the lightweight 'Outlaw Blues'
and the panoramic insanity of '115th Dream,' 'On the Road
Again' has not really received its fair due. It is something of a

minor masterpiece. And Dylan himself clearly felt there was something worth preserving in this account of a home life that reads like some long lost episode of *The Addams Family* written by Luis Buñuel. Having run the song down acoustically on the thirteenth, when it came to its electric cousins on the fourteenth and fifteenth, something kept tripping the man up. Of the thirteen takes at the final *Bringing It . . .* session, just three were complete (including the first, as it happens). But he remained determined to make it work, and when he did, it sprang the springs of his kaleidoscopic mind. He never chanced his arm again, though, and the song remains just one of two songs from this truly groundbreaking album never performed in concert.

{144} YOU DON'T HAVE TO DO THAT

Known studio recordings: Studio A, NY, January 13, 1965 – 1 take.

Dylan must have been working on the songs for *Bringing It . . .* until the very last minute, for here is one song idea he never quite finished up. (And there may have been others, now lost. Photographer Daniel Kramer says Dylan 'brought eighteen new songs with him,' yet he apparently only recorded sixteen.) Recorded as the eleventh song on the thirteenth, 'You Don't Have to Do That' – or as it is logged, 'Bending Down on My Stomach Looking West' – is clearly a work in progress (at best), and/or proof positive that sometimes there really is no success like failure. Dylan's commitment to the idea seems fairly marginal. He calls out to Wilson at the song's start, 'I'm not gonna do it!' before vamping a verse about someone who runs around 'piking / like a chicken with his head off.'

After less than a minute, he's had enough and announces he's 'going to play on the piano.' Which is rather odd, because the only song Dylan definitely performed at the piano on this day was 'I'll Keep It with Mine,' which he'd already recorded (as 'Bank Account Blues'). To add to the mystery, CO85280 (a.k.a. 'Bending Down . . .') times out on the session sheet at two minutes and forty-two seconds, about two minutes longer than the fragment in circulation. So either he recut the song at the piano, or there is another 'lost' song yet to be discovered on the session tape, one that also conjured up that unique perspective accorded by anyone on his stomach, looking west.

{145} MAGGIE'S FARM

Published lyrics: Writings and Drawings; Lyrics 1985; Lyrics 2004.
Known studio recordings: Studio A, NY, January 15, 1965 – 1 take [BIABH].
First known performance: Newport Folk Festival, July 25, 1965 [NDH] [OSOTM].

A central song in Dylan iconography, 'Maggie's Farm' may well have been hastily penned the night before the final *Bringing It . . .* session. It was overlooked on the thirteenth, when the remainder of the album – acoustic epics excepted – got a test run. If so, it was heaven sent. He cut the song in a single take, knowing any further foray would be futile. According to Daniel Kramer, 'When the playback of "Maggie's Farm" was heard over the studio speakers, we were all elated. There was no question about it – it swung, it was good music, and, most of all, it was Dylan.'

An *electric* reworking of the traditional 'Down on Penny's Farm,' 'Maggie's Farm' (re)inverted the country/city dynamic of 'Hard Times in New York Town,' making the lady's farm a place where exploitation is rife, rebellion is imminent, and escape to the city a dream. The one song not cut acoustically at these sessions, it was nonetheless tried in an acoustic setting a few months later, at a June 1 rehearsal for his solo BBC-TV special. Unconvinced it worked that way, Dylan held off playing the song live until fronting the Elston Gunn Blues Band at Newport, where it was largely lost in the feedback off and on the stage (though not on the recent DVD, where it *soars*).

Generally, though, this twelve-bar blues has struggled to recapture the spark ignited at Newport, it being dropped from the set shortly after the Hawks, a.k.a. The Band, came on board in September 1965. It didn't even pass muster when Dylan worked up an arrangement for the British leg of the 1981 European tour, surely as a nod to then–Prime Minister Maggie Thatcher. But with Mr. D one can generally find an exception to any rule. So when, in September 1985, it was tagged onto the end of an exhilarating set at the first Farm Aid, a massive TV audience was reminded why he wrote the song in the first place, and, indeed, what words like, 'They say, sing while you slave,' were meant to mean. It proved a temporary reinvigoration. When the song reappeared in 1987, he again sang, 'I just get bored!' like he meant it.

{146} PHANTOM ENGINEER

Known studio recordings: Studio A, NY, June 15, 1965 – 10 takes [TBS – tk.10] [NDH – tk.9?].

First known performance: Newport Folk Festival, July 25, 1965.

[= IT TAKES A LOT TO LAUGH, IT TAKES A TRAIN TO CRY]

Published lyrics: Writings and Drawings; Lyrics 1985; Lyrics 2004.

Known studio recordings: Studio A, NY, July 29, 1965 – 7 takes [H61 – tk.7]

First known performance/s: Madison Square Garden, NY, August 1, 1971 [CFB].

The pace of Dylan's helter-skelter existence and scale of personal fame may have accelerated at an exponential rate through the winter and spring of 1965, but he seems to have reached something of an impasse when it came to further songwriting. He admitted as much to *Melody Maker*'s Ray Coleman at the end of his first English tour in May: 'I have these things ready . . . nothing's finished. . . . I know I'll write a lot of stuff, but exactly what shape it'll take has yet to be decided.' He was fully entitled to take a breather. After all, he'd completed *Bringing It All Back Home* just four months earlier. And he was clearly not worried about any temporary drought. He had experienced a similar three-month respite after *The Times They Are A-Changin'*, following it with two breakthrough songs in rapid succession.

Ideas still crowded his head. A wealth of new footage from the English tour, released on the deluxe DVD edition of *Don't Look Back*, suggests he still couldn't walk past a piano without vamping a tune (two hours of outtakes also appeared on a Japanese bootleg DVD beforehand, which director Pennebaker decided to leave in the bootleg domain). It would appear that Dylan was increasingly inclined to work out melodies on the ol' stand-up. When Tom Wilson came to call at his Savoy suite at tour's end, Dylan sat at the stand-up and played him (and D. A.'s camera) a new song he was hoping to record – 'Phantom Engineer.' Wilson, delighted at the thought of a Dylan R & B single, soon set up a session in London.

The tape log for the May 12, 1965, session at Levy's Recording Studio, backed by John Mayall's Bluesbreakers, is now lost, so we cannot know for sure whether Dylan attempted to record this new song at this west-end studio (we do know the Bluesbreakers were paid £28 for the session). But 'Phantom Engineer' *was* just the kind of electric blues the Bluesbreakers could play in their sleep; and the one contemporary report of the session, in *Record Mirror*, states that they recorded *two* songs – along with some (unspecified) blues material – until 'one of the huge tape reels . . . was almost filled.'

The guitarist on that session was a young Eric Clapton, whose own memory is that 'it was just a jam session. . . . We played for about two hours. There was a lot of stuff down on tape. . . . We did a lot of blues songs which . . . [suggested] he was making it up. He was sitting at the piano and we just joined in.' This sure sounds more like 'Phantom Engineer' than 'If You Gotta Go, Go Now' – especially if one applies some significance to the fact that Dylan and Clapton decided to do a joint version of 'It Takes a Lot to Laugh,' as the song became, at the October 1992 'Bobfest' concert. (Though the song was cut at the last minute, video exists of them running the song down a number of times at the dress rehearsal the previous day.) I suspect they'd been down this road before.

As for Clapton's suggestion that 'he was making it up,' parts of 'Phantom Engineer' sound like Dylan is doing exactly that. Having already transposed a pair of lines – 'Don't the clouds look lonesome across the deep blue sea / Don't my gal look good, when she's coming after me' – from 'Alabama Woman Blues' to 'Rocks and Gravel' back in 1962, it was but a short journey from there to here. However, there is no doubt that the final verse is all Dylan, including a second couplet that wouldn't have been out of place on 'From a Buick Six':

I've just been to the baggage car, where the engineer's been tossed.
I've stomped out forty compasses, God knows what they cost.
Well, I wanna be your lover baby, I don't wanna be your boss.
I just can't help it if this train gets lost.

The May 12 session may have been a bit of a bust, but it taught Dylan something – he need not hijack entire blues bands, just elements thereof. When he and producer Tom Wilson met again at their usual stomping ground, Columbia's New York Studio A, a month later, Dylan brought along guitarist Mike Bloomfield from the Paul Butterfield Blues

Band, a white Chicago bluesman who had done his apprenticeship when knee-high to the great Joe Williams.

As at the May 12 session, Dylan elected to play piano, leaving Bloomfield to let rip with the electric guitar. He attached just one caveat, instructing the young bluesman, 'I don't want you to play any of that B. B. King shit.' Bloomfield had already been shown the ropes, having spent a weekend in Woodstock letting Dylan demonstrate his new songs to him. Bloomfield found the whole experience 'very weird, he was playing in weird keys which he always does – all on the black keys of the piano.'

And though June 15, 1965, may have gone down in history as the day Dylan recorded the fabled 'Like a Rolling Stone,' that song proved a mere afterthought that spilled over to the following day. It was 'Phantom Engineer' that occupied most of the first afternoon, requiring ten takes – six complete – as Dylan worked at getting a new sound outta his head and onto tape. No longer 'making it up' on the spot, he was still not happy with the opening to the second verse, which at this point read, 'Don't the moon look good, shinin' down through the trees / Don't the ghost child look good, sitting on the madman's knee.'

Seemingly happy with the final take, he continued to tinker with the song as June turned to July. A typed version of the song from this period, which somehow ended up among the Margolis and Moss papers, along with 'I'll Keep It with Mine,' showed he had yet to give up on either song. 'Phantom Engineer' is how it is identified at the top of the page. On this typescript, that 'ghost child' couplet has been changed to fit the rest of the song's train motif – 'Don't the break [sic] man look good / Being where he wants to be' – which is how he sings it on its live debut, at what the organizers still thought of as America's premier annual *folk* festival.

The Newport version in every other way remained the dose of R & B medicine recorded back in June (listen closely between songs and you can hear someone onstage call out 'Phantom Engineer'). It would take until a lunch break at the third *Highway 61 Revisited* session, four days later, for the song to slow down to an uphill crawl, for the brakeman to 'look good / Flagging down the double E,' and for the windows to be 'filled with frost.' Before that break Dylan recorded three more takes of 'Phantom Engineer' (while also running through another song debuted at Newport, 'Tombstone Blues').

According to eye-witness Tony Glover, who stayed on in New York after Newport: 'As most of the musicians and [studio] crew split [for lunch], Bob sat down at the piano and worked over "Phantom Engineer" for an hour or more. When the crew was back in place, Bob ran down how he wanted it done differently – and in three takes they got the lovely version on the album . . . with some tasty guitar and piano builds in it.' It also got a new name, 'It Takes a Lot to Laugh, It Takes a Train to Cry,' though the studio engineer continued to log the song by its original title.

'Phantom Engineer' continued waiting in the wings, and when the song was restored to the live set as a roustabout replacement for an electric 'A Hard Rain's A-Gonna Fall' on the latter stages of the 1975 Rolling Thunder Revue, it reverted to the kind of up-tempo midnight stomp that rattled sabers at Newport. Since then Dylan has occasionally allowed blues guitarists to cut their teeth on the song, giving Mick Taylor the opportunity to have a wail at Nantes in 1984, allowing G. E. Smith the same privilege in Spain in 1989, and even letting 'E. C.' show the world what he might have done back in 1965 at the 1992 'Bobfest' rehearsals. Said train, though, has recently got lost.

{147} SITTING ON A BARBED-WIRE FENCE

Published lyrics: Writings and Drawings; Lyrics *1985;* Lyrics *2004.*

Known studio recordings: Studio A, NY, June 15, 1965 – 6 takes
[TBS – tk.6].

The song title 'Barb Wire' appears to have been used for
'Outlaw Blues' at the first *Bringing It* . . . session – probably
because it (originally) featured a line, 'Well I paid fifteen
dollars . . .' which is similar to the first line of this song, 'I
paid fifteen million dollars . . .' Evidently, that shorthand
title was written at a later date, probably in 1970, when these
tapes were reviewed by the record label. There are no (other)
allusions to 'Sitting on a Barbed-Wire Fence' – or, as it is
listed on the studio sheet, 'Over the Cliffs Part One' – before
its appearance at the June 15 New York session.

Personally, I have always preferred the title under which
it was bootlegged, 'Killing Me Alive.' But whatever its actual
title, this song is very much in the vein of 'Outlaw Blues'
and 'On the Road Again' – a series of scrambled lines, interchangeable at will (the Arabian doctor is destined to reemerge
as the best friend in 'Just Like Tom Thumb's Blues'). It also
shares the driving barroom piano of the studio version of
'Phantom Engineer.' And as with that song, the so-called
Goldmine acetate, from the June 15 session – which sounds
like a monitor mix, with Dylan's piano being mixed *way* to
the fore – allows one to hear just how our aspiring bar pianist
is coming along. In all likelihood, the song was penned at
the same Woodstock piano where Dylan had played his new
songs to Bloomfield the weekend before.

What convinces me to put it 'ahead' of 'Like a Rolling
Stone' – also apparently composed at *that* piano – is the
way it fits Dylan's description (to Coleman) of something
whose 'shape . . . has yet to be decided.' The words, like the
tune itself, are 'just a riff.' Dylan is grappling with a new
methodology that is still only coming through in dribs and

drabs. Even the defining line, 'The girl I'm loving, I swear she's killing me alive,' can't help but recall the earlier 'Hero Blues.' If anything, the direction in which he's heading ends up being put on hold by the synaptic swerve towards Miss Lonely, only truly blooming on the Big Pink basement tape, after the midsixties madness had abated. Consider this verse, from one of the earlier takes on June 15:

> I was walking down the street one day,
> And saw her sitting all alone on the shelf,
> Right away she gave all my shoes to her mother,
> But she kept all the bread for herself.

The earlier take lacks any barbed-wire fence. Rather, at song's end, he is trying to avoid falling over 'any screwdriver cliffs.' Actually, none of the lines have been nailed into place, and one senses Dylan was using the song largely to establish the credentials of the band, since he evidently intended to make this sixth album a belated collection of the kinda Bob Dylan blues that owed as much to Arthur Rimbaud as Robert Johnson.

Note: The version in *Writings and Drawings* has received a revamp, and not a particularly good one. She is no longer killing him alive, she's 'thrilling me with her drive'; and instead of being 'not even twenty-five,' he has a woman who calls him 'Stan' and 'Mister Clive.' 'Gotta Serve Somebody' awaits.

{148} LIKE A ROLLING STONE

Published lyrics: Writings and Drawings; Lyrics 1985; Lyrics 2004.
Known studio recordings: Studio A, NY, June 15, 1965 – 5 takes [TBS]; June 16, 1965 – 15 takes [H61 – tk.4].
First known performance: Newport Folk Festival, July 25, 1965 [OSOTM].

I wrote 'Rolling Stone' after England. I boiled it down, but it's all there. . . . I knew I had to sing it with a band. I always sing when I write, even prose, and I heard it like that. – Dylan to Ralph J. Gleason, December 1965

In March 1965, speed-rapping with Paul Jay Robbins, full-time hipster and part-time L.A. journo, Dylan openly admitted he still hadn't got where he wanted: 'I've written some songs which are kind of far out, a long continuation of verses, stuff like that – but I haven't really gotten into writing a completely free song.' It was a theme he was now warming to, telling others about these 'songs which are . . . a long continuation of verses,' without ever demonstrating what he had in mind. One suspects he didn't know himself. He probably had in mind a song that distilled elements of 'A Hard Rain's A-Gonna Fall,' 'Mr. Tambourine Man,' and 'It's Alright, Ma.'

Earlier Beat aspirations now became attached to the tutorial he'd already had in tradition. Making a musical Molotov cocktail of the two, he jettisoned page-bound poetry for good. He now knew one could be a songwriter and a poet utilizing the same medium. As he told Nat Hentoff privately, a matter of months after he cracked the code, he could still 'remember . . . writing those [other] things. The other stuff I was doing didn't even resemble those [earlier songs] at all. They resembled more what I'm writing today, in terms of songs.' The schema adopted for *Tarantula* by the summer of 1964 contained its fair share of song-like rhythms. Refusing to be hidebound by line breaks, Dylan wrote screeds of speed, all amphetamine alliteration, as he demonstrated in a short correspondence with the late Tami Dean:

> An god's own pillars've even turned t rust
> sugar tastes bitter. Salt is sweet
> ramming bali ligosi girls on the tails of mice

rats ring the bells
truth don't lie in the alley dead
bums don't die
cleopatra's sister opens her mouth at the manhole
tries t grab mayor wagner's son.

Just as John Lennon needed to write two books of offbeat poetry to get to 'Nowhere Man' and 'In My Life,' Dylan's year-long jag of speed-writing helped him adopt a more intuitive approach to the song form, integrating everything around the malleable framework of a tune and arrangement. As he told Nat Hentoff the second time around, '"Like a Rolling Stone" changed it all; I didn't care any more after that about writing books or poems or whatever. [Here] was something that I myself could dig. . . . My songs are pictures and the band makes the sound of the pictures.'

Dylan did not arrive at this defining song easily. Shortly after completing the *Highway 61* set of songs, he described the tortuous process: 'Every time I write a song [now], it's like writing a novel . . . [but] I can get it down, you know . . . down to where I can re-read it in my head.' 'Like a Rolling Stone' was his first song to condense the whole life story of a Miss Lonely down to just four verses. At this stage, if we are to believe things he said in the day, Dylan wrote the whole thing out longhand. And again, if we attach credence to contemporaneous utterances, it came after he decided he'd gone as far with song as he could: 'I'd literally quit singing and playing, and I found myself writing this . . . long piece of vomit about twenty pages long and out of it I took "Like a Rolling Stone." . . . And I'd never written anything like that before and it suddenly came to me that that was what I should do.'

This admission rings a lot truer than his 1991 claim to Elliott Mintz that the song in question 'is not any better or worse than any of the other songs I'[d] written in that period. It just happened to be one of the ones that was on the Hit Parade.' Actually, it was the *one* that opened the doors of perception. In the months immediately after its composition, he felt no shame communicating its importance a number of different ways: onstage, when he sang it with an intensity and gusto he never came close to again; in interviews, whenever he felt he had a sympathetic ear; and on the radio, where he aimed to reach those (at)tuned. For now, it was everything he thought a song could be. As he told writer Jules Siegel in one of the more memorable interviews of the era:

> It was [originally] ten pages long. It wasn't called anything, just a rhythm thing on paper all about my steady hatred directed at some point that was honest. In the end it wasn't hatred, it was telling someone something they didn't know, telling them they were lucky. . . . I never thought of it as a song, until one day I was at the piano, and on the paper it was singing, 'How does it feel?' in a slow motion pace. . . . It was like . . . in your eyesight you see your victim swimming in lava . . . in the pain they were bound to meet up with. I wrote it. I didn't fail. It was straight.

All this fevered activity provided Dylan with the very shape he told Ray Coleman, in mid-May, had 'yet to be decided.' The process itself probably occupied much of the five weeks that separate Dylan's aborted 'single' session on May 12 from the successful 'single' session/s. Having 'quit singing and playing,' his overactive mind puked up a 'long piece of vomit' between ten and twenty pages long, quite possibly a conscious effort to emulate Kerouac's fabled 'scroll version' of *On the Road*, and composed in a similar span of time. Having set about turning said technicolour yawn into a song, he taught it to Michael Bloomfield. Only then did he turn up at Columbia's Studio A ready to create a thing called rock music in a single afternoon.

In all likelihood, Dylan started on his original 'piece of vomit' while laid up in his $500-a-day hotel suite in London the last week in May, suffering from a bout of 'food poisoning' acquired on a trip to Europe with Sara. (Respected rock historian Peter Doggett points out that the pair attended the same Parisian party that resulted in rock & roller Vince Taylor acquiring a messianic delusion, and suspects that Dylan was also 'dosed' with some bad acid.)

With the typewriter on his lap, he again set about putting himself in 'Homesick Blues' mode. We know Dylan was still tapping out many a *Tarantula*-esque 'rhythm thing on paper.' In *Don't Look Back* he can be seen banging away at the typewriter in his Savoy suite before London shows, and we *know* what he was typing: a piece called 'Alternatives to College,' originally intended for *Esquire* magazine but not published until the 1985 edition of *Lyrics*. Anyone looking for evidence of 'a rhythm thing on paper, all about my steady hatred directed at some point that was honest,' I present Exhibit A: 'yonder at your funeral, you will see this pauper – dressed like your face, he will have a wedding present for you – it will be a mirror & in it, you will see the world as it sees you?'

We have Marianne Faithfull's 'autobiographical' word that such a speed-screed was no exception. Whenever she visited his suite, 'day after day . . . Dylan was constantly going over to the typewriter and pounding away. . . . In the middle of a conversation he would tear himself away and toss off a song, a poem, a new chapter of his book, a one-act play. It was a wonder to behold.' Unfortunately, when she clumsily spurned his advances, 'without warning, he turned into Rumpelstiltskin. He went over to the typewriter, took a sheaf of papers and began ripping them up into smaller and smaller pieces, which he let fall into the wastepaper basket.'

Which makes one wonder whether this girl on her 'chrome horse' could be the Miss Lonely who, in rejecting the great poet-singer, prompted him to imagine some kind of pain she was 'bound to meet up with.' (And did.) His description of someone who had 'gone to the finest school alright, Miss Lonely / But... only used to get juiced in it,' concisely describes Marianne's well-documented convent-school upbringing.

But this broken English gal is hardly the only candidate for Miss Lonely. Joan Baez may have been no princess, but she fancied herself the Queen of the Folk Revival, and when her name came up in conversation with Robert Shelton nine months later, Dylan still described her as someone heading for a fall: 'I feel bad for her, because she has nobody to turn to that's going to be straight with her. . . . She hasn't got that much in common with street vagabonds who play insane instruments.' Or mystery tramps, I suspect.

There is another candidate Dylan only belatedly recognized as the song's possible target – himself. As he candidly told his first biographer, it took the motorcycle accident for him to realize 'that when I used words like "he" and "it" and "they," and talking about other people, I was really talking about nobody but me.' And he had, after all, sung, 'I'm a rolling stone,' to Pennebaker's camera at an impromptu hotel room session earlier in the month – the opening line of Hank Williams's 'Lost Highway,' which Dylan made a part of a twenty-minute 'country' medley. Also, in conversation with an English journalist before the tour, he spoke of a time when he could be invisible again and have 'no secrets to conceal': 'In a couple of years I shall be right back where I started – an unknown.'

'Like a Rolling Stone' on one level operates as just another interior mirror, at least while it remained 'just a rhythm thing on paper.' The moment when Dylan 'thought of it as a song' came not in London but in 'a little cabin in

Woodstock, which we rented from Peter Yarrow's mother,' where he found himself 'at the piano, and on the paper it was singing, "How does it feel?"' When the paper actually started singing perhaps the most famous line in rock, it was to a rather familiar tune. As he later said, 'It started with that "La Bamba" riff.'

'La Bamba' was a frat-rock classic made famous by Ritchie Valens, whom Dylan had seen at the Duluth Armory three days before he became a footnote to the great Buddy Holly's death in a plane crash. He even instructed his 1978 band during tour rehearsals to do his most famous song 'like "La Bamba."' But the words he set in stone were a million miles away from the innocent world of frat rock: 'How does it feel? / To be on your own? / A complete unknown? / Like a rolling stone??!?'

It was as another piano song that Dylan initially planned to record it. But this was no Golden Chords high school debut. He would be fronting the kind of band of 'street vagabonds' who could make 'the sound of the pictures' in his head. He hoped that the choice of musicians alone would ensure that the song acquired some necessary textural architecture. Yet its final shape would be as much of a mystery to Dylan as its intended audience. As he opined four decades later, 'I'm not thinking about what I want to say [at this point], I'm just thinking, "Is this okay for the meter?" . . . It's like a ghost is writing a song like that. It gives you the song and it goes away. You don't *know* [my italics] what it means.'

Yet it was only after an afternoon spent auditioning the studio band on the likes of 'Phantom Engineer' and 'Killing Me Alive' that Dylan introduced the assembled throng of soundmen and sound men to the song. It is something of a mystery why he'd been holding back, but when Wilson finally did begin rolling tape, it is Bloomfield whom one hears directing the musicians, not Dylan. It is as if its *auteur* cannot bear to reduce this particular song down to mere chords, bars, and keys.

Thirty years later, Dylan told Kurt Loder, 'I don't think a song like "Rolling Stone" could have been done any other way. What are you gonna do, chart it out?' Yet his reliance on serendipity – again – almost proved as much a disaster as his date with the Bluesbreakers had been. As it is, all five takes attempted on that first June afternoon – including the one in 3/4 time included on *The Bootleg Series* – petered out before the musicians got the sound of revolution in their heads. As Greil Marcus has recently written in his book-long study of the song, 'At this point, "How does it feel?" is very nearly the whole song.'

Only on June 16 – a session he probably hadn't planned on, hence why the studio log continued to be dated the fifteenth – did 'Like a Rolling Stone' acquire some flesh on its bare bones. And it only happened because Dylan held back from punctuating the song's intro with that trademark harmonica whine, while surrendering the piano to the ever-capable Paul Griffin and switching to a barely-audible electric rhythm. Griffin, in turn, allowed himself to be supplanted at the organ by Al Kooper, a friend of Tom Wilson who had snuck into the session as a 'stand-by' guitarist only to hi-jack it with a stopgap organ sound that proved unique largely because it was born of intuitive ineptitude. As Kooper put it in his own unreliable memoir, he was 'like a little kid fumbling in the dark for a light switch.'

Thankfully, he was allowed a couple of rehearsal takes and a false start to figure his part out before, on take four, lightning struck. The confluence of important words, that frat-rock melody, its steady rhythm of hatred, a happen-stance of masterful musicians, and the hippest producer on the block fused together, and stayed together, for the six solid minutes it took to break all the rules. For all time.

Yet Dylan still wasn't sure whether lightning might strike twice, so he put the band through eleven more takes, without even finishing the song a second time, let alone surpassing this one radical, nay revolutionary, moment. The song has already passed beyond his and their command, as take eight decisively demonstrates. Marcus's description of that version suggests just how fortunate they had been to catch lightning in a bottle:

Dylan leads on harmonica, the bass is strong – and the drums have turned martial and busy, undermining the song from the start. It's a mess, but it's alive, scattershot, everyone reaching in a different direction. The more oppressively Gregg plays, Griffin plays more foolishly. 'WHOOAA – you've gone to the finest schools,' Dylan shouts, riding the bucking line. The second verse is crackling. . . . Dylan is flying solo. His rhythm guitar is pushing; Bloomfield is all but silent. Then Bloomfield picks up a theme from the piano – he has lost his own hold on the song. *Budda bump, budda bump*, say the drums, and by now that's all they say. The take breaks off two words into the last verse.

Undaunted, Dylan drove yet more nails into Miss Lonely's coffin, until everyone present had almost forgotten how great the song had been just an hour or two earlier. Even then he couldn't resist seeing if he might make up something equally mercurial on the spot, running through the never-to-be-finished 'Why Do You Have to Be So Frantic?' Only when Wilson rolled the tape back, cutting an acetate of take four for the songwriter to take with him, did what had been achieved truly sink in. As Dylan recalled twenty-two proud years later, 'We [then] took an acetate of it down to my manager's house on Gramercy Park and different people kept coming and going and we played it on the record player all night.'

Dylan learned an important lesson that afternoon – never flog a song to death, eke out its essence, and, if it won't yield it up, be stoic in the face of any resistance. It is another irony that he realized perhaps his most perfect studio recording by relying wholly on intuition, and then later found it nigh on impossible to get back to that feeling in subsequent performances. He has come close to redefining other breakthrough songs from the pre-accident era onstage. But 'Like a Rolling Stone' has almost always proved beyond post-accident Bob.

Even its live debut at Newport teeters on the edge of disaster, despite Dylan's best efforts (and the recent DVD shows just how *much* he is pushing himself). Thankfully the furore over the gesture itself, playing electric blues at a goddamn folk festival, soon overtook any question regarding the actual quality of the set. For a while afterwards, though, 'Rolling Stone' continued to scale the heights – just as long as Dylan had sufficient reason to focus on that 'steady hatred' that originally inspired it, as he did at most stops along the way throughout his 1966 world tour. The legendary Manchester performance soars because he found himself compared to a false apostle (which made a change from the Messianic types he generally encountered) and so was again obliged to tell 'someone something they didn't know.'

And the gobsmacking (to use a good Geordie word!) footage of his performance in Newcastle a couple of days later, included entire on the *No Direction Home* DVD, proves no less maelstromic. Here we can see he is visibly speeding out of his brains and probably more than a little miffed that the Mr. Jones puffing on his pipe in the front row thinks he's attending a poetry recital. But of all the songs written within the vortex, 'Like a Rolling Stone' is the one that should have been pensioned off along with the remains of the Triumph Bonneville he mangled on that back road leading up to the rustic retreat where he first heard a piece of paper singing to him, 'How does it *feeeeeeeeeeeeeeeel?*'

{149} WHY DO YOU HAVE TO BE SO FRANTIC?

Known studio recordings: Studio A, NY, June 16, 1965 – 1 take.

Recorded last at a session that had become a series of frustrations after the sublimity that was 'Like a Rolling Stone' take four (remake), this weird little one-verse fragment was assigned a CO reference number (CO 86449) and even circulates among collectors, yet was still omitted from Michael Krogsgaard's online sessionography. Admittedly not a substantial addition to the canon, it nonetheless hardly deserves to be written out of history, providing a presentiment of all the problems that would dog Dylan in the studio in the months separating *Highway 61 Revisited* from its successor.

Dylan once told holy man Allen Ginsberg, as he started coming out of his post-accident haze, that he sometimes used to 'go into a studio and chat up the musicians and babble into the microphone then rush into the control room and listen to what [I] said, and write it down, and then maybe arrange it a little bit, and then maybe rush back out in front and sing it [again]!' Such an approach seems like the only credible explanation for this babbling lyric:

> Why should you have to be so frantic, you
>   always wanted to live life in the past,
> Now why [d'ya wanna] be so Atlantic, you
>   finally got your wish at last.
> You used to be oh so modest, with your arm
>   around your cigarette machine,
> Now you lost it all, I see, an' all you got is your
>   two-dollar bill and your hat full of gasoline.

From this veritable freefall of random words, maybe one line would have been worth transferring to one of the new songs he had started writing ('with your arm around your cigarette machine'). The whole attitude, though, would survive intact on most *Highway 61* songs. Yet again he is laying into some 'victim, swimming in lava,' telling her/ him, 'Now you lost it all.' Here is the same man who told the Bay Area press, later in the year, that he wrote such songs because he wanted 'to needle 'em.' The song, like the session, peters out, but the riff will hang around, as this 'holy slow train' ultimately transforms itself, fourteen years on, into *Slow Train Coming* – for here, in the raw, I kid you not, is the 'Slow Train' riff, writ rough.

{150} TOMBSTONE BLUES

Published lyrics: Writings and Drawings; Lyrics *1985;* Lyrics *2004.*
First known performance: [Newport Folk Festival, July 24(?), 1965]
Forest Hills, NY, August 28, 1965.
Known studio recordings: Studio A, NY, July 29, 1965 – 12 takes
[H61 – tk.12] [NDH – tk.9].

> I've stopped composing and singing anything that has either a reason to be written or a motive to be sung. . . .
> My older songs, to say the least, were about nothing. The newer ones are about the same nothing – only as seen inside a bigger thing, perhaps called the Nowhere. – Bob Dylan, January 1966

Should it be true that Dylan wrote almost all of *Highway 61 Revisited*, plus his next two singles, in the six weeks that separate the 'Like a Rolling Stone' session from the 'album sessions,' then genius is the *mot juste* for this man-on-the-edge. According to Dylan, all these songs were written in the new home he had acquired in Woodstock for him and his already pregnant partner, Sara (and assuming Jesse was conceived in May, he didn't yet know he was about to be a father). As he told Shelton, 'When I got back from England . . . I bought me a thirty-one room house. . . . I wrote *Highway 61 Revisited* there.'

Dylan had been visiting Woodstock since 1963, staying either at the home of Peter Yarrow or in a cabin on the estate of his manager Albert Grossman. And he had already written some important songs there – especially the previous summer, when 'entertaining' Joan Baez and her in-laws, the Fariñas. But he had yet to use Woodstock as a base for the rigorous regime required when writing an entire album in one inspirational spurt – as he had tried with *Another Side* (London and Vernilya) and *Bringing It All Back Home* (Carmel, Woodstock, and New York). Now, after 'Like a Rolling Stone' opened everything up, he believed he could to do the same with his next offering.

Dylan later said he felt 'inspired' to buy this extravagant edifice after a visit to the Lennons' while in London. John and Cynthia's suburban retreat, in Esher, Surrey, was full of the bric-a-brac of a compulsive collector. And though he did not share Lennon's penchant for clutter, he had found a woman who understood his need for solitude; he needed the time and space to write a whole album of songs that not only rewrote the book, but ripped up a number of esteemed 'how to write a song' textbooks.

'Tombstone Blues' – the one post-'Rolling Stone' song he tried out on the Newport throng (albeit during an acoustic workshop!), and the first song completed when work resumed at Studio A on July 29 – was probably the first song he finished after being struck by lyrical lightning. Indeed, on *Highway 61 Revisited* he placed it directly after his new hit single. 'Tombstone Blues' represents the formal unveiling of what would become the stock scenario for a midperiod electric Dylan song, or as Paul Cable put it, 'the typical melee of totally unrelated events involving totally unrelated weirdo characters.'

In this particular instance, these characters include the likes of Paul Revere's horse (though not Revere himself), Belle Star (who reappears twenty years later on *Empire Burlesque*), Jack the Ripper (now enough of a worthy to join the Chamber of Commerce), John the Baptist (who is torturing a thief – possibly in the night), and Gypsy Davey (who carries a blowtorch, in case the 'glamour' doesn't work). The whole madcap menagerie culminates in an inspired deconstruction of the kind of moralizing coda he used to rely on:

> Now I wish I could write you a melody so plain
> That could hold you, dear lady, from going insane
> That could ease you and cool you and cease the pain
> Of your useless and pointless knowledge.

Such magnanimity proves all too rare on the remainder of the album, as ever more Byzantine works poured forth in the weeks to come. Clearly feeling that 'Tombstone Blues' was another important statement, Dylan used it as the opener to his electric set for the remainder of 1965, having found the bar band he'd always wanted. In 1984, when he reverted to the bar-band aesthetic with more mixed results, the song returned to live duties. And it enjoyed a third wind in 1995, when he rekindled the kind of punchy delivery that made such a methodology aurally apposite.

{151} DESOLATION ROW

Published lyrics: Writings and Drawings; Lyrics 1985; Lyrics 2004.
Known studio recordings: Studio A, NY, July 29, 1965 – 1 take
[NDH]; August 2, 1965 – 5 takes; August 4, 1965 – 4 takes [H61].
First known performance: Forest Hills, NY, August 28, 1965.

> If I just came out and sang 'Desolation Row' five years ago,
> then I probably would've been murdered. – Dylan to Nat
> Hentoff, October 1965

What does one do the month after inventing an entirely new form of popular song? One does it again. With 'Desolation Row,' Dylan manages something even he'd never pulled off before – writing a song as long as 'Tam Lin' (and in that classic ballad meter) but without any such narrative thread. Instead, Dylan relies almost solely on placing familiar characters in disturbingly unfamiliar scenarios, revealing a series of increasingly disturbing canvases. Being Dylan, he unravels no ordinary tale. This is the same world he talked about in a number of interviews from the second half of 1965, at which he regularly claimed he'd 'never written anything . . . as far out as some of the old songs,' and how inspired he had been by 'all these songs about roses growing out of people's brains and lovers who are really geese and swans that turn into angels.'

This 'far out' vision depicts a totalitarian world where one's only escape is to the ominously named Desolation Row (an idea David Bowie borrowed for his own magnificent 'All the Madmen'). With Dylan's reading beginning to branch out beyond the Beats and French symbolists – and the drugs *temporarily* helping to open yet more doors of perception – he draws on the likes of Nietzsche (cited in the album sleeve notes), Kafka, and Kierkegaard to fuel a bleak, dystopian worldview. (There can be little doubt that the castle where the insurance men keep the kerosene is Kafka's.)

Dylan later suggested (to *Rolling Stone* publisher Jann Wenner) that 'Desolation Row' – along with everything from 'that kind of New York type period, when all the songs were just "city songs"' – was heavily influenced by his good friend, Beat poet Allen Ginsberg – 'His poetry . . . sounds like the city.' Well, one of Ginsberg's achievements in writing *Howl* and *Kaddish* was to reintroduce oral rhythms to poetry (hence their suitability for record). 'Desolation Row' went further still, returning the words of popular song to a time when they had a power no other media could match. Or as Ginsberg himself put it, 'It was an artistic challenge to see if great art can be done on a juke box. And he proved it can.'

Despite displays of literary ambition, one must be wary (as others have not been) of reading too much into Dylan's name-dropping of literary sources in midsixties songs, a list of which would imply an awfully well-read twenty-four-year-old university dropout. References to the likes of Ophelia, the Hunchback of Notre Dame, T. S. Eliot, and Ezra Pound in this oral epic in no way affirm an intimate knowledge of Shakespeare, Victor Hugo, or the authors of *The Waste Land* and *The Cantos*, respectively. Dylan wants these familiar cultural icons to provide him with a series of archetypes he can place in his own wasteland.

Dylan actually had something of a fierce anti-intellectual streak running through him in these years. As he told Hentoff a couple of months after the composition of 'Desolation Row': 'We have the literary world . . . [and] the museum types . . . which I also have no respect for. . . . In my mind, if something is artistic or valid or groovy . . . it should be out in the open. It should be in the men's rooms.' When asked about the prospect of critical acceptance by another journalist friend, Ralph J. Gleason, the following December, Dylan retorted, 'They should use the new ones, like "Desolation Row" [if they want to study me].'

It seems clear that, even in his midsixties heyday, Dylan drew more from the world of painting than from any extra-curricular reading – or from frequenting men's rooms. 'Desolation Row' was, in Dylan's mind, an aural painting, 'a picture of what goes on around here sometimes,' as he suggested on the sleeve of his previous album. Were it to have a visual equivalent, it would have been something like Bosch's *Garden of Earthly Delights*, a triptych vision of heaven and hell certainly familiar to Dylan's former girlfriend, Suze (who attended one of the *Highway 61* sessions). A similar incongruity regarding its characters ('Einstein, disguised as Robin Hood') and locale ('They're selling postcards of the hanging') suffuses 'Desolation Row.' And whereas a song like 'On the Road Again' was intended to be humorous, here the results are as oppressive as anything Hieronymus ever daubed on canvas.

Yet it would appear that some contemporaries found 'Desolation Row' a riot of sorts. When it was debuted at Forest Hills and the Hollywood Bowl, a month before the album's release, there is audible laughter from each audience. And one suspects that one more line that would have induced mirth at these shows would have been, 'They're spoonfeeding Casanova / The boiled guts of birds.' But it was the one significant change Dylan made to the lyrics between July 29 and August 2, when the song went from electric to acoustic, 'their' motive for spoonfeeding now being 'to get him to feel more assured.'

Writing a song of this length was only half of the challenge – recording and performing it quite another. For all of Dylan's early immersion in epic narratives like 'Matty Groves' and 'Tom Joad,' his longest studio recording to date had been 'Percy's Song.' As such, Dylan must have been both surprised and delighted when he recorded it, backed by electric guitar and bass, in a single take at the end of the first album session on July 29. (Krogsgaard dates the 'electric' version of the song to the July 30 session. He is clearly wrong. The session sheet for the July 29 session has an untitled song that times out at eleven minutes and forty-seven seconds, the exact time of the take on the *Highway 61* test-pressing.)

His own performance is almost faultless, singing the words like a man in the captain's tower on a personal voyage of discovery. Yet something convinced Dylan to redo the song, and I doubt it was the slightly out-of-tune guitar (Tony Glover, in his *Live 1966* notes, has suggested it was *wildly* out of tune, and that Dylan didn't notice). So at the end of another extraordinarily productive session on August 2, he cut the song acoustically, allowing producer Bob Johnston to overdub some flamenco guitar fills (which may or may not have been provided by Bloomfield or Charlie McCoy) at a session two days later, before editing together the released version from four incomplete takes and the only complete take. And even though it would generally be hard to fault his judgement at this juncture, I am not sure the acoustic version is more captivating than the electric one. What it did mean was that the song became *Highway 61*'s 'Restless Farewell.'

That Dylan seriously considered using the electric take is confirmed by the existence of a test-pressing of all the songs on his shortlist, presumably cut at the end of the August 2 session. One must presume it was for Dylan's own benefit, allowing him to decide which songs and sequence to go with. This remarkable artifact (subsequently boot-legged as *Highway 61 Revisited Again*) doesn't utilize the acoustic 'Desolation Row' but rather the earlier, electric take, implying that Dylan and/or his producer still preferred the electric version, even after recording its acoustic alter ego (thus debunking Glover's suggestion that Dylan was annoyed to find himself out of tune).

The sequence of songs on this test-pressing does not resemble the order in which they would have appeared on the original reels. Nor does 'Desolation Row' come last. This, and the fact that Dylan ended up releasing the songs in pretty much the order they *were* recorded, suggests that neither he nor producer Bob Johnston ever settled on an ideal album sequence, and 'Desolation Row' ended up as the album closer largely by default. ('Desolation Row' is also 'out of place' in *Writings and Drawings*, appearing before 'Highway 61 Revisited' and 'Just Like Tom Thumb's Blues.')

In concert 'Desolation Row' was never the finale, even though Dylan performed it at every show from Forest Hills to the Albert Hall nine months later. Those performances showed just how sure he was of the power these plentiful words had to hold his audience/s. Post-accident, he has been less convinced, performing the song exactly three times between 1974 and 1986: once in St. Louis in 1974, once in Rome in 1984, and once with the Grateful Dead gumming up the works in Washington in 1986. (Where are the super-human crew when you need them?) In each case the song was trimmed of at least two of its ten, twelve-line verses (in truth, they are thirty four-line verses in traditional ballad meter).

Only in 1987, with the Heartbreakers on hand, did Dylan rediscover 'Desolation Row.' Trimmed down to even slimmer proportions, performed in seven- and eight-minute versions, this semi-electric tour de force almost resembled that fabled outtake from July 29. Even when he mastered the song sufficiently to perform an eleven-minute semi-acoustic arrangement – such as the one manifested at Bethlehem, PA, in December 1995, it was still pruned of three verses (including the penultimate 'Praise be to Nero's Neptune . . .' stanza). Other Never Ending Tour performances suggest he has never quite resolved its acoustic/electric status, and also that the full ten-verse original is long gone. At least the release of the electric outtake in 2005 meant everyone could finally savour that first studio vocal, when Dylan could still recall the thrill of it all.

{152} FROM A BUICK 6

Published lyrics: Writings and Drawings; Lyrics 1985; Lyrics 2004.

Known studio recordings: Studio A, NY, July 30, 1965 – 4 takes
[H61 ver.1 – tk.3; H61 ver.2 – tk.4].

First known performance: Forest Hills, NY, August 28, 1965.

Highway 61 Revisited is hardly an album littered with filler, but 'From a Buick Six' is definitely one that Dylan put there for light relief. Another 'she's killing me alive' lyric, it may well be what came out when he decided to rework 'Sitting on a Barbed Wire Fence.' Another barroom blues, it relies on the band's sound to convince us he is doing more than just listing the number of ways in which this 'graveyard woman' is both a lifesaver and a death-giver, handy with a shroud should she ever need one.

At least the song was not one that either held up or hung up its author, being recorded in two takes (after a couple of false starts) at the start of business on July 30. As if to prove that both takes served their purpose just as well, Columbia managed to release the earlier take accidentally on the album's initial U.S. pressing (and every Japanese pressing for years to come). Dylan also tried out the song at both Forest Hills and the Hollywood Bowl (where she walks like Rimbaud, as opposed to Bo Diddley), before dropping it and Her, never deigning to invoke the woman with the blanket again.

{153} CAN YOU PLEASE CRAWL OUT YOUR WINDOW?

Published lyrics: Writings and Drawings; Lyrics 1985; Lyrics 2004.

Known studio recordings: Studio A, NY, July 30, 1965 – 21 takes
[45]; October 5, 1965 – 2 takes; ?November 30, 1965 – 10 takes [45 –
tk.10] [probably recorded on October 5 in reality].

Dylan's claim that he abandoned writing sequel songs after the now-lost 'Mr. Tambourine Man Part 2' does not bear a great deal of scrutiny. He wrote a couple of sequel songs to 'Like a Rolling Stone' in the months following, issuing them as a series of singles that produced progressively more disappointing chart positions. The first of these was almost certainly 'Can You Please Crawl Out Your Window?' – a song he did not release until December 1965, but first recorded at the second-album sessions in late July. Its twenty-one starts and five finishes occupied a large chunk of studio time on July 30, and even then he wasn't entirely happy.

The reason this song occupied Dylan and the musicians so long is unclear, though Bloomfield had his own chaos theory about the sessions as a whole that seems particularly pertinent here: 'No one had any idea what the music was supposed to sound like. . . . The sound was a matter of pure chance. . . . The producer did not tell people what to play or have a sound in mind. . . . It was a result of chucklefucking, of people stepping on each other's dicks until it came out right.' Bassist Harvey Brooks confirms that new producer Bob Johnston – who replaced Wilson after he and Dylan had a fundamental falling out, as artists and producers some-times do – was largely a bystander to proceedings: 'Johnston was there just to keep it going. He was supposed to say if somebody was in tune or out of tune, but that was a useless concept.'

In the case of 'Can You Please Crawl Out Your Window?' Dylan seemed to *want* the thing out of tune. After twenty-one takes, the one that was put on the *Highway 61* test-pressing features an off-key rhythm guitar (Dylan's, I suspect) throughout. That a more musical take was available was confirmed when Columbia managed to accidentally release another July 30 take of the song on the A side of early copies of 'Positively Fourth Street.'

For once, one has some sympathy for the label. With a song title like this, who knew what it actually sounded like?

'Can You Please . . .' certainly wouldn't have been much of a clue, as that particular phrase doesn't appear anywhere in the song. Dylan generally sings, 'Ah, c'mon, crawl out your window.' In Columbia's cardex system it was initially filed under the title on the studio sheet – 'Look at Barry Run' – while 'Positively Fourth Street' had itself been filed under 'Black Dalli Rue.' Gee, I wonder why they mixed 'em up?

The song demonstrates very little compassion for this particular Miss Lonely, even when she seems to be on the receiving end of a rather violent man ('your face is so bruised'). For those who consider Dylan's sixties symbolism to be entirely consistent (e.g., A. J. Weberman), there is doubtless mileage to be found in his use of that 'window' again, presumably the very one from which he told an ex-lover, 'It Ain't Me, Babe,' and beneath which a fearful Ophelia sits in 'Desolation Row.' But Bloomfield probably had a better handle on the song's theme as a reflection of the changes Dylan was going through personally, when he told Larry Sloman, 'I would see him consciously be that cruel, man, I didn't understand the game they played, that constant insane sort of sadistic put down game.' For now, he also enjoyed being consciously cruel in song.

Though 'Can You Please Crawl Out . . .' was the one song from the July/August sessions not issued the following month either as a single or on album, Dylan still felt it could be another potential 'hit,' and in October he attempted to record the song a second time with his new Canadian pick-up band, the Hawks. On this version he even threw in a little aside in the fade – the opening line to 'Positively Fourth Street' – probably a dig at Columbia for not telling the difference between the two.

According to Hawks drummer Levon Helm, the single version was recorded shortly after their October 1 Carnegie Hall show (for which it was apparently rehearsed). A

November 30 studio date, assigned by others, is decidedly unlikely, both because Helm had left the band by then and because it left no time to get a single out in the pre-Christmas rush. (Yes, the studio logs suggest multiple takes on that date, but for a stereo mix, which would not be issued for many years, and then only in Japan, on *Masterpieces*.) The Band's own *Musical History* box-set, issued in 2005, clearly attributes it to October 5.

The Hawks give their all on this single version, the word-play is quintessential midperiod Dylan, and his vocal is a delight, but the song showed no obvious advance on an album's worth of dispositions reflecting that 'sadistic put-down game' his sustained amphetamine habit was merely exacerbating. It failed to replicate the success of the previous two Dylan 45s, both of which went Top Ten Stateside. Dylan himself never gave the song a live debut and, when asked about it in the lead up to *Biograph*, claimed, 'I was pressured into doing another single.' By whom?

Note: Dylan is surely singing, 'religion of little tin women,' not, as the published lyric suggests, 'religion of the little ten women.'

{154} POSITIVELY FOURTH STREET

Published lyrics: Writings and Drawings; Lyrics 1985; Lyrics 2004.
Known studio recordings: Studio A, NY, July 29, 1965 – 12 takes [45 – tk.12].
First known performance: [University of Vermont, Burlington, October 23, 1965] Berkeley Community Theater, December 4, 1965.

It may be hard to be any more precise than June/July for the majority of songs recorded at the July 29 to August 2 album sessions, but 'Positively Fourth Street' sure sounds like the product of a post-Newport Dylan, mightily pissed off for the second year running by those shouting, 'Which Side Are You On?' This time it is clear the gloves are off, Dylan dishing out his audible disdain with added vocal relish. It still stands up as one of his greatest-ever vocal performances in a studio setting.

Should my assumption be correct, he wrote the song in the three-day period between the postshow party and his return to Studio A, i.e., with an immediacy that made the emotion real but also kept second thoughts in check. In this sense, it is another 'Ballad in Plain D.' This time he leaves us guessing as to his unnamed target/s. But I think we can assume they still wake with a start whenever they hear that exquisite organ intro.

Like in 'Plain D,' his main beef seems to be against the female of the species ('I do not feel that good / When I see the heartbreaks you embrace' sure doesn't sound like a guy thing). He almost admitted as much two decades on, when he accurately described 'Positively Fourth Street' as 'extremely one-dimensional. I don't usually purge myself by writing anything about any type of so-called relationships.' Which rather suggests the song should be placed somewhere between 'Ballad in Plain D' and 'Idiot Wind,' and that Miss Lonely is still very much in his sights.

'Positively Fourth Street' may even be a belated reworking of (unused parts of) the vomit version of 'Like a Rolling Stone,' already edited down to its poetic core. Rather than inducing a feeling that one is reading someone else's mail, it invokes a sense of stumbling in on a particularly bitter argument with Miss X. Like most Dylan arguments-in-song, this is one long *j'accuse*. He had found the perfect medium for saying what he thought without worrying about the subject of such 'verbal bayonets' talking back. Not that he entirely accepted the power of such words or that they were even *meant* to wound, telling Hentoff shortly after the single charted:

I don't want to hurt anybody like that . . . but then again,
I know a lot of people are hurt, but it's not really me that
hurts them . . . like, they're just deceived. But I haven't hurt
them any. . . . I don't really worry too much about people
who say they've been hurt by me because, ninety-nine times
out of a hundred it's not me that hurts them.

Here is the retort of someone equipped with his own
state-of-the-art psychological armour. He simply cannot
conceive of the pain his barbs might be causing others. As
long as he remained wired on speed, he retained the same air
of invincibility. And 'Positively Fourth Street' would be his
way of winding himself up for 'Like a Rolling Stone' at the
ensuing North American live shows. Only after the regime
of daily drug transfusions had ceased did Dylan examine
the wreckage he'd left behind. 'Positively Fourth Street'
itself was performed exactly once, at a benefit show for
'Hurricane' Carter in Houston in January 1976, in the twenty
years before the Heartbreakers convinced the songwriter
to take the spitting old jalopy for another few spins round
the block. Since that time Dylan has tapped into the song's
sarcastic self a fair few times, but never with anything like
the venom unleashed in Studio A, when the wild mercury
sound had a real merry-go-round feel.

{155} HIGHWAY 61 REVISITED

Published lyrics: Writings and Drawings; Lyrics *1985;* Lyrics *2004.*
Known studio recordings: Studio A, NY, August 2, 1965 – 9 takes
[H61 – tk.9][H61 – tk.6].
First known performance: Isle of Wight, August 31, 1969.

On the evening of Monday, August 2, 1965, Dylan
re-entered Studio A feeling he still had a lot of work to do
if he was going to 'eclipse anything I've ever done before.'
Only three of the half-dozen songs already on tape would

make the finished album. Having originally planned to spend the weekend in Woodstock recuperating from two days of sustained work in Studio A, he found himself too cranked up to chill and returned to the city to work further on the songs.

Ever a man in a hurry, he now attempted to finish the album in one soulful, bounding leap, using the midnight-shift musicians who had already worked wonders. The studio log suggests the session on the second started at eight in the evening and ended around three thirty in the morning. In that time he would lock down four songs with a rare, iridescent inspiration – 'Highway 61 Revisited,' 'Just Like Tom Thumb's Blues,' 'Queen Jane Approximately,' and 'Ballad of a Thin Man' – before re-recording an acoustic, twelve-minute 'Desolation Row' (presumably after the other musicians had crawled home to bed).

And the first song he elected to run through on that eventful evening would become the title track of this revolutionary collection. For 'Highway 61 Revisited,' Dylan had assembled the wildest collection of song characters this side of Jacques Brel. From the outset he is ready to roust another herd of sacred cows, starting with the father, the son, and an angry God:

> God said to Abraham, 'Kill me a son.'
> Abe said, 'Man, you must be putting me on.'
> God said, 'No.' Abe said, 'What!'

Has there ever been a more memorable dialogue to open a 'pop' song? Adhering to another popular ballad convention – setting up the action by getting the protagonists to tell their story – Dylan finds a wholly original way to retell the story of Abraham in hip patois (an idea probably inspired by the memorable Lord Buckley skit, 'The Nazz').

This time there is a more credible outcome. An incredulous Abraham only agrees to murder his own flesh and blood when God out-and-out threatens him, like the boss of a mob family. When Abraham asks where he must do the deed, God replies, 'Out on Highway 61,' the road that traverses the country, weaving past Dylan's Minnesota home – where his father, Abraham, was doubtless wondering what his prodigal son was up to.

Dylan has not picked out a random dialogue between the Big J and a religious father. He is actually indulging in a philosophical speculation – one Kierkegaard had already addressed at length in *Fear and Trembling* – which is, What kind of a person would it take to make the leap of faith required to murder one's own son at the command of one's God? Whereas Kierkegaard indulged in a book's worth of contemplation, Dylan cuts to the chase and sees it not as a test (or indeed an ethical dilemma, as Soren K. did) so much as a demonstration of power: 'Next time you see me comin', you better run.'

He is informing listeners they have entered a world where one cannot even rely on God to be good – the world the characters in this (title) song, and by implication its narrator, inhabit. As he wrote in response to a university newspaper questionnaire back in May, 'I have no faith in better world coming. I live now in this world.' The world he finds himself in is a worried one, where a rovin' gambler might try and 'create a next world war'; where 'the second mother' is lying incestuously 'with the seventh son,' and the father only finds out because he goes off to tell the mother that her 'fifth daughter' is with child. Here all one can do is grimace – or grin. Dylan even has a little joke at tradition's expense. The daughter does not tell her father she is pale and wan, as the convention demands, but rather, 'My complexion . . . is much too white.' Emphasizing the idea that the song is something of a hoot is the spontaneous inclusion of a kid's toy police siren in the mix, surely the most unusual 'instrument' found on a sixties Dylan album.

Preparing to travel down another restless highway, Dylan found no place for this title track in the live set (it was down as a possible encore at Forest Hills, but never played). It took a most incongruous setting – the 1969 Isle of Wight festival, where he appeared in a snow-white suit and sang 'Like a Rolling Stone' like he was chewing the cud – for him to try out the song on the common folk. Thankfully, the 'Highway 61 Revisited' that night was the cry of a raucous recidivist stuck in a border-town bordello, making it the one hint that the pre-accident Bob lived on (an audience video of the performance suggests he is really starting to loosen up by song's end).

Subsequently revived as an occasional encore on the 1974 tour and as a nightly opener in 1984, it took G. E. Smith's Never Ending Tour combo to find a reliable way of whipping the crowd up and holding on to any failing energy. The downside of this Never Ending Tour incarnation – as a Good Time Charlie of a song – is that one would be hard pressed to glean evidence of the metaphysic raising so many philosophical questions while the boys in the band were whooping it up.

{156} JUST LIKE TOM THUMB'S BLUES

Published lyrics: Writings and Drawings; Lyrics *1985;* Lyrics *2004.*
Known studio recordings: Studio A, NY, August 2, 1965 – 16 takes [H61 – tk.16][NDH – tk.5].
First known performance: Forest Hills, NY, August 28, 1965.

I write inside out and sometimes the dimensions cross.
– Dylan, responding to Cambridge *Varsity* questionnaire,
May 1965

Of the songs Dylan recorded at this historic August session, 'Just Like Tom Thumb's Blues' took the most work, as Dylan sought to get his audience experiencing it in a visceral way. As he said in 1965, referring to all of these songs, 'The point is not understanding what I write, but *feeling* it.' The early takes of the song did not do it for him. The release of *No Direction Home* allows us to hear one of these early takes – take five, the second full version recorded. Taken in isolation, it is rather wonderful. The sedentary, almost mournful pace rather suits the song, and Dylan's vocal sounds like a man awakened from a dream.

However, what really separates it from the sixteenth and final take is the studio personnel. It sounds like a more tentative drummer and less fluid pianist. And according to the log, there *was* a musician changeover around eleven in the evening, from Sam Lay to Bobby Gregg on drums and from Frank Owens to Paul Griffin at piano. If that is Griffin playing those great piano fills on the released version, he comes close to deserving a co-composing credit, while the drums acquire a jazziness they lack on that earlier take. So it wasn't all serendipity! Someone was paying enough attention to realize that Sam Lay's drumming, while fine for an up-tempo rocker like 'Highway 61 Revisited,' merely shuffled on a slow blues.

Dylan knew 'Tom Thumb's Blues' deserved all the loving care it could get, the lyrics skirting the edge of reason. 'Your gravity fails / And negativity don't pull you through' communicates as a 'feeling,' nothing more. It was surely such songs Dylan had in mind when he told Shelton later that month, 'If anyone has imagination, he'll know what I'm doing. If they can't understand my songs, they're missing something. If they can't understand green clocks, wet chairs, purple lamps or hostile statues, they're missing something, too.' In 'Juarez' (as the song was originally called) no hostile statues were needed to experience the kind of dislocation that could lead a singer to exclaim, 'I'm going back to New York City / I do believe I've had enough.'

Again Dylan has allowed himself to be drawn to 'witchy women' exuding that gypsy air. Yet rarely has he conjured up a creature as enticing as 'sweet Melinda . . . the goddess of gloom,' a close relative of the 'She' who belonged on *Bringing It All Back Home*. But this is a song with a moral, and this time it comes in the first verse, not the last: 'They got some hungry women there / And they really make a mess out of you.' As for any direct inspiration from the women of Juarez, we have no documented evidence Dylan visited Mexico at this time, though its influence was felt long before he spent the winter of 1972–3 in Durango.

As performed live in 1965–6, 'Tom Thumb' became an inferno of pain. As if pain were indeed art. At the American shows Dylan claimed the song was specifically written 'about a painter. Not too many songs about a painter. This one lived in Mexico City. . . . He lived with Indians in jungle. Will live to be a ripe old age. Was famous in his era. Called Tom Thumb. Did same things as other painters. Had his periods. This is about his blue period. It's called Tom Thumb's Blues.' Introduced in a similar way in Melbourne, it induced the odd hormonal girl to scream. I guess they breed their women hungry in Australia.

But the song got no such reception in Liverpool a month later, when Dylan sounded like he'd been doing some sword swallowing, lacerating the audience with every hurled syllable. Issued as the B side to 'I Want You,' this was for many years the only official evidence of just how close to the edge Dylan came on that tour. It is still one of the most harrowing and compulsive cuts. Thankfully, his fondness for the song endured beyond those wild mercury days. Even now he can generally be relied on to treat that prophetic final verse ('I started out on burgundy / But soon hit the harder stuff . . .') with an appropriate degree of respect for someone who had no right to come out the other side, synapses intact.

{157} QUEEN JANE APPROXIMATELY

Published lyrics: Writings and Drawings; Lyrics 1985; Lyrics 2004.
Known studio recordings: Studio A, NY, August 2, 1965 – 7 takes [H61 – tk.7].
First known performance: Foxboro, Mass. July 4, 1987.

For many years 'Queen Jane Approximately' was the forgotten lady of *Highway 61*. Sandwiched between 'Just Like Tom Thumb's Blues' and 'Ballad of a Thin Man' at the August 2 session, and subjected to a painfully dry mix on the released stereo album (the mono mix is less painful, though one can still hear the band playing in at least three tunings), it seemed like the least memorable of those songs suffused with a 'steady hatred directed at some point that was honest.'

The only interviewer to ever ask about this song was then-journalist Nora Ephron who, at a September 1965 gathering, inquired as to Queen Jane's identity. Dylan's response was suitably cryptic: 'Queen Jane is a man.' Dylan may, of course, have been pulling Ephron's leg. On the other hand, an androgyny bordering on out-and-out transvestism flickers on and off throughout songs of the period. Homosexual imagery abounds in 'Ballad of a Thin Man,' as it does in a number of songs circa 1965–6, notably 'Just Like a Woman,' where Dylan takes great delight in mixing up genders.

The central figure in 'Queen Jane' may even be the same queen bitch Bowie later portrayed in song. Andy Warhol was certainly someone whose path crossed Dylan's at this time. As the pop artist writes of the songwriter in *Popism*, 'He was around 24 then and the kids were all just starting to talk &

act & dress & swagger like he did. But not so many people except Dylan could ever pull off this anti-act. . . . He was already slightly flashy when I met him, definitely not folky anymore. I mean, he was wearing satin polka-dot shirts.' By November 1965, after a year in which their supra-hip enclaves intersected at will, Dylan willingly sat for a silent film portrait at Warhol's Factory.

Nor is there a shortage of lines in 'Queen Jane' that could be applied to our regal pop art exponent. May I offer up: 'When . . . you're tired of yourself and all of your creations,' 'When all the clowns that you have commissioned,' 'When all your advisers heave their plastic,' and so on. Written when all his songs were 'city songs,' this could have been Dylan's way of saying he was not impressed by the hangers-on Warhol seemed to like accumulating.

Yet it was not a song to which Dylan developed any attachment. At the time Warhol died in February 1987, he had still to give the song a live debut. Since 1987, though, 'Queen Jane' has been given another lifetime. Dylan has also turned the song inside out, adding inflections of sorrow and pity to that original, slightly sinister plea, 'Won't you come see me, Queen Jane?' Obliged to survive the Grateful Dead, who insisted on giving the 'lady' a good seeing-to at joint summer shows, Jane was miraculously revived by the Heartbreakers the following fall.

Born again, the song has gone on from strength to strength. The version on the penultimate night of an October 1989 New York residency at the Beacon Theatre might even get my vote over its 1965 archetype. Though it takes time to build some momentum – and Dylan can only hold on for as long as he sticks to the song itself, and not some imaginary harmonica fugue he adds as a coda – those five minutes transport his entire expressive range back in time. Its semi-acoustic incarnation at the November 1993 Supper

Club shows almost rekindles the same emotional range. And these days the members of the band even usually play in the same key.

{158} BALLAD OF A THIN MAN

Published lyrics: Writings and Drawings; Lyrics 1985; Lyrics 2004.
First known performance: Forest Hills, NY, August 28, 1965.
Known studio recordings: Studio A, NY, August 2, 1965 – 3 takes [H61 – tk.3].

Just as 'Positively Fourth Street' may have been 'inspired' by events at Newport, another song on *Highway 61 Revisited* could be a post-Newport rant, according to one barely credible source. Rock journalist Jeffrey Jones claimed, some years after the event, that he interviewed Dylan at the festival and that it was his annoying line of questioning that prompted Dylan to write that memorable refrain, 'Something is happening, but you don't know what it is, do you, Mr. Jones?' But it is hardly likely that Dylan would have remembered this innocuous individual's name in the whirlwind of events that weekend, let alone make him an archetype for his own Mr. Clean. Nor would it be like Dylan to be quite so prosaic.

If Dylan did make an exception and it was a specific journalist he was targeting, the one credible candidate would have to be *Melody Maker's* Max Jones, whom he had first attempted to contact in December 1962. He was the first British music journalist to interview Dylan, in May 1964, and he was someone he specifically asked about at his first London press conference in April 1965. By 1966 Jones had become the slightly crumpled character seen in the tour documentary, *Eat the Document*, asking Dylan why he doesn't sing protest songs anymore – though he is *not* seen during the sequence where a live 'Ballad of a Thin Man' is intercut with footage of assorted candidates for the position.

The essential problem with such a theory is that Dylan

liked Jones. He was never a victim of Mr. Send-Up, as one London journalist called Dylan after a classic 1965 demolition interview. Though Jones was strictly old school, so were Nat Hentoff, Robert Shelton, and J. R. Goddard, all of whom were more than just 'pressmen' in Dylan's mind. However, it is possible that his name sprang to mind when the idea for 'Ballad of a Thin Man' came to him, and Dylan liked the way it fit. He *has* suggested that the song was directly inspired by events in England that spring. In March 1986, while onstage in Japan, he delivered one of the most credible explanations of what made him separate the world into neophytes and neophobes:

> This is a song I wrote in response to people who ask questions all the time. You just get tired of that every once in a while. Y'don't wanna answer no more questions. I figure a person's life speaks for itself, right? So every once in a while you gotta do this kinda thing – gotta put somebody in their place . . . it's not a bad thing to be put in your place. . . . Actually it's a good thing. It's been done to me once in a while, and I always appreciated it. So this is my response to something that happened over in England – I think it was about '64 [*sic*]. Anyway, the song still holds up. Still seem to be people around like that, so I still sing it.

Ain't it just like our man to provide such a cogent explanation to ten thousand bemused Nippon fans, prefacing a performance in Nagoya. Twenty years earlier, in March 1966, performing it for a Canadian audience, he was not so helpful, introducing it with an offbeat biographical sketch: 'Mr. Jones lives in Lincoln, Nebraska – to prove I don't make these things up. He hangs around bowling alley there. Also owns water mill rights, but we don't talk about that when we're in Nebraska. We just let Mr. Jones have his little way.'

Six months earlier, with the song only just in the shops, he told a Carnegie Hall audience at the song's conclusion – and before another cathartic 'Like a Rolling Stone' – 'That was about Mr. Jones, this one is *for* Mr. Jones.' One contemporary confidant immersed in pill-popping paranoia was a Rolling Stone called Mr. Jones. Brian Jones's insecurities led him to believe Dylan was having a go at *him*, though one would be hard-pressed to ever describe the hedonistic Stone as straight-laced. Perhaps Dylan was sending up Jones's effete homophobia, *if* one interprets the song as one long catalogue of homosexual innuendo (as has been suggested).

The song certainly convinced an awful lot of people that there was a real Mr. Jones behind the song (hence the Canadian rap). As such, although not a single interviewer in the months after *Highway 61*'s release asked Dylan about the identity of Miss Lonely, it seemed like every journalist had a burning need to know the true identity of Mr. Jones, starting with Nora Ephron, then of the *New York Post*, in early September 1965. Dylan ducks her question beautifully, while storing up a whole lot of trouble for himself in the near future:

He's a real person. You know him, but not by that name. . . . I saw him come into the room one night and he looked like a camel. He proceeded to put his eyes in his pocket. I asked this guy who he was and he said, 'That's Mr. Jones.' Then I asked this cat, 'Doesn't he do anything but put his eyes in his pocket?' And he told me, 'He puts his nose on the ground.' It's all there. It's a true story.

Three months later the question popped up again, at a press conference in San Francisco. Again Dylan suggests he is a real person, just not someone you'd want to meet at the dark end of the street: '[Who's] Mr. Jones? I'm not gonna tell you his first name. I'd get sued. He's a pin boy. He also wears suspenders.' Uncomfortable with explaining the unexplainable, he began to develop a rap like the one he used in Vancouver, placing Mr. Jones in Lincoln, Nebraska, which was precisely where he was when Robert Shelton also summoned up the nerve to ask him about the Thin Man's identity. And because it was Shelton, Dylan tempered his usual tendency to ridicule the questioner:

> I could tell you who Mr. Jones is in my life, but, like, every-body has got their Mr. Jones. . . . Mr. Jones's loneliness can easily be covered up to the point where he can't recognize that he is alone . . . suddenly locked in a room. . . . It's not so incredibly absurd, and it's not so imaginative, to have Mr. Jones in a room with three walls, with a midget and a geek and a naked man. Plus a voice, a voice coming in his dream.

Try as he might to deflect such speculation, this fascination with finding out the *exact* person who triggered such a judgemental song continued to pique people's curiosity. Dylan finally put the whole absurd game of naming names in its proper context in 1985, talking to Bill Flanagan: 'There were a lot of Mr. Joneses at that time. . . . It was like, "Oh man, here's the thousandth Mr. Jones."'

Dylan earlier claimed he had been running into Mr. Jones ever since his days in the North Country, in another in-concert rap, offered to audiences on the American leg of his 1978 world tour:

> In the mid-West during the Fifties, you'd have carnivals come through town, and every carnival would have what you'd call a geek. A geek is a man who eats a live chicken, he bites the head off [first]. Working a job like that, he got insulted most of the time by lots of people who would [then]

pay a quarter to see him. I never did get too tight with him, but I did learn one interesting thing, and that was, he used to look at these people who came to see him as *very* freaky. I always remembered that as I traveled through some of the stranger places . . .

For Dylan to feel an impulse to explicate *any* song to audiences in 1966, 1978, *and* 1986 suggests that the song 'bothered' him as much as his ever-curious fans. And though the 1986 rap seems to address the real trigger for the song's composition, the 1978 rap, which featured at a number of shows on the three-month U.S. tour, provides its own intriguing backdrop. One, it re-creates the young, rebellious Dylan who hung out with carnival freaks, a wholly fictional alter ego of the dutiful son, Robert Zimmerman. Two, it suggests that the whole song can be seen from the vantage point of the geek, specifically the one who, in verse three, walks up to Mr. Jones and asks him a line straight out of the 'vomit version' of 'Like a Rolling Stone': 'How does it feel to be such a *freak*?' Three, it sends us back to a song Dylan says he wrote during his first few months in New York, 'Won't You Buy My Postcard?' about 'this lady I knew in a carnival. . . . They had a freak show in it' (see #40).

By July 1965 Dylan felt he was part of a mighty similar 'freak show.' As he told one journalist, the month after he recorded 'Thin Man,' 'I don't call myself a poet. . . . I'm a trapeze artist.' At least he wasn't one of the multitude of working stiffs represented by the journalist with pencil in hand in verse one, and/or the anonymous person who pays to 'go watch the geek.' And herein resides the true source of the depiction of a straight man lost amid a cavalcade of freaks. When, a couple of months earlier, he got into a heated debate with a *Time* reporter, Horace Judson (now an esteemed professor at George Washington University – really!), Dylan suggests the weekly magazine is aimed at 'Mr. C. W. Jones, on the subway going to work.' It is a characterization he repeats, almost verbatim, in another rant he directed at journalist Jules Siegel almost a year later.

In keeping with other songs of the period, 'Thin Man' dishes it out to the schools and universities that its author likened to 'old people's homes' in one interview (except that more people die in the former). Having questioned the purpose of college education as far back as 1960, he delivers the knockout punch in 'Ballad of a Thin Man': 'You've been with the professors / And they've all liked your looks.' It really is not so very far to go from ridiculing someone for 'going to school reading and writing and taking tests' – as Dylan did in one 1965 conversation – to becoming the preacher man at Tempe in 1979 telling attendant nonbelievers, 'You're paying a lot for your education. Get one.'

Whatever its immediate trigger, Dylan had been storing up such feelings for a long time. But when it came time to let it all out in Studio A, 'Thin Man' came fast and furious. The album take came after a single false start and a full run-through. Unfortunately, Dylan (and/or Johnston) appears to have decided that Al Kooper was getting carried away with the old ghost-in-the-machine organ fills and stripped them from the album mix. It makes one concentrate more on the words and some percussive piano playing (that sounds like Dylan's own), but it makes for a more monochromatic sound-picture. The original, rough mix can be found on the *Highway 61 Revisited Again* bootleg CD, and is well worth the price of admission.

Naturally, such a forensic diagnosis of Mr. Jones's doubts and fears made 'Ballad of a Thin Man' the perfect prelude to 'Like a Rolling Stone' at the shows on the world tour, which occupied Dylan for the nine months after *Highway 61*'s release. He even asked for hush at some shows, keen for the audience to hear every laser-directed word. And this time organist Garth Hudson was given free rein to embellish the song as much as he liked, as the (slightly histrionic) singer directed each performance from the piano, like some grand circus master.

Even after Dylan calmed down, post-accident, this remained a song that lent itself to some demonstrative performances, complete with hand gestures. In 1978 he often sang the song with only a handheld microphone (something not repeated until 1995), and in 1981 at Earl's Court he punched the air on every chorus like a man possessed. The song has rarely left Dylan's live set for long; nor has that feeling that the world is inhabited by some 'very freaky' people.

{159} MEDICINE SUNDAY

Known studio recordings: Studio A, NY, October 5, 1965 – 2 takes.

Dylan had allowed himself just two months' respite from the studio when he booked three days of sessions in early October 1965, suggesting that breaking in two different live bands – the Forest Hills outfit and the Hawks – hadn't stopped him refining some techniques explored on the latest album. However, those three days of sessions would prove an optimistic allocation of studio time. The results disproved the theory that the boy genius had only to turn up with any half-baked idea to leap ahead of the folk-rock fraternity once again.

As with the June 15 session, the purpose of the October 5 session seems to have been twofold: to get another single to follow up 'Positively Fourth Street' and to see how his new band, the Hawks, responded to his working methods in the studio. Like that June session, the results were mixed at best. Having turned up with three half-ideas for songs, Dylan seems to have simply jammed with the Hawks on each of them, before deciding which he would flesh out into a potential single.

The two losers – 'Medicine Sunday' and 'Pilot Eyes' (a.k.a. 'Jet Pilot') – would remain as one-verse workouts that never worked out. In the case of 'Medicine Sunday,' at least the punch line would be preserved, appearing five months down the line in an entirely different song, 'Temporary Like Achilles,' though I have to agree with author Paul Cable that 'the one verse you get to hear [here] has a much more attractive melody than its successor.' The lyrics, though, do rather suggest something scribbled on the back of a packet of cigarette papers:

> Well, that midnight train pulled on down the track,
> You're standing there watching, with your hands tied behind
>   your back.
> And you smile so pretty, and nod to the present guard.
> Well, you know you want my loving, but mama you're so
>   hard.

One of those instances of Dylan 'go[ing] into a studio and chat[ting] up the musicians and babbl[ing] into the microphone,' f'sure.

{160} JET PILOT

Published lyric: Words Fill My Head
Known studio recordings: Studio A, NY, October 5, 1965 [BIO].

If 'Medicine Sunday' was the first half-idea that day to falter two feet from the well of inspiration, Dylan's next foggy notion wasn't even deemed worthy of a name or a CO number. The tape log makes no mention of 'Jet Pilot' until a later hand has written beneath, 'Jet Pilot 2nd leader on tape UNANNOUNCED. Has been lifted off on to SW 63115' (a project undertaken in 1970 to catalogue 'interesting' unused Dylan studio material, for purpose/s unknown). And yet, according to Krogsgaard's sessionography, there were seven attempted takes of this unlogged song, a claim I find rather hard to credit.* The version on *Biograph* sure sounds like a one-off, as Dylan again demonstrates a keen fascination with transvestism:

> Well, she's got jet pilot eyes, from her hips on down,
> All the bombadiers are tryin' to force her out of town.
> She's five feet nine and she carries a monkey-wrench,
> She weighs more by the foot than she does by the inch.
> She's got all the downtown boys, all at her command
> But you got to watch her closely, 'cause she ain't no woman,
>> she's a man.

Was Dylan just flirting with something he considered transgressive? Or could it be that his desire to recast himself as a Rimbaudian seer – increasingly evident in all that he did – included getting familiar with a modern-day Paul Verlaine? (After all, what is one to make of his allusion to relationships 'like Verlaine's and Rimbaud,' on 1974's 'You're Gonna Make Me Lonesome When You Go'?) Whatever the case, Dylan continued to introduce queer elements into his songs. She of the 'jet pilot eyes,' though, never got to use her monkey wrench. Dylan dispensed with the idea and turned his attention to another song that blurred the gender lines, 'I Don't Want to Be Your Partner.'

{161} I WANNA BE YOUR LOVER

Published lyrics: Writings and Drawings; Lyrics *1985*; Lyrics *2004*.

---

* The seven takes 'of' 'Jet Pilot' attributed by Krogsgaard I suspect may be the missing versions of 'Can You Please Crawl Out Your Window.'

327

Known studio recordings: Studio A, NY, October 5[–6?], 1965 – 7 takes [BIO].

When Dylan began recording 'I Wanna Be Your Lover,' it was another half-idea called 'I Don't Want to Be Your Partner,' and perhaps he was already despairing of getting anything useful from the night's session/s. Aside from the two half-ideas that stayed that way, he had already attempted to record 'Can You Please Crawl Out Your Window?' with his new band, a song they apparently rehearsed in Woodstock in late September. They finally got this fully fledged song down on tape here (though possibly not until the following day).

The portents for 'I Don't Want to Be Your Partner,' another song that stalled after a single verse on take one, were not auspicious. At this point he hadn't even gotten a chorus that worked – just, 'I don't wanna be your partner, I wanna be your man,' sung twice. (Is he proposing?) And yet, a couple of hours/nights later, the song had four full verses and a largely revamped chorus, 'I wanna be your lover, baby, I wanna be your man [x2] / I don't wanna be hers, I wanna be yours,' or *'yerrrs'* as Dylan sings it, a curious form of reassurance given the man's polygamous lifestyle.

As with 'It Ain't Me, Babe,' Dylan took great delight in parodying a Beatlesque chorus, though it is doubtful that Lennon or McCartney would have had the audacity in 1965 to rhyme 'hers' with 'yours.' The transformation justifies organist Al Kooper's claim, in the *Biograph* notes, that '[t]he songs changed all the time. We would try different tempos, he would try other words. Most of the songs [even] had different titles.'

Presumably that hour-and-a-half break the band took in midsession on the fifth (from ten to half past eleven, according to the session log) allowed Dylan to do a 'Takes a Lot to Laugh,' turning 'I Don't Want to Be Your Partner' on its head and making it sing. He certainly demonstrated a remarkably rapid way with words, even assuming he sketched out the direction the song might go in advance. Unfortunately, its 'success' convinced him he could do the same for half of the songs on his next album. The cast of characters he came up with by the time they recorded take seven – which *ain't* the version issued on *Biograph* – share the same caboose with other personae from this remarkable year: 'the rainman . . . with his magic wand,' 'the undertaker in his midnight suit,' 'jumpin' Judy,' and, best of all, 'Phaedra with her looking glass.' One can't help but wonder why it never even made it onto a single B-side.

Dylan wondered too, telling Cameron Crowe in 1985, 'I always thought it was a good song, but it just never made it onto an album.' What its inclusion on *Biograph* fails to resolve is whether the two full versions in circulation, one widely bootlegged, the other unknown till *Biograph*, both come from the session on the fifth, or whether – as *Biograph* itself claims – there was a further session later, at which the song was attempted again, along with 'Can You Please Crawl Out Your Window?' (Personally I'd go with a session on the sixth, with the tape log from the fifth carrying over, as had been the case with 'Like a Rolling Stone.' But I could be wrong.)

{162} BABY LET ME FOLLOW YOU DOWN [1965]

First known performance: [Burlington, October 23, 1965] Back Bay Theater, Boston, October 29, 1965.

Dylan probably came to regret his spoken introduction to the first-album version of 'Baby Let Me Follow You Down' – in which he verbally acknowledged his debt to Eric Von Schmidt – almost as soon as he recorded it. As a result it was not included in his first songbook, along with 'rearrangements' of 'Gospel Plow,' 'Man of Constant Sorrow,' and 'Pretty Peggy-O.' Two years later the Animals displayed no such scruples, crediting their own 1964 Britpop revamp of *his* version, 'Baby, Let Me Take You Home,' to 'B. Russel–W. Farrell,' though neither were ever known aliases of the Reverend Gary Davis, its 'original' source, or Von Schmidt, its conduit.

By January 1964 Dylan decided to have another stab at copyrighting the song, recording a rather nice fingerpicked demo for Witmark. But the registration hit a problem (presumably because of prior registration by Von Schmidt, who had got around to recording it himself) and Dylan's copyright was subsequently withdrawn. As of October 1965 he still had no claim on the song. But during rehearsals with the Hawks, he worked up a full-blooded electric arrangement that warranted the nightly introduction to 'I Don't Believe You' far more than that song: 'It used to go like that, and now it goes like *this!*' He also extracted two new verses from his scrapbook of *Highway 61* women:

> I'll buy you a broken twine, honey, just for you to climb,
> I'll do anything in this God almighty world, if you just once
>   drive me out of my mind.
> I'll buy you a purple shirt, I'll buy you a velvet skirt,
> I'll do anything in this God almighty world, if you just don't
>   make me hurt.

This belated claimant to the 'original' folk-rock template would remain part of the Dylan/Hawks set right up to those Royal Albert Hall meltdowns at the end of May 1966 without ever being copyrighted in its own right, even though Dylan could now stake a claim to a 'Baby Let Me Follow You Down' that was largely his own. Indeed, according to a 1973 *Rolling Stone* interview, Carly Simon was given a copy of Dylan's 'new' version to record at some point in 1967–8 by Albert Grossman, who was probably still hoping to make the song the property of Dwarf Music. Her version, though, was never released, so it was left to Dylan to resurrect his 'original' variant for The Band's 'farewell' performance, *The Last Waltz*, in November 1976, when he fondly but fleetingly recreated the sound of folk-rock for another generation.

{163} LONG DISTANCE OPERATOR

Published lyrics: Writings and Drawings; Lyrics *1985;* Lyrics *2004.*

First known performance: [Arie Crown Theater, Chicago, October 26, 1965] Berkeley Community Theatre, December 4, 1965.

The first time anyone not witness to the fall 1965 shows knew of 'Long Distance Operator' – which came and went in the veritable twinkling of an eye – was when it appeared in *Writings and Drawings* among the set of songs marked 'From *Blonde on Blonde* to *John Wesley Harding*,' i.e., the basement tapes. Though not one of the nineteen 'basement' songs to have been bootlegged before 1973, it did seem to contain the strange melange of pastiche teen lyrics ('Long distance operator, place this call / It's not for fun') and *Highway 61*–like dislocation ('I'm strangling on this telephone wire'), which could suggest a kinship with the likes of 'Lo and Behold' and 'Million Dollar Bash.'

Not so. The song was one of those Dylan wrote exclusively for performance (like the long-forgotten 'Who Killed Davey Moore?' and 'Tell Me, Momma,' the immediate successor to 'Long Distance Operator'). And it made its debut in late October 1965 during the electric set (the first documented performance was in Chicago on the twenty-sixth, when he evidently introduced the song, because local journalist Bruce Plowman mentions it in his *Tribune* review). In this incarnation the song served as replacement for 'Phantom Engineer' and 'From a Buick Six,' allowing the Hawks to demonstrate their R & B credentials to those unfamiliar with their earlier work with Ronnie Hawkins and John Hammond Jr. And it ran to five verses, the fourth of which was later omitted from the published text:

> Well, she don't need no shotgun,
> Blades are not her style, [x2]
> She can poison you with her eyes,
> She can kill you with her smile.

Quite why the singer is so keen to get in touch with another woman capable of killing him alive, the song fails to explain. After all, he was about to become a married man for the first time (he and Sara tied the knot on November 22). Thankfully, 'Long Distance Operator' survived to the West Coast jaunt in December when the handy tape recorder of Allen Ginsberg, in the front row of Berkeley Community Theatre, captured the only known *Dylan* recording. He had not taken the opportunity to cut a quick studio take during the November 30 'Freeze Out' session – when the Hawks were again his session mates. As such the song duly fell off the map until January 1971, when it was belatedly copyrighted by his music publisher, Dwarf Music.

By then, Dylan wasn't about to record the song himself, and it would be rather early for its copyright to relate to *Writings and Drawings* (some songs *were* copyrighted during the compilation of that collection, but most old songs copyrighted in 1970–1 appear to belong to some Columbia-related project/s). It begs the obvious question, What version was used to copyright the song? The Band had recorded their own studio version in February 1968, which would feature on the 1975 *Basement Tapes* set (a misnomer all along), but unless they intended to include the song on *Cahoots*, why copyright it in 1971?

As it happens, the version The Band did ultimately release corresponds to the lyrics in *Writings and Drawings*, suggesting that the 1968 recording is in some way bound up with its 1971 copyright (its Dwarf Music status explaining why it was assigned to the basement tapes section in Dylan's collected lyrics). However, there is another possibility: Dylan recorded the song at the Big Pink sessions in 1967, and this take became the basis for both the later Band studio version and the published lyrics. Maverick musicologist Rob Bowman suggests as much in his notes to the recently remastered *Music from Big Pink* CD. Assuming Bowman has some basis for his claim that 'it had . . . been recorded with Dylan singing as part of [t]he Basement Tapes,' one awaits the emergence of said recording with barely contained anticipation.

{164} VISIONS OF JOHANNA

Published lyrics: Writings and Drawings; Lyrics 1985; Lyrics 2004.
Known studio recordings: Studio A, NY, November 30, 1965 – 14 takes [NDH – tk.8]; Studio A, Nashville, February 14, 1966 – 4 takes [BOB – tk.4].
First known performance: [Berkeley Community Theater, December 3, 1965] Westchester, NY, February 5, 1966.

Dylan really had to work at 'Visions of Johanna' – which many, myself included, consider Dylan's finest work/song – in the studio before capturing the sublimity of the *Blonde on Blonde* recording. In keeping with previous instances when he stepped beyond the paradigms of popular song, he initially seemed in something of a hurry to get the song captured in the studio, as if the inspiration would fade as quickly as the night vision he sought to contain.

It had been less than four months since completing his sixth album, but already Dylan was feeling the strain. The songs had not come, which was fast becoming a source of frustration. Indeed, it is awfully tempting to see Johanna as his muse, who at the start of the song is 'not here,' but by the final line is 'all that remain[s]' (other possible incarnations of said lady include 'Dirge' and 'What Was It You Wanted'). It is certainly one of the oddest songs ever written by a man who has just tied the knot and is enjoying a brief honeymoon in the city.

It would appear he had already abandoned his Woodstock mansion, unhappy with the vibe of the place and superstitious about the possibility of writing more breakthrough songs there. As he told Shelton the following March, 'I don't believe in writing *some total other thing* [my italics] in the same place twice. It's just a hang-up, a voodoo kind of thing. I just can't do it. When I need someplace to make something new, I can't go back there.'

As a result, on his return from Texas at the end of September, Dylan again immersed himself in New York's nightlife, holing up at the Chelsea Hotel on 23rd St. Its *fin de siècle* feel would provide a redolent backdrop to the songs he wrote, or began to write, that winter. The Chelsea was (and still is) hardly the Ritz. But Dylan liked the vibe and the centrality of this mauve-bricked edifice. As late as 1985 he still had fond memories of this place (and time), telling Scott Cohen, 'Me and my wife lived in the Chelsea Hotel on the third floor in 1965 or '66, when our first baby was born. We moved out of that hotel maybe a year before [Warhol's] *Chelsea Girls*. When *Chelsea Girls* came out, it was all over for the Chelsea Hotel. You might as well have burned it down.'

That first baby, Jesse, a son and heir, would be born the following January. Sara, six months pregnant when they were married, was no longer the secret backwoods girl. She was at Dylan's side on (or around) November 8, when they were photographed by Don Paulsen at a Young Rascals show with Jerry Schatzberg and Brian Jones. So, should these visions really be set in this *déclassé* hotel – and, rest assured, the heat pipes *still* cough at the Chelsea – we can be fairly sure it was not *her* absence that set him musing.

Unlike a number of other songs Dylan wrote during this *annus mirabilis*, few folk have stepped forwards to claim they are Johanna, evidently another of Dylan's goddesses of doom, but not necessarily a corporeal entity. Strangely, though, Joan Baez has been one such claimant, telling Scaduto, 'He'd just written "Visions of Johanna," which sounded very suspicious to me. . . . He had never performed it before, and Neuwirth told him I was there that night and he performed it.'

While it is true that he debuted the song at the Berkeley Community Theatre on December 4, a show Baez attended, this was his first opportunity to play the song since writing it. And if he was playing it for anyone that night, it was Allen Ginsberg and fellow Beat poet, Lawrence Ferlinghetti, who were sitting in the front row surrounded by Hell's Angels. He considered Ginsberg a profound influence on his songwriting at this juncture. And though he had stopped 'auditioning' breakthrough songs to those he admired in late-night, sitting-room sessions, he still wanted their bene-diction, and Ginsberg was not cagey about dispensing it. (He may even have known that Allen planned to tape the show.)

But before he could play the song in Berkeley, Dylan set out to record it himself, with the typewriter ribbon not yet dry. Which is where the fun begins. The session he booked for November 30 in New York must have been slotted in very much at the last minute because Dylan and the Hawks were due to fly to the West Coast the following day. An evening session (according to the log, it broke up around ten-thirty P.M.) hardly qualifies as an obvious way to rest and relax before embarking on an important West Coast tour, espe-cially with a new drummer to break in (Bobby Gregg had been hastily drafted after Levon Helm cried 'Enough' at the end of the East Coast dates). But Dylan was determined to get the song down before time quelled the fire in his fingertips. As he complained to journalist Jim Jerome almost exactly ten years later, 'I write fast. The inspiration doesn't last. Writing a song, it can drive you crazy. My head is so crammed full of things I tend to lose a lot of what I think are my best songs.' He didn't want to lose this one.

Convening at Columbia's New York studio at two-thirty in the afternoon, Dylan intended to concentrate on this one song. The first order of the day was to teach the band the song itself, since they would hardly have had time on the road to learn it (though guitarist Robbie Robertson, now firmly attached to Dylan by bonds of mutual self-interest, probably heard it in some hotel room).

Dylan's faith in his new band to translate his thought patterns quickly and efficiently in the studio had already been dampened by his experience at the October session/s. And this was an era when it was the norm to have bands teach arrangements to session musicians who efficiently executed said licks on their behalf at the session itself (the Byrds' 'Mr. Tambourine Man' and Them's 'Baby Please Don't Go' being two good examples of session musicians doing the actual playing 'on record,' though the arrangement remained the same).

So this time Dylan hedged his bets, drafting in just about every key player from previous 1965 sessions to step in should they be required. As such, Joe South and Bruce Langhorne were standing by on guitar, while Al Kooper was there to play 'supplementary organ,' and Paul Griffin constituted an additional pianist. With Bobby Gregg now the temporary Hawks drummer, Dylan effectively brought two separate bands to the studio to make sure there was an imprint of the song on tape while the vision remained. Which certainly helps explain the slightly schizophrenic nature of the versions recorded here.

Quite when the rehearsing process ended and tape started rolling is not clear, but there was clearly a point when the two crossed over. According to Sean Wilentz, who gave a talk on the *Blonde on Blonde* sessions at the Morgan Library in 2006 that was interspersed with excerpts from the session tapes: 'On the session tape, he and the Hawks change the key and slow the tempo at the start of the second take, if only to hear more closely; "that's not right," Dylan interrupts. He speeds things up again – "like that" – and bids Gregg to go to his cowbell, but some more scorching tests are no good either: "That's not the sound, that's not it," he breaks in. . . . Two more broken attempts feature Richard Manuel playing on the harpsichord: "Nah," Dylan decides, though he keeps the harpsichord in the background. [Then] out of nowhere comes a slower, hair raising, bar band rock version.'

This 'bar-band rock version,' the earliest take in circulation, was cut to an acetate auctioned by *Goldmine* in 1980 and is both rehearsal and recording. A marathon performance, in every sense of the word, it demonstrates a Dylan mustering all of his creative focus just to keep the song on the rails, determined not to lose his train of thought in the recording process. Clocking in at eight minutes and twenty-seven seconds, it is also the longest of the four studio performances in circulation.

Yet it may *not* be the longest of the lot; the November 30 studio log times the song at nine minutes and twenty-three seconds. Locating this version presents a real problem because the song actually got shorter – not longer – as Dylan started to refine the arrangement. The previously uncirculated version released on *No Direction Home* – which, according to the accompanying notes, is take eight (of the fourteen recorded) – sets another kind of record by clocking in at just six minutes and thirty-eight seconds, though lyrically it is almost identical to its more expansive predecessor. They shave two minutes off the song just by playing with greater assurance and singing with renewed confidence.

The musicians strip the song bare first time around, with nary a fill to be heard. Even with Dylan singing with a precision last heard on 'Mr. Tambourine Man' at the Festival Hall, the song does slightly drag, and I find the *NDH* version preferable, even though Dylan's vocal sounds a little rushed, as he fails to linger on the words in the way he manages consummately on the 1966 world tour. But there is far more of a contribution from the musicians, either because they have figured out how to play their parts or because they have been belatedly introduced into the mix. (Paul Griffin apparently arrived at the session around five, some two-and-a-half hours after work began.)

According to the studio log, the one on *NDH* was the fourth complete take. One may even wonder why this didn't signal an end to proceedings (until one remembers how Dylan kept hammering away at 'Rolling Stone' long after the *moment* had passed). The song had come a considerable way in a short time. Yet work continued, with four more false starts following immediately afterward. Finally Dylan and the other musicians realized the song again – twice – and then called it a night.

If, as appears to be the case from the session sheets, one of those two later takes is the one that has been in circulation since the early seventies – when it appeared (under its original title, 'Freeze Out') on a couple of very famous bootleg LPs, *Seems Like a Freeze Out* and *Forty Red, White & Blue Shoestrings* – then Dylan executed quite an about turn. He suddenly stopped trying to make 'Visions' into a rock song, reverting to almost a jazz-rock arrangement. This 'third' version is dramatically different from both what came before and the Nashville version later released on *Blonde on Blonde*. Clocking in at seven minutes and twenty-eight seconds, it retains the so-called 'nightingale's code' set of lyrics, Dylan jamming in an extra line on that final verse (à la 'Hard Rain'):

> The peddler now steps to the road
> Knowing everything's gone which was owed
> He examines the nightingale's code
> Still written on the fish-truck that loads
> My conscience explodes . . .

The lyrics have subtly changed from earlier in the session, this so-called 'L.A. Band' version* making two significant shifts. The addition of 'knowing' before 'everything's gone which was owed' provides the peddler with a reason for stepping 'to the road.' Also, the line that on the record became, 'She's delicate, and seems like the mirror,' has gone from, 'Like silk, she seems like the mirror' – which is how it was sung on previous takes – to, 'She's steady, and seems like the mirror.' Assuming that this version *is* from November 30 (and not January 1966), one must assume it is one of these last two takes. Which still leaves another mystery: Whatever happened to the nine-minute-and-twenty-three-second version listed on the tape log?

Thankfully, Dylan treated the song as something of a gift, cherishing it accordingly. As with 'Mr. Tambourine Man,' he refused to settle for second best (and impressive as they all are in their own special ways, the New York versions are just signposts on the way to its final destination). So he took the song with him to Nashville, where it was the second song to be cut at the bona fide *Blonde on Blonde* sessions. After three false starts, it just slid into the

---

* The so-called 'L.A. Band' session was a compilation tape made up by Columbia in the early seventies from the New York sessions in October and November 1965 and January 1966 with the Hawks. How it got this moniker is unclear, but it probably has something to do with a comment Dylan made at the San Francisco press conference in early December, about having just recorded 'Freeze Out.'

same groove as the musicians themselves, who effortlessly executed an inner intent Dylan's touring band had struggled to discern. Hence, perhaps, why the song appeared only as an acoustic performance throughout 1966. Indeed, even on its Berkeley debut, four days after the Hawks recorded six complete studio takes, Dylan chose to do it all by himself, certain that *he* could tease out any subtleties frozen out in the studio setting.

But the real triumph on 'Visions' is the way Dylan manages to write about the most inchoate feelings in such a vivid, immediate way. For now, it must have seemed like he didn't even have to *try* writing something this great. As he said to the ever-attentive Hentoff only a matter of days before he wrote the song, 'I'm not trying to say anything, any more. Once upon a time I tried to say, "Well, I'm here. Listen to me. . . . Will you let me stay at your house tonight?" . . . I don't have to say that any more. . . . [The new songs]'d be there if anybody listened to them or not. They're not manufactured songs.'

This particularly luminous vision has generally remained acoustic, or semi-acoustic, in performance, save for its Never Ending Tour debut in 1988 – a rollicking rendition that unexpectedly opened a September show in San Diego. It sounds like he'd finally figured out where that New York 'rock' version could have gone if time had been on its side. Post-accident – but before its Never Ending Tour debut – he had generally held off performing the song, singing it exactly twice to a paying audience: once in Denver in February 1974, and again in Lakeland, Florida, in April 1976. The former is predictably painful, while the latter proves a perfect way to introduce his finest tour in a decade. Since 1990, the song has become far more familiar to regular Dylan concert-goers, while whoops of recognition suggest it has yet to slip from its position as many fans' favourite. Generally, though, he has struggled to realize the vision almost as much as he did that night in late November 1965.

Note: The published lyrics print the penultimate line as, 'The harmonicas play the skeleton keys and the rain.' Cute, but every critique I've ever read hears the line as, 'The harmonicas play the skeleton keys in the rain.'

1966

{ Blonde on Blonde }

Of the songs used to fill up rock's first double-album, Blonde on Blonde, *just one ('Visions of Johanna') had certainly been written by the turn of the year. But by mid-March Dylan had already recorded four sides of new ditties, without even touching two of his finest compositions ('She's Your Lover Now' and 'Tell Me, Momma'), both composed before the first set of Nashville sessions in February. The legend of Dylan writing songs on airplanes, in motels, and even in the studio starts here. And even when the work was completed, the river of song was still flowing strong until he (literally) crashed and (metaphorically) burned on an upstate country road in late July – if one extrapolates from the tantalizing evidence of two taped hotelroom sessions and reports of at least one other from the world tour, which concluded on May 27 in London. For the remainder of the year, though, the sound of silence and the dust of rumours vied for ascendancy . . .*

Published lyrics: Writings and Drawings; Lyrics *1985;* Lyrics
2004 [complete version: Words Fill My Head; Telegraph *#2].*
*Known studio recordings: Studio A, NY, January 21, 1966 – 19
takes [TBS].*

One element of 'Visions of Johanna' that aligns it to the
almost equally magnificent 'She's Your Lover Now,' another
major composition, comes in verse three ('Little boy lost,
he takes himself so seriously . . .'). Such a line could easily
have transferred from one to the other, something we know
happened on other *Blonde on Blonde* compositions. 'Visions of
Johanna' almost certainly prompted Dylan to continue this
line of reasoning, writing a song specifically about 'little boy
lost' and his lady friend (which may explain why he ultimately
rejected 'She's Your Lover Now,' not even attempting it at the
Nashville sessions).

The two compositions certainly appear to have been
written very close to each other – 'Visions . . .' in late
November, 'She's Your Lover Now' in late December. A
sense pervades 'Visions of Johanna' that, at any minute, the
dissolute aesthete sitting there stranded may come out of his
(opiate?) daze and start telling it like it is. In 'She's Your Lover
Now,' he does exactly this, alternating between a wistful
regret for 'her' and an ill-disguised disdain for 'him.' With
'Visions of Johanna' any barely contained disgust is reserved
for the various women, real and imaginary, whose only
crime is that they are not Johanna – 'Louise, she's alright,
she's just near,' 'Mona Lisa musta had the highway blues,'
and 'Madonna, she still has not showed.' Whereas with 'She's
Your Lover Now' Dylan is merciless in his dissection of *every*
combatant: 'I see you're still with her, well, that's fine, 'cause
she's comin' on so strange, can't you tell?' and, 'I ain't the
judge, you don't have to be nice to me.'

A comment Dylan made on Bob Fass's radio show the

night of the last January 1966 session (the twenty-seventh) suggests he had originally hoped to record a good chunk of his next album at these sessions.* This was not such an outlandish idea, given that he had recorded *Bringing It . . .* and *Highway 61 Revisited* – 'Like a Rolling Stone' excepted – in three days apiece. But in both cases he had arrived at the sessions with a locker full of songs. The three new songs recorded at sessions on the twenty-first, twenty-fifth, and twenty-seventh hardly suggested he had a similar-sized armoire of raw material.

'She's Your Lover Now,' the one major work recorded on this occasion, is shattering enough. Like 'Visions of Johanna' in November, it was the immediate priority when he arrived at the January 21 session, and he imme-diately set about getting the groove right before all drama drained from this cathartic composition. After a successful West Coast tour, he had removed the safety net of session musicians, and it was with the Hawks (now on their third drummer, Sandy Konikoff) that he set about recording the song in all its raging glory, Konikoff's rat-a-tat drum-ming driving the song forwards on wave after wave of recrimination.

According to the studio logs, they worked at the song all night long, trying it nineteen times, five of them complete, one with just Dylan at the piano. In fact, we can be pretty damn sure there never was a 'complete' 'Band' version of the song. When it was finally released in 1991, compiler Jeff Rosen used (an edit of) the regular bootlegged take that breaks down on the final verse, as Dylan mixes his meta-phors (he sings, 'Now your mouth cries wolf,' rather than,

---

* Dylan tells Fass, on his radio show, that they have just done three days of album-sessions, but that they have just a single to show for it.

'Now your eyes cry wolf,' though it sounds like someone has already dropped out before he trips over the words).

Wilentz, who before his talk on these sessions heard the session tape, never heard any full electric version. The session he describes suggests Dylan was rapidly running out of patience with his touring buddies: 'The first take rolls at a stately pace, but Dylan is restless and the day has just begun. On successive takes, the tempo speeds, then slows a bit, then speeds up again. Dylan tries singing a line in each verse accompanied only by Garth Hudson's organ, shifting the song's dynamics, but the idea survives for only two takes. After some false starts, Dylan exclaims, "It's not right . . . it's not right," and soon he despairs, "No, fuck it, I'm losing the whole fucking song." He again changes tempos and fiddles with some chords and periodically scolds himself as well as the band: "I don't give a fuck if it's good or not, just play it together . . . you don't have to play anything fancy or nothing, just . . . just together."'

According to Wilentz, after the *Bootleg Series* take collapses, Dylan says he has had enough. When he complains, 'I can't hear the song anymore,' it is his way of saying, 'Pack up guys, and go home.' However, he does have the presence of mind to run down the song solo, and Bob Johnston has the wit to set the tape machine going again, capturing all four verses, sung by a Dylan who knows that his voice 'is really warm / It's just that it ain't got no form / It's just like a dead man's last-pistol shot, baby.' However, when the song was copyrighted in 1971, and published in 1973, it was missing that final verse, suggesting that the recording Dylan and/or Columbia referenced – the song being one of those pulled for the SW63115 project – did not contain that crucial concluding stanza. And what a stanza it is:

Why must I fall into this sadness?
Do I look like Charles Atlas?
Do you think that I still got what you still got, baby?
My voice is really warm,
It's just that it ain't got no form.
It's just like a dead man's last pistol shot baby.
Ah, your mouth used to be so naked,
Your eyes used to be so blue,
Your hurts used to be so nameless,
Your tears used to be so few,
Now your eyes cry wolf, while your mouth cries,
'I'm not scared of animals like you.'
And you, there's really nothing 'bout you I can recall,
I just saw you that one time and you were just there, that's all,
But I've alreay been kissed,
I'm certainly not gonna get into this,
I couldn't make it anyhow.
You do it for me, she's your lover now.

Even the emergence of the solo piano take in 1980, on the *Goldmine* acetates, failed to convince the 'editor/s' to add it to subsequent editions of *Lyrics*. As such, the published lyric remains crucially incomplete, as does the released take on *The Bootleg Series*. Without this resolution – in which the singer allows himself to remember a time when her 'tears used to be so few' – 'She's Your Lover Now' comes across as just another demonstration of Dylan's 'verbal bayonet.' Yet that exquisite solo take is tinged with genuine regret in his voice, as he sings of the girl he once knew. One can only imagine how frustrated he felt when the song broke down so close to its finishing end. Next time around, the safety net would be back in place.

Published lyrics: Writings and Drawings; Lyrics 1985; Lyrics 2004.
Known studio recordings: Studio A, NY, January 25, 1966 – 19
takes [BOB – tk.19+insert].
First known performance: [Westchester, NY, February 5, 1966]
Corpus Christi, May 10, 1976.

'I didn't mean to treat you so bad / You shouldn't take it
so personal . . .' is the seductive way Dylan opens this coda
to the final verse of 'She's Your Lover Now.' In keeping with
his 1965 persona, though, 'One of Us Must Know' ends up
as nothing of the sort. Rather, it becomes a 1966 version of
Dylan's 1963 poem 'Message to ECLC.' Nineteen years later,
discussing (his) songwriting with Bill Flanagan, he admitted,
'A lot of people . . . come up with a line that sums up everything and then they have to go backwards and figure out
how to fill it in. With me, I usually start right at the beginning and then wonder where it's going.' 'One of Us Must
Know' sounds like a song that started out as one thing and
mutated into another. Here we can hear his more remorseful
Blonde on Blonde self struggling to shed his 'Positively Fourth
Street' skin. He wants to make amends but can't quite stop
himself from remembering why things didn't work out – 'I
didn't mean to make you so sad / You just happened to be
there, that's all.'

Now where did we hear that last line before? The answer,
my friend, is in the last verse of the song he recorded just four
days earlier. On 'Sooner or Later,' the spirit of 'She's Your
Lover Now' has not quite dissipated. The final couplet of the
third verse would hardly have been out of place in the former
song: 'An' I told you, as you clawed out my eyes / That I
never really meant to do you any harm.' Dylan even holds
onto that final word like a lovelorn leech.

Unlike either 'She's Your Lover Now' or 'Visions of
Johanna,' Dylan had not quite located the song's narrative

thrust when he entered Studio A. According to Wilentz, 'The title chorus did not even appear until the sixth take.' Like previous installments from Dylan's farewell to his footloose self, 'One of Us Must Know' proved a bitch of a song to get down. It required nineteen takes, occupying three consecutive three-hour sessions in one single exhausting day, to capture Miss So and So. By the final session Dylan had fired most of his touring Band, recording the final two takes – both complete – with Bobby Gregg, Paul Griffin, Al Kooper, and William E. Lee – all veterans of those groundbreaking 1965 sessions. Rick Danko and Robbie Robertson are the only two Hawks who make the released cut.

As he complained to Robert Shelton six weeks later, the problem had been staring Dylan in the face all along: 'It was the band. But you see, I didn't know that. I didn't want to *think* that.' At the same time, he learned one shouldn't try to make a single and an album at the same time. And he always intended to make 'One of Us Must Know' (as) a single, as he made plain to WBAI's Bob Fass. But recording his new single 'took me away from the album. The album commands a different sort of attention than a single does. Singles just pile up and pile up; they're only good for the present.'

Actually 'One of Us Must Know' wasn't even 'good for the present.' It failed to chart at all in the United States (though it did well enough in the UK), a failure that, coming hard on the heels of 'Can You Please Crawl Out . . . ,' convinced him to abandon the form. As he subsequently explained to *Rolling Stone*'s Jann Wenner, 'We cut two or three [songs] right after "Positively 4th Street", we cut some singles and they didn't really get off the ground. . . . They didn't even make it on the charts. Consequently, I've not been back on the charts since [those] singles. I never did much care for singles, 'cause you have to pay so much attention to them.'

At the time, though, he was convinced he had hit a righteous vein by combining his unique brand of folk-rock with a biting misogyny. But the times were a-changing, and even the Stones had started to tone down their single-minded brand of putative putdown. As with 'Can You Please Crawl Out Your Window?' Dylan failed to be convinced 'One Of Us Must Know' slotted into the current live show. According to A. J. Weberman, he did perform the song at the first show that winter, in White Plains, New York, but if so, the audience-taper missed it by leaving early. He never did play it again with the Hawks.

Piqued by the single's failure, he insisted on putting it at the end of *Blonde on Blonde*'s first side, between the twin beacons of 'Visions of Johanna' and 'I Want You.' And there it remained until journalist Larry Sloman informed him, at the end of the first Rolling Thunder tour, 'Most of the time I would much rather listen to you sing "One of Us Must Know" than get a blow job.' Dylan decided to test Sloman's theory by (re)introducing it, alongside several other *Blonde on Blonde* songs, on the second Rolling Thunder leg the following spring, at a time when his marriage to Sara no longer restrained him from playing the field.

It remained a feature of almost every show on the Far East and European legs of the 1978 world tour, after separation had become divorce. Since then, this melodic melodrama has joined the forgotten few from this fertile period, making only two further appearances across thirty years of steady touring. At a show in Scranton, Pennsylvania, in August 1997, he introduced an arrangement of the song a lot more worked-out than the one he brought to Studio A in January 1966. Sadly, it proved to be (almost) another White Plains one-off (he did it the following night).

Published lyrics: Writings and Drawings; Lyrics *1985;* Lyrics *2004.*
Known studio recordings: Studio A, NY, January 25, 1966 – 2
takes [NDH – tk.1]; January 27, 1966 – 4 takes; Studio A,
Nashville, February 14, 1966 – 13 takes; Studio A, Nashville,
March 10, 1966 – 1 take [BOB – tk.1].
First known performance: Westchester, NY, February 5, 1966.

Dylan has gone to great pains to stress that he wrote
'Leopard-Skin Pill-Box Hat' with no one specific in mind,
telling Scaduto in 1971 that he was 'coming down hard on
all the people, not just specific people.' But the fact that
he felt like insisting on such an abstract form of inspiration damns him. One suspects he was fully aware that
people were suggesting the exact opposite (hence Scaduto's
question). Nico felt she knew the truth, telling oral historian Jean Stein, '"Leopard Skin Pill-Box Hat" is written
about Edie [Sedgwick]. Everybody thought it was about
Edie because she sometimes wore leopard. Dylan's a very
sarcastic person. . . . It was a very nasty song, whoever the
person in it may be.' Having received an altogether kinder
song from the man before arriving at Warhol's Factory
of stars, Nico knew all about Edie's infatuation with the
folk-rocker.

No one disputes that the newly married Dylan and Edie
had been spending time together, after being introduced by
a mutual friend. According to sidekick Bobby Neuwirth,
that first meeting took place 'in the bar upstairs at the
Kettle of Fish. . . . It was just before the Christmas holidays.
It was snowing.' Assuming we are talking 1965, it seems
more likely it was around Thanksgiving, rather than
Christmas. Dylan spent most of December 1965 on the West
Coast, as did Neuwirth. And so, perhaps, did Edie.

In his account of the period, *Popism,* Warhol describes
how the three friends ended up sharing the Castle, a wholly

incongruous 'large imitation medieval stone structure in the Hollywood Hills . . . which rock musicians often rented for $500 a week.' According to Warhol, he, Nico, and the Velvet Underground rented the place in the spring of 1966, after 'Dylan had just been there with Edie Sedgwick.' Warhol could have been talking about Dylan's visit to the city of angels in early April (as his use of the word 'just' implies), but that trip was a short one, and Dylan appears to have been accompanied by his wife.

If Edie and Bob shared time at the Castle the previous December, it might also explain the trio of songs Dylan set about recording at the January 1966 sessions. The subject matter of all these new songs seemed disturbingly similar – a cloyingly persistent female being detached from her vanity and ego brick by brick. None of them were the kind of song one might have expected from a recent honeymooner. But as Dylan spent ten December days buzzing around the L.A. music scene, he seems to have found himself caught in the middle of one lady's meltdown. Never at his best around fragile egos, Dylan sped through the experience before dismantling the guilty party/s in song, probably after his return East. (And in 'She's Your Lover Now' he makes two separate mentions of the Castle.)

Edie was possibly the source of a falling out between Dylan and long-time sidekick Neuwirth, who was singularly absent from the world tour the following spring. The old friend apparently became quite infatuated with the gal. When Jean Stein was doing interviews for her best seller *Edie*, Neuwirth described Sedgwick as 'always fantastic.' It was also probably him who convinced Patti Smith that 'she was the real heroine of *Blonde on Blonde*,' a line Smith used in her first collection of poetry, *Seventh Heaven*. If Neuwirth was stuck on someone crazy about the other Bobby, it would explain a number of ménage à trois–like references in the

1966 lyrics (if not the psychodrama Todd Haynes extrapolates from that section of my biography).

Yet I doubt Dylan's live-wire mind ever considered 'Leopard-Skin Pill-Box Hat' to be 'a very nasty song.' Though he takes a certain delight in ridiculing the affectations of this nonspecific fashion victim, he does no more than the Kinks' Ray Davies in the contemporary 'Dedicated Follower of Fashion.' Just like 'On the Road Again,' the song was another sarcastic blues that Dylan struggled to inject with the necessary feeling in the studio. Looking for something specific, he made four separate attempts at the song, two with the Hawks (and standby session musicians) in January, and one each at the February and March Nashville studio sessions.

The first of these forays served more as the warm-up for 'One of Us Must Know.' Recently released on *No Direction Home*, it is interesting, if unrealized. Taken at the tempo of 'It Takes a Lot to Laugh,' the song clocks in at six-and-a-half minutes, with Dylan electing to improvise extra verses after exhausting the usual five. The first of these additional stanzas has Dylan singing what sounds like: 'I'm so dirty, honey / I been working all day in a coal bin.' But as the pace picks up, he slips into the frame of mind required to parody his favourite pop band, the Beatles, who had only just released the infectious 'Drive My Car':

> Honey, can I be your chauffeur [x2]
> Oh, you can ride with me.
> I'll be your chauffeur,
> Just as long as you stay in the car.
> If you get out and start to walk,
> You just might topple over,
> In your brand-new leopard skin pillbox hat.

This extended take allows the Hawks to demonstrate the kind of chops they'd begun to display live, Robertson unleashing a guitar solo in the class of Bloomfield for the first time. Dylan, though, does not persevere with the song, leaving it till he can play with some Nashville cats. As for the Hawks, as Dylan himself said in 1978, 'We never did capture the *Highway 61* sound on stage. What we did get on stage was something different, that we never recorded [in the studio].'

He still seemed disinclined to take the song seriously in Nashville, the new version providing mere light relief during both sets of sessions. According to Wilentz, 'Numerous takes . . . reworked "Leopard-Skin Pill-Box Hat" into a sort of "knock knock" joke complete with a ringing doorbell, shouts of "Who's there?" and car honks.' It was only when the song was cut, in a single take, almost an afterthought at the final *Blonde on Blonde* session (March 10), that Dylan returned it to base, letting Robertson loose again, a gesture that prompted bassist Charlie McCoy to exclaim at take's end, 'Robbie, the whole world'll marry you on that one.'

Robbie was just getting warmed up. On each succeeding night of the resultant world tour, he seemed to get more and more steamed up in his playing, sending furious folkies scurrying for the hills. Dylan, though, clearly loved the results, and considered the song as much his guitarist's as his own. On the first part of the Never Ending Tour, G. E. Smith got his bottleneck out and even dared to come up with a more modern variant on that '*Highway 61* sound.'

{168} TELL ME, MOMMA

Published lyrics: Writings and Drawings; Lyrics 1985; Lyrics 2004.
First known performance: Westchester, NY, February 5, 1966.

In 1971 Dwarf Music, the music publishing company Dylan and Grossman formed after the Witmark deal expired at the end of 1965, belatedly copyrighted five unreleased songs from his midsixties heyday – 'Long Distance Operator,' 'I Wanna Be Your Lover,' the instrumental 'Number One,' 'She's Your Lover Now,' and 'Tell Me, Momma.' As such, these songs constituted a part of the canon for which Grossman would continue to collect his pound of flesh even after their business relationship formally ended, also in 1971.

The lyrics to the songs in question were clearly transcribed from existing tapes, all save the first of these coming from Columbia. In the case of 'Tell Me, Momma,' it was a live recording made at Columbia's behest, from the same Liverpool show as 'Just Like Tom Thumb's Blues' (already issued on single). This was less satisfactory than something with studio fidelity, but they had no option. No studio version had ever even been attempted. Which doesn't excuse getting the lyrics transcribed by a cloth-eared illiterate with a hollow tin for a hearing aid. As a result the published lyrics feature couplets so silly they make basement tape songs read like *The Wasteland*:

> Ol' black Bascom, don't break no mirrors, cold black water
>   dog, make no tears . . .
> Oh, we bone the editor, can't get read, but his painted sled,
>   instead it's a bed.

Who, pray tell, is 'ol' black Bascom'? Yes, the song does present problems to the would-be transcriber. And some lines were simply never finished, even though the song constituted the nightly opener to the electric set from February through May 1966. But the opening couplet does not fall into this category, Dylan consistently singing the perfectly intelligible, 'Cold black glass don't make no mirr'r / Cold black water don't make no tears.'

Thanks to some very fine soundboards from Australia and England, it *is* possible to piece together the various lyrical stages with a degree of confidence, even if it is quite clear that of the three eight-line verses, just the first maintained a clear trajectory all the way through. As for the final verse, by the time Dylan got to Manchester in mid-May, Momma has stopped 'pounding lead,' as she did back in Sydney. The singer has also grown tired of her cries for attention. After singing, 'Everyone sees you're really on the edge,' in Australia, he now tells her straight:

> Everybody sees you on your window ledge,
> How long's it gonna take for you to get off the edge?

Dylan, it seems, had decided to stop using the studio to flesh out half-formed ideas, inflicting them on largely hostile audiences instead. And 'Tell Me, Momma' is a perfect way to piss off the already alienated – it is loud and frenetic, and despite a perfectly intelligible *pop* chorus, it serves its immediate purpose: to disorientate the discontented while demonstrating the musical muscularity he had at his command with Mickey Jones now pounding out the beat.

Dylan's failure to fully finish the lyrics may explain why he never even made a pass at the song in the studio, though it entered the live set before the *Blonde on Blonde* sessions. Fourteen years later he would repeat the trick, performing another song featuring an ever-changing set of lyrics, designed to alienate those imbued with Unbelief: 'Ain't Gonna Go to Hell (for Anybody),' which was also never subjected to a studio situation.

{169} FOURTH TIME AROUND

Published lyrics: Writings and Drawings; Lyrics 1985; Lyrics 2004.
Known studio recordings: Studio A, Nashville, February 14, 1966 – 20 takes [BOB – tk.20].
First known performance: Hempstead, NY, February 26, 1966.

The first week of December 1965 saw the Beatles release their finest collection to date, *Rubber Soul*. Though the U.S. edition was again pruned of several songs on the British original, one song that stayed the course had a largely Lennon lyric. Originally known as 'This Bird Has Flown,' it was released as 'Norwegian Wood.' The song was an important one to Lennon (he later said of it, 'I was trying to be sophisticated in writing about an affair. But in such a smokescreen way that you couldn't tell'). For the first time he was writing about something deeply personal – his clandestine affair with attractive journalist Maureen Cleave, whom Dylan also knew – using the kind of code the American had made something of a trademark.

Dylan undoubtedly recognized the influence and decided at some point to acknowledge it with his own version of 'This Bird Has Flown.' For the past eighteen months he had enjoyed dropping in the occasional lyrical nod with a wink to his new-found friends – a gesture they reciprocated on 'With a Little Help from My Friends' the following year. But 'Fourth Time Around' was also a way of showing he could raise the bar lyrically on Lennon, the one Beatle to have aspirations beyond being a pop poet. 'Fourth Time Around' is an altogether darker, more disturbing portrait of an affair, though it emulates 'Norwegian Wood' in its circular melody and structure.

At song's end it turns out that Dylan has been telling his tall story to someone who knew both of the participants – the clue is a 'picture of you in your wheelchair / that leaned up against / Her Jamaican rum' – and who still 'took me in' and 'loved me then.' He informs said lady that his first offering to her came as a result of rifling through the dead girl's drawers. In the song's last lines, delivering his most deadpan 'moral' to date, he reveals both of them to be cripples inside: 'I never asked for your crutch / Now don't ask for mine.'

Presumably Dylan penned this impenetrable pastiche only days (or hours) before he began recording it in Nashville, Tennessee, nine days after returning to the road with the Hawks. Lyrics like these would have left most singer-songwriters tripping down their own stairs. But according to Wilentz, the song 'evolved little in the studio,' where synchronizing the lyrics to an archaic waltz presented the real challenge. Just three of the twenty takes make it to the end, most false starts breaking down before they've really begun.* Yet by the time he left Nashville, Dylan felt comfortable enough with the song to introduce it into the solo half of his shows, where it stayed to the bitter end at the Albert Hall in May.

There is one particular 1966 version one would pay a king's ransom to hear: the occasion when he played the song to Lennon in the privacy of a hotel suite. Lennon's response was predictable. Dylan asked, 'What do you think?' and he replied, 'I don't like it.' He never did learn to like it. Nor was he flattered by Dylan's interest. But Dylan was not dissuaded from playing it to him again, along with the six thousand other souls who filled the Albert Hall for the final night of that whirlwind world tour. If Dylan said his farewell to the song that night, it was still subjected to a harpsichord overdub a couple of weeks later back in Nashville, making it both the first and last song recorded for the landmark LP his label got around to releasing in July.

Requiring the band to follow the words more than the melody made it a tough song to do electric, which presumably explains why it took until April 1999 for Dylan to attempt a band arrangement live. When he did, though, on April 18 in Granada, he delivered one of the great triumphs

---

* According to the studio log, just takes five, eleven, and twenty (incorrectly labelled as nineteen) were complete, with ten long false starts, and seven short false starts.

of the Never Ending Tour, caressing every line like he was back at the Royal Albert Hall playing to the gallery. He may even have improved the song by inverting the lines 'You, you took me in' and 'You loved me then.'

Prior to this 1999 revisitation, though, 'Fourth Time Around' had been a song Dylan only sang when he was in the mood. And that mood came upon him just thrice, post-accident. The one time he attempted it on the Rolling Thunder tours, at Augusta, November 26, 1975, he came caressingly close to its corrosive core. But one-off acoustic versions in 1974 and 1978 rank among Dylan's worst-ever live performances, a drastic contrast to the way he put himself at the service of the song on each and every '66 performance.

{170} SAD-EYED LADY OF THE LOWLANDS

Published lyrics: Writings and Drawings; Lyrics *1985;* Lyrics *2004.*
Known studio recordings: Studio A, Nashville, February 15, 1966 – 4 takes [BOB – tk.4].

> **Journalist:** Are you making up as many songs as you used to?
> **Bob Dylan:** I'm making up as many words as I used to.
> – London Press Conference, May 3, 1966

'Sad-Eyed Lady of the Lowlands' is a thirteen-minute one-trick pony of a song – quite literally just 'chains of flashing images' – and possibly the most pretentious set of lyrics the man ever penned. It is also a captivating carousel of a performance, set all on its own on side four of the positively gregarious *Blonde on Blonde.* Transforming a veritable concordance of nouns into adjectives, Dylan sets out to describe the indescribable 'sad-eyed lady of the lowlands.' After thirteen songs in which his new bride hardly seems to have featured, Dylan remembered to include his first wedding song.

And 'Sad-Eyed Lady of the Lowlands' is very much his

Song of Songs. Like that ancient lyric, his intent seems to be both to abase himself before Her ('Sad-eyed lady, should I wait?') and to suggest that no one else is worthy of Her ('How could they ever, ever persuade you?'). For once, there can be little doubt that Sara Dylan is the immediate subject of his paean. Dylan says so, albeit in 1975's 'Sara,' a song that adheres to facts about as well as the first volume of his autobiography. Who can forget the roar that greeted those lines – 'Staying up for days in the Chelsea Hotel / Writing "Sad Eyed Lady of the Lowlands" for you' – whenever he sang them on the Rolling Thunder tour several weeks before the song's release?

In fact there is an overwhelming amount of anecdotal evidence that suggests Dylan did nothing of the sort. He may have come up with that magnetic chorus at their Chelsea love nest, but the bulk of the song was written in Tennessee from February 15 through the wee hours of the next morning, while Nashville's most expensive session musicians played cards and wondered what kind of songwriter turns up to record a song he's not yet written. Bassist Charlie McCoy told biographer Bob Spitz, 'When he first came in, he had his manager Al Grossman and his organ player Al Kooper. Everybody was introduced and he asked us if we'd mind waiting a . . . minute while he worked on a song. So we all went out and let him have the studio to himself. He ended up staying in there working on that song for six hours.' Actually it was eight hours, but who's counting?

Three years later, being uncharacteristically sincere, Dylan suggested he lost his way during the writing process and forgot what it was he had set out to do: 'It started out as just a little thing, "Sad-Eyed Lady of the Lowlands," but I got carried away somewhere along the line. I just sat down at a table and started writing. At the session itself. And I just got carried away with the whole thing. . . . I just started writing and I couldn't stop. After a period of time, I forgot what it was all about, and I started trying to get back to the beginning.'

He never figured out a suitable resolution, driven as he was by an all-consuming desire to stretch (beyond) the bounds of song itself. 'Carried away' or not, it seems Dylan consciously set out to make the song something else. He had informed one press conference, two months earlier, that he was interested in 'writing [a] symphony . . . with different melodies and different words, different ideas, all being the same, which just roll on top of each other and underneath each other . . . the end result being a total[ity]. . . . They say my songs are long now. Some time [I'm] just gonna come up with one that's gonna be one whole album, consisting of one song.' 'Sad-Eyed Lady of the Lowlands' was not quite 'one whole album.' Nor is 'the end result' symphonic – it never departs from a single melodic idea – but it was nonetheless a daunting experience for the musicians when Dylan finally got them to put down their cards and start earning their keep, around four o'clock the morning of the sixteenth (the musicians had been there since six the previous evening).

Drummer Ken Buttrey explains the extent of Dylan's instructions: 'We'll do a verse and a chorus then I'll play my harmonica thing. Then we'll do another verse and chorus and I'll play some more harmonica, and we'll see how it goes from there.' This being Nashville, no one supposed the song would last longer than your average pop song, though they should perhaps have considered the seven-minute song recorded the day before, 'Visions of Johanna.' Buttrey says, 'After about ten minutes of this thing, we're cracking up at each other, at what we were doing, I mean, . . . where do we go from here?' Yet keep going they did. The very first take is logged as complete, as are two of the other three versions recorded in just an hour and a half, after an exhausting day (and night) of inactivity. While the musicians crawled off to bed, Dylan began working on the lyrics to the next song he was hoping to record.

Initially, Dylan was convinced he'd pulled off something quite remarkable (which in a way he had). He told Robert Shelton a couple of weeks later, on a flight to Denver, '["Sad-Eyed Lady"] is the best song I've ever written. Wait till you hear the whole thing.' (He would get a personal preview later that evening. Dylan pulled out his guitar and began to play it. After the second breakdown, he informed Shelton, 'I hope you're getting the idea.') When the acetates were cut for the (almost) finished album in Los Angeles in early April, the first song he elected to play was 'Sad-Eyed Lady.' Attendant journalist Jules Siegel recalls that when the song came on, 'he said, "Just listen to that! That's old-time religious carnival music!" He was just thrilled with his own work.'

Not surprisingly, though, it was never a song that lent itself to live recreation. Having written and recorded it in under a day, he simply couldn't conceive of conditions auspicious enough to divine a similar inspiration. However, it was a song he occasionally liked to rehearse. There is a haltingly marvellous stab at it in Dylan's 1977 movie, *Renaldo and Clara*, part of the lengthy 'Woman in White' sequence. Derived from 1975 rehearsals with Rolling Thunder core musicians Scarlet Rivera, Rob Stoner, and Howie Wyeth, Dylan mixes up his lines, and slurs everything but the chorus, yet still seems on the verge of tapping into that wild mercury moment again. In January 1978 the song was again rehearsed for another travelling medicine show, though no recording of that moment is known. By then, the sad-eyed lady had returned all of her hero's votive offerings.

Published lyrics: Writings and Drawings; Lyrics *1985;* Lyrics *2004.*
Known studio recordings: Studio A, Nashville, February 16,
1966 – 20 takes [BOB – tk.20][NDH – tk.5].
First known performance: Pensacola, FL, April 28, 1976.

> I used to have to go after a song, seek it out. But now, instead
> of going to it, I stay where I am and let everything disappear
> and the song rushes to me. Not just the music, the words,
> too. . . . What I'm doing now you can't learn by studying,
> you can't copy it.
> – Dylan to Margaret Steen, January 1966

Generally the *Blonde on Blonde* songs recorded after
'Visions of Johanna' do not take that song as a template
for their own ventures into the unknown (what Rimbaud
called that 'ecstatic flight through things unheard of, [and]
unnameable'), making it a breakthrough song he never
took any further. Even Dylan felt he was fast approaching
the outer limits of this particular region. Barely days before
that inspired vision came he had told a friend, 'I'll continue
making the records. [But] they're not gonna be any better
from now on. They're gonna be just different, that's all. . . .
When I made my last record before this [one], I still knew
what I wanted to do on my next record. I don't know what
I'm gonna do on my next record, but I know it's gonna be the
same kind of thing.'

'Stuck Inside of Mobile' is the one song recorded in
Nashville that suggested Dylan might still go further
exploring both his own psyche and the form he'd made a
habit of reinventing. A masterpiece of the first order, it was
proof positive, were it needed, that his claim he'd given up
any attempt at perfection (on the rear sleeve of *Bringing It*

. . .) hadn't stopped him pursuing it. And yet the surviving draft to the song – part typed, part handwritten, in keeping with most songs from this period – hardly suggests another 'ecstatic flight.' The page begins with 'honey but it's just too hard,' an image Dylan had been trying to jam into a song since the previous October. Then, as Wilentz observes, 'the words meander through random combinations and disconnected fragments and images ("people just get uglier"; "banjo eyes"; "he was carrying a 22 but it was only a single shot"), until, amid many crossings-out, there appears, in Dylan's own hand, "Oh MAMA you're here IN MOBILE ALABAMA with the Memphis blues again."' The blue touch-paper had finally been lit.

Dylan still dared to think he could flesh out the song in the studio, before *and* during the recording process. In fact, the fifth take recently issued on *No Direction Home: The Bootleg Series Vol. 7* (*sic*) suggests he was trying to do both. On a superficial level, it is the same song it would be fifteen takes later, minus the little organ fugue Kooper initially played between the verses, and with the refrain tightened up. 'This might be the end / I'm stuck down in Mobile / with the Memphis blues again' becomes that most pregnant of queries, 'Can this *really* be the end? / To be stuck inside of Mobile . . .,' the change to 'Stuck *inside of* Mobile' actually occurring midtake. (He starts singing this on the fourth verse of the take and never goes back.)

So despite using the studio as a writing lab – it was four in the morning before the record button got pushed again – it is the song's arrangement, and not its lyrics, that occupies the musicians through the wee small hours. With a plane to catch, he knew he had just one three-hour session to get it right, but just as frustration begins to set in, they turn mercury to gold on the twentieth take (listed as take fourteen!).

Dylan knew 'Stuck Inside of Mobile' was one of those fortunate instances where the song rushed to him when required. Like 'Visions of Johanna,' it was never going to be one that lent itself to the blunderbuss blast of the Hawks, and was never attempted live with them. It was only when Dylan realized he was a day or two away from playing a show in Mobile, Alabama, in the spring of 1976, that he decided to work out an arrangement with the Rolling Thunder veterans that would suit both the sound of Guam (the band's nickname) and those psychedelic syllables.

The 1976 arrangement, almost as raucous as a contemporary 'Lay, Lady, Lay,' might have suited a basement-tape song better, but at least it reminded Dylan of the song's enduring allure. He was further reminded of the need to coax the song's charms out in July 1987, when the Grateful Dead defused all the drama at the half-a-dozen shows they shared with a curiously disembodied Dylan. The Heartbreakers gave it some much-needed resuscitation at European shows three months later. And then, for the first six years of the Never Ending Tour, Dylan tried to give it that onstage *Highway 61* sound. Generally, though, these versions resembled a phantom engineer struggling to get back to Memphis.

{172} **WHEN YOU WALKED AWAY**

{173} **YOU CAN'T GET YOUR WAY ALLA TIME**

{174} **LIKE A RICH MAN'S SON**

#172 – Published in Isis *#46 in Xerox form; photographically reproduced in* Isis *#120.*

After the February sessions, Dylan had just three weeks before another ninety-six-hour block of studio time, in which he was determined to complete *Highway 61 Revisited*'s successor. In that period he would write the eight songs that bulk up *Blonde on Blonde* and start at least three others, listed above, none of which ever got onto tape. Initially he concentrated on typing out 'song ideas,' perhaps hoping to ensure there would be a thematic balance to the material released.

What we have here, on three separate sheets of paper, are jumping-off points for songs. I've put the number at three, but one could easily double that. We also get a verse apiece to two songs he would record and release ('Absolutely Sweet Marie' and 'Most Likely You Go Your Way') scribbled across the typed pages, along with stray lines later found in 'Obviously Five Believers' and 'Temporary Like Achilles.' These sheets thus form part of the same set of papers as drafts of 'Stuck Inside of Mobile,' 'Absolutely Sweet Marie,' 'Just Like a Woman,' 'I Want You,' and 'Obviously Five Believers' known to collectors – plus the 'clean copy' of 'Temporary Like Achilles' auctioned in the mideighties (reproduced in my 1987 edition of *Stolen Moments: Dylan Day-by-Day*).

The person who acquired all of this material chose, for financial reasons, *not* to keep everything together, preferring to break it up and sell it off piecemeal at assorted auctions, spanning almost a decade, doing something of a disservice to any future Dylan scholar. Like the Dude, the suspicion abides that these papers were obtained surreptitiously. Perhaps Dylan left them behind at his hotel (or had them stolen from his room) on his second trip to Nashville in March. Nowhere near as complete as the *Another Side* materials, the drafts are either the product of a single waste-bin or Dylan *really* did write a lot in the studio.

Two sets of ideas can be found at the bottom of one typed page, headed by what was probably a provisional song title, 'You Can't Get Your Way Alla [i.e., all of the] Time.' Whether this title relates in any way to a first set of disconnected lyrics is unclear, but none of the lines link to any known completed song. Each line of thought is left hanging, including, 'I'd go all the way with you, but . . .,' and, 'when the dawn comes, i am not alone anymore.' Perhaps he is already taking too much 'powerful medicine' (to use his own phrase). One line reads more like a shorthand diary: 'vibrate / chemicals . . . lazy afternoon'; another couplet is pure country: 'I'm sitting here thinking / after doing [some] drinking.'

Below this he begins to type not lyrics per se, but rather possible titles and *themes* for songs (presumably not yet written). These begin with 'PLEDGING MY TIME' (capitalized) and 'mama youre so hard' (lowercase) and are followed by 'White Love & . . . song,' 'Yellow Monday . . . Song' and 'i did it so you wouldnt have to (do it) SONG.' Things get stranger still as he types out what appear to be six further song titles, numbered:

1. Corss fire [Cross fire]
2. Hey Baby
3. Jullieta
4. You Go Your Way, I'll Go Mine
5. Love Will Endire [Endure]
6. Little Baby

One might be inclined to discount these song-titles were it not that one of these became a known song (#4). I'd be curious to know what happened to 'Jullieta' and friends. Meanwhile, another scrawled couplet at the top of the page reads, 'Going down to [?tractor] parts / Fix all these women broken hearts to run.' At the bottom of the page, Dylan has written out by hand the bridge to 'Absolutely Sweet Marie' ('the riverboat captain' section). Further evidence of a mile-a-minute mind.

All of this would be tantalizing enough in its own right. But there is another typed sheet, headed by the couplet, 'like a rich man's son / like a poor fool in his prime' – a recognizable prototype for what *became* 'Temporary Like Achilles' (the 'rich man's son' being converted to 'a rich man's child'). Yet the song in question no more became 'Temporary Like Achilles' than 'Medicine Sunday' did. A reference to 'five fevers / & fourteen believers' suggests he is still cross-breeding lines to various songs. The first image appears in 'Absolutely Sweet Marie,' the second in 'Obviously Five Believers.'

He then sets about developing something around a repeated refrain that informs some unfortunate lass, 'You know I'm running with the devil / running with your lover.' Still being cruel to be kind, he reminds 'her' of her once-virgin charms: 'it's nothing to be ashamed about . . . when you lost your innocence.' The idea peters out, though, or perhaps migrates to another song, for at the bottom of the page is another random couplet, 'you say disturb me & you don't deserve me / well honey some-times you lie' – a starting point for 'You Go Your Way, I'll Go Mine.'

A third sheet from the same cache of papers, offered for auction shortly before the others (circa 1991), confirms that a lot of the ideas he generated in this manic phase wandered down dead-end streets. It also suggests that like the *Another Side* songs two years earlier, Dylan was starting songs on one sheet then wandering off at a tangent, only to return to the original idea on another piece of paper. The 1966 page comprises a typed set of verses on one side, the first two numbered, and a handwritten lyric bearing a familiar refrain ('how does it feel?') on the reverse. (The use of this familiar refrain led to the sheet in question being auctioned as an unknown lyric circa 1965, but it clearly comes from 1966.) The first handwritten verse is perfectly intelligible, suggesting a song that still has some-where it might go:

When you walked away, I just excused you,
Tho' you said you'd stand by me,
When I had to tell the people
Cho[o]se between the ground and the sea.

The opening line to another verse continues the same thought flow, 'I must cho[o]se between the forest and the ocean' – an allusion to the coda from 'Once I Had a Sweetheart' previously adapted for 'Ballad in Plain D.' But after this the song quickly loses all sense of direction, meandering off into the woods, as Dylan tries to tie together images of 'my home . . . carved in wood' and 'setting fire to the water.'

Over the page Dylan continues typing paradoxical couplets similar to those that had served him well in the past year. '[N]ow the scorpion & the sandmen . . . when they find their eyes can't speak' (a promising train of thought) becomes 'i got a bluebird with one lonesome scorpion' (less promising), only to descend into the kind of recrimination/s he could slot into any old song: 'I've followed your instructions & I'm here now / just like you told me to be / for seeing things they say i do not see. . . .' Left there, it becomes another tantalizing thought dangling in the breeze.

{175} ABSOLUTELY SWEET MARIE

Published lyrics: Writings and Drawings; Lyrics 1985; Lyrics 2004.
First known performance: Concord Pavilion, June 7, 1988.
Known studio recordings: Studio A, Nashville, March 7, 1966 – 3 takes + insert [BOB].

The musicians who awaited Dylan's return to Nashville three weeks on from the first set of gruelling sessions must have been pleasantly surprised to find that this time he had a more traditional set of songs he hoped to record. 'Absolutely Sweet Marie,' the first of these, recorded in a single session on the evening of the seventh, also exists in manuscript form. Entirely handwritten on a single page, the lyrics are largely complete, save for the first verse, which lacks its 'railroad gate,' having 'your eagle's teeth' instead (the line survives to the first studio take, when Dylan sings, 'And the eagle's teeth / Down above the train line').

He also had yet to figure out how to make 'the promises you left, that [he] gave to me' less of a mouthful, while 'Yes, I can see you left him here for me' is clearly intended to rhyme with that redoubtable refrain, 'Where are you tonight, sweet Marie?' Indeed each verse ends with the -ee rhyme, and the song is logged as 'Where Are You Tonight, Sweet Marie?' Yet the line appears nowhere in the manuscript or on that first, tentative take.

Also absent from the initial draft is a four-line bridge invoking the riverboat captain, though he suggests it's there in his head by scribbling two lyrical prompts: 'they all know my fate' and 'they gonna have to wait.' And as we know, the bridge appears on another draft page (see above), so it presumably came to him while he was thinking about other songs. With the bridge in place, he cut the song with minimum fuss at the first March session. Though the band changed keys between takes, it took just four takes (and an insert) to realize one of Dylan's most melodically inviting songs.

Despite its obvious pop sensibility and compulsive melody (so compulsive it served Steve Harley for his own number-one single, 'Come Up and See Me (Make Me Smile)'), Dylan duly left the song behind in Nashville, refraining from playing it live for some twenty-two years. In that time it acquired garage-punk status thanks to two memorable cover versions. The Flamin' Groovies put it on 1979's *Jumpin' in the Night*, and five years later Jason and the Scorchers kicked off their debut mini-album *Fervor* with their compulsive cow-punk rendition. The Scorchers' radio-friendly revival probably reminded Dylan just what he had discarded, because on the opening night of the Never Ending Tour, at Concord Pavilion on June 7, 1988, he finally took his own Marie out of the garage.

{176} JUST LIKE A WOMAN

Published lyrics: Writings and Drawings; Lyrics *1985;* Lyrics *2004.*
Known studio recordings: Studio A, Nashville, March 8, 1966 [BOB].
First known performance: Vancouver, March 26, 1966.

'Just Like a Woman' is another song found among the *Blonde on Blonde* papers, though this time it is some way away from the finished song, with no evidence of a chorus to be seen for love nor money. What Dylan does have is most of the first verse (minus 'from her curls'); a single couplet from the second ('nobody has to guess / baby can't be blessed'); another from the final verse ('when we meet again, introduced as friends / don't let on you knew me when'); and just a single line of the bridge: 'I'm dying here of thirst . . .' All of these lines he tapped out on a single sheet, the last of which is typed the other way up, apparently part of a separate set of lyrics – for yet another *ménage à trois* in song – to which the lines, 'how come you both lied to me,' and, 'he never said he'd live forever / he'd just make a fuss over all of us / but it's just you and me,' also apparently belonged.

Rather than going further with this line of thought, Dylan takes the 'dying here of thirst' line, turns the page over, takes up a pen, and begins to write out what he clearly marks as '(bridge)': 'it was raining from the first / And I'm dying here of thirst / what's worse is this pain in here / I won't stay in here,' to which he attaches an unrelated couplet, 'she's my friend / see her again.' But there is still no sign of that memorable chorus, 'She takes / aches / breaks just like a woman / little girl.'

In all likelihood, 'Just Like a Woman' was one song Dylan continued writing in his Nashville hotel room (from whence said papers probably came) as Al Kooper sat at the piano playing the melody over and over again. If the draft does come from Nashville, then the song's chorus was another last-minute formulation. Wilentz's recent lecture on the *Blonde on Blonde* sessions seemingly confirms this. He describes an early take in which Dylan is singing what can only be described as dummy lyrics. As he states, 'On several early takes, Dylan sang disconnected lines and semi gibberish. He was unsure about what the person described in the song does that is just like a woman, rejecting "shakes," "wakes," and "makes mistakes."'

As with his 'first' electric session fifteen months earlier, Dylan refused to get bogged down by just one song, and around two in the afternoon, he took a break from 'Just Like a Woman' – after trying 'a weird, double time fourth take, somewhere between Bo Diddley and Jamaican ska.' Only after recording 'Pledging My Time' does he return to 'Just Like a Woman,' around nine in the evening. But the song still needed work, being fifteen takes away from the finished version.

Dylan has never felt inclined to elucidate what exactly it is 'Baby' can learn from 'Queen Mary.' The reference to Baby's penchant for 'fog . . . amphetamine and . . . pearls' (which he originally sang as, 'I gave you those pearls') again suggests Sedgwick, or some similar debutante. Queen Mary herself certainly could be a confidant of the androgynous Queen Jane. And the one time Dylan prefaced the song in concert with a short rap, at the Warfield in San Francisco in November 1980, he implied the song's subject was another 'woman' with jet-pilot eyes:

The other night I was standing out backstage, and this guy came up to me and said, 'Do you remember that woman that came up to you about an hour ago with long red hair?' And I said, 'Yes, I remember that woman.' He said, 'She sure was pretty, wasn't she?' 'Yes, she was alright.' He said, 'That was me.' . . . 'Nobody feels any pain. . . .'

The theory that the 'woman' in 'Just Like a Woman' is actually a man has been around since the early seventies, appearing in the crank theories section of Michael Gray's (very first) *Song and Dance Man*. And one should never discount the possibility Dylan was having a little fun at fans' expense in his 1980 rap. But the song *was* completed within days of 'Temporary Like Achilles,' which explicitly refers to one character as 'hungry like a man in drag.'

Something risqué *is* clearly going on in the song, but Dylan ain't saying what. Even thirty-eight years later, he firmly told Robert Hilburn, 'Even if I could tell you what ["Just Like a Woman"] was about, I wouldn't. It's up to the listener to figure out what it means to him. . . . This is a very broad song. . . . It's like a lot of blues-based songs. Somebody may be talking about a woman, but they're not really talking about a woman at all. . . . It's a city song. . . . I don't think in lateral [*sic*] terms as a writer. . . . I always try to turn a song on its head. Otherwise, I figure I'm wasting the listener's time.'

One thing is apparent: Dylan felt a personal connection to this song from the first. As late as 1995 he was singing it with all the passion and persistence of a still-hungry man. And though it is one of his most-covered songs, he told old friend Mary Travers on a 1975 radio show, 'Personally, I don't understand why anybody would want to do ["Just Like a Woman"] – except me.' And yet barely had he written the thing when he turned up at the Whisky a Go Go in Hollywood, hoping to convince Otis Redding he should record it. Sadly he never did, though the little organ intro Redding uses on his version of 'White Christmas' sounds awfully familiar.

'Just Like a Woman' is also one of just two Dylan songs Van Morrison has consistently performed live. Intriguingly, every time the c*** elects to sing it (and he was still singing it in 2000), he sings, 'There's a queer in here,' instead of, 'I can't stay in here.' Does he know some scuttlebutt about the song's composition that he can't resist alluding to? He did, after all, spend a lot of time hanging with the guys from The Band in Woodstock, circa 1969–70.

Any whisper Morrison heard would surely have come from Robbie Robertson, who accompanied Dylan to Nashville and was there when he played the song to Robert Shelton in a Denver hotel room four days after recording it. None of the other Hawks were at the Nashville sessions, nor were they party to any of the 1966 live performances, which were solo acoustic (and intensely introspective). A recent addition to YouTube has been a complete performance of the song from Dublin (the one on the famous *While the Establishment Burns* bootleg). Anyone who doubts that this is a Song of Experience should just watch this particular harmonica break, which really does sound like a little girl sob-sob-sobbing.

{177} PLEDGING MY TIME

Published lyrics: Writings and Drawings; Lyrics *1985;* Lyrics *2004.*
First known performance: Modena, September 12, 1987.
Known studio recordings: Studio A, Nashville, March 8, 1966 [BOB].

'PLEDGING MY TIME if nothing comes outa this, you'll soon know' is just one of the single-line 'song ideas' on the 'You Can't Get Your Way' sheet. It is perfectly possible that all Dylan had at this stage was the title (surely a knowing reference to the Johnny Ace classic, 'Pledging My Love'); a single couplet he could incorporate into a third verse ('And if it don't work out / You'll be the first to know'); and the idea of making a pledge to a girl, hoping she'll also come through. Another song constructed from leftover strands from the blues, this song came together with no great birth pangs, being cut in four takes while the band took a breather from 'Just Like a Woman.'

Yet 'Pledging My Time' was not what the song was called when Dylan and the Nashville musicians made their first pass at it, after struggling to extract *l'essence de jusqu' à la femme (sic)*. According to the studio log, the song was called 'What Can You Do for My Wigwam?' which would be weird enough were it not the name of the very song country-picker Pete Rowan recalled witnessing Dylan record in Nashville, when interviewed in July 1966 (the interview was not published until December 1978, and the studio logs were not accessed until the midnineties).

Rowan said that when he arrived, Dylan was recording a long blues, with one line that went 'the lady took a trip with a tramp, that's a hobo,' and that Dylan's wife was at the session, as were two drummers, one of whom was badly out of time. And he remembered Dylan calling out the title of the song, 'What Can I Do for Your Wigwam, Right?' Wilentz makes no mention of an alternate lyric or two drummers, but he does confirm that the song was quite different at the outset, being a 'boogie-woogie piano number' before Robertson and pianist 'Pig' Robbins started pledging themselves, too. I presume the song took shape before any tape started rolling, so what Rowan heard may well no longer exist.

Another *Blonde on Blonde* song that Dylan seemingly forgot for two decades, 'Pledging My Time' was revisited in September 1987, when Dylan again seemed in the grip of 'a poison headache,' but was refusing to hold back. Subsequent Never Ending Tour versions have been little more than an excuse for a blues jam, though the debt to Jimmy Reed's 'Bright Lights, Big City' has become a lot more obvious with these later live incarnations.

Note: The only real loss on the album take is that dynamite harmonica coda, which has been needlessly truncated. A longer fade can be found on the Dutch *Greatest Hits Vol. 3*.

{178} MOST LIKELY YOU GO YOUR WAY (AND I'LL GO MINE)

Published lyrics: Writings and Drawings; Lyrics *1985;* Lyrics *2004.*
First known performance: Chicago Stadium, January 3, 1974.
Known studio recordings: Studio A, Nashville, March 9, 1966 [BOB].

Another song that Dylan name-checked on one of the draft song lists, 'Most Likely You Go Your Way' constitutes part of the 'Rich Man's Son' typescript, Dylan again tuning his receiver to this song's setting while musing about another. When the song comes through, it is slightly scrambled. He has most of the second verse ('you say you disturb me and you don't deserve me') and the fourth ('you say you're sorry for telling stories'), plus one key element from its chorus ('let you pass / time will tell / who has fell'). But just like 'Just Like a Woman' and 'Sweet Marie,' he refrains from revealing the song's punch line – already listed as 'You Go Your Way, I'll Go Mine.'

The released version was recorded on March 9 as part of another marathon session. According to the session sheets, the studio was block-booked from six in the evening to seven the following morning. In that time Dylan recorded five new songs, while also finding time to cut a satisfactory 'Leopard-Skin Pillbox Hat.' Unfortunately, we lack studio logs from the session/s, but 'Most Likely You Go Your Way' was recorded between six and nine in the evening. And it made a perfect opener for the third side of the double-album Dylan was now able to produce.

It also served as the first and last song on most nights of

the 1974 tour, which announced his live return. Between that false dawn and the start of the Never Ending Tour, fourteen years later, it was only tried out during rehearsals for a TV 'in concert' in April 1976 and at rehearsals for the 1978 world tour, never gaining live relief. It was eventually restored to performance duties in 1989, initially as a show opener. By then time had told who'd been felled.

{179} TEMPORARY LIKE ACHILLES

Published lyrics: Writings and Drawings; Lyrics *1985;* Lyrics *2004.*
Known studio recordings: Studio A, Nashville, March 9, 1966 [BOB].

There is plenty of evidence that Dylan had been looking to write a song containing the *double entendre* 'Honey, why are you so hard?' as its refrain since at least October 1965. As for the line, 'Hungry like a man in drag,' Dylan used that very expression in conversation with a listener on Bob Fass's radio show in late January 1966. Both lines appear on the draft list of possible songs before Dylan connects the two, initially typing, '(you're so hard) man in drag,' then adding, as a second image, 'helpless like rich man's child.' On another typescript he had already chanced upon the couplet, 'like a rich man's son / like a poor fool in his prime,' lines he now adapted to Achilles' cause. Not only is 'Mama you're so hard' put down as a working title, but Dylan also adds a beautiful telegraphed description of the song he's planning to write: a 'guilty for being there (or else – man feel down –) "song."'

By the time the song was recorded on the ninth, Dylan had four verses and a bridge, every line of which is riddled with guilt and depression. He also had a title, 'Like Achilles.' But what becomes another *ménage à trois* song, with a dose of that faintly debauched *BOB* atmosphere, still awaits last-minute changes. A clean copy of the finished lyrics has Achilles 'pointing to the flag,' not 'the sky' (thus rhyming with 'hungry like a man in drag'). And the narrator, who begins by 'lean[ing] against your window' – asking, 'How come you send me out and have me barred?' – ends up on the receiving end of far worse treatment: 'I get beat up and sent back by the guard.' Also, when the narrator encounters Achilles 'in your hallway,' he demands of Her, 'How come you get *him* to be your guard?'

Even here, though, the patriotic-transvestite Trojan is destined to win the day. We are back in 'Fourth Time Around' territory – the protagonists even share the same hallway. And this time, the narrator finds himself on the wrong side of 'your velvet door.' Once the song has used up a number of stray sexual innuendos – even the scorpion from 'When You Walked Away' makes an appearance – Dylan moves on. Of the *Blonde on Blonde* songs, 'Like Achilles' is the only one that has never even appeared in tour rehearsals, being left alone 'like a poor fool in his prime.'

{180} RAINY DAY WOMEN #12 & 35

Published lyrics: Writings and Drawings; Lyrics 1985; Lyrics 2004.
Known studio recordings: Studio A, Nashville, March 9, 1966 [BOB].
First known performance/s: Isle of Wight, August 31, 1969.

It may open his seventh album, but 'Rainy Day Women #12 & 35' always seemed like one of those songs Dylan largely made up on the spot to fill out the double-album he now seemed set on. Using a fairly lame pun to avoid being banned on the radio – the idea of being physically stoned for committing a sin, as opposed to being stoned on 'powerful medicine' – it represents his first overt drug song. This gives him leave to construct a series of activities, both banal and bizarre, on which he can hang the song's simple but subversive message, 'Everybody must get stoned!'

According to Al Kooper in *Backstage Passes*, it was not actually Dylan's idea to turn the song into a revivalist sing-along: 'Dylan was teachin' us [the] song one night when [producer Bob] Johnston suggested it would sound great Salvation Army style. Dylan thought it over and said it might work. But where would we get hornplayers at this hour? "Not to worry," says Charlie McCoy and grabs the phone. It's 4.30 a.m. when he makes the call. . . . At 5 a.m. in walks a trombone player. . . . He sat down and learned the song, they cut three takes, and at 5.30 he was out of the door and gone.' Actually the song appears to have been cut around one in the morning, but that's close enough for Al.

Given its Old Testament connotations, the 'Salvation Army style' backing served to make the joke that much better. And Dylan reinforced these connotations with the assigned song title. He knew he could never get away with calling it 'Everybody Must Get Stoned!' The Byrds were about to get wiped off the airwaves for calling their latest masterpiece 'Eight Miles High.' And the working title, 'A Long Haired Mule and a Porkepine,' was probably not a serious contender. He culled its eventual title from chapter 27, verse 15, of the book of Proverbs, which contains a number of edicts for which one could get genuinely stoned, one of which reads, in the King James version, 'A continual dropping in a very rainy day and a contentious woman are [much] alike.' Ever the wit, Dylan does not actually call the song 'Rainy Day Women #27 & 15,' though we clearly have another 'mathematical song' here.

Amazingly, this afterthought to the sessions duly became the man's biggest hit. Climbing to number two in the U.S. singles chart, it would provide a soundtrack of sorts to the silence that ensued after the accident. After he returned to the stage in 1974, it received a raucous Band arrangement at every single show on that tour, as Dylan mixed his metaphors up some more. Even after he wrote the song's sequel, 'Gotta Serve Somebody,' in 1979, the song continued to enjoy sporadic favour. Indeed, on one occasion in 1992 (Warfield Theatre, San Francisco, May 4), he decided not to sing any of the lyrics but left it as one long instrumental opener. On another occasion, in 1991 (South Bend, Indiana, November 6), he even sang the lyrics to 'Watching the River Flow' over the original 1966 tune (I kid you not).

{181} OBVIOUSLY FIVE BELIEVERS

Published lyrics: Writings and Drawings; Lyrics *1985;* Lyrics *2004.*
Known studio recordings: Studio A, Nashville, March 9, 1966 – 4 takes [BOB – tk.4].
First known performance: Palm Springs, May 15, 1995.

A handwritten 'working manuscript' of 'Obviously Five Believers,' auctioned by Christie's in the early nineties, provides another valuable scrap from the *Blonde on Blonde* hoard. Again the song is largely complete, though there are plenty of crossings-out, including an abandoned sixth verse. He also refrains from mentioning 'five believers.' At this stage he confines himself to 'just on[e] midget' and 'sixteen jugglers dressed like men,' who are 'all [his] friends.' The final line of the first verse also makes a more direct plea – 'I could make it without you, but I do wish you'd come home.' But rather than continuing the first rumination (and indeed the chorus to 'Rainy Day Women'), he ends up recording, '. . . if I just didn't feel so all alone.' Otherwise, the scrawled lyrics are pretty much as Dylan recorded them, under the working title of 'Black Dog Blues.'

The third 'straight' blues recorded at the March sessions, 'Five Believers' was the one that occupied him least, being the kind of song he could write while not quite asleep, but on the nod. Though every song recorded in Nashville is to some extent reliant on the Music Row musicians for its magic – even 'Visions of Johanna' – 'Five Believers' is entirely *dependent* on them. Dylan wasn't prepared to get hung up by the song, and when it initially broke down, he told the musicians, 'This is very easy, man. . . . I don't wanna spend no time with this song.' The musicians pick it up almost immediately, and in four takes we have 'Five Believers,' one of three songs recorded from midnight to three on that final morning (along with 'Rainy Day Women' and the released 'Leopard-Skin Pillbox Hat').

Twenty years on, Dylan finally decided to play the song – on the radio phone-in show, *Rockline* – claiming it was one of his favourites. Yet he had not felt the slightest urge to run through a live version during a decade of almost solid touring. It would take another ten years for a concert performance to occur, but when it did, it was in good company, alongside equally welcome restorations of 'Tombstone Blues' and 'Pledging My Time.'

{182} I WANT YOU

Published lyrics: Writings and Drawings; Lyrics 1985; Lyrics 2004.
Known studio recordings: Studio A, Nashville, March 9, 1966 – 5 takes [BOB – tk.5].
First known performance: San Antonio, May 11, 1976.

'I Want You' was apparently the last song recorded for *Blonde on Blonde*, occupying the last four hours – from three to seven A.M. on the tenth – as the clock ticked down to Dylan's departure for St. Louis to resume his American tour. After recording loose-end blues and a 'Sally Army' sing-along, Dylan finally returned to the kind of edgy excursion that had occupied him with songs like 'Just Like a Woman' and 'One of Us Must Know.' 'I Want You' certainly has that three A.M. feel about it, as he admits to a physical desire previously kept abstract ('Sad-Eyed Lady') or asexual ('Love Minus Zero').

According to Kooper, it was a song Dylan had been playing around with for some time, deliberately leaving it last 'to bug him.' The existing manuscript suggests, rather, that Dylan was still working on the song, containing lines like, 'The deputies I see they went / Your father's ghost . . . to ha[u]nt / Just what it is that / Want from you,' indicating a sketch in progress. When he does start recording, however, the lyrics are largely in place, and it takes just five takes to wrap up his latest, substantive dream.

'I Want You' suggests someone still tempted to love the one he's with, even when he'd 'like to be' somewhere else. Again he can't resist introducing a queen to the proceedings, 'the Queen of Spades,' who along with her chambermaid provides displaced solace for the lonely narrator. Nor does he refrain from reinstating the archetypal 'other suitor' – this one a 'dancing child with his Chinese suit' – who dogs his steps throughout.

Dylan's lyrical depiction of the 'dancing child' has fueled the theory that he is describing Brian Jones of Rolling Stones fame. The 'Chinese suit,' the 'flute' (Jones being the Stones' multi-instrumentalist), and the reference to how 'time was on his side' ('Time Is on My Side' being the Stones' first U.S. hit) lends some substance to this supposition. Dylan had spent a great deal of time with Jones the previous November, finding out firsthand how insecure this fellow pop star could be. So whom did 'the dancing child' take 'for a ride'? Both Jones and Dylan were still friendly with Nico. Or are we back to 'the real heroine of *Blonde on Blonde*'? Intriguingly the verse has generally been omitted in its live incarnations, as if no longer relevant.

The Dylan who delivers the chorus is *hurtin'*. The need is real – real enough for Dylan to generally give the song an inflection of real interest when he performs it. The gorgeous tune helps, being a perfect illustration of what he was talking about when he told one reporter, as he started work on *Blonde on Blonde*, that he tended to 'think of [a song] in terms of a whole thing. It's not just pretty words to a tune or putting tunes to words. . . . [It's] the words and the music [together] – I can hear the sound of what I want to say.'

It would take Dylan ten more years to resurrect 'I Want You,' which he finally did on the second Rolling Thunder stint – a series of shows that could qualify as the *Blonde on Blonde* tour (he performed seven of the thirteen songs at these shows). Here it is given more of a clippety-clop arrangement, with pedal steel and audible acoustic guitar providing more of a Nashville feel than the original. Two years later he stripped the song back down – much as Bruce Springsteen had in the winter of 1975 – making a torch ballad of it. Then, in 1987 it was sped up again. Throughout the early stages of the Never Ending Tour, Dylan veered from soulful to speedy, before deciding it (and his vocal cords) might prefer the song as a ballad. By the time of the Supper Club shows in November 1993 (and *Unplugged* shows in 1994) he had returned to doing it in a way that emphasized the agony and ecstasy of his need: 'I wasn't born to lose you. . . . I want you *sooooooo* bad.'

{183} DEFINITIVELY VAN GOGH

Recorded by Robert Shelton in a Denver hotel room, March 13, 1966.

Having started recording the 'last' *Blonde on Blonde* song around three A.M. on March 10, Dylan set about recording more new songs just three days later, at a quite different three A.M. session. This one was in a Denver hotel room, designed to impress would-be biographer Bob Shelton, who had already interrogated the singer for a couple of hours on their flight from Lincoln to Denver. The session provides the first audio evidence of a process Dylan had first adopted the previous fall. As he told one December 1965 press conference, 'Robbie, the lead guitar player, [and I], sometimes we play the guitars together . . . something might come up. . . . I'll be just sitting around playing, so I can write up some words.'

Frustratingly, we have just two *audio vérité* documents of such sessions, though both come *after* the 'completion' of *Blonde on Blonde*, as Dylan continued to use this method to generate new ideas. Australian Rosemary Gerrette has also described a session from Sydney in April 1966: 'I was able to listen to a composing session. Countless cups of tea; none of the group drinks. Things happened, and six new songs were born. The poetry seemed already to have been written. Dylan says, "Picture one of these cats with a horn, coming over the hill at daybreak. Very Elizabethan, you dig? Wearing garters." And out of the imagery, he and the lead guitarist work on a tune.'

The session that Shelton was privileged to witness followed similar lines, Dylan extemporizing around three distinct 'song-ideas.' He also uses it to play Shelton two of the more personal songs just recorded in Nashville, 'Just Like a Woman' and 'Sad-Eyed Lady of the Lowlands.' The first of the brand-new songs he plays for his old buddy is also almost realized. Though it has no obvious title, he ends each verse with a different reference to the painter Vincent Van Gogh ('can he paint like Van Gogh,' 'if she ever sat for Van Gogh,' and so on).

For all his extemporizing skills, it seems quite clear that this quixotic song, which runs to six eight-line verses, cannot be another on-the-spot invention. When he trips over the opening line of verse five – 'It was either her or the straight man who introduced me . . .' – he starts again from the same point, without changing the line. Even when he tries a different melody line he sticks to his earlier account, which he prefaces by telling Shelton, 'This is a great part here. This is the part about Camilla.' The rhymes also sound generally too sophisticated ('Kathleen' with 'half-breed' and 'over' with 'four-leaf clover') to be spur of the moment.

This is a song, and a long one, that Dylan has worked on

before Shelton was allowed to hear it. Which could mean it was a song he had started, but not finished, before the March sessions (was Camilla a close relation of Julietta?) or that he carried on writing songs even after he boarded the plane for St. Louis. Could it be that Dylan had not yet finished working on his seventh set of songs? According to Shelton, Dylan phoned Grossman from the Denver hotel room to inform him, 'I've got five new songs to tape,' which must have taken Albert by surprise. It had been less than seventy-two hours since his folk-rock phenomenon completed eight songs in three days of recording. Yet there *was* a session booked in Dylan's name at Columbia's L.A. studio – now with eight-track capability – for the end of the month (March 30). The session was subsequently cancelled, perhaps because Dylan realized his latest glass of water was brimming over.

For now, though, he continued to stockpile 'song ideas' for this album – or its successor. And stylistically, 'Definitively Van Gogh' stands foursquare with other songs of the period, right from its evocative opening line, 'And I'd ask why the painting was deadly,' down to the unfinished sixth verse, in which we learn that 'Camilla's house stood out of bounds for you / How strange to see the chandelier destroyed.' The relationship between Maria the cook, the half-breed boy who 'makes trips to the north,' and 'a very crooked straight man' is left typically opaque. One senses that Dylan has almost finished the song when the tape cuts (after recording the first four verses at 3 3/4 ips, Shelton knocked the speed of his tape recorder down to 1 7/8, reducing the sound quality of the second part of the tape dramatically). However, it will not be done in Denver. If it ever did make it to the finishing end, no tape recorder was there to capture the moment. When the tape starts up again, Robbie Robertson is making his presence felt, and the pair have started working on another song entirely.

Both songs recorded in a Denver hotel room, March 13, 1966.

As Shelton presses record on his reel-to-reel again, Dylan and Robertson have moved onto a bluesier piece, with a simple enough refrain: 'Don't tell him, tell me.' When that 'song idea' is exhausted, they start on a similar one, 'If you want my love.' The quality of the recording, combined with a great deal of lyrical bluffing from Bob, all but defeats analysis, making a rather frustrating listen. Both songs suggest his muse is back on cruise control, demonstrating no real surges of imagination. Neither song was destined for greater things, and were it not for Shelton's trusty Uher, both would doubtless have been forgotten in the cold glare of a Denver day. Dylan, meanwhile, seemed surprisingly blasé about those songs that slipped away with the dawn, telling one set of pressmen at the time, 'The songs I don't publish, I usually do forget. . . . I have to start over all the time. I can't really keep notes or anything like that.'

{186} WHAT KIND OF FRIEND IS THIS?

Recorded in a Glasgow hotel room, May 19, 1966.

Dylan's decision not to 'keep notes or anything like that' means we have very little idea what kind of songs he continued composing between Denver and the 'last hair-pin curve,' five months away – the same amount of time it took Dylan to write *Blonde on Blonde*. Even touring with a camera crew throughout May failed to yield a great deal, perhaps because filmmaker D. A. Pennebaker felt that, 'unlike *Don't Look Back* . . . this film centred on the stage – he came to life in the middle of that stage and . . . that was really the kind of film we started to make.'

The one exception, a hotel-room session on a rainy afternoon in Glasgow before another night's catharsis, was not filmed by Pennebaker, who was returning from a couple of days in Europe, but by second cameraman and editor, Howard Alk, who had quite different ideas about what they should be filming (it was Alk's idea to interrogate the audience as it left the Free Trade Hall). Thanks to director-for-a-day Alk, Dylan and Robertson are caught on camera working on three 'song ideas' together. And like the Denver hotel session, the first song idea they are working on seems to be fairly fully developed, with a clear structure, just requiring some lightly seasoned lyrics.

Perhaps this is because Dylan acquired the basic idea from Koko Taylor's 1964 recording of 'What Kind of Man Is This?' as Michael Krogsgaard suggests in *Twenty Years of Recording*. I'm not entirely convinced. Original or not – and the song was copyrighted to Dylan alone – it has its share of arche-typal themes for a midsixties Dylan composition: betrayal ('What kind of friend is this? / Laughs at me behind my back'); an inability to take a hint ('Make me holler to and fro. . . . Who wants to go everywhere I wanna go'); and the destructive capabilities of women ('I give her everything and she come back with it all to bits'). Hardly the kind of themes Koko made into a trademark.

Yes, the recorded lyrics are slightly garbled, but nowhere near as garbled as the version transcribed and copyrighted in December 1978 (when *Eat the Document* was due to be broad-cast for the first and last time). The transcriber manages to transmute one line into, 'Well, she ain't good-looking but she keeps on turtle-doving in the backyard bed.' Very *Highway 61*, but not remotely what Dylan sings ('Well, she ain't good lookin' / But she knows how to get [a turtledove] / In a pack of beans'!?). OK, not a whole lot more cogent, but then Dylan is making most of these lyrics up, as indicated by the fuller version available on audio, where he and Robbie can be heard doing a dry run of the first verse, which is merely the sound of syllables clashing, before running the song down for the benefit of Alk's camera.

{187} I CAN'T LEAVE HER BEHIND
{188} ON A RAINY AFTERNOON

Both songs recorded in a Glasgow hotel room, May 19, 1966.

Like 'What Kind of Friend Is This?,' both these 'songs' were copyrighted in 1978, in readiness for broadcast. And like that song, the transcripts are hopeless. Yes, Dylan slides in and out of coherence on both 'songs,' particularly 'On a Rainy Afternoon,' but like 'Tell Me, Momma,' there are telling phrases that shouldn't have defeated His Deafness. In fact, copyrighting them as two separate songs is a slight swindle. They are two streams drawn from the same river, as a more complete tape of the session – acquired from The Band's own booty and bootlegged in the nineties – makes clear.

The *Eat the Document* version of 'On a Rainy Afternoon,' it turns out, is only the first half of the performance, which continues in a slightly more coherent vein after Dylan suggests that Robertson play the same chords but 'twice as slow,' moving ever *sooooo slowly* towards 'I Can't Leave Her Behind.' Even the 'lyrics' are now leaning in that direction: 'I'll be on my way to get it to you / I'll be with my sister, too / I can't find [?] what to do / I'm trying to get a message to you.'

When they finally get to the fragment later copyrighted as 'I Can't Leave Her Behind' – which apparently only exists as the minute-long snippet seen early on in *Eat the Document* – Dylan has decided that, even though she 'leads me where she goes,' he can't live without her. If necessary he will 'stay here night and day,' but he just 'can't leave her behind.' The similarities shared by both 'songs' proved sufficient for Martin Scorsese to include what purported to be a complete 'I Can't

Leave Her Behind' as a bonus feature on the *No Direction Home* DVD. Unfortunately it is no such thing – it is the version of 'On a Rainy Afternoon' already featured in *Eat the Document*. Oops.

1967: I

{ The Basement Tapes }

'When it all came crashing down / I became withdrawn,' the man later claimed. Just not yet. 1967 is qualitatively, and may even be numerically (if we ever get our hands on those missing basement reels), Dylan's most productive year as a songwriter, topping even 1965. It is so creative that I have divided it into two sections, one covering the spring and summer, the other the fall. The basement tape sessions – which began some time in the spring and ran for several months – seem to have taken place in stages, first in Dylan's Red Room, then at the fabled Big Pink house The Band were renting in West Saugerties, and, finally, on Wittenberg Road.

Any order applied to these songs is speculative, though at least in my case it is based on the reels themselves and the order they came in. But, oh, for Garth taking a pen and putting a date or even a number on those precious boxes. No less confusing is how many basement songs there were. Certainly somewhat more than the sixteen songs released officially in 1975. Ten of the fourteen acetate songs, copyrighted pre–John Wesley Harding, form *the cream of the year's homegrown output. Some of these acetate songs – 'I Shall Be Released,' 'The Mighty Quinn,' and 'This Wheel's on Fire' – would become signature songs for other artists, but the original versions stayed underground. Then there are those eternal mysteries, 'I'm Not There' and 'Sign on the Cross,' seemingly among the earliest of the Dylan originals which qualify as more than bacchanalian jams. All in all, a mystery in need of unravelling . . .*

{189} YOU CAN CHANGE YOUR NAME

Rumoured to be recorded in Woodstock, circa spring 1967.

The Dylan of *Chronicles* may well suggest he couldn't get no peace post-crash – even in Peacenik Central, a.k.a. Woodstock – but it actually took nine months after his motorcycle accident before any reporter bothered tracking him down to ask, What gives? It is hard to imagine a figure as central to today's *zeitgeist* being accorded the same respect, if that's the right word. By the spring of 1967, though, the natives were becoming restless, and two New York journalists did make the trek upstate. One was an old friend, Al Aronowitz, and the other a workaday scribe for the *Daily News*, Michael Iachetta, who had interviewed the man once before, four years earlier.

Both found a Dylan talking about writing songs again – but not admitting to recording them! To Iachetta, Dylan proved surprisingly forthright, claiming, 'Songs are in my head like they always are. [But] they're not goin' to get written down until some things are evened up.' Evidently, he had been spending some of his down time reading the contracts he'd signed with his record label and manager. But whereas Dylan had told the *Daily News* reporter he was going to 'have to get better before I do any singing on records,' he was already soliciting Aronowitz's opinion about two songs he had in his head that he'd not yet 'written down.'

Only one of them, though, seems to have had a title – or at least the nub of a song in the making. The lines quoted in Aronowitz's article 'A Family Album,' published in the short-lived *Cheetah*, suggest a re-evaluation of personal goals had definitely occurred during Dylan's recuperation. 'You can change your name / But you can't run away from yourself' sounds like the same man who just told Iachetta, 'What I've been doing mostly is . . . thinkin' about where I'm goin' and why am I runnin' and am I mixed up too much and what am I knowin' and what am I givin' and what am I takin'.' When Aronowitz expressed a preference for the unnamed song over the one quoted, Dylan told Robertson, 'We shouldn't keep any music critics around here. We just lost another song.'

The songs Aronowitz heard firsthand that spring were played to him solo by Dylan, 'sitting at an electric piano . . . [in] a rambling American chateau of mahogany-stained shingles that clung to a mountaintop,' i.e., at his Byrdcliffe home. As an intriguing aside, Aronowitz states elsewhere in his article that 'Dylan [is] writing ten new songs a week, [and] rehearsing them in his living room with Robertson's group [*sic*], the Hawks,' providing confirmation that Dylan and the Hawks were already working in the Red Room, as it was called, rather than the Big Pink basement (actually a garage), where they would relocate later in the summer.

One presumes Aronowitz heard evidence of these 'ten new songs a week' on tape. Hence his enthusiasm. Yet despite allowing Garth's trusty portable reel-to-reel recorder to roll *some* of the time, Dylan stayed true to his word, refusing to let the new songs 'get written down until some things are evened up.' As a result, quite a few more song ideas would slip through the cracks.

{190} **WILD WOLF**

{191} **BETTER HAVE IT ALL**

{192} **YOU OWN A RACEHORSE**

All songs rumoured to have been recorded at either Red Room or Big Pink, West Saugerties, Spring/Summer 1967.

Although rumours of further basement tape excavations won't go away (nor should they – there *are* more reels, at least another nine), there have been no more surprises since the early nineties, when the five-volume *Genuine Basement Tapes* bootleg set first appeared. Alternate mixes, yes. New songs (or takes), no. However, at least two more songs from this period have been copyrighted by Dylan's music publisher, Special Rider, bearing the titles, 'Better Have It All' and 'You Own a Racehorse.' The existence of a recording of the latter was confirmed during a 2002 interview with Band archivist, Garth Hudson, who tantalizingly told one reporter, 'There may still be some things in there. There's one by Bob called "Can I Get a Racehorse?" He thought I had it and I thought he had it. It's there somewhere.' (Sid Griffin, in his *Million Dollar Bash*, adds another title, 'Chilly Winds,' though he does not provide the basis for his information.)

Of other songs covered in this ferric dust, there's just one more we can be pretty sure resides somewhere safe (and hopefully dry). 'Wild Wolf' was one of five 'basement tape' songs copyrighted by Dwarf Music in September 1973 (along with 'Bourbon Street,' 'Santa Fe,' 'Silent Weekend,' and 'All-American Boy'). Quite why these particular songs were copyrighted at this juncture is not clear. Columbia had no rights to the recordings, so it can't have come from them. And as far as we know, Dylan wasn't looking to revisit this material. (When he *did* revisit the tapes – to dig The Band out of a financial hole of their own making, in June 1975 – none of these five songs made the released double-album. 'Wild Wolf' wasn't even one of the thirty-five songs pulled to 'composite' reels producer Rob Fraboni and Robbie Robertson compiled, probably as a short-list of sorts for the projected album.)*

'Wild Wolf' sounds like one of the more enticing oddities of the era, though. Clearly copyrighted from tape, it includes the instruction, '(spoken throughout),' which suggests a relationship to 'basement' songs like 'Stones That You Throw' and 'Clothesline Saga.' It also shares with other original basement-tape songs a tenuous hold on linear thought, making explication all but impossible, though at song's end it would appear that the 'wild wolf' is 'howling his way to morning,' ready to descend into the ruins of a lost city. Meanwhile the singer renounces his role as saviour of said city, suggesting, 'If I was a missionary leader, I would attempt to laugh and rage / Yet the wild wolf he's still bubbling under, and not a babe.' All very ominous, and decidedly left field, even for a cave song.

---

* The full track-listing for those Fraboni-Robertson reels is: 'Odds and Ends,' take 1; 'Nothing Was Delivered,' take 3; 'Odds and Ends,' take 2; 'Get Your Rocks Off'; 'Clothesline Saga'; 'Apple Suckling Tree,' take 1; 'Apple Suckling Tree,' take 2; 'Try Me Little Girl'; 'Young But Daily Growin''; 'Tiny Montgomery'; 'Don't Ya Tell Henry'; 'Bourbon Street'; 'Million Dollar Bash,' take 1; 'Yea! Heavy and a Bottle of Bread,' take 1; 'Million Dollar Bash,' take 2; 'Yea! Heavy and a Bottle of Bread,' take 2; 'I'm Not There'; 'Please Mrs Henry'; 'Crash on the Levee,' take 1; 'Crash on the Levee,' take 2; 'Lo and Behold,' take 1; 'Lo and Behold,' take 2; 'Song for Canada'; 'Baby Ain't That Fine'; 'You Ain't Going Nowhere,' take 1; 'This Wheel's on Fire'; 'You Ain't Going Nowhere,' take 2; 'I Shall Be Released'; 'Too Much of Nothing,' take 1; 'Too Much of Nothing,' take 2; 'Tears of Rage,' take 3; 'Quinn the Eskimo,' take 1; 'Open the Door Homer,' take 3; 'Nothing Was Delivered,' take 1; 'Folsom Prison Blues'; 'Sign on the Cross'; 'Santa Fe'; 'Silent Weekend'; 'Silouette'; 'Bring it on Home'; 'King of France'; 'Going to Acapulco'; 'Gonna Get You Now'; 'Banks of the Royal Canal.'

Published lyrics: Writings and Drawings; Lyrics *1985;* Lyrics *2004.*
First known performance: Isle of Wight, August 31, 1969 [SP].
Known studio recordings: Basement Tape?

'Minstrel Boy' appears to be one basement-tape song that took a couple of years to 'get written down,' Dylan performing it as an encore at the 1969 Isle of Wight festival (that live version appearing on *Self Portrait* the following summer). It seems to be very much about getting 'things . . . evened up,' with a number of lines in its two verses lending themselves to autobiographical interpretation ('With all of them ladies, he's lonely still'; 'With all this trav'lin, I'm still on that road'). But it is the thrice-sung chorus that really acquires extra resonance by being applied to its author:

> Who's gonna throw that minstrel boy a coin?
> Who's gonna let it roll?
> Who's gonna throw that minstrel boy a coin?
> Who's gonna let it down easy to save his soul.

A few months later, Dylan would be asking some unspecified 'landlord' to please not 'put a price on my soul.' In the interim he began copying some songs down, but not this one. Whether Dylan even played the song to his erstwhile personal manager, Al Grossman, to whom he was still bound contractually, is not known. Grossman was noticeably absent from the Isle of Wight jamboree at which it received its one public performance. And the song was not copyrighted by Dwarf Music, the music publishing company Dylan and Grossman jointly set up at the end of 1965, to which all other known basement-tape songs were copyrighted. Indeed, 'Minstrel Boy' was only registered at the time of *Self Portrait,* and then to Big Sky Music.*

---

* Big Sky only began copyrighting Dylan's songs in 1969.

And yet when he came to compile *Writings and Drawings* in 1972, Dylan placed 'Minstrel Boy' in the 'basement tape' section – a clear indication that this is where he thought it belonged. (Needless to say, he has second-guessed himself in subsequent editions of *Lyrics*, where the song has been reassigned to 1969.) The fact that it went uncopyrighted at the time hardly sets it apart from the likes of 'I'm Not There' and 'Sign on the Cross,' both (also) composed early in the process, when Dylan was not yet acknowledging a growing pressure to deliver 'something' as he continued seeking refuge from the world. Though he began copyrighting some songs in September, he told one journalist a decade later, 'When I stopped working, that's when the trouble started. . . . When you stop working, they want more – those people always want more. It's not what have you done for me yesterday, but what can you do for me today. They always want more.' 'Minstrel Boy' may have been his idea of a righteous retort.

{194} **LOCK YOUR DOOR**

{195} **BABY, WON'T YOU BE MY BABY**

{196} **TRY ME LITTLE GIRL**

{197} **I CAN'T MAKE IT ALONE**

{198} **DON'T YOU TRY ME NOW**

{199} **ONE FOR THE ROAD**

{200} **ONE MAN'S LOSS**

#194–200 – Known studio recordings: Red Room, Woodstock, spring 1967.

These seven 'songs' had all gone undocumented when they appeared *in toto* on a set of reels passed to collectors by a former Band roadie in 1986. This should not really be surprising, given that none of these songs had been copyrighted in 1967, 1968, 1970, 1971, 1973, or 1975 – when various batches from the basement *were* registered with Dwarf. All seven betray varying stages of incompleteness, as one might expect, from the half-minute fragment 'Lock Your Door' to the almost-realized 'I Can't Make It Alone' (which Dr. Marcus intimates is 'perhaps a sketch of "This Wheel's on Fire."' – maybe not).

As I have suggested elsewhere, what we have here are snapshots from an ongoing process, as Dylan eases himself back into songwriting via a panoply of musical styles that directly influenced him, all the while showing The Band how they might integrate such influences themselves. In all seven instances, probably recorded at two or three sessions in Dylan's living room early on in said process, he seems to be grabbing his ideas from song titles – not his own, but others lodged in this land's lexicon.

'One for the Road' is lifted from Johnny Mercer's memorable 'One for my Baby (One More for the Road),' first featured in the Fred Astaire movie, *The Sky's The Limit* (1945). Though the two songs couldn't be more different, Dylan's vocal does betray a despair similar to the one that had caused Astaire to single-handedly destroy a bar at the climax of his song-and-dance rendition of the song (on the verses, Dylan uses the kind of seductive vocal he would later use on the altogether more rarified 'I'm Not There').

'I Can't Make It Alone' is another kind of catchphrase that has titled many a song. Of the likely debtees, P. J. Proby's minor hit the previous year was probably one known to Dylan. 'Try Me,' a song title that had already given James Brown a chance to wail, here supplies Dylan with two song ideas, 'Try Me, Little Girl' and '(Don't You) Try Me Now.' Likewise, 'One Man's Loss' nicks its nomenclature from Dick Thomas's 1950 country pastiche, 'One Man's Loss Is Another Man's Gain,' but promptly swerves across to the darker side of that particular highway, Dylan garbling the verses but unmistakably enunciating its repetitive chorus: 'One man's loss always is another man's gain / One man's choice always is another man's pain.' Here is someone absolutely intending to even things up.

However, the most intriguing song within this mini-series – and the most frustrating (because it cuts after two minutes, forty-seven seconds, just as an organ break threatens to raise the stakes) – is 'Baby, Won't You Be My Baby,' which draws its title from the '(Won't You) Be My Baby' high-school of songs, but takes it into uncharted territory. Blending those elements of pop he liked to pastiche, the odd traditional commonplace ('I looked east, I looked west / There was nothing I could see that I liked the best'), and a whiff of apocalypse ('East and west / The fire will rise'), Dylan starts ploughing the furrow that leads to a bleak watchtower. He has also begun coining the type of aphorisms that will mark out the songs demo-ed for Dwarf later in the summer: 'Drop your load / Don't look back, it's a dead-end road.'

As these songs make plain, one must be wary of retrospectively applying a seriousness of intent that a communal jocularity audible on the session reels repeatedly belies. They are having a ball, making a lot of this up as they go along. As Dylan later told two female inquisitors, 'It was just songs which we'd come to this basement out in the woods and record. . . . These songs . . . were written in five, ten minutes' (to Mary Travers – of Peter, Paul, and Mary – April 1975); and, 'I thought they were what they were – a bunch of guys hanging out down in the basement making up songs' (to author Denise Worrell, eighteen years later).

Dylan once suggested they spent as much time 'planting gardens and just watching time go by' as they did 'making music.' Actually, the only horticulture that really interested *these* backwood boys involved cultivation of weed. But then one must not forget that the first order of the day was healing some deep psychological scars formed over eighteen months in hell. Chronologically speaking, Dylan may be off the mark when claiming, 'We'd just come off a ferocious tour,' but his mind was bound to take its time catching up with a healing body. Hence why they were just as likely to spend an afternoon immersed in 'homespun ballads' of a certain vintage as in trying to work up their own remake/remodel/s. But try they did and, praise be, a lot of the time the Uher was rolling.

{201} KING OF FRANCE

Known studio recordings: Red Room, Woodstock, spring 1967.

Most of the basement-tape songs defy analysis because of the way Dylan contorts imagery, indulging in lateral shifts from nonsense to clarity and back again. 'King of France' defies analysis for a more straightforward reason – the recording is hopelessly distorted. Which is not to say that its imagery wouldn't be impenetrable if a state-of-the-art recording did exist; just that there is an insuperable aural obstacle stopping us from assessing this song. (If Dr. Marcus can find 'dim echoes of . . . Child Ballad 164' herein, then we really are in trouble!)

'King of France' does at least fit Dylan's 1978 description of the kind of song he was trying out that summer: 'At that time psychedelic rock was overtaking the universe and so we were singing these homespun ballads. . . . They said it was ahead of its time, but actually it was behind its time.' The song purports to be just such a 'homespun ballad' about the famous occasion (*sic*) 'the King of France came to the USA,' feeling 'he had something to say.' To these ears it contains certain messianic elements, reiterated on 'Quinn the Eskimo,' in its depiction of someone who claims to 'know what it was all about' (a line Dylan repeats at the end of every verse). The king initially attracts an audience ('There was a whole lotta [folk?] waiting for him / Thinking he had something to say'), only for them to 'walk out' when 'he opened his mouth.' Could Dylan himself be the King of France? Maybe we are in fact back at the Olympia, a year earlier, when folk-rock 'was overtaking the universe,' but paying Parisians were not amused.

To add to the mystery, the song circulates from a generational dub of the compilation reels made by producer Rob Fraboni in 1975, when an official release was slated. It seems unlikely that such a poor recording was ever under consideration for a CBS record. Robertson later informed Marcus he wasn't even sure it was a song, but the fact that it is the only one of the dozen or so sonically challenged Dylan originals recorded at Big Pink to appear on these reels suggests it had some significance to its compiler/s. However, the song got no closer to official release, nor was it ever copyrighted. Whatever the King of France had to say, Dylan has stayed *schtum*.

{202} ON A RAINY AFTERNOON
{203} I CAN'T COME IN WITH A BROKEN HEART
{204} UNDER CONTROL

#202–4 all recorded at Big Pink, West Saugerties, summer 1967.

These three songs appear to have been recorded at a single session, all displaying the same distorted high-end that comes from pushing the levels a little too much. The needles may not all be on red, but they're definitely a darker shade of pink. Aside from providing evidence that Dylan and the guys could still crank it up when so inclined, this particular trio of tunes largely serves to demonstrate that not every day spent in the basement crackled with creativity.

The one song that threatens to get off the ground is 'On a Rainy Afternoon,' which (on tape) starts midway through, betraying something resembling a song structure, though dummy lyrics are well in evidence again. 'I Can't Come In with a Broken Heart' suggests that all those country covers are taking their toll, thankfully breaking down before Dylan does. What is not clear is the basis for the song title, written on the original tape box. The line in question is not a discernible feature of the song. 'Under Control' is a throwback to, of all things, the 'Why Do You Have to Be So Frantic?' / 'Pilot Eyes' type of improvisation abandoned back in '65, the singer unconvincingly suggesting that she is finally 'under control.'

{205} THE SPANISH SONG

Known studio recordings: Big Pink, West Saugerties, summer 1967.

Now *this* is nuts. Were one looking to demonstrate the sheer perversity of Dylan's decision making regarding which songs from Big Pink got documented and which didn't, 'Spanish Song' is evidence for the prosecution. Having told Garth Hudson to turn the tape recorder off as he grappled with the timeless 'Hills of Mexico' – apparently because he felt they were 'just wasting tape' – he proceeds to record not one but two 'complete' takes of this drunken revelry on all things Spanish. What starts out as a parody of the Spanish ballad 'Adelita' (a song Dylan later recorded for *Planet Waves*) quickly mutates into a cacophony of innuendo, as Band-member Richard Manuel goads Dylan into making farce from tragedy. A good time was had by all. Not copyrighted. I wonder why.

{206} I'M A FOOL FOR YOU
{207} NEXT TIME ON THE HIGHWAY
{208} I'M YOUR TEENAGE PRAYER

#206–8 all recorded at Big Pink, West Saugerties, summer 1967.

Pop pastiches remain an integral part of 'the process' for as long as Dylan shared time with The Band at Big Pink, achieving its full bloom on one of the last songs recorded at Big Pink, 'Clothesline Saga.' On the pair of reels that provide the first three copyrighted songs of the sessions ('Tiny Montgomery,' 'Sign on the Cross,' and 'All-American Boy'), much tape is given over to songs that either start out as pastiches par excellence ('I'm Your Teenage Prayer' and 'All-American Boy') or soon surrender to the impulse ('See You Later Allen Ginsberg,' 'The Spanish Song,' 'The Big Flood,' and 'Next Time on the Highway').

'See You Later Allen Ginsberg' is more of a rhyme than a song, a little piece of spontaneous wordplay around the idea of 'See You Later Alligator,' changed to 'See You Later Croco-gator' before they give the nod to the basement boys' mutual friend, Allen Ginsberg, who had recently shared a stage with The Band in New York. 'Next Time on the Highway' does more with the idea, even if it does little more than tie together a series of chain-gang commonplaces before collapsing in a drunken heap as Dylan (playing the kettle) accuses the piano player (a.k.a. the pot) of being 'shit-faced.'

'I'm Your Teenage Prayer' is one of those pastiches that is so engaging it codifies all that is good about both these sessions and everything they are parodying. Like the (non-Dylan) song 'Acne,' a party piece at early New York gigs, 'I'm Your Teenage Prayer' shows both an innate love of the form – the teen love songs he grew up on – and a delirious desire to lampoon said form. Though Dylan starts off with the basic idea, 'Take a look at me, babe, I am a teenage prayer / When it's cloudy all the time / All you gotta do is say you're mine / I'll coming running anywhere,' it is Richard Manuel who becomes the child molester in the night, whispering lascivi-ously into the girl's inner ear, upping the ante on the singer, until he too must raise his game. Finally Dylan becomes Luke the Preacher, intoning a middle eight while eight miles high and four sheets to the wind. One imagines lines like 'I

401

know what you need. . . . I can feel it on my throne' would have had the gals scampering for the hills. Yet there is just so much good humour in the performance, it is almost a shame Dylan did not claim the song for his Dwarfish own.

'I'm a Fool for You,' on the other hand, belongs more with the seven Red Room songs (#194–200), as it takes another popular song title and twists it till it snaps. Loosely based on those 'Rolling Stone' chord changes that, lest we forget, had once been 'La Bamba,' the recording of the song provides a rare instance of Dylan allowing the tape to run while he makes changes to both the chord sequence and the tempo he wishes to take the whole thing at. The song itself has a certain amount of promise, as do the lyrics ('Every night when I come back, well, I don't make my return / Every heart shall rise, every banner shall burn / I'm a fool for you . . .'), though one senses Dylan becoming frustrated with the thing, getting ready to toss it out. Which he duly does.

{209} ALL-AMERICAN BOY

Published lyrics: Words Fill My Head.

Known studio recordings: Big Pink, West Saugerties, summer 1967.

On the brink of another breakthrough, Dylan decided to record one last parody of a fifties pop song – and a specific one at that, country singer Bobby Bare's 'All-American Boy' – before letting Luke the Preacher gaze upon that ol' 'Sign on the Cross.' Again he can't resist making the song refer to his own predicament, as opposed to Elvis Presley, the all-American boy Bare himself had originally lampooned back in December 1958 when he first cut the song. As a result Dylan turns the song into the kind of morality tale that would have made Frankie Lee proud. Where Bare satirizes the standard 'star is born' fare – 'Up stepped a man with a big cigar / He said, "C'mon cat, I'm gonna make you star. . . . Sign here kid!"' – Dylan's copy-righted lyrics suggest an altogether more Faustian pact: 'Drink this sonny, it comes in a cup / Yeah, he'll take you out to his farm / Where he's fixing it up.'

Dylan had always distrusted the star-making machinery, tearing a strip off a bemused British reporter back in May 1965 for suggesting he had bought into the process by becoming a star himself: 'Build up your own star! Why don't you get a lot of money and bring some kid out here from the north of England and say, "We're gonna make you a star. You just comply with everything we do. Every time you want an interview, you can just sign a paper that means we can have an interview and write what we want to write. And you'll be a star and make money!"' This facet of the man is now given air using the Bobby Bare original he ostensibly adapts.

In fact that Bobby Bare original did not bear its author's name, having been cut as a demo for Bill Parsons as news of Elvis joining the army threatened to shake the very founda-tions of rock & roll (it was initially attributed to Parsons on the original single). After the songwriter sold all rights to the recording for fifty cents to Fraternity Records, it rose to number two in the charts. And Dylan's debt to the original is evident throughout, though no more so than with Bare's opening verse, from which he extemporizes at least four couplets of his own:

> Gather round cats, and I'll tell you a story
> Of how to become an All-American boy.
> Buy you a guitar and put it in tune,
> You'll be rock & rollin' soon.
> Impressing the girls, picking hot licks.
> All that jazz.

Written out like this, Bare's 'original' rings the odd bell of debt itself. This is clearly another talkin' blues, and this is exactly how Dylan elects to do it, riffing on lines like 'making the girls wiggle . . . in their socks / in their britches,' while Richard Manuel again becomes the whispering devil in disguise. With a licence to play around with the idea, Dylan really does create a very different song, one he felt fully justified in copyrighting *solely in his name* in September 1973 – which, frankly, is going a bit far, Bare having provided the bare bones for his namesake, thus warranting a co-credit.

When Dylan recorded it in the summer of 1967, it was a moot point because he had no intention of copyrighting the song at all. Remember, he was just passing time. But by 1973 he seems to have decided to fully render the song unto himself, rewriting his original reworking. As such, when offering to 'tell you the story about how to become / an All-American Boy,' he adds, as a glossary, 'instead of a bum.' And instead of playing 'hot licks' over the ocean, he is 'kicking up hot shit.' And while rewriting some lines to lessen the debt, he adds a whole section to the first verse, which is rather basement-esque:

> Bought a hot dog and smelled it, and I smelled the crowd
> Everybody was a-down on this side of a cloud
> There was a holy cow and a medicine man
> And a sacred cow and an iron jaw that wouldn't break.

That is not all. When Dylan introduces his own cigar-chomping boss, the man has a wife who's 'there and in her way / She sure does like the things you play.' This here ain't no Colonel Parker. But it could be the manager still retaining a share of the publishing company to which this song was now registered. So who were these '1973 rewrites' for? Though Dylan made similar changes to certain lyrics in that year's *Writings and Drawings*, 'All-American Boy' was copyrighted five months *after* the book was published – and two years before *The Basement Tapes* double-album appeared (for which 'All-American Boy' was not even short-listed). Weird.

{210} TINY MONTGOMERY

Published lyrics: Writings and Drawings; Lyrics 1985; Lyrics 2004.
Known studio recordings: Big Pink, West Saugerties, summer 1967.

At some point towards the end of August or, more likely, the beginning of September, Dylan chose to lodge ten of the songs written that summer with his current music publisher, Dwarf Music. He had evidently already decided these tracks would not constitute his next album, and having resolved his differences with his long-standing record label (for a while there he nearly skipped over to MGM), he no longer needed to supply the fourteen cuts he still owed them from his 1961 contract. As such, the songs in question were put up for grabs to other artists, much as his earlier publishing demos for Witmark had been, for he continued to recognize the commercial benefits of being covered. Hence his comment to *SongTalk* a quarter of a century later: 'If you've got songs that you're not going to do, and you just don't like them [!], . . . show them to other people.'

Almost immediately a tape copy was made (in mono) from which acetates could be cut and sent to interested parties. The ruse was a rousing success. Dylan enjoyed one of his most successful spells as a songwriter thanks to the legions queuing up to cover a set of songs he didn't rate highly enough to do himself. While 'This Wheel's on Fire' would be a number one single for Julie Driscoll and the Trinity, 'I Shall Be Released' set about becoming Dylan's third-most covered song. Yet with every band from Fairport Convention to Thunderclap Newman racing to record something from

405

this new set of Dylan demos, there was one song that seems to have been largely ignored: 'Tiny Montgomery.' Which seems to be the song that kicked off the whole enterprise, as well as providing one of the most enticing performances from the whole Big Pink carousel of song.

'Tiny Montgomery' is *the* prototype for a number of standout songs in a new-found style, utilizing the kind of wordplay that would have had Edward Lear reaching for the smelling salts. Lines like 'Scratch your dad / Do that bird / Suck that pig / And bring it on home' demonstrate an even greater love for nonsense than the *Highway 61 Revisited* songs, and now Dylan was unabashed about it. All pretence of sense is scattered to the wind in this song of celebration, as Tiny Montgomery 'says hello' to 'ev'rybody down in ol' Frisco' (great rhyme!).

Of course, what works on tape won't necessarily sing on the page – nor is it meant to – and before the song was published in *Writings and Drawings*, Dylan red-penned some of its funnier lines. So although 'Pick that drip / And bake that dough' makes marginally more sense than 'Pink that dream / And nose that dough' – and the same goes for 'Now grease that pig / And sing praise,' as opposed to what he *really* sings, 'Grease that gig / And play it blank' – I somehow prefer the originals in all their nonsensical glory.

Any attempt to render sense from the published lyrics to these songs just strikes me as *against* the whole spirit of the sessions. Quite why Dylan turns T-Bone Frank into Half-track Frank, Bob alone knows. Apart from anything else, it loses the link to 'Please Mrs. Henry,' in which the narrator is 't-boned and punctured,' a connection that reinforces the sense that every character in these songs is somehow in the same basement barroom (duly enhanced by the cover to the official *Basement Tapes* album, the best thing about the set). Fulsome as the fare is for Tiny Montgomery's homecoming, it proves to be just a starter course for the basement banquet to come.

{211} SIGN ON THE CROSS

Published lyrics: Writings and Drawings; Lyrics *1985;* Lyrics *2004.*
Known studio recordings: Big Pink, West Saugerties, summer 1967.

> Some [songs] were old ballads . . . but others Bob would make
> up as he went along. . . . We'd play the melody, he'd sing a
> few words he'd written, and then make up some more, or
> else just mouth sounds or even syllables as he went along.
> It's a pretty good way to write songs. – Garth Hudson

Coming at the end of the same reel as 'Tiny Montgomery' and 'All-American Boy,' 'Sign on the Cross' represents the first unalloyed masterpiece of the summer. Oddly enough, though, the song was *not* one of the fourteen songs sent out on the publishing demo in the winter of 1968, nor was it part of the 'safety' reel compiled by producer Elliott Mazur at some point in late 1969. When the song was finally copyrighted in 1971, along with 'Don't Ya Tell Henry,' it came across as an afterthought. Only after the song was respectfully covered by McGuinness Flint on their all-Dylan 'covers' album, *Lo & Behold*, did the song's reputation begin to pick up speed.

Shortly afterwards, the original basement 'demo' began to circulate – in stereo! – and proved to be every bit the equal of 'Tears of Rage' and 'This Wheel's on Fire.' Its appearance in 1973's *Writings and Drawings* seemed to imply acceptance into an 'approved' canon of basement originals, only for the song to then be omitted from the official double-album two years later. A chance of official dispensation came again in 1991, when it was included on the original four-CD version of *The Bootleg Series*, due for release that winter. But again it got chopped at the roots, when that set was reduced – in an act of symptomatic stupidity on Sony's part – to three volumes. And so, as of 2007, it remains one of those grade-A Dylan classics which resides solely in the bootleg domain.

Dylan himself has never commented on the song. And though it was included in *Writings and Drawings*, he seems to have left it to the same transcriber-with-tinnitus who was let loose on the likes of 'Tell Me, Momma' and 'Sitting on a Barbed Wire Fence.' Even I am at a loss to explain how the couplet, 'There's some who're in prison / And there's some in the penitentiary, too,' becomes, 'There is some on every chisel / And there is some in the championship, too.' More cloth-eared still is 'The bird is here and you might want to enter it,' which has been transmuted from the perfectly intelligible, 'Later on you might want to enter it, but, of course, the door it might be closed.' Quite a trick.

So why has Dylan treated such a major song with scant regard, and what exactly is the man's problem with this testimony to that indivisible link between singing and salvation? It is probably the exact same problem he has with that other captured-on-the-cusp-of-creation classic, 'I'm Not There.' Both songs are clearly semi-improvised. In the case of 'Sign on the Cross,' the entire spoken bridge bespeaks an incantation born of the moment – and a dose of medicinal weed, which has done more than just smoke his eyelids.

Dylan may even have felt faintly embarrassed by this (premature) expression of religious yearning – hence the 'rewrite' given it in *Writings and Drawings*. Something, it seems, was paining him; no one to date has been entirely successful nailing it down. Even the song title itself does not convey a clear meaning. What, one wonders, *is* this sign on the cross that has begun to worry him? Is it, as has been suggested, the sarcastic words posted on the cross, according to Matthew 27:35 – 'This is Jesus The King of the Jews'? And if so, how have these words begun to 'worry' the singer?

One thing is certain – Dylan was once again immersing himself in the Bible, and not just the Old Testament. When he talks of wanting to enter 'the kingdom,' but 'the door, it might be closed,' he seems to be making a direct reference to Luke 13:25: 'You will begin to stand outside and to knock at the door, saying, "Lord, open to us." He will answer you, "I do not know where you come from."' Dylan's mother told Robert Shelton that, when she and husband Abraham had visited her son's family in Woodstock late that summer, she had seen a Bible prominently displayed.

The question then arises whether it is Dylan or Luke the Drifter (Hank Williams's down-home alter ego) who is worrying about that 'sign on the cross, just layin' up there in top of the hill' (presumably Calvary). Because although he may well know in his head 'that we're all so misled,' he can't resist signing off with the kind of moral that the later Luke would've liked: 'Sing a song / And all your troubles will pass right on through.'

{212} SANTA FE

Published lyrics: Lyrics *2004;* Words Fill My Head.

{213} SILENT WEEKEND

Published lyrics: Lyrics *1985;* Lyrics *2004.*
Known studio recordings [212+213]: Big Pink, West Saugerties, summer 1967 [#212 TBS].

As already stated, the last set of basement songs copyrighted prior to the release of the official double-LP were registered in September 1973, representing five more previously undocumented Dylan 'originals' added to the ever-growing stockpile from Woodstock. None of the five, though, made the official set; and just three songs, the two songs above plus 'Bourbon Street,' were placed on the composite reels by its producer/s.

And though neither 'Santa Fe' nor 'Silent Weekend' were deemed important or interesting enough for official dispensation on the 1975 LP, 'Silent Weekend' popped up in a lavish, all-encompassing songbook, *The Songs of Bob Dylan 1966–1975*, the following year (sandwiched between 'I Wanna Be Your Lover' and 'Tell Me, Momma'). No explanation for its inclusion was forthcoming, and it remained unheard until the early nineties, when the composite reels passed into collecting circles.

As with 'All-American Boy' and the three other 1973 copyrights, the lyrics to 'Silent Weekend' on the original 1967 recording are largely spur-of-the-moment spins on another silent weekend, with well-placed gargles replacing the odd line. Its closest kin, basement-wise, would have to be 'Please Mrs. Henry.' But in 'Silent Weekend' he is pleading for his woman to drop the silent treatment; whereas in 'Please Mrs. Henry' he needs another kind of relief. Yet the published lyrics are neither guesswork, nor what he sang at the time. And a couple of the lines are pretty good; 'She's uppity, she's rollin' / She's in the groove, she's strolling / Over to the jukebox playin' deaf and dumb' rank among the best. So either some rewriting had again been done back in 1967, or, more likely, in 1973.

Just as 'Silent Weekend' began to circulate among diehards, 'Santa Fe' was also being dispersed to one and all on 1991's *The Bootleg Series*, in a sound quality that left a great deal to be desired. Of all the 'missing' basement-tape originals that could have been included on that three-CD set, 'Santa Fe' hardly represented an A-list candidate. Just another discarded ditty, it relies on the usual wordplay and slurred diction to obscure any pretence to a deeper meaning, making it ripe for a rewrite in 1973.

And it seems to have gotten one. The copyrighted lyrics –
which also serve as the published lyrics when they finally
appear in the 2004 edition of *Lyrics* – repeatedly depart from
those he sang in the summer of love. Those original lyrics
revolve around 'dear, dear, dear, dear Santa Fe' – intended to
be both a woman's name and the town in New Mexico. After
five verses of rolling said words around, he moves on.

The copyrighted lyrics evince a dramatic reworking, and
a later one. In 1973, musing in Malibu, Dylan might well have
envisaged a time when he would 'build a geodesic dome and
sail away,' but not in 1967. Likewise, 'My shrimp boat's in the
bay / I won't have my nature this way,' sounds like someone
sitting on the dock of a bay, not up on Meads Mountain. As
to why Dylan would rework five basement-tape songs at this
juncture, I guess that's one more log to toss on the enigma
fire.

{214} BOURBON STREET

Published lyrics: Words Fill My Head.

{215} DON'T YA TELL HENRY

Published lyrics: Writings and Drawings; Lyrics *1985*; Lyrics *2004*.
Known studio recordings: Big Pink, West Saugerties, summer 1967.
First known performance: Academy of Music, NY, December 31,
1971 [ROA].

Neither 'Bourbon Street' – another of those 1973 copyrights – nor 'Don't Ya Tell Henry' (copyrighted in 1971)
constitute part of the two circulating sets of session tapes
from the summer of 1967. They only appear on compila-
tions made later. So placing them is an even more purified
form of guesswork than most other songs recorded that
summer. Marcus states unequivocally that 'Bourbon Street'
(or as he calls it, for no obvious reason, 'Gimme Another
Bourbon Street') comes from 'the last cycle of recordings,

those made with Levon Helm,' meaning around November 1967, presumably because it is 'of a piece' with that other drinking song, 'Don't Ya Tell Henry,' a song recorded with and without Helm at the helm.

The fact that 'Bourbon Street' was copyrighted with other unfinished songs suggests an earlier assignment. And this time the copyrighted lyrics represent a fair transcription of the recording, save for the onanistic reference to bagging 'it / Down in bitter sweet / I don't beat the meat . . . On my Bourbon Street.' The one known recording, found on the 1975 composite reels, cuts abruptly and, the copyrighted lyrics would suggest, prematurely. Absent is a final verse, which descends into the same oblivion the singer seeks in the French Quarter:

> Let me have another Bourbon Street
> Talk to your brother, mother
> I want a Bourbon Street, Mr Bartender
> I'll have another Bourbon Street.

So, not so much one for the road as one for the sidewalk; whereas 'Don't Ya Tell Henry' could be the fishing trip the morning after. If so, hair of the dog has already been applied, because the spirit of mayhem continues to reign. The song is subsequently adopted by The Band, but with nothing like the same sense of bacchanalian excess.

{216} MILLION DOLLAR BASH

First known performance: Brixton Academy, London, November 21, 2005.

{217} YEA! HEAVY AND A BOTTLE OF BREAD

Published lyrics: Writings and Drawings; Lyrics 1985; Lyrics 2004.
Known studio recordings: Big Pink, West Saugerties, summer 1967 – 2 takes each [BT – tk.2 x 2].

#217 – First known performance: Madison Square Garden, New York, November 27, 2002.

These two classic basement-tape compositions were recorded on a single reel, both requiring just two takes to reveal their enigmatic selves. In keeping with that summer's spirit, the element of spontaneity evident on each is fortuitous, but no accident. Talking about the whole experience in 2002, Garth Hudson, the tape operator, recalled Dylan's methodology: 'He would go in with us, play a new song only part way through. We wouldn't much rehearse or much less play it all the way through to learn it. And he'd turn on the tape and we'd get it down in a first or second take. He just knew the material.'

'Million Dollar Bash' may be taken at much the same tempo both times around, but Dylan's vocals are night and day. On take one he is a participant in the insanity, revelling in the party atmosphere and thoroughly mashed. The second go-round he is getting ready for 'Clothesline Saga,' sounding as laconic as a pipe smoker on his porch. As for the song itself, it begged to be covered as a doo-wop ditty, even alluding to the Coasters twice ('Along came Jones' – a song title in itself – and 'emptied the trash' – a reference to 'Yakety Yak'), but the best anyone managed was Fairport Convention's free-for-all on their third album, *Unhalfbricking.*

As for 'Yea Heavy,' one suspects Dylan had a whole string of non sequiturs he could have pulled out of his hat, but decided to stop at four verses, giving it a chance to be the psychedelic hit it never was. Though Dylan later claimed he consciously opted out of the brand of 'psychedelic rock . . . overtaking the universe,' songs like this suggest a psychedelic breakfast was still the meal of choice for these guys. Again Dylan tried out alternate vocal styles on the two takes – one hard, the other more resigned – though he changed little else, save replacing 'a nose full of blood' with 'a nose full of pus,' and repeating the first verse at the end of the second take. It remains the least covered of the basement-based publishing demos, being left to ex–Pink Fairy Twink to accord it solitary recognition.

{218} I'M NOT THERE

Published lyrics: The Telegraph *#24;* Words Fill My Head; *'Some Other Kinds of Songs.'*
Known studio recordings: Big Pink, West Saugerties, summer 1967 [INT].

> There are times you just pick up an instrument – something will come . . . some kind of wild line will come into your head and you'll develop that. If it's a tune on the piano or guitar . . . you'll write those words down. And they might not mean anything to you at all, and you just go on. . . . Now, . . . if I do it, I just keep it for myself. So I have a big lineup of songs which I'll never use. – Dylan, *Sing Out!* June 1968

Of the 'big lineup of songs which I'll never use' dating from this rich period, the most legendary would have to be 'I'm Not There,' a song that it took forty years and a $40 million film to put into the official domain. Dylan himself has consistently been baffled by the song's enduring appeal. When asked in 1985 why the song had never been released, he replied, 'It wasn't *there!*' He stood alone with this opinion in 1967, 1970, 1975, 1985, and 1991 – all occasions when the song could have emerged, but didn't.

The Band always loved this song, and not just because they play like their lives depend on it. When the 'safety' reel was compiled, circa 1969 (see my *Recording Sessions*), some wise soul (presumably Garth) decided it must be on there, even though it had yet to be copyrighted, and the likes of

'Tiny Montgomery' and 'Sign on the Cross' were over-looked. It is from this 'safety' that the 2007 film soundtrack derives its version. It had already been under consideration for *The Basement Tapes*, *Biograph*, and *The Bootleg Series*, but Dylan baulked at its inclusion on the first of these, while the lack of a good copy counted against it when it came to later archival sets (the 'safety' having been mislaid all the way to Neil Young's Californian ranch – a long story, partially related in Sid Griffin's commendable basement book, *Million Dollar Bash*).

Meantime, it was obliged to rely on the kindness of collec-tors and commentators to build up a wellspring of demand. Because it was not part of the fabled 'acetate' – the fourteen-track publisher's demo compiled in early 1968 – 'I'm Not There' did not feature on any of the early bootleg LPs that stoked the legend (neither did 'Sign on the Cross'). For the whole of the seventies it was essentially a taper's treasure. All the while, it was known to the few. Of its early advocates, Paul Cable was probably the one who furthered the myth most, specu-lating that 'the [circulating] tapes of it start some way into the song, [and] possibly several verses are missed.' Actually, Dylan simply employed his usual trick of not telling his fellow musi-cians when he was about to start a song, and Hudson had to hastily lean over and press 'record' on the reel-to-reel.

Where Cable becomes his usual insightful self is in suggesting, 'In places you get the impression that he is making the words up as he goes along. It is possible, even, that the incomprehensible bits are not real words at all but slurrings to fill in where inspiration temporarily runs out.' Though he has only his ears to go by, Cable is spot-on. Evidence, were it needed, that Dylan was once again 'sing[ing] a few words he'd written, and then mak[ing] up some more, or else just mouth[ing] sounds or even sylla-bles,' comes from a most unlikely source – a typed draft that arrived anonymously at Wanted Man HQ in the late eighties.

The late John Bauldie and I agreed that the draft had all the hallmarks of authenticity (evinced by the use of the *x* key for deletions; the way Dylan suddenly resorts to capital letters; and even the funny little misspellings, like 'yesta-day' and 'shUD,' for 'should'). As such, we ran it in issue 24 of *The Telegraph*. My view has not changed. But even this type-script could be a fragment. A tear at the bottom of the page obscures one couplet: 'heaven knows the answer – don't call nobod[y] . . . / i go by the lord BEWARE BE[WARE].' These lines appear in the recorded version at two separate points: 'And I go by the Lord and she's on my way / But I don't belong there,' and then, a verse later, 'Heaven knows that the answer, she don't call no one.' While missing entirely are thirteen of the most elliptical – and most discussed – lines in the Dylan canon:

Now I'll cry tonight like I cried the night before
And I'm leased on the *height* but I still dream about the door
It's alone he's forsaken by fate, who can tell
It don't *hang 'proximation*, she's my all, fare thee well.
Now when I *treat* the lady I was born to love her
But she knows that the kingdom weighs so high above her
And I run in that race, it's not too fast or *slim*
But I don't perceive her, I'm not there I'm gone.
It's all about diffusion as I cry for her veil
I don't need anybody now beside me to tell
And it's all affirmation I *receive*, but it's not
She's a lone hearted beauty but don't like the spot
And she's gone.

These lines could exist on another page of typescript, but I suspect not. I believe Dylan to be simply in the zone, flying

416

the flag of a wild fancy, improvising on the spot. The lines in question slip in and out of clarity; threatening illumination but really straddling the border between non sequitur and nonsense (the words in italics proving particularly difficult to rationalize). Just as the song spirals into wordlessness, Dylan drags it back with a verse that appears in the typescript midsong, sung like the resolution it patently is not. As typed it reads thus:

> SHES GONE
> SHES GONE ! ! ! ! Like the rainbow shinin yesta-day
>   an now shes here with me an i want her to stay
> shes a lone forsaken beauty an she don't trust anyone
> i wish i was beside her but im not there im gone.

The typescript then ventures down avenues left unexplored on tape. 'I could take a trip to mount st[reet] but i don't know if i SHUD' is particularly tantalizing. Which Mount Street? A number of other verbal cues he also chooses to transmute. '2 hearts mistaken / i don't far believe / its so bad / for its amusing / an shes hard [too hard] to please / its a low / its a crime / [the way] she drags me around' becomes – with the bracketed additions – the first three lines of the penultimate verse.

But the final line of the typescript, 'shes a drag queen / shes a drag-a-muffin / shes a drag,' is a strand he left dangling, while the final verse has no precedent on its page-bound prototype, as Dylan works his way towards that final, forsaken line, 'I wish I was there to help her, but I'm not there, I'm gone.' As he sings it, it is the only possible resolution, as mystical as the 'lone forsaken beauty,' and equally bereft of hope. Satisfied with the exercise, Dylan can't imagine any reason to revisit it. Or give it a title. On the tape box it is called 'I'm Not There, I'm Gone.' On the safety reel it is known as, 'But It's Not Here.' For its 1970 copyright registration, it is entitled 'I'm Not There (1956).' (The addition of this date served to convince many folk that Dylan was delving into his wild youth. Maybe.) Finally, for its fortieth birthday, it received an official release under the same name as the film it unwittingly inspired, 'I'm Not There.' Hallelujah.

{219} PLEASE MRS. HENRY

Published lyrics: Writings and Drawings; Lyrics *1985;* Lyrics *2004.*
Known studio recordings: Big Pink, West Saugerties, summer 1967 [BT].

Back on the bourbon, Basement Bob seems in need of relief, but he lacks the means ('a dime,' as in 'buddy, can you spare a . . .'). That Dylan should put the 'tip' in *tipsy* immediately after – in tape terms – the sublimity of 'I'm Not There' suggests an ongoing ambivalence as to the purpose of the sessions, not to say the unbounded expectations of serious-minded fans. It is purely physical relief he craves from Mrs. Henry – a relief that is as sexual ('won't you take me to my room?') as it is scatological ('I'm startin' to drain / My stool's gonna squeak').

Though it may strain credulity, there is a rich literary tradition for lyrics *this* immersed in innuendo. Among Dylan's favourite poets, the French symbolists Verlaine, Rimbaud, and Baudelaire were hardly shy of getting down and dirty with their language ('Be ye novices or pros, plain or fancy / In your cracks and crannies I'd live out my days and nights' – not a lost basement lyric, one of Verlaine's). And according to Allen Ginsberg, Dylan had been reading a lot of French literature during his recuperation from the motorcycle crash. Though it came out austere on his next album, for now that delight in language knew no proprietorial bounds.

{220} CRASH ON THE LEVEE (DOWN IN THE FLOOD)

Published lyrics: Writings and Drawings; Lyrics 1985; Lyrics 2004.

Known studio recordings: Big Pink, West Saugerties, summer 1967 – 2 takes [BT – tk.2]; Studio B, NY, September 24, 1971 – 2 takes [MGH – tk.2].

First known performance: Academy of Music, NY, December 31, 1971 [ROA].

Should the order of reels represent the process remotely accurately, Dylan hit a very rich vein of inspiration shortly before the September copyright registration of ten originals.* He was quite literally reeling them off, with song after song approaching the human condition from an offbeat angle (all cut in two takes, tops), as he approached the end of a journey *back* to where he left off when that back wheel locked. But Dylan still suspected that these songs he was writing – albeit no longer just to pass the time – were not enough of a statement to mark his re-immersion in the mainstream. Seemingly unaware of the quality of what he was now writing, he decided to place the best basement cuts with his publishers as demos. One result was an unbecoming scramble to 'cover' 'Crash on the Levee,' an obvious highlight of that initial ten-track demo.

Quite an artistic distance separates Dylan's dissolute deconstruction of John Lee Hooker's 'Tupelo' (a.k.a. 'The Big Flood'), early on in the sessions, from this first-person account of the biggest flood *ever*. But there is no such distance between 'Crash on the Levee' – a.k.a. 'Down in the Flood' – and 'All Along the Watchtower.' Both use a particular type of English vernacular (one conversational,

---

* The ten songs copyrighted in September 1967 (registration date: October 9, 1967) were: 'Down in the Flood,' 'I Shall Be Released,' 'Lo and Behold!,' 'Million Dollar Bash,' 'Please Mrs Henry,' 'This Wheel's on Fire,' 'Tiny Montgomery,' 'Too Much of Nothing,' 'Yea! Heavy and a Bottle of Bread,' and 'You Ain't Goin' Nowhere.'

the other Jacobean) to convey with real immediacy a threat from nature that might be more than just another catastrophe. In 'Down in the Flood,' like 'Watchtower,' the apocalyptic reality is driven home on the final line of the final verse: 'It's gonna be the meanest flood / That anybody's seen.' And though we get the ubiquitous Big Pink chorus, this one offers no reassurance to its audience – or his 'mama':

> But oh mama, ain't you gonna miss your best friend now?
> You're gonna have to find yourself another best friend, somehow.

By the fall of 1971, with his songwriting faucet having been temporarily turned off again, Dylan was no longer so immune to the song's merits. After re-recording it for a second *Greatest Hits* set in September, he performed a passionate, slightly punch-drunk rendition with The Band during their residency at the Academy of Music, on New Year's Eve. The next time it was performed, in Prague in March 1995, it was no less dramatic or unexpected. Opening the delayed first show of the year – and his finest show in a decade – Dylan wailed away at the harmonica as if 'that high tide' was visibly starting to rise. It would stay the set opener throughout one of the outstanding Never Ending Tour legs.

{221} LO AND BEHOLD!

Published lyrics: Writings and Drawings; Lyrics 1985; Lyrics 2004.
Known studio recordings: Big Pink, West Saugerties, summer 1967 – 2 takes [BT – tk.2].

'Lo and Behold!' comes at the end of another inspired reel of songs that give precedence to wordplay over sense, opined by characters caught in a contagion of chaos to such an extent that down is now up. The dialogue between Molly and Moby Dick exemplifies everything that makes these songs such fun (its residue survives in the 'Three Kings' sleeve notes to *John Wesley Harding*, though not on the album itself):

> 'What's the matter, Molly dear, what's the matter with your
> mound?'
> 'What's it to ya, Moby Dick? This is chicken town.'

Once again the chorus fails to provide any shelter from the storm breaking over its verses. The singer is not the only one to be caught 'looking for my lo and behold!' A sense of just how much fun they are having with this stuff and nonsense comes during the final verse on take one. Dylan blows the line after 'Goin' back to Pittsburgh.' Cracking up, he shouts, 'Again!' Cue much merriment and a disorganized end to proceedings. Take two is just fine. By now Dylan had figured out what to do with the herd of moose somehow acquired in the second verse: 'Round that horn and ride that herd, / Gonna thread up!' One imagines that the revelries continued into the evening, maybe even unto the wee hours.

{222} YOU AIN'T GOIN' NOWHERE

Published lyrics: Writings and Drawings; Lyrics *1985*; Lyrics *2004 [1971 version:* Words Fill My Head].

Known studio recordings: Big Pink, West Saugerties, summer 1967 – 2 takes [BT – tk.2]; Studio B, NY, September 24, 1971 – 6 takes [MGH – tk.6].

First known performance: Portland, Maine, April 10, 1997.

Having decided to let the songwriting process stop short of the usual conclusion – a set of studio sessions – Dylan continued to play the wise fool with his new lyrics. Relying on a different kind of public dissemination, he gave these songs hooks and choruses along with a surfeit of innuendo. The sense of freedom permeating his finest work songs meant that, whatever Dylan's opinion, some proved just as enduring as the very best of his pre-accident canon.

'You Ain't Going Nowhere' is one of those songs where Dylan never quite settled on a single set of lyrics. The one the Byrds put on *Sweetheart of the Rodeo* was how he felt one particular day he stopped by Big Pink to play with The Band. This acetate version, which circulated rapidly in the eighteen months preceding its appearance on *Great White Wonder*, and even more rapidly since, comes across as another example of Dylan delivering pearls of wisdom wrapped in riddles.

But it turns out that this was the second take. The first take was a dummy run in the true sense of the word. At that stage Dylan had a tune, the last line of each verse (i.e., the title), and the chorus. And unlike most other double takes at Big Pink, there is a clear break on the reels between the two performances of 'You Ain't Going Nowhere,' Dylan recording the incendiary 'This Wheel's on Fire' in the interim. So he might well have gone away and written a set of verses, having decided 'You Ain't Going Nowhere' justified a more linear treatment. However much the first take resembles an Edward Lear concordance, the recording demonstrates how adept Dylan had become at versifying on the spot. Though I don't doubt there is a PhD student out there working on the exact meaning of 'I seen you out there beatin' on your hammer / You ain't no head of lettuce,' Bob knows it just sounds good. As does:

I don't care if your name is Michael, you're gonna need some
    boards,
Get your lunch, you foreign bib, you ain't going nowhere.

Whether Dylan went away and strapped himself to his writing desk in order to pen a new set of verses or, as Robbie Robertson suggests was often the case, just took 'a stab at some ideas and things via a typewriter,' a second take achieved the requisite amount of profundity ('Strap yourself to a tree with roots' could come straight from the book of Proverbs), mixed with the usual irreconcilable contradictions found at West Saugerties that summer ('Pick up your money and pack up your tent / You ain't going nowhere').

Either way, Dylan almost certainly spent less time on the lyrics that afternoon than he spent reworking them a third time, four years later, having decided to re-record the song for a second *Greatest Hits*. And having had it in for Michael back in 1967, he now had it in for Roger McGuinn, whom he commanded to 'pull up your tent.' Perhaps he didn't feel the Byrds did the song, or country-rock, justice on *Sweetheart of the Rodeo*. McGuinn claims Dylan was having a go because he accidentally inverted a couple of images on the Byrds' version. Save that he doesn't. Something else also set Dylan off, these reconstructed verses demonstrating the sheer malleability of the basement template, notably:

> Buy me some rings and a gun that sings, a flute that toots
> and a bee that stings
> A sky that cries and a bird that flies, a fish that walks and a
> dog that talks.

Such riddles, wisely expounded, came easily enough. But by the time the song was revived in the spring of 1997, Dylan had pretty much stopped tweaking the templates of yesteryear. Though he could still sing it with gusto, what one wouldn't have given for another 'head of lettuce'!

{223} THIS WHEEL'S ON FIRE

Published lyrics: Writings and Drawings; Lyrics 1985; Lyrics 2004.
Known studio recordings: Big Pink, West Saugerties, Summer 1967 [BT].
First known performance: Madison, Wisconsin, April 13, 1996.

'This Wheel's on Fire' would appear to be the first time Dylan gave the boys in The Band some homework. Unexpectedly, it was not sidekick-guitarist Robbie Robertson but Rick Danko whom he recruited to write a tune that suited these weird and rather wonderful lyrics (perhaps he felt Robertson had had enough free lessons already), as he started separating out lyrics and the tunes to which he set them.

We are now moving full steam towards the next Immaculate Conception, *John Wesley Harding*. At the outset Dylan even whispers into the recorder the song's working title, 'If Your Memory Serves You Well' – a direct allusion to the opening line of Rimbaud's *A Season in Hell* (*Une Saison En Enfer*), 'If my memory serves me well . . .' Re-invoking Rimbaud reinforces the sense of returning darkness, which Dylan had been shutting out with songs of revelry and absurdity. Like the young Arthur, he seems to be documenting a very specific season in hell when he sings, 'This wheel's on fire, rolling down the road / Best notify my next of kin, this wheel shall explode!'

Back in the spring of 1965 he had suggested to one English music journalist that 'catastrophe and confusion are the basis of my songs.' He was evidently returning to base. A memorable chorus and the usual elusive imagery in the verses are tied to first- and last-line rhymes of 'serves you well' and 'to tell,' while thematically the song is almost an update of 'Fourth Time Around.' Again there is a secret, a story, and a debt to be repaid, in this case from 'the one / that called on me to call on them / to get you your favours done.'

In a surprisingly generous mood, Dylan not only donated half the publishing rights to Danko but also let The Band bolster their own debut collection, *Music from Big Pink*, with the song. In fact, 'This Wheel's on Fire' was destined to become one of the most-covered songs from this lexicon of demos, providing a number-one 45 for Julie Driscoll and the Trinity and a Top-Ten hit, a decade later, for Siouxsie and the Banshees, as well as a fitting theme tune for the dysfunctional characters in Jennifer Saunders's nineties sitcom, *Absolutely Fabulous*. By this time Dylan had also begun taking the song through its paces, as he continued rolling down the Never Ending road.

{224} I SHALL BE RELEASED

Published lyrics: Writings and Drawings; Lyrics 1985; Lyrics 2004 [1986 version: In His Own Words 3].
Known studio recordings: Big Pink, West Saugerties, summer 1967 [TBS]; Studio B, NY, September 24, 1971 – 4 takes [MGH – tk.4].
First known performance: Plymouth, MA, October 31, 1975.

Prisons of the body and the mind seem to have preyed on Dylan's mind throughout his time spent with the boys on retainer. Among the songs recorded at early basement sessions were covers of 'Folsom Prison Blues' and 'The Banks of the Royal Canal' (the latter is particularly affecting), both songs written – metaphorically – from inside prison walls. Dylan then takes a leaf from Johnny Cash and Brendan Behan (brother of Dominic), authors of those earlier songs, by writing his own prison song, 'I Shall Be Released.' He is characteristically careful not to confuse simplicity of construction with a commensurate simplicity of meaning. The release that he is singing about – and that Richard Manuel echoes – is not from mere prison bars but rather from the cage of physical existence, the same cage that corrodes on 'Visions of Johanna.'

Ten years later, with 'I Shall Be Released' a regular highlight on a 115-date world tour, he still felt the same way, informing Phillip Fleishman, 'The whole world is a prison. Life is a prison, we're all inside the body. . . . Only knowledge of either yourself or the ultimate power can get you out if it . . . . Most people are working toward being one with God, trying to find him. They want to be one with the supreme power, they want to go Home, you know. From the minute they're born, they want to know what they're doing here. I don't think there's anybody who doesn't feel that way.' Before the year was out, Dylan would find God reflected in a (silver) cross.

Dylan here returns to deeper concerns. Songs like 'I Shall Be Released' suggest their author was again tempted to put his head in a guillotine. Yet he gave the song away, allowing his backing musicians first use of it. It concludes *Music from Big Pink*, an all Band album that was not so much *from* Big Pink as a by-product of the summer tutorials there. Even in such a favourable context, it is a pale shadow of the introspective masterpiece recorded in the Big Pink basement. Like a number of Dylan's greatest songs – including that other reluctant rabble-rouser, 'Knockin' on Heaven's Door' – its solipsistic self would be turned inside out by simpletons (after The Band, that is) as this highly personal song was made a communal anthem by organizations like Amnesty International, for which it was always a song with one meaning alone.

It was perhaps in direct response to Amnesty's use of it as the nightly finale to a particularly overblown stadium tour in the fall of 1985, featuring Bruce Springsteen, Peter Gabriel, and the like, that Dylan decided to rework the song himself. The version he debuted the following January, at a live telecast celebrating Martin Luther King Day, may not display the same full-on poetic sensibility as its precursor, but it left less room for doubt about the relationship between the sinner man and He who saves:

> It don't take much to be a criminal,
>   Just one more move and they'll turn you into
>   one.

At first the pain is just subliminal,
  You protect yourself, and you're forever on the run.
He will find you where you're stayin',
  Even in the arms of somebody else's wife,
You're laughing now, you should be praying,
  This being the midnight hour of your life.

Fans still preferred the original set of lyrics, which were restored the following year and from which Dylan has not since departed, save on the one occasion when he added the final verse of the 1986 rewrite as a coda (Helsinki, September 23, 1987). Despite being one of his most covered, and emulated, songs (Van Morrison, rather than challenging The Band's version, rewrote it as 'Brand New Day'), that original quintessential rendition – in its unadulterated, living, breathing, stereo self – remains unavailable (a generational mono dub of a dub was deemed adequate for 1991's *The Bootleg Series*). Any day now.

{225} TOO MUCH OF NOTHING

Published lyrics: Writings and Drawings; Lyrics 1985; Lyrics 2004.
Known studio recordings: Big Pink, West Saugerties, summer 1967 – 2 takes [BT – tk.1].

'Too Much of Nothing' was probably the last of the ten basement songs copyrighted in September to be recorded. Yet it was the first to be released. In November it became the new Peter, Paul, and Mary single. It would be reasonable to assume that their relationship to Dylan, and a shared management, gave Yarrow and company 'dibs' on the new songs. As such, they presumably did not need to wait for a copy of the full demo-tape before purloining this new Dylan original. They probably got an earful around the first week in September (which tallies with its copyright registration on October 6).

The song completes one cycle on the wheel of fire, as Dylan allowed himself to become a serious man again. He even expressed a surprisingly forthright evaluation of previous shortcomings ('When there's too much of nothing / It just makes a fellow mean'). Perhaps it was too damn honest. The two takes he recorded down those stairs – of which the patently inferior first take was preferred on the 1975 set – were the first and last times he sent his regards to Valerie and Vivian. As such, many fans initially had to make do with Fotheringay's and/or Spooky Tooth's journeys into nothingness, both preferable to Peter, Paul, and Mary's.

{226} TEARS OF RAGE

Published lyrics: Writings and Drawings; Lyrics *1985;* Lyrics *2004.*
Known studio recordings: Big Pink, West Saugerties, summer 1967 – 3 takes [BT – tk.3].
First known performance: Patras, Greece, June 26, 1989.

'Tears of Rage' and the three songs that succeed it on the same inspired reel do not constitute part of the ten songs copyrighted in September. They may have been recorded in just two sessions, all four songs being copyrighted as a group in December 1967,* a couple of weeks after the *John Wesley Harding* songs. Added to the ten-song publishing demo, they then made up the fabled fourteen-song acetate. Given the copyright date, one certainly cannot discount the possibility that they were written and recorded *between* sessions for *John Wesley Harding.* The likelier scenario, though, is that they precede the first *John Wesley Harding* session (October 17) by a matter of days. They were almost certainly recorded before

---

* The five songs copyrighted in December/January 1968 (registration date: January 16, 1968) were as follows: 'Get Your Rocks Off!,' 'Nothing Was Delivered,' 'Open the Door, Homer,' 'Quinn, the Eskimo,' and 'Tears of Rage.'

drummer Levon Helm returned to the fold at the end of October, but were presumably not copyrighted immediately because of other distractions (Bob was recording an album, the reconstituted Band were demo-ing one).

All of which suggests that, for all his claims that it was just a way to kill time, Dylan wasn't quite done with the Big Pink process. There was a new seriousness to the process – no diversions, rambunctious or otherwise, occupy the reel in question, just original compositions. In each instance Dylan and The Band indulge in two or three takes not because they haven't quite nailed the song, but because they want to experiment with the arrangement. These alternate arrangements divide opinions, with some astute folk preferring the first take of 'Tears of Rage' (the one on the acetate) to the third (the one Robertson picked for the official LP), and most folk preferring the first take of 'Open the Door, Homer' to the two that followed.

To my mind, the one indisputable masterpiece on this reel is 'Tears of Rage,' which again demonstrates a Dylan comfortable with writing lyrics to a song *before* he found a tune, stole a tune, or asked for a tune. In this instance he turned to Richard Manuel, who was a little nonplussed by Dylan's faith in him: 'He came down to the basement with a piece of typewritten paper. . . . It was typed out – in line form – and he just said, "Have you got any music for this?" I had a couple of musical movements that fit . . . so I just elaborated a bit, because I wasn't sure what the lyrics meant. I couldn't run upstairs and say, "What's this mean, Bob: 'Now the heart is filled with gold as if it was a purse?'"'

Dylan was pushing The Band to go their own way, donating another obtuse lyric to the cause, which is presumably why he never even knocked out a sly single take at the *John Wesley Harding* sessions. Yet it clearly shares similar preoccupations. By asking, 'Why must I always be the thief?'

he seems to be answering the joker in the watchtower. And it is the poor immigrant he is addressing when he sings of how 'the heart is filled with gold / As if it was a purse.' That telltale chorus, though, confirms a song assigned to the Big Pink locker. To Dylan's warped (1984) thinking it was just one of those 'songs we had done for the publishing company, as I remember. . . . I wouldn't have put them out. . . . People have told me they think it's all very Americana and all that. I don't know what they're talking about.'

'Tears of Rage' certainly has a lot more of Elizabethan England about it than a creationist construct like 'weird ol' America.' But this sense, that the song was not really part of his core 'canon,' took a long time to leave Dylan. Only in June 1989, with The Band barely a going concern and a need for songs to fill out the ever-changing sets that made the G. E. Smith–era so exciting, was 'Tears of Rage' given an overdue resuscitation. At his first-ever Greek show, Dylan summoned up the strength to give it his best shot, forty-eight-year-old vocal cords notwithstanding. Its coauthor had already demonstrated that life is indeed brief, making his friends cry 'tears of rage, tears of grief' by hanging himself in March 1986.

{227} QUINN THE ESKIMO (THE MIGHTY QUINN)

Published lyrics: Writings and Drawings; Lyrics 1985; Lyrics 2004.
Known studio recordings: Big Pink, West Saugerties, summer 1967 – 2 takes [BIO – tk.1].
First known performance: Isle of Wight, August 31, 1969.

At one end of the basement tapes we find 'Tiny Montgomery,' a figure who sends his regards to the folks 'down in ol' Frisco,' while making it clear he's staying put. At the other end resides 'Quinn the Eskimo.' This time everyone expectantly awaits the mighty one's arrival, when all will be set right and 'ev'rybody's gonna jump for joy.' Yet, just like Tiny (and Johanna), Quinn stays absent at song's end. Unsurprisingly, certain commentators have imbued Quinn with messianic, or false messianic, properties. Not all of them have noticed that the narrator, wholly detached from the hubbub surrounding Quinn's arrival, has already expounded his own philosophy of life: 'Guarding fumes and making haste / It ain't my cup of meat.'

Again Dylan elects not to settle for a single take. However, the first take is noticeably more lethargic, and it is the second take that ends up on the acetate (and *Biograph*). Though not one of the *musical* highlights of the sessions, the song was then singled out by Manfred Mann when they were played the publishing tape at the London offices of Dylan's publisher. Mann's band decided they could hear some potential, especially if they gave it a gung-ho chorus.

They also renamed it 'The Mighty Quinn' – inverting the original's title and subtitle – restoring both them and Dylan to the UK Top Five at a time when the latter's singles profile was at an all-time low. And Dylan must have been keeping tabs, because he encored with the song at the Isle of Wight. Thanks to its sing-along chorus, perfect for football fans, it remains one of Dylan's best-known pop songs. Like the many who loved the Byrds' 'Tambourine Man,' though, few of those who bought Mann's 'Mighty Quinn' paid a great deal of attention to the actual lyrics, which warned one and all not to trust wicked messengers.

{228} OPEN THE DOOR, HOMER

Published lyrics: Writings and Drawings; Lyrics *1985;* Lyrics *2004.*
Known studio recordings: Big Pink, West Saugerties, summer 1967 – 3 takes.

Dylan returns to writing riddle songs. He even puts a riddle in the title, calling it 'Open the Door, Homer,' not 'Open the Door, Richard,' which is what he actually sings on all three takes (and which he knew had been a hit for Louis Jordan back in 1947) – though not according to *Lyrics*. 'Homer' was apparently a nickname given to the late Richard Fariña, who had died in a motorcycle crash on April 30, 1966, on his way home from a launch party for his debut novel, *Been Down So Long It Looks Like Up to Me*.

And it could well be that the song is an obtuse homage to an old friend, one who would not have been shy of including a character called Mouse in his novel. But perhaps Dylan was also thinking about a spill of his own, which he was lucky to have survived. Either way, when he proclaims that he 'ain't gonna hear [those words] said no more,' he sounds like someone exorcising a certain kind of ghost. As for the song's two morals, one is phrased just like a Luke the Drifter platitude – 'Take care of all your memories . . . for you cannot relive them' – the other like a Biblical proverb – to 'heal the sick / one must first forgive them.'

He attempted the song three times on tape, each version moving further and further away from the spirit originally invoked (the second take has spoken verses but a sung chorus, a trick he repeated in 1983 on the original version of 'Don't Fall Apart on Me Tonight'). The country licks on take three might have suited the song if it had been intended for *John Wesley Harding*, but for the publishing demo, take one sufficed. Something of a lost 'acetate' song, it has rarely been covered and even more rarely covered well, though Thunderclap Newman produced a thoroughly respectable version on their fine 1969 LP, *Hollywood Dream*.

{229} NOTHING WAS DELIVERED

Published lyrics: Writings and Drawings; Lyrics 1985; Lyrics 2004.
Known studio recordings: Big Pink, West Saugerties, summer 1967 – 3 takes [BT – tk.1].

'Nothing was Delivered' could be the last basement recording made before Dylan got on that nine-carriage train bound for Tennessee. It may also mark the point at which the four-piece Hawks gave way to the five-piece Band. According to Levon Helm, he returned just in time to cut a version of this song with him on the kit (such a version exists, sandwiched between alternate 'Odds and Ends'). The two known complete versions, however, were cut without Helm. On these drummer-less takes, the same seat-of-the-pants spirit found on most basement songs inhabits the recordings – one is wholly successful (take one), the other less so (take two).

It would appear that Dylan had again turned up with a typewritten sheet containing a proverb disguised as a chorus: 'Nothing is better, nothing is best / Take heed of this and get plenty [of] rest.' As to whether the melody arrived spontaneously at the session or came courtesy of a stray country riff Dylan had once heard, I know not. But 'Nothing Was Delivered' was another song where Dylan intended to donate the results. As he said to John Cohen in 1968, 'It used to be, if I would sing, I'd get a verse and go on and wait for it to come out as the music was there and sure enough, something would come out, but in the end, I would be deluded in those songs. Besides singing them, I'd be in there acting them out. . . . Now I . . . just write [those songs] for somebody else to sing, then do it – like an acetate.'

Recutting the song with Helm suggests The Band probably had their eye on this one, too. In this instance, though, it was Roger McGuinn who snagged the song for *Sweetheart of the Rodeo*. More mysteriously, the Byrds used as their template the 'rejected' second take, part spoken, part sung, rather than the so-called acetate version. Perhaps the little neighbour boy knows how this came to be.

1967: II

{ John Wesley Harding; The Basement Tapes }

By the fall of 1967, the silence had been deafening [sic]. Oblivious to Dylan's restored faculties, known only to those invited into the Big Pink basement, the world at large is wondering where in the hell the next Dylan album might be. Indeed, fans want to know just what extraordinary response he has up his sleeve to 'top' Sergeant Pepper *and other like-minded hippie recruits. Less is more, it would appear, as he wrote, recorded, and cut* John Wesley Harding *in just six weeks. Such fecundity proved to be just a part of the man's recording activities, as he continued to work with The Band, and their tape recorder, now that they too had a specific goal in mind – to prepare the groundwork for a debut Band album; which Dylan continued to shape with the songs he was still writing. Everything, it seemed, was now smooth like a rhapsody. Then someone pulled the switch.*

Published lyrics: Writings and Drawings; Lyrics 1985; Lyrics 2004.

Known studio recordings: Studio A, Nashville, October 17, 1967 – 1 take [JWH].

First known performance: JFK Stadium, Philadelphia, July 10, 1987.

> There's mystery, magic, truth and The Bible in great folk
> music. I can't hope to touch that, but I'm going to try.
> – Dylan to Michael Iachetta, May 1967

Supposedly, Dylan travelled down to the sessions in Nashville by train, a two-day ride, and used the time to write (or complete) songs he planned to record there. Since it would appear that his producer Bob Johnston had booked two days of sessions, he perhaps expected Dylan to have more songs than he actually had (or at least wanted) to record. Having visited the artist in Woodstock, Johnston was convinced that his once-productive progeny was ready to start recording again, even if he still subconsciously feared another *Blonde on Blonde* – songs written in the studio while the musicians pulled out their playing cards. This time, though, Dylan knew where he wanted to go, and 'Frankie Lee' – the narrative starting point – kicked off proceedings in a single take. This was *not* gonna be another *Sgt. Pepper*, an album that took more studio time to record than Dylan had *ever* spent behind closed studio doors.

Dylan has spoken a number of times about the pressure he was feeling to produce another album that fall, an era when *no one* took eighteen months off between albums. Most of this pressure he placed on himself. And not just because of his natural desire to prove that the flame still burned. He had finally re-signed to Columbia the previous August, cleverly negotiating a deal with no specific delivery dates, giving Columbia very little say as to what and when he delivered, or what they could do with it. Unfortunately for his emotional well-being, though, this new deal meant he only got paid a whopping new royalty of 10 percent – twice the norm even for 'name acts,' and more than the Beatles were getting – as and when he produced said album/s. If nothing was delivered, nothing was owed.

Yet Dylan disingenuously spun a yarn to *Sing Out!* the following June, claiming external pressure was the reason he returned to the studio in mid-October to record an album of 'folk songs': 'If I didn't have the recording contract and I didn't have to fulfill a certain amount of records [*sic*], I don't really know if I'd write down another song as long as I lived. . . . I didn't want to record this last album. I was going to do a whole album of other people's songs, but . . . the song has to be of a certain quality for me to sing and put on a record. One aspect it would have to have is that it didn't repeat itself. I shy away from those songs which repeat phrases, bars and verses, bridges. . . . The folk songs are just about the only ones that don't . . . – the narrative ones.'

Dylan may start with a lie here, but he then proceeds to reveal the genesis of his most integrated album in surprising detail. An interview given in close proximity to the album's release – but at a distance from the process itself – it confronts a number of issues the album only raised in hindsight. Crucially, it addresses the creative *volte-face* that left nary a residue from a summer's worth of form-shattering songs. Those 'repeat phrases, bars and verses' that had been propping up most of the material recorded back in Woodstock he eliminated entirely. He is now back to his 'homespun ballads,' even knowing 'psychedelic rock was overtaking the universe.'

The notion that he was even considering 'a whole album of other people's songs' – and *Self Portrait* was just a couple of years away – suggests he'd decided not to use *anything* already written, even songs like 'This Wheel's on Fire,' 'Tiny Montgomery,' and 'Yea Heavy and a Bottle of Bread,' which would have made a fair few choke on their psychedelic breakfasts. Yet, if we accept what he later said to Matt Damsker at face value, he *had* previously considered doing them: 'We were up there in Woodstock . . . and at that period of time we were laying down all these songs on tape. We were writing 'em and singing 'em onto tape, and I was going to have to go in and make a record, and I figured . . . I'd sing the [same] songs. . . . But then I went back and wrote just real simple songs.'

What Dylan appears to be saying, admittedly some ten years apart, is that he felt an obligation to start recording again but had nothing he desperately wanted to record. As such, having initially considered re-recording 'all these songs [already] on tape,' he then thought about an album of covers. Finally, and disarmingly close to the start of scheduled sessions in Nashville, he decided to write what, to that rewired mind, seemed like 'just real simple songs' – songs that 'didn't repeat' themselves; the kind of song he described on *Biograph* as 'definitely not pussy stuff . . . songs [which] are filled with more despair, more sadness, more triumph, more faith in the supernatural, much deeper feelings.' (The one specific example he cites, the traditional 'Young but Daily Growin',' he had recorded that summer, filling it with the full range of those raw emotions.)

Where else could he turn save to them old 'folk songs . . . the narrative ones'? It was this kind of song that had got him started a lifetime ago. Perhaps they could kick-start things again. Sure enough, most of the songs on *John Wesley Harding* are narratives (of a sort) – just as many of the covers recorded with The Band had been. Those that abandon the narrative approach were contrived at the end of the process, perhaps for the sake of variety or resolution (all three were recorded

437

at the final album session). There is also a fair share of 'faith in the supernatural' on the album (e.g., 'Drifter's Escape' and 'The Wicked Messenger').

One practice that *did* carry over from Big Pink was typing out lyrics first and then finding a tune to which it could be set. As he told Damsker, 'It was the first time I ever did an album . . . [where most] of the songs were written out on paper, and I found the tunes for them later. I didn't do it before and I haven't done it since. . . . It was special.' This time he allowed himself no real opportunity to work anything up in rehearsal, as The Band were otherwise engaged, making the album itself almost a demo. And all the better for it.

Where 'Frankie Lee and Judas Priest' departs from other kith and kin on *John Wesley Harding* is by sticking to that narrative, albeit one that resembles a medieval mystery play – with a mystery worth unravelling. Its closest relative can be found on the album, not in it. The sleeve notes, 'Three Kings,' tell a parable in prose. 'Frankie Lee' tells a parable in song (the moral/s of the parable, given at song's end, 'If you see your neighbour carrying something / Help him with his load,' is suitably trite, but sets up the real message of the album, 'Don't go mistaking paradise for that home across the road'). The post-accident Dylan claimed that 'the only parables that I know are the Biblical parables. I've seen others . . . [but] I have always read the Bible, though not necessarily always the parables.'

As it happens, the sleeve notes already told us that the 'key is Frank.' They do not tell us, though, whether Frank might be shorthand for Frankie Lee. Vera calls Frank 'a moderate man,' which would suggest that he is not. The Frankie Lee in the ballad overreacts to just about everything he is told. After asking his friend not to 'stare at [him] like that!' he is left alone, feeling 'low and mean.' When he is told his friend is 'stranded in a house,' his response is equally out of all proportion: 'He panicked / He dropped ev'rything and ran.' Eventually he loses 'all control'; 'foaming at the mouth he began to make his midnight creep,' until finally 'he died of thirst.'

Here, in unexpurgated form, is the world all the album's characters are obliged to inhabit. And though Dylan knew this world-gone-wrong well, he hadn't visited it in a while and did not plan to linger ('I knew I wasn't going to stay there very long' – Dylan to Damsker, 1978). He later put his concerns to Jonathan Cott: '*John Wesley Harding* was a fearful album . . . dealing with the devil in a fearful way, almost. All I wanted to do was to get the words right.'

Fear – and loathing – ripple through the first ten songs on *John Wesley Harding* like rats in a cornfield. And perhaps that was why Dylan shied away from developing the songs in concert. Prior to 1987 – with the obvious exception of 'All Along the Watchtower' – songs from this album almost never received a live outing. Even at the Isle of Wight, when it was one of just two albums released since the last UK tour, he performed only three *JWH* songs.

'Frankie Lee and Judas Priest' itself was obliged to wait twenty years for its meandering live debut on the July 1987 tour with the Grateful Dead. Reminded what a great little narrative he had written, Dylan persevered with it, performing a more compelling version on the Temples in Flames tour later the same year, set to the same arrangement as 'Shelter from the Storm.' Perhaps feeling more redemptive, he suggests on this occasion that Frankie Lee might not have died of thirst, the little neighbour boy carrying 'him home to rest,' rather than laying him 'to rest.' But Frankie and friend have been cruelly treated on the Never Ending Tour. Since rare but worthy excursions in 1988, when it has been performed, and it suffered a dozen or so performances in 2000, it has sounded like a song dying of thirst.

{231} DRIFTER'S ESCAPE

Published lyrics: Writings and Drawings; Lyrics 1985; Lyrics 2004.

*Known studio recordings: Studio A, Nashville, October 17, 1967 –
5 takes [JWH – tk.2].*

First known performance: Eugene, OR, April 30, 1992.

If it took 'Frankie Lee and Judas Priest' two decades to receive its live due, the sentence for 'Drifter's Escape' was twenty-five years. Were it not for the riotous release of racial tension that the 'not guilty' verdict in the trial of the officers who assaulted Rodney King sparked, we still might not have heard this microcosmic masterpiece in a concert setting. Instead, on April 30, 1992, Dylan unveiled the song in Oregon, having clearly worked it up in a hurry, without having quite mastered the compressed narrative.

As has often proven the case, it was only by performing the song that Dylan reminded himself how beautifully honed and economical this forgotten work was. As a result, he set about working up a proper arrangement (he even learned the lyrics), which he was ready to unveil by the time he arrived in San Francisco four days later; by which time the whole country 'was stirring' at a rank injustice. As Dylan sang nightly, 'The trial was bad enough / But this was ten times worse.'

Back in October 1967, mired in a similar climate of fear, Dylan once again demonstrated his distaste for the legal process, preferring to leave Judgement to Him on high. Reversing 'Percy's Song' and 'Seven Curses,' he makes the judge compassionate but powerless. He also sets the drifter free, not at the whim of the judge, but via that most traditional of devices, the *deus ex machina*. A bolt of lightning causes everyone else to pray, allowing the (presumably faithless) drifter to escape. Dylan had found a way to tell a five-act story in just three verses. Enthused by what he had achieved, he began writing a whole set of songs along similar lines.

Published lyrics: Writings and Drawings; Lyrics *1985;* Lyrics *2004.*

Known studio recordings: Studio A, Nashville, October 17, 1967 –
4 takes [JWH – tk.4].

First known performance: Isle of Wight, August 31, 1969.

The third and last song recorded at the first *John Wesley*
Harding session, 'I Dreamed I Saw St. Augustine' was also
the first to place a real historical character in circumstances
that failed to resemble any previously documented (a dry
run for *Chronicles?*). Like Tom Paine (in 'As I Went Out
One Morning') and John Wesley Harding, St. Augustine
finds himself in a most incongruous setting. Attempting to
dispense good advice ('Go on your way / And know you're
not alone'), he is 'put . . . to death' for his troubles.

The song's martyr is clearly neither Augustine of Hippo
nor the St. Augustine who brought the Word to the heathen
Brits, and Dylan knows it. He is a cipher, serving to inform
Dylan's audience that nothing on *John Wesley Harding* is as it
seems. Neither early Christian father was put 'out to death.'
Nor would either have ever adopted as a catchphrase, 'No
martyr is among ye now.' So Dylan has another martyr in
mind, one who *was* 'put out to death,' and whose dying
words were meant to offer hope and solace.

Not one inclined to mention martyrs at the drop of a hat,
Dylan did enthuse about one such person who was a bit of
a songwriter, in a September 1978 interview, shortly after
discussing the merits of his 1967 LP: 'Now those were good
songs that Joe Hill wrote. He wrote some real good songs,
but . . . in those days martyrs were easy to find. . . . Things
were pretty simple.'

Joe Hill was a union organizer for the Industrial Workers
of the World (IWW) who was convicted of the motive-
less murder of a complete stranger on the grounds that he
had sustained a bullet wound he could not explain. He was

executed in November of 1915. Some fifteen years later, Alfred Hayes wrote a poem about Joe Hill's fate, which Earl Robinson duly set to music. The poem, which was called 'I Dreamed I Saw Joe Hill Last Night,' contained the following opening verse:

> I dreamed I saw Joe Hill last night,
> Alive as you and me.
> Says I 'But Joe, you're ten years dead'
> 'I never died' said he.

Decades later, in *Chronicles*, Dylan admitted that the idea of writing a song about Joe Hill had long appealed to him: 'Protest songs are difficult to write without making them come off as preachy and one-dimensional. You have to show people a side of themselves that they don't know is there. The song "Joe Hill" doesn't even come close, but if there was someone who could inspire a song, it was him.' And that song is . . .

'St. Augustine' is, in fact, written from the point of view of a member of the jury who 'put him out to death' and now sees the terrible error he has made. The parallels are clear. Just not exact. One should be wary of overstating Joe Hill's resemblance to the august saint, for St. Augustine is as much a cipher for Dylan as he is for Hill. Having been cast as a messiah of sorts himself, Dylan recognized the importance of telling any obvious believers that '[no] martyr is among ye now.' After all, here was a man who had already written a number of epitaphs, including one that read, 'here lies bob dylan / murdered / from behind.'

Not only is 'St. Augustine' a eulogy of sorts, it is exquisitely sung (even if Dylan and his fellow Americans don't know how to pronounce the saint's name, rhyming it with 'mean,' not 'sin'). 'St. Augustine' also seems to have been one of the few *JWH* songs he could bring himself to play, applying a slow waltz arrangement at the Isle of Wight, thus providing a possible insight into what a Band-embellished *John Wesley Harding* might have sounded like.* It also became a regular feature of the Rolling Thunder Revue as a Dylan/Baez duet (Baez having covered 'Joe Hill' *and* 'St. Augustine'). In the eighties it enjoyed another welcome revival at the hands of the Heartbreakers, but in the nineties, just as the rest of the album returned to the fold, our martyr fell from grace.

{233} ALL ALONG THE WATCHTOWER

Published lyrics: Writings and Drawings; Lyrics *1985;* Lyrics *2004.*
Known studio recordings: Studio A, Nashville, November 6, 1967 – 3 takes [JWH – tk.3+insert].
First known performance: Chicago Stadium, January 3, 1974.

Two three-week gaps separate the three sessions from which Dylan's eighth album was culled. In that time he found a willing muse and a surprising facility for filling in gaps *to order.* The only other album where he started every session knowing which songs he would record, aiming to place all of them on the finished artifact, would be *Street-Legal*, another album for which the lyrics were written first. But that album gestated for nine months, whereas the writing *and* recording of *John Wesley Harding* took six weeks. For *John Wesley Harding*, Dylan wrote exactly twelve songs, recorded exactly twelve songs, and released exactly twelve songs, while telegraphing his next move on the last two.

Of these three sessions, the most productive would be

---

* According to Robbie Robertson, there were discussions with Dylan about him and Garth Hudson doing some overdubbing of the *John Wesley Harding* cuts, but nothing came of it. (See *Behind The Shades: Take Two*, pp. 287–8.)

the second. On November 6, in just three and a half hours, Dylan recorded five strong songs. And he began with the most carefully crafted (and best-known) song on the released album, 'All Along the Watchtower.' Recorded with minimal fuss, the song set the listener up for an epic ballad with its first two verses, only to cut, after the briefest instrumental interlude, to the end of the song, leaving the listener to fill in his or her own (doom-laden) blanks. It was a technique he employed a couple more times on *John Wesley Harding* – notably on 'The Wicked Messenger' – but as Dylan told John Cohen some months later, this particular song 'opens up . . . in a stranger way':

> The scope opens up, just by a few little tricks. I know why it opens up, but in a ballad in the true sense, it wouldn't open up that way. . . . See, on the album, you have to think about it after you hear it, that's what takes up the time, but with a ballad, you don't necessarily have to think about it after you hear it, it can all unfold to you. . . . The third verse of 'The Wicked Messenger' . . . opens it up, and then the time schedule takes a jump and soon the song becomes wider. . . . The same thing is true of . . . 'All Along the Watchtower,' which opens up in a slightly different way, in a stranger way, for here we have the cycle of events working in a rather reverse order.

Much has been made of this song's supposed circularity – i.e., the last line could be the first, and vice versa. Dylan's comment about 'the cycle of events working in a . . . reverse order' does suggest there is something to this. Indeed, in performance he has occasionally played with the order of the verses (not always knowingly). One particular night in the fall of 1989 in New York's Poughkeepsie, he sang the opening two verses a second time, as if the nightmare would never end, i.e. there really is no 'way out of here.'

Folk have also gotten very excited at the handful of allusions the song contains to the apocalyptic sections of the Bible. The late Bert Cartwright, the most knowledgeable of Dylan-Bible scholars, cites five biblical references for 'All Along the Watchtower' in his seminal study, *The Bible in the Lyrics of Bob Dylan*, quoting in full the section from the Book of Isaiah that foretells the fall of Babylon (21:6): 'For thus hath the Lord said unto me, "Go set a watchman, let him declare what he seeth." And he saw a chariot with a couple of horsemen . . .'

Cartwright was hardly alone in suggesting that the thief in 'All Along the Watchtower' is probably the messianic One foretold by St. John the Divine in Revelations, who 'will come on thee as a thief, and thou shalt not know what hour I will come upon thee.' Which might mean that Dylan is the joker complaining of 'too much confusion,' and this song is a conversation between the lapsed Jew and his Redeemer. On the other hand, the thief could as easily be the Dylan of yesteryear ('you and I, we've been through that, and this is not our fate') – i.e., the pre-accident Bob, the thief of fire who had taken Rimbaud's dictum to heart ('Why must I always be the thief?' he asks on the contemporaneous 'Tears of Rage').

Should one depict the song as apocalyptic – and the End appears to be evident everywhere the joker looks – it is the Apocalypse of 'When the Ship Comes In.' At the head of the queue for those who shall be judged are all those 'businessmen [who] drink my wine.' This is the same Dylan who had told Michael Iachetta in May, 'Songs are in my head . . . [but] they're not going to get written down until some things are evened up.' He was even blunter to Kurt Loder in 1984: 'I had that motorcycle accident which put me outta commission.

Then, when I woke up and caught my senses, I realized I was just working for all these leeches.' Hence, one suspects, the sense of retribution that permeates the entire album – as well as contemporary songs like 'Down in the Flood' and 'I Shall Be Released.' As Dylan told the *L.A. Times*' Robert Hilburn semi-seriously in November 1991, when he finally let the song linger awhile: '"All Along the Watchtower" may be my [only] political song.'

How ironic, then, that it should receive an arrangement by guitar-God Jimi Hendrix – recorded just a couple of months after Dylan's own version – that conveyed all that terrible beauty in the tenor of the *music* (which prompted Dylan to write of Hendrix's covers of his songs: 'he played them the way i would have done them if i was him'). That 'cover' version became another radio hit in which the import of the song was lost in the translation. Few might consider Dylan's subtler, more worldly-wise rendition preferable, but the many in this instance would be wrong. Hendrix turns it into a rock anthem, when it was written as the very antithesis of that. The song, written as a 'homespun ballad,' had been hijacked by psychedelic rock's talisman.

Disappointingly, even Dylan was swept up by its success. His own ubiquitous live treatments have generally adhered to the Hendrix template, making the music sound vaguely apocalyptic but losing the power and precision those 129 words originally brought to the process. Only in the eighties did he begin to consider the error of his ways. In 1985 he set the less ambiguous 'When the Night Comes Falling from the Sky' to the 1978 live arrangement of 'All Along the Watchtower,' while in 1987 he set 'Watchtower' to the same, slow-burn setting as his first post-conversion song, 'Slow Train,' making a point on each occasion.

{234} JOHN WESLEY HARDING

Published lyrics: Writings and Drawings; Lyrics 1985; Lyrics 2004.
*Known studio recordings: Studio A, Nashville, November 6, 1967 –
2 takes [JWH – tk.2].*

Dylan's abiding fascination with outlaws, particularly cowboys like Billy the Kid and Jesse James, is well documented. So the decision to write a cowboy ballad about the notorious gunfighter John Wesley Hardin should have come as no surprise. Hardin was another cold-blooded murderer who bragged that he had killed forty-four men, including one he shot for snoring too loudly, before being cornered in 1875 on a train bound for Pensacola. Amazingly, he was not executed, but served seventeen harrowing years in a penitentiary before emerging from jail with a law degree. He practised law until 1895 when an argument over his prostitute girlfriend led one John Selman to return later, while Hardin was playing dice in a saloon, and shoot him three times in the back ('he was shot in the back / by a hungry kid . . .').

None of this sounds much like 'a friend to the poor,' or someone likely 'to lend a helping hand.' Or indeed a person who was 'never known to make a foolish move.' And Dylan knows this. He is back in the mythological hinterlands leading off from Highway 61 – self-consciously opening the album with a figure who has already passed beyond history, into the mythic soundscape that now bears his name. Hence, one suspects, Dylan's choice of outlaw. Even the one incident he specifically refers to – 'Down in Chaynee County . . . With his lady by his side / He took a stand' – is lifted straight from medieval romance, via nineteenth-century dime-store fiction. No such incident occurred, at least not where Hardin was concerned.

Again Dylan enjoys setting up the listener for the classic broadside ballad, complete with moralizing coda. But all we get is the raw outline for such a ballad. According to Dylan, talking to Jann Wenner in 1969, he simply gave up on the story: '"*John Wesley Harding*" . . . started out to be a long ballad . . . like maybe one of those old cowboy [ballads]. . . . But in the middle of the second verse I got tired. I had a tune, and I didn't really want to waste the tune . . . so I just wrote a quick third verse and recorded that. . . . It was the one song on the album which didn't seem to fit in.' Another classic Dylan smokescreen! The idea that he simply 'got tired' of the song might be more credible (and it couldn't be less) if he hadn't used the same technique – setting up a ballad narrative, before removing all its innards – on two of the four songs he'd already recorded.

Yet he continued to claim the title track 'didn't seem to fit in,' informing Cameron Crowe that even after he'd recorded the whole album, 'I didn't know what to make of it. . . . So I figured the best thing to do would be to put it out as quickly as possible, call it *John Wesley Harding*, because that was the one song that I had no idea what it was about, why it was even on the album. . . . It was never intended to be anything else but just a bunch of songs really.' Just to prove he'd lost none of his comic timing, Dylan delivers the perfect punch line: 'Maybe it was better than I thought.'

Not only couldn't the album have been more perfectly constructed, but in keeping with long-standing practice, Dylan used the opening song to demonstrate which stylist the listener could expect this time around. Like Frank, he was enticing the listener to venture in 'just far enough so's we can say that we've been there' – and what better way than to give them a simple cowboy ballad that was nothing of the sort. By now he knew what sound fit, cutting the song in two takes, both complete, each considered for the album. That sound wasn't the next big thing – country-rock. He left that to the Byrds. It was as simple as the songs seemed.

Published lyrics: Writings and Drawings; Lyrics 1985; Lyrics 2004.

Known studio recordings: Studio A, Nashville, November 6, 1967 –
5 takes [JWH – tk.5].

First known performance: Toronto, January 10, 1974.

After a cowboy ballad, Dylan decided to try his hand at
a lyric of love unrequited. Once again he is determined to
have a little fun with folk commonplaces. And there is no
greater commonplace than 'As I went out one morning,'
the folk equivalent of the classic blues opening, 'Woke up
this morning.' However, this time the maiden in question
is not in peril; the singer is. Nor is he saved from this siren-
like seductress by any conventional traditional device – like a
bird flying to tell the king, or a harp singing of her guilt – but
by the entry of famed libertarian and author Tom Paine, who
comes 'running from across the field . . . commanding her
to yield.' After succeeding in releasing the narrator, Paine
mysteriously apologizes 'for what she's done.' As the man
said, 'Mystery is a traditional fact.'

Here, then, is that basement-esque contagion of chaos
in popular ballad form. And just like in the Big Pink songs,
Dylan prefers to leave its meaning unexplained. 'As I Went
Out One Morning' begins like the opening chapter of a book,
or the opening scene of a modern thriller; but if the popular
ballad is a musical play that starts in Act Four, as has been
stated a number of times, Dylan Wesley Harding preferred
to jump from Act One to Act Five. Having recognized that
'with a ballad, you don't necessarily have to think about it
after you hear it, it can all unfold to you,' he elected to write
songs that obeyed balladic forms but *required* the listener 'to
think about it after you hear it.'

Dylan, though, did not dally long with the song in question, cutting it in just five takes before forgetting it for good,
save for one enticingly captivating rendition delivered with

full Band accompaniment (and some lovely Robertson licks) at a show in Toronto in January 1974. Here, again, a word-perfect Dylan sings the song with a real relish for what he has wrought, spitting out the lines like he realizes how close he came to another encounter with Johanna. The following night, though, he was back on autopilot, and the song has not popped up since.

{236} I AM A LONESOME HOBO

Published lyrics: Writings and Drawings; Lyrics *1985;* Lyrics *2004.*
Known studio recordings: Studio A, Nashville, November 6, 1967 – 5 takes [JWH – tk.5].

A popular mainstay of the broadside presses throughout the eighteenth and nineteenth centuries were the last words of criminals on the gallows, in rhyming doggerel, recanting their wanton ways and warning others 'not to do what I have done.' Dylan himself performed a magical version of one of the more popular, 'Newlyn Town' (a.k.a. 'A Wild and Wicked Youth'), at a show in Reims in 1992, having apparently learned the song in Minneapolis thirty-two years earlier (see *Chronicles,* p. 239).

And even though we can't be sure that the Lonesome Hobo is about to swing, he has decided to make a similar confession of misdeeds – 'before I do pass on.' In so doing, he does not spare us any of his wrongdoings in his litany of crimes: 'Bribery, blackmail and deceit / And I've served time for ev'rything / 'Cept beggin' on the street.' No longer only a hobo, the lonesome one is a wicked messenger, a poor immigrant, and a mystery tramp rolled into one.

Dylan again sets things up with the couple of verses allocated to most *John Wesley Harding* songs, before delivering the moralizing coda that was an obligatory part of every wrongdoer's potted history-in-rhyme. After the playful proverb in 'Frankie Lee and Judas Priest,' the moral in 'I Am a Lonesome Hobo' takes on quite a different hue, asserting individuality over social morés: 'Live by no man's code / And hold your judgement for yourself / Lest you wind up on this road.' Here is the same man who once vouchsafed that 'to live outside the law you must be honest.'

{237} I PITY THE POOR IMMIGRANT

Published lyrics: Writings and Drawings; Lyrics 1985; Lyrics 2004.
Known studio recordings: Studio A, Nashville, November 6, 1967 – 10 takes [JWH – tk.10].
First known performance: Isle of Wight, August 31, 1969.

At what exact point did Dylan outline the architecture for this, his most perfectly realized album? By the end of the second session, he was already two-thirds into the process, with an album opener, a big ballad, and a potential single (which he refrained from releasing, resulting in an argument with new Columbia president Clive Davis, who pointed out the commercial realities of AM airplay). All that really remained was for him to hit the home stretch of that path, 'thick beset wi' briars,' which leads from retribution to salvation. Simple.

Before that, though, he required one more parable-in-song, focusing on the fate of tenants, hoboes, tramps, and hawkers. The latter two formed the subject of a traditional ballad Dylan knew well, which he may or may not have learned from Scottish folksinger Jean Redpath. As she told Radio Scotland in 2001, 'Bob and I were out-of-towners . . . in the back end of the summer of 1961, ' we had the same roof over our heads, thanks to the generosity of a woman called Mikki Issacson. . . . [And] I know I had "Tramps & Hawkers" and "Davy Farr," of course the same tune, and "The Bonnie Lass of Fyvie" in my own active repertoire about that point. But who can tell what damage that did.'

The last of these served as the original for 'Pretty Peggy-O,' a song Dylan put on his debut platter (and donated in kind to the Dead), while 'Tramps and Hawkers' was another simple song that did not quite suffice for Dylan's polemical purpose, but had a tune that did. The song itself was a jaunty celebration of life on the road, not the tortured tale of a 'poor immigrant / who wishes he would've stayed home':

> Sometimes noo I laugh tae mysel'
> when dodgin' alang the road
> Wi' a bag o' meal slung upon my back,
> my face as broun's a toad
> Wi' lumps o'cheese and tattie scones
> or breid an' braxie ham
> Nae thinking whar' I'm comin' frae
> nor thinkin' whar I'm gang.

It had been a while since Dylan allowed himself to put a traditional tune to the words he was spinning (a process he then carried back to Woodstock). As with the equally jaunty 'I've Been a Moonshiner,' which he transformed into the wrist-slashing 'Moonshine Blues' for the *Times . . .* sessions, he again turned a fine traditional tune to a darker purpose – writing the *John Wesley Harding* equivalent of 'Tears of Rage,' a song written within a couple of weeks of 'I Pity the Poor Immigrant.'

'I Pity the Poor Immigrant,' though, relies more on the language of Milton's *Paradise Lost* or the King James Bible than ballads of a similar vintage. Not just the language but also the specific follies the song details can be found scattered across the Old Testament, whether it be Leviticus ('Your strength shall be spent in vain: for your land shall not yield her increase' – 26:20; 'Ye shall eat, and not be satisfied' – 26:26) or Deuteronomy ('Thou say in thine heart, My power and the might of mine hand hath gotten me this wealth' – 8:17).

Of a piece with 'The Wicked Messenger,' which follows it on the album (and may have already been written), 'Immigrant' took Dylan ten takes to sing and be satisfied.

One of three *John Wesley Harding* songs to receive its live debut at the Isle of Wight, 'I Pity the Poor Immigrant' is blessed with another sympathetic Band treatment, a wash of accordion overseeing its stately procession. However, Dylan's attempt to blend *Nashville Skyline* and *John Wesley Harding* 'voices' makes for one of the least effective vocals on that strange evening. Seven years later, the song was redeemed by the glorious honky-tonk arrangement it received on the second leg of the Rolling Thunder Revue, this time delivered by a Dylan who almost snarls the lyrics, while Joan Baez gamely tries to hold her own. This last, sardonic reincarnation, also a highlight of the *Hard Rain* concert film, seemingly sufficed.

{238} THE WICKED MESSENGER

Published lyrics: Writings and Drawings; Lyrics 1985; Lyrics 2004.
Known studio recordings: Studio A, Nashville, November 29, 1967 [JWH].
First known performance: Giants Stadium, Meadowlands, July 12, 1987.

> A wicked messenger falleth into mischief: but a faithful ambassador *is* health. – Proverbs 13:17

Dylan knew precisely what kind of album he was making, and probably had the sequence in his mind by the time he arrived at the last *John Wesley Harding* session on November 29. Before recording the last three tracks, Dylan elected *not* to end the album on a downbeat note. And so, having written the better part of another song dealing with deception, betrayal, and general 'mischief,' Dylan allowed 'the third verse of "The Wicked Messenger" . . . [to] open it up.' Not just the song, but the album, too.

An interviewer once asked Dylan if he wrote 'Dear Landlord' just to get to the last line ('If you don't underestimate me . . .'). The journalist probably should have asked the same about 'The Wicked Messenger,' the way 'the time schedule takes a jump' being nowhere near as abrupt as in 'All Along the Watchtower.' 'Oh the leaves began to fallin' / And the seas began to part,' signifying the passing of the seasons, the ballad equivalent of the movie montage, beautifully sets up the denouement to come: 'If you cannot bring good news, then don't bring any.'

As with 'All Along the Watchtower,' it took a rugged rock arrangement to remind some listeners of both the musicality and the dramatic potential of such a song. The Faces' *First Step*, their 1969 debut LP, opens with the song, the beginning of a career-long Dylan fixation for frontman Rod Stewart. Yet for Dylan it was another piece in the *JWH* jigsaw that, once completed, held little allure. Eventually, the Grateful Dead pushed him to perform it to the great unwashed and permanently dazed in 1987, and it actually worked. Dylan even transferred their arrangement to the Heartbreakers later that year, before deciding that that was enough good news for now. It took another ten years – and another storming arrangement of the song by the Patti Smith Group on the joint Dylan/Smith *Paradise Lost* tour in the fall of 1995 – for the seas to part again. East Coast audiences in the spring of 1997 were thus blessed with the return of the redeemed messenger.

{239} DEAR LANDLORD

Published lyrics: Writings and Drawings; Lyrics *1985;* Lyrics *2004.*
Known studio recordings: Studio A, Nashville, November 29, 1967 [JWH].
First known performance: Providence, RI, October 25, 1992.

Still not quite done with calling the feckless to judgement, Dylan had one more target in his sights. Though on 'Dear

Landlord' he never explicitly names the culprit, it didn't take long for others to surmise that the 'landlord' was Albert Grossman, someone who had once 'put a price on [his] soul.' By this point, contact between Dylan and Grossman was kept to a bare minimum, Sara often finding herself obliged to act as go-between. At the January 1968 Woody Guthrie memorial, CBS president Clive Davis recognized a changed dynamic, and even the less astute Bob Shelton noticed a real distance between Dylan and his manager.

Dylan almost admitted that Grossman *was* 'the landlord' in a 1971 conversation with A. J. Weberman – another person who wanted to put a price on Bob's soul – but smartly stopped short of giving it this one, narrow meaning: '["Dear Landlord"] wasn't *all the way* [my italics] for Al Grossman. In fact, he wasn't even in my mind. Only later, when people pointed out to me that the song might've been written for Al Grossman, I thought, well, maybe it could've been.' In fact, he was already planning to even things up by pulling the plug on Grossman's half share of the publishing – terminating Dwarf Music at the end of 1967.

He had certainly been aiming to make such a statement for a while (see #209). Between songs of resolution, he switched over to piano to pound out this valedictory to a relationship whose lease has expired. 'Dear Landlord' duly became another song on *John Wesley Harding* that sneaked under the wire of most listeners' sensibilities, though it struck a chord with a number of fine singers, notably Joe Cocker and Sandy Denny, who both recorded the song the following year. Dylan himself seemed faintly embarrassed by the song, insisting to Crowe that it 'was really just the first line. . . . Then I just figured, what else can I put to it.'

'Dear Landlord,' one more Dwarf song put into cryogenic storage, did not come in from the cold until October 1992, when he at last presented a full band arrangement of it at a

New England soundcheck, unveiling it the following night to whoops of delight from the Dylan devotees.

Note: The recent Super Audio CD 'remaster' of *John Wesley Harding* is a travesty of the original LP. Typically bright, it centres everything, losing the piano/vocal symmetry of the original recording of 'Dear Landlord.' An original stereo vinyl copy (not the crappy Sundazed 'mono' reissue) should sit in every Dylan fan's collection.

{240} I'LL BE YOUR BABY TONIGHT

Published lyrics: Writings and Drawings; Lyrics *1985*; Lyrics *2004*.
Known studio recordings: Studio A, Nashville, November 29, 1967 [JWH].
First known performance: Isle of Wight, August 31, 1969.

{241} DOWN ALONG THE COVE

Published lyrics: Writings and Drawings; Lyrics *1985*; Lyrics *2004*.
Known studio recordings: Studio A, Nashville, November 29, 1967 [JWH].
First known performance: Eugene, Or, June 14, 1999.

In every sense imaginable, these two songs belong together. Recorded in reverse order, at the end of the last *John Wesley Harding* session, they bid farewell to all the recriminations and garment-rending that came before. They also, as Dylan admitted to Matt Damsker, were the 'only two songs which came at the same time as the music.' Whether or not he knew at the time that he was composing 'tasters' for the next album is less clear. He says not, insisting in 1978 that on *'John Wesley Harding, . . .* we did two songs which the whole next album was like the last two songs on that album. [But] I didn't even realize it at the time.'

Yet, by laying Pete Drake's pedal steel across these tracks, Dylan does seem to be suggesting that he – and/ or his producer – were looking to go 'more country.' The voice, too, has started to undergo its metamorphosis into a cross between Rodgers's twang and 'all the Hanks,' fully previewed on the basement-tape version of 'See That My Grave Is Kept Clean.' Yet all this could be hindsight toying with us. As Dylan mockingly observed in 1981, 'The older albums don't really mean something to some people until they're hearing the new one, and in retrospect they go back and hear something else from the path that'll seem like it takes the steps that leads up to the new one.'

At the end of 1967, no one was predicting that Dylan would venture further down this ol' dirt road. And had he felt so inclined, he could easily have put these two AM-friendly songs out as a single, thus reinforcing a change in direction. But Dylan only went the whole hog after Johnny Cash reinvented country's commercial credentials with his *Folsom Prison* LP. When Dylan performed 'I'll Be Your Baby Tonight' at the Isle of Wight, he sang it in that cud-chewing *Skyline* voice (some boozy backing vocals at least act as a reminder of those basement days). As if apologizing for this artistic crime, his subsequent live versions (of which there have been many) have generally removed the 'tree' from *country*.

'Down Along the Cove' has enjoyed less favour than 'I'll Be Your Baby Tonight,' from either Dylan or the cover merchants. A mere footnote to the era until 1999, it became the tenth song from *JWH* to receive a live debut and the fifth to be so revived since 1987. In 2003 the song received a further makeover before being reintroduced into the live set. This would barely warrant comment had Dylan not set this inconsequential incursion to new lyrics and then included them as an 'alternate version' in the 2004 edition of *Lyrics* – the only such instance of a 'live' rewrite featuring in any authorized edition of the man's lyrics. This 2003 version, still unreleased in any form – unlike, say, the 1976 'Lay, Lady, Lay' or the 1984 'Tangled Up in Blue' – from a purely literary view barely warranted the effort expended transcribing it.

Yet its inclusion was apparently at Dylan's insistence. Shame that he allowed another half-wit to do the transcription, thus turning the famous gambling boat 'the Jackson River Queen' into 'Jacks and the River Queen.' I trust it went down in the flood.

{242} ODDS AND ENDS

Published lyrics: Writings and Drawings; Lyrics *1985;* Lyrics *2004.*
Known studio recordings: Big Pink, West Saugerties, summer 1967 – 2 takes [BT – tk.2].

The basement reel that features 'Odds and Ends,' 'Get Your Rocks Off,' 'Clothesline Saga,' and 'Apple Suckling Tree' is even more difficult to place in the order of things than its immediate predecessor, the 'Tears of Rage' reel. The key question, again, is whether any of these songs predate the start of *John Wesley Harding?* Or had Helm returned to the fold? There *is* somebody pounding the kit with more than the timekeeping manner adopted on the basement bulletins that came before. Yet neither Griffin nor Marcus thinks this is Levon Helm, who found his way to Woodstock by early November.

Helm himself suggests, in his autobiography, 'When [Dylan] came back after Thanksgiving [i.e., after the *last JWH* session], we cut "Nothing was Delivered."' And the only possible candidate for said recording of said song lies between the two takes of 'Odds and Ends' (Helm refers to hearing 'a great rock & roll song called "Odds and Ends"' on his arrival, just to confuse things further). Even if these recordings predate Helm's return (in which case, hats off to Richard), methinks it is only by a matter of days. This reel probably still comes after activities moved from Big Pink to Wittenberg Road – which would make the inclusion of 'Odds and Ends' as the opener to the 1975 double-album of 'Big Pink' recordings an ironic choice indeed.

The reel demonstrates that Dylan continued to revel in nonsense, whether in the folk-song mode of 'Apple Suckling Tree,' improvising a slow blues ('Get Your Rocks Off'), or writing his first basement ballad ('Clothesline Saga'). But 'Odds and Ends,' for all its musical spirit, suggests that when it came to spouting catchphrase choruses while espousing mock profundities in verse, the process had just about run its course. Dylan admits as much by singing, 'I've had enough, my box is clean / You know what I'm sayin' and you know what I mean.'

{243} GET YOUR ROCKS OFF

Published lyrics: Writings and Drawings; Lyrics 1985; Lyrics 2004.
Known studio recordings: Big Pink, West Saugerties, summer 1967.

A 'Rainy Day Women' for the basement tapes, 'Get Your Rocks Off' is the least successful of the 'later' home recordings. Yet of those recordings, it, and it alone, was among the five songs copyrighted in January 1968, indubitable proof that the song – and companions of the reel – were recorded by early December at the latest. The perversity that suggested it should be copyrighted immediately – when 'Clothesline Saga,' 'Odds and Ends,' 'Apple Suckling Tree,' and 'Goin' to Acapulco' were cast aside – cannot be attributed to its 'hit' potential. It was omitted from the publishing demo compiled from the other songs registered at this time.

Nor was 'Get Your Rocks Off' restored to favour when the official album appeared – though it featured all four of the songs overlooked in January 1968. As for the song itself, it is largely a way to riff on the double entendre 'rocks' – as, literally, the kind of rocks used to stone someone, and also the testicular rocks inside a man's pants. As such, a source of amusement to one and all after an afternoon spent sending smoke signals, but not something to savour through those Woodstock winters.

Published lyrics: Writings and Drawings; Lyrics *1985*; Lyrics *2004*.
Known studio recordings: Big Pink, West Saugerties, late summer 1967 [BT].

The fabled 'safety' of the basement songs was most likely compiled in the fall of 1969 from session masters – save for the four songs copy-righted in January 1968 [#226–9], which audibly derive from a generational copy. Its compilation also revealed four uncopyrighted songs worthy of preservation. 'I'm Not There' was one of these. The other three were all to be found on the 'Get Your Rocks Off' reel, notably 'Clothesline Saga,' another highlight of these sessions, and as deadpan a deconstruction of Bobbie Gentry's 'Ode to Billie Joe' as 'Fourth Time Around' had been of 'Norwegian Wood.' Gentry's account of how she came to write her song shows a particular kind of structural sophistication, similar to Lennon's, that Dylan admired (the man usually only parodying something he *liked*):

> The story of Billie Joe has two . . . underlying themes. First, the illustration of a group of people's reactions to the life and death of Billie Joe, and its subsequent effect on their lives, is made. Second, the obvious generation gap between the girl and her mother is shown, when both women experience a common loss . . . and yet Mama and the girl are unable to recognize their mutual loss or share their grief.

As with 'Fourth Time Around,' 'Clothesline Saga' – or, as it was called on the safety reel, 'Answer to Ode' – has a lot more ambition in its lyrical loins than just parodying a crossover chart-topper. Dylan wanted to address country music's capacity to develop a narrative about real people and still make people 'think about it after [they] hear it.' As he wrote decades later, in *Chronicles*, 'Folk songs were the underground story. If someone were to ask what's going on, "Mr. Garfield's been shot down, laid down. Nothing you can do." That's what's going on. Nobody needed to ask who Mr. Garfield was, they just nodded, they just knew.'

'Clothesline Saga' thus functions as both a folk song *and* an underground story. In this version of the six o'clock news, an event in the wider world impinges – 'The vice-president's gone mad!' – but the response from these people who are entirely detached from world-shaking events is stoic: 'There's nothing we can do about it.' It is the narrative of neighbours over the fence, people who just get on with their daily chores. This is not the Dylan of 'Black Diamond Bay,' where apathy has bred ignorance. He is on *their* side. Just as he is when Happy Traum endeavors to get an opinion on the Vietnam 'police action' the following summer. Dylan responds by reinventing himself as Everyman: 'I know just as much about [events] as the lady across the street does, and she probably knows quite a bit. Just reading the papers, talking to the neighbors, and so forth.'

But it is also the way Dylan delivers the whole 'saga' in the most laconic manner imaginable that lets the song take root in the subconscious, planting its seeds. He had already test-run this persona on a number of songs that summer – notably 'Sign on the Cross,' 'Nothing Was Delivered' (take two), and (one suspects) 'Wild Wolf.' But its archetype can be found on his cover of Hank Williams's '(Be Careful of) the Stones That You Throw,' a moralistic monologue Williams recorded using his Luke the Drifter alter ego. Dylan had been living with Luke a long time (as he recently wrote, 'The Luke the Drifter record I just about wore out'). If learning to play the preacher would come in handy later, for now it allowed him to concisely capture the routine of country living at a time when he still believed that 'this must be what it's all about.'

Published lyrics: Lyrics *1985;* Lyrics *2004.*

Known studio recordings: Big Pink, West Saugerties, late summer 1967 – 2 takes [BT – tk.2].

Back in love with his traditional roots, Dylan decided it was high time he wrote his own folkloric nursery rhyme. And like Newton, he fell to musing 'underneath that apple suckling tree,' penning this delicious piece of nonsense around a melody line that had served for four hundred years or more at the behest of 'Froggy Went A-Courtin.' That song – obliquely mentioned in a 1549 Scottish text before becoming a popular seventeenth-century broadside – depicts a fanciful procession of animals invited to the wedding of a frog and a mouse. So it was bound to have the edge on 'Apple Suckling Tree' in the surreal stakes. But Dylan doesn't give up without a fight, coming up with the immortal sentiment on the second take:

> Aloysius was sold at seven years, uh-huh, [x2]
> If I die, bury me in the ground
> I'll catch your mane by the hare and hound.

Or words to that effect. It is this second take that appears, quite correctly, on the official album. The other take barely qualifies as a run-through, but it is from this 'rehearsal' take that the song was copyrighted and the lyrics in *Lyrics* transcribed. Both lyrics are of the moment and largely slurred. But the rehearsal *only* has dummy lyrics, which are not greatly improved by transcription. At least in their original form, as published in *The Songs of Bob Dylan 1966–1975*, they are faithful to the original, the final couplet reading, 'Who shall I tell, oh, who should I tell? / The forty-nine of you [can] go burn in hell.' But by 1985 he'd been at the meat loaf: 'The forty-nine of you like bats out of hell.' I don't think so. On take one, 'Apple Suckling Tree' had yet to yield its crop, but the spontaneity and invention on take two comes through loud and clear. As Danko told Marcus, 'We didn't rehearse. One or two takes, from conception, on paper, to the finish.'

Like 'Odds and Ends,' 'Goin' to Acapulco,' and 'All You Have to Do Is Dream,' 'Apple Suckling Tree' has a drum accompaniment absent from earlier basement recordings. Marcus and Griffin credit Robertson with being the little drummer boy, relying primarily on their ears. The first take sure sounds sloppy enough to be a guitarist sitting in on drums. But the second take has someone who knows how to play in front of the beat and in swing time; it even has a proper drum ending worked out. Could it be Helm's handiwork? Either way, take two captured all this tree was likely to yield – and they knew it.

{246} GONNA GET YOU NOW

Known studio recordings: Big Pink, West Saugerties, late summer 1967.

A three-chord warm-up that warmed up sufficiently for Garth to hit record – albeit some way in – 'Gonna Get You Now' is one song that never went from 'conception, on paper, to the finish.' Nor did it warrant a second, more measured representation on those precious dime-a-dozen reels. Another blurred snapshot that could have become something more – as a plaintive plea for a roll in the hay, it actively anticipates the equally licentious 'Lay, Lady, Lay' – it again has that drummer boy barracking from the back.

{247} GOIN' TO ACAPULCO

Published lyrics: The Songs of Bob Dylan 1966–1975; Lyrics 1985; Lyrics 2004 [BT version: Words Fill My Head].
Known studio recordings: Big Pink, West Saugerties, late summer 1967 [BT].

It does seem that every time somebody has returned to the treasure trove Bob and The Band buried in the Big Pink basement, they have uncovered yet another remarkable Dylan original that he couldn't be bothered to copyright, let alone release. In truth *almost* all the real gems had been excavated by the time *Writings and Drawings* codified these 'lost' recordings for the first time in 1973. There are really only two exceptions – both songs of the first degree, 'Goin' to Acapulco' and 'All You Have to Do Is Dream,' which appeared in 1975 and 1986 respectively. Both are several notches up from the likes of 'Bourbon Street,' 'Santa Fe,' and 'Don't Ya Tell Henry,' throwaways that had already been puzzlingly copyrighted.

It was the fresh perspective of Rob Fraboni and Robbie Robertson, sifting through the reels for gold before the 1975 LP, that allowed 'Goin' to Acapulco' to appear in all its dissolute glory. But 'All You Have to Do Is Dream' never made Fraboni's 'composite' reels, perhaps suggesting an even later composition date. I suspect neither song constituted part of the 'basement tapes' proper, Dylan feeling he had already fulfilled his obligations to Dwarf Music ('Minstrel Boy' could also date from a post-*JWH* session – hence its Big Sky copyright).

'Goin' to Acapulco' is found on the same reel as that disarming 'See That My Grave Is Kept Clean,' on which Dylan drops into his *Nashville Skyline* voice as if he'd been storing it up for years (which he had). This alone suggests *John Wesley Harding* is done and dusted, and we are heading towards the Guthrie Memorial Concert on January 20, 1968 – his first post-accident performance – when Dylan was again backed by The Band. In every other way, though, it is a quintessential Big Pink song – featuring the usual debauched narrator, rambunctious harmonies, and euphemistic ribaldry.

When it came time to copyright the song in 1975, though, on the verge of its release, Dylan backed away from such boozy bawdiness, rewriting two verses where on the original he'd let it all hang out. But then, as Robertson once told a Japanese TV crew, 'We made the basement tapes with a freedom unknown to man. . . . [W]e thought nobody will ever hear this, so it doesn't matter what we do.' Such freedom had now been taken away, so Dylan saw fit to censor himself in retrospect.

Thus, on the first verse he clearly sings, 'I'm just the same as anyone else / When it comes to scratching for my meat,' whereas, on the second, he finds a wholly original way to describe the opposite of popping her cherry: 'I can blow my plums, and drink my rum, and go on home and have my fun.' In *The Songs of Bob Dylan 1966–1975*, though, the former has been transformed into, 'And I'm just the same as the Taj Mahal / When it comes to standing on my meat,' while for the latter he substitutes a couplet he could have saved for another rewrite of 'Tangled Up in Blue': 'If the wheel don't drop and the train don't stop / I'm bound to meet the sun.' Surreal stuff. Nor was this the last coat of prim paint he applied to the Big Pink original. By the time of *Lyrics* (1985), he'd decided to have another go at that first verse, which was still dedicated to the Eastern monument:

It's a wicked life but what the hell, the stars ain't falling down
I'm standing outside the Taj Mahal, I don't see no-one around.

Unless this is some covert reference to the finale of old friend Mason Hoffenburg's novel *Candy* – in which Candy, having travelled to the Taj Mahal, ends up giving herself to the Buddha and her father at the same time – the rewrite hardly revels in the delicious degeneracy of the original. And having allowed the song to appear on the official double-album, where it attracted a great deal of attention simply by being the only song previously unknown to collectors, Dylan was wasting his time denying the good-time intent underlying that original, exuberant performance.

{248} ALL YOU HAVE TO DO IS DREAM

Known studio recordings: Big Pink, West Saugerties, late summer 1967 – 2 takes.

There are two known versions of 'All You Have to Do Is Dream,' both found at the end of the 'roadie' reels that slipped into circulation circa 1986, and both of which seem somewhat divorced from the other contents – i.e., Red Room run-throughs and acetate songs. In keeping with other latter-day basement recordings, the two versions are quite different in approach, the first one relying on some Kooperesque organ fills, the second one driven on by a jagged guitar and a more assured vocal. (The latter cuts in part way through, Garth again caught unawares.)

Unlike 'You Ain't Going Nowhere' and 'Apple Suckling Tree,' though, both takes of 'All You Have to Do Is Dream' are clearly taken from the same lyrics page. That page contained a fully worked-out set of words, even if they make no more sense than previous songs. Dylan is still in 'Acapulco' mode, at one point suggesting he'd returned North to a rolling-pin welcome: 'Look at what an earful I get, when I go get a tickle.' He also manages to apply an altogether cruder meaning to the ballad commonplace, 'blow thy horn,' which here becomes another way of going about blowing one's plums:

> Destruction causes damage; and damage causes lust.
> Come little girl, blow this horn, hard as any horn I've seen,
> It's very easily done, actually – all you have to do is dream.

Some folk are also still arguing about what the hell 'floorbirds' are, and why they 'fly from door to door.' One suspects these floorbirds were originally floorboards, or door birds, or what have you, but the smoke rings of Dylan's mind suggested another candidate for the basement lexicon of nonsense. The drummer this time must be Helm, or someone who'd taken lessons from Levon. It is certainly not Robertson, who on the second take plays his guitar with the kind of attack last seen on the stage of the Royal Albert Hall, when the Beatles shouted, 'Shut up and let him sing!' (Not to Robbie, to the booing fans). And so, with this last enticing taster of what might have been, the Woodstock idyll fades to black.

1968–9

{ Nashville Skyline; Self Portrait }

Plenty of singer-songwriters would consider a couple of years in which they wrote the likes of 'Lay, Lady, Lay,' 'I Threw It All Away,' and 'Tonight I'll Be Staying Here with You' to be something of a golden era, but for the preeminent singer-songwriter of his time, these were dark days. Those songs, none of which were exactly 'Like a Rolling Stone,' were the cream of a very thin crop. On the verge of becoming a parody of his former self, Dylan turned off the tap, preferring to parody others, beginning work on a most unbecoming Self Portrait . . .

{249} LAY, LADY, LAY

Published lyrics: Writings and Drawings; Lyrics *1985*; Lyrics *2004 [1976 lyrics:* Words Fill My Head].

Known studio recordings: Studio A, Nashville, February 13, 1969 – 4 takes; February 14, 1969 – 5 takes [NS – tk.5].

First known performance: Isle of Wight, August 31, 1969.

At some point during the summer of 1968, the producers of a film about two small-time hustlers, *Midnight Cowboy*, got in touch with Dylan to ask if he had some songs they could use. He did have one song he'd been tinkering with, but by the time he played it to John Schlesinger, the director had already settled on Harry Nilsson's cover of Fred Neil's 'Everybody Talkin'' (which then went on to win an Oscar for best song). Quite how much Dylan knew at the time about the film's subject matter is not clear, but the idea of writing such an overtly romantic song for a would-be gigolo might well have sent cinema-goers mixed messages.

All the evidence suggests Dylan was not even thinking about another collection of songs through 1968, demonstrated by his appearance backstage at an Everly Brothers Carnegie Hall concert that fall. Still looking for someone to lay the song on, he played Don and Phil the same composition, hoping they might cover it, but was spurned by these one-time teen idols (they later covered 'Abandoned Love' as a form of recompense). The song, which ultimately received one of his most memorable melodies, at this stage probably sounded quite unlike the released version, which would itself define another dramatic switch in style. Dylan again credited happenstance in conversation with Ron Rosenbaum in 1977: 'I recorded it originally surrounded by a bunch of other songs on the *Nashville Skyline* album. That was the tone of the session. Once everything was set, that was the way it came out. And it was fine for that time.'

Actually, it was the other way 'round. This song *defined* the *Nashville Skyline* sound and set the agenda for these sessions. It was also the only song he went back to at consecutive sessions, feeling that he had a song with some real potential, one of only two compositions he had been sitting on since the previous year. And so, despite cutting three complete takes at the first session, he returned to it at the end of the following day's exertions, presumably to remind himself that 'Country Pie' and 'Peggy Day' did not represent the extent of his range, even as a country crooner.

According to drummer Kenny Buttrey, they then began experimenting with different kinds of percussive sounds, but nothing seemed to work until Dylan suggested bongos. Producer Bob Johnston topped that with cowbell. The fifth and final take on the fourteenth has both, and as a thoroughly sceptical Buttrey now admits, '[When] we started playing the tune . . . I was just doodling around on these bongos and the cowbell, and it was working out pretty cool.'

Despite 'working out pretty cool,' 'Lay, Lady, Lay' was not Dylan's choice for his first new single since 1966 (which would be 'I Threw It All Away'), only being issued in July as an afterthought, after picking up extensive radio play as an album track. But it quickly outstripped its predecessor in chart position, peaking at number five in the U.S. and at number seven in the UK. It also received one of the biggest cheers of the evening at the Isle of Wight in August.

Over the years the song has come to define this era for every classic rock 'jock.' Ever the Gemini, though, Dylan seemed faintly embarrassed by the song's startling success, even though it validated his country persona in a way that the album (and initial single) failed to do, reaching an audience his earlier, more complex work had not reached. As such, when he returned to the road in the winter of '74, though he preserved the song's original, coaxing lyric, he gave the song a vocal that could have stripped paint. His excuse at the time? 'You'll always stretch things out or cut [an old song] up, just to keep interested.'

But he still felt he hadn't gone quite far enough to erase

the sickly sweet original from people's minds, and in 1976 he gave the song a real rollicking, combining a caustic vocal with a set of words that suggested he had run out of patience with the song and its subject – making it more 'Please Mrs. Henry' than 'To Be Alone with You':

> Forget this dance, let's go upstairs,
> Let's take a chance, who really cares.
> Why, don't you know, you got nothin' to prove,
> It's all in your eyes and the way that you move . . .

No longer content to let love (or lust) take its course, the Dylan of 1976 took the song to another level – albeit one lower on any scale of nobler emotions. And he was happy enough with the rewrite to let it appear on the official live album, *Hard Rain*, even boasting to *Playboy* the following year, 'I rewrote "Lay, Lady, Lay." . . . A lot of words to that song have changed. . . . I always had a feeling there was more to the song than that [original].'

Having explored his own emotional response to the song thoroughly, Dylan dispensed with it, only returning to it on a magical night in Barcelona in 1984, when he played it as a request and remembered even less of the original lyric than eight years earlier. On Never Ending Tour performances Dylan has generally remembered more of the words, but a whole lot less of the tune, one of his most beautiful, and therefore one he seemingly wishes to strike from the record – a reminder that he is still the man who wrote many moons earlier, 'The symbol "beauty" still struck my guts / But now with more a shameful sound / An I rebelled twice as hard an ten times as proud . . .'

Published lyrics: Writings and Drawings; Lyrics *1985;* Lyrics *2004.*

Known studio recordings: Studio A, Nashville, February 13, 1969 – 4 takes [NS – tk.4]; Studio B, New York, May 1, 1970.

First known performance: Isle of Wight, August 31, 1969.

'I Threw It All Away' is one of two songs on *Nashville Skyline* that demonstrates enough attention to lyrical detail to suggest that he had lived with it for more than a week. He had even remembered what it was like to coin an image that shone like the sun: 'Once I had mountains in the palm of my hands / And rivers that ran through every day.'

On the release of the recording, he told *Newsweek's* Hubert Saal that, before *Nashville Skyline*, 'everyone expected me to be a poet so that's what I tried to be.' In truth the amnesia had now set in, and 'I Threw It All Away' was one last, self-conscious flash from the old gun. Dylan was clearly proud of the song after he wrote it because he played it to George Harrison when he and wife Patty came to visit in November 1968. Harrison was sufficiently impressed to learn the song himself, breaking into a version during one of the terminally tedious Twickenham sessions with his fellow Beatles the following January. It was presumably at Harrison's request that Dylan did the song at their joint May Day session the following year, while warming themselves up for an evening of proper work by running through (and, in most instances, over) some old favourites. (This version was later offered as a download by Sony, trumpeted as a previously unknown outtake – a full decade and a half after it was bootlegged.)

But this was one song Dylan did not feel like donating to Harrison, or the Everlys. Instead, he was looking to record it right out of the block on February 13, 1969, when he resumed his recording career in Nashville – having warmed up with the tepid 'To Be Alone With You.' And in just four takes, he had set this luscious lyric to a tune even Hank would have been proud of (though I don't think he'd have done it this way). Bob was enthusiastic enough about his own version of the song – the kind he grew up listening to – that he performed it on Johnny Cash's TV show. He also couldn't wait to sing it second at the Isle of Wight, having raced through a quite different portrait of his muse, 'She Belongs to Me.'

Writing a song about a true love in the style of his first musical love was something he had been threatening to do for a while. Hence all those covers of country songs like 'I'm Guilty of Loving You,' 'You Win Again,' 'Confidential to Me,' 'Still in Town, Still Around,' 'I Don't Hurt Anymore,' and 'I Forgot to Remember to Forget' recorded by Garth at Big Pink. Unfortunately the style did not suit him as well as traditional folk, something he only realized part way through recording *Self Portrait*.

Proving that he had not stayed in such a place very long, he was reluctant to re-explore similar territory throughout the seventies, when reestablishing himself as one of the great contemporary live performers. When he did go back there, he would lacerate his larynx jolting such songs out of their bobby sox. He gave 'Tonight I'll Be Staying with You' a sturdy Rolling Thunder rock-out, in addition to the lashing he gave 'Lay, Lady, Lay' in 1976. As for 'I Threw It All Away,' it personified the raging glory unleashed on the second Rolling Thunder tour, as he put the song out on the ledge and left it there, awaiting *Hard Rain*. And yet, somehow, as he sang it that May night in Fort Worth, with his marriage to the muse who originally inspired it in tatters, it never made more sense.

A less frazzled Dylan worked up a more musical arrangement for the world tour he embarked on in February 1978. And he got playful with the lyrics, trying out his *Street-Legal* persona on this earlier song. In self-reproach mode, he asked rhetorically, 'What did I do? I started looking at you,' doing away with the cliched 'cruel/fool' rhyme in verse one. At the finishing end, love no longer made 'the world go round' but rather felt like a disease: 'One thing's for sure / You won't find a cure / If you throw it all away.' Disappointingly, 'I Threw It All Away' departed from the set after the Australian leg (save for a rearranged two-gig reprise in September). It would take a return to Oz, twenty years on, for him to revive the song again, a worldly-wise gravel voice replacing the tenor's twang he'd imposed in February 1969.

{251} I DON'T WANT TO DO IT

Published lyrics: In His Own Words 2.

Dylan presumably informed Harrison – while they were swopping songs after Thanksgiving turkey – that he had earmarked 'I Threw It All Away' for his own use. But he was still in a song-giving mood, and he had another for which he had no use himself. 'I Don't Want to Do It' suggested an interesting direction, a bridge between the past and present that would lead on to *Planet Waves* and *Blood on the Tracks*. But its autobiographical elements did not suit its author, who was backing away from releasing anything that reflected real life.

Here is a song that from line one is 'looking back upon my youth,' cross-referencing the 'wish in vain' of 'Bob Dylan's Dream' – which materializes as 'To go back in the yard and play / if I could only have another day' – with those 1963 *Joan Baez in Concert/2* liner notes: 'in my younger days I used t kneel / By my aunt's house on a railroad field.' This time he remembers things clearly:

> To go back on the hill beside a track, and try to concentrate,
> On all the places that I want to go,
> You know it shows you that I could not wait.

When he sings the chorus, 'I don't want to do it / I don't want to say goodbye,' one can't help wondering whether he is more determined to cling to a lost youth than to his present love. It seems like even he is not so sure. Finally, though, he surrenders to the moment, and her: 'So come back into my arms again / This love of ours, it has no end.' Happily ever after. Yet he still can't resist thinking about a time when he 'always knew the truth.'

All in all, an important demonstration of abiding concerns, and proof that those 'amazing projections when I was a kid' – as he later put it – were still sometimes 'strong enough to keep me going.' Yet the song was not one he ever recorded himself, and though Harrison demo-ed the song, along with 'If Not for You,' for his first solo album, he had more than enough of his own songs for such a symbolic statement. Only in 1985 did Harrison come upon the demo again, which he decided to re-record for a film about youthful hijinks, *Porky's Revenge*. Though Dylan gave his blessing, he still omitted the song from that year's edition of *Lyrics* (and indeed its 2004 successor).

{252} I'D HAVE YOU ANYTIME

Published lyrics: Writings and Drawings; Lyrics *1985*; Lyrics *2004*.

By November 1968, when he shared a notepad and a couple of guitars with his friend Bob, George was no longer the quiet Beatle when it came to songwriting. Indeed, he was becoming rather vociferous about the boys recording more of his songs, one of many festering issues making the decade's biggest stars no longer much of a going concern. The others had found room on *The White Album* for McCartney's risible 'Rocky Raccoon,' but not Harrison's acidic 'Sour Milk Sea,' and by the time of the January 1969 *Let It Be* sessions, Harrison knew he was bringing as many songs of quality as either Lennon or McCartney.

One of these could have been the song he'd cowritten with Dylan, still an idol to the others. Yet through all the mind-numbing filming sessions, Harrison did not play 'I'd Have You Anytime' once. He'd happily pull out a basement song or two, even 'All Along the Watchtower,' in between pushing for the likes of 'All Things Must Pass' and 'Isn't It a Pity' to make the final cut. But he had evidently earmarked this co-composition for his first (proper) solo album, already in the planning stages. And sure enough, 'I'd Have You Anytime' opens that ambitious debut, *All Things Must Pass*. By the time he recorded the song with producer Phil Spector in the summer of 1970, he had been sitting on it for eighteen months or more. Yet the song itself had come easily, Harrison describing its composition in his book, *I Me Mine*:

> I was hanging out at his house, with him, Sara and his kids. He seemed very nervous and I felt a little uncomfortable – it seemed strange, especially as he was in his own home. Anyway, on about the third day we got the guitars out and then things loosened up and I was saying to him, 'Write me some words.' . . . And he was saying, 'Show me some chords. How do you get those tunes?' I started playing chords . . . and the song appeared as I played the opening chord (G major 7th) and then moved the chord shape up the guitar neck (B flat major 7th). . . . I was saying to Bob, 'Come on, write some words.' He wrote the bridge:
>
> > All I have is yours
> > All you see is mine
> > And I'm glad to hold you in my arms
> > I'd have you anytime.
>
> Beautiful. And that was that.

Dylan continued to provide bridgework for friends, contributing a few more lines of a similar hue to a Roger

McGuinn song the following spring. But he remained some way short of a full album's worth of original songs when he began his first set of sessions in fifteen months, in mid-February – less than a fortnight after the Beatles 'completed' their own, failed, 'basement-tape' experiment, *Let It Be*.

{253} TO BE ALONE WITH YOU

Published lyrics: Writings and Drawings; Lyrics *1985*; Lyrics *2004*.
Known studio recordings: Studio A, Nashville, February 13, 1969 – 8 takes [NS – tk.4].
First known performance: Tower Theatre, Philadelphia, October 15, 1989.

Nashville Skyline was barely in the shops when Dylan informed Jann Wenner, 'The first time I went into the studio I had, I think, four songs.' Sure enough, he and the band cut four songs on the first day in Studio A, February 13. Of those four songs, two date from 1968. The other two – 'To Be Alone with You' and 'One More Night' – sure sound like they were written on the way down to Tennessee, as had been the case with parts of *John Wesley Harding*. The previous afternoon he had met with producer Bob Johnston at his hotel to discuss the upcoming recording sessions. He had even booked a session for the evening, attended by bassist Charlie McCoy and drummer Kenny Buttrey, those stalwarts of previous Nashville sessions, perhaps to run through a few songs, or even indulge in a spot of impromptu songwriting a la *Blonde on Blonde*. (Sadly no tape was running.)

But he was no longer in that Big Pink basement, and the songs he'd been writing were not 'right on target, so direct,' just plain simplistic. As he later put it, he had 'never [previously] gone and done something with no tradition behind it. When I finally broke [away from] it at *John Wesley Harding*, I started out again.' So here he was writing the kind of song he could have given to one of his high school bands, or Bobby

Vee. 'To Be Alone with You,' the first of the four songs he recorded on this session, took eight takes as Dylan expanded his sound, if not his horizons, to include dobro, piano, organ, and at least three guitars. Though he was sleepwalking most of the time, it would take a decade, and the penetrating interview technique of Jonathan Cott, for him to admit, 'I was trying to grasp something that would lead me on to where I thought I should be, and it didn't go nowhere.'

Imagine the surprise, then, two decades after one whole section of fans chucked in their hand upon hearing *Nashville Skyline*, when he opened a show in Philadelphia designed to highlight the terrific new songs on *Oh Mercy* with 'To Be Alone with You.' And, divorced from the soppy lyrics by a spotty sound system, and from *Skyline*'s treacly tenor by fifteen years of almost solid touring, the song threatened to go somewhere real. One wonders what that night's support act, cow-punkers Jason and the Scorchers, might have made of it. As it is, it became the first of a number of Never Ending Tour debuts for the lesser *Skyline* songs.

{254} ONE MORE NIGHT

Published lyrics: Writings and Drawings; Lyrics 1985; Lyrics 2004.
Known studio recordings: Studio A, Nashville, February 13, 1969 – 6 takes [NS – tk.6].
First known performance: Sunrise, FL, September 29, 1995.

> Now I have enough time to write the song and not think about being in it. – Bob Dylan, June 1968

'One More Night' stands as the best of the songs Dylan wrote in haste to fulfill his (nonexistent) contractual obligations in the days/hours leading up to the *Nashville Skyline* sessions. Unfortunately, the vocal utterly fails to convince us that there is even the slightest heartache underlying the singer's claims. When he sings, 'Oh I miss that woman so / I didn't mean to see her go,' he sounds like someone 'not think[ing] about being in it.' *Detached* is the word.

In September 1995, when he revived the song for a single performance with Alison Krauss, another soft-shoe surprise on the receiving end of a Never Ending Tour treatment, he still failed to sing it like it was 'written in my soul / from me to you.' The one man who could have done the song justice – and for whom it was probably written 'in kind' – by then had been eighteen years in the ground (there is even a nod to one of Elvis's fifties classics, 'One Night with You,' in the title). When Dylan said he always wanted to be Elvis, here is the evidence. Elvis *always* epitomized country-rock for the boy from Minnesota, as he had explained to Nat Hentoff three years earlier, when the term was unknown: 'Country-rock *was* Elvis Presley. . . . You listen to Elvis Presley's first records. . . . There isn't a better name.'

{255} COUNTRY PIE

Published lyrics: Writings and Drawings; Lyrics *1985;* Lyrics *2004.*
Known studio recordings: Studio A, Nashville, February 14, 1969 – 2 takes [NS – tk.2].
First known performance: Anaheim, March 10, 2000.

{256} PEGGY DAY

Published lyrics: Writings and Drawings; Lyrics *1985;* Lyrics *2004.*
Known studio recordings: Studio A, Nashville, February 14, 1969 – 3 takes [NS – tk.3].

{257} TELL ME THAT IT ISN'T TRUE

Published lyrics: Writings and Drawings; Lyrics *1985;* Lyrics *2004.*
Known studio recordings: Studio A, Nashville, February 14, 1969 – 8 takes [NS – tk.8].
First known performance: Anaheim, March 10, 2000.

The crooner in Bob must have been happy with how the February 13, 1969, session had gone. Every one of the four songs he sketched out in advance had been captured on Columbia recording tape. He could now return home and work on enough 'simple songs' to make a worthy successor to *John Wesley Harding*. But return home he did not. Instead, as he put it to *Rolling Stone*, 'I pulled that instrumental one out. . . . Then Johnny [Cash] came in and did a song with me. Then I wrote one in the motel. . . . Pretty soon . . . we had an album. . . . It just manipulated out of nothing.'

Actually, the recordings of the instrumental ('Nashville Skyline Rag'), the song with Cash ('Girl from the North Country'), and the motel-composed song ('Tonight I'll Be Staying Here with You') *all* postdate the second *Nashville Skyline* session, when Dylan recorded three more originals, re-recorded 'Lay, Lady, Lay,' and really did conspire to produce 'an album . . . out of nothing.' And boy, does it show. 'Peggy Day' and 'Country Pie' are, frankly, embarrassing. One can't help but wonder what the Nashville cats thought about such un-Dylanesque drivel. They could tell a B side when they heard one, and it must have struck them that Dylan was stockpiling a whole slew of 'em (actually, 'Peggy Day' became a B side – to the hugely successful 'Lay, Lady, Lay').

'Tell Me That It Isn't True,' the one song introduced on the fourteenth to suggest any kind of ongoing career for this forgetful songwriter, was probably finished in the Ramada Inn the night before (or in the afternoon – the session on the fourteenth didn't start until six in the evening). At least Dylan spent a great deal longer recording this eminently singable song than the two other examples of this new country *schtick*. He subsequently suggested to Wenner that he'd been obliged to rearrange it, having written it in the style of all those Hibbing polka bands: '"Tell Me That It Isn't

True" . . . came out completely different than I'd written it. It came out real slow and mellow. I had written it as a jerky kinda polka-type thing. I wrote it in F. I wrote a lot of songs on this new album in F. That's what gives it a kind of a new sound.'

What he didn't tell Wenner was that the song represented another of his little pop parodies, in the same vein as 'Answer to Ode,' though lacking the latter's grasp of dialogue. It was also patently inferior to the hit single he was emulating this time around. Marvin Gaye had been at number one for a staggering seven weeks in December/January with his recording of the Whitfield-Strong classic, 'I Heard It Through the Grapevine.' Dylan could hardly have escaped it. Thus, like one of those Brill Building refugees he ridiculed on 'Bob Dylan's Blues,' he decided to write a country version of the same song.

'I bet you're wond'rin how I knew / 'Bout your plans to make me blue' becomes, in *Dylan Country*, 'I have heard rumors all over town / They say you're planning to put me down.' But the chunka-chunk non-arrangement and a vocal delivery that sounds like it was phoned in make 'Tell Me That It Isn't True' a wholly appropriate companion to 'Country Pie' and 'Peggy Day.' And it was as a companion to the former that it resurfaced in March 2000. Dylan decided to debut both songs at a two-show residency in Anaheim. The band had even been briefed, delivering the original stop-start ending without a trace of irony. One suspects the same could not be said of Nashville's finest, in the days of '69.

{258} TONIGHT I'LL BE STAYING HERE WITH YOU

Published lyrics: Writings and Drawings; Lyrics *1985;* Lyrics *2004;* The Telegraph #7 *(1975 lyrics).*
Known studio recordings: Studio A, Nashville, February 17, 1969 – 11 takes [NS – tk.5].
First known performance: Waltham, MA, November 22, 1975.

Having decided to stay on in Music City USA for one more weekend, awaiting the arrival of his old friend Johnny Cash, Dylan thought he might yet pad out the seven songs already recorded with enough material to make up a full album. However, after two days at the hotel stationery, he had just one more song, albeit a good 'un – 'Tonight I'll Be Staying Here With You' (a handwritten copy of the lyrics, on Ramada Inn paper, is extant). And so he turned to his own back pages, planning to plaster over the gaps with countrified arrangements of 'One Too Many Mornings' and 'Don't Think Twice, It's Alright,' both of which had already been released in versions as perfect as any recording has a right to be. Neither of the Nashville takes proved good enough to make *Self Portrait*, let alone *John Wesley Harding* vol. 2 (as *Nashville Skyline* was almost called).

Maybe he had this original album title in mind when he wrote 'Tonight I'll Be Staying Here With You,' which constitutes a marginal rewrite of the previous album's closer, 'I'll Be Your Baby Tonight.' A song of reassurance for a woman who knew all about that 'restless, hungry feeling,' 'Tonight . . .' became the third single from the album and a minor hit in its own right. However, it had to wait until the fall of 1975 to receive its first live outing, by which time it was almost unrecognizable (though the fake, looped whoops of recognition on *The Bootleg Series* vol. 5 seem designed to make listeners think otherwise). An exuberant full-on arrangement and a superior set of lyrics, name-checking the tour itself ('You came on to me like rolling thunder'), provide a double delight:

> I could have left this town by noon,
> By tonight have been in some place new,
> But I was feeling a little bit scattered,
> And your love was all that mattered,
> So tonight I'll be staying here with you.

New words or not, its message of reassurance remained, addressed to the same concerned lass for whom the Rolling Thunder tour was further evidence that she had lost her man to the lure of the world, wedding songs (and vows) notwithstanding. One doubts it was a coincidence that the revamped song was introduced after Sara elected to tag along. But, whereas Dylan undoubtedly meant every word in February 1969, the man (in him) singing in 1975 of an enduring devotion comes across as someone trying to convince himself almost as much as his suspicious spouse. And, save for a spontaneous one-off, minus a lyric sheet, at the final show of his landmark February 1990 Hammersmith Odeon residency, the Revue proved to be the last time Dylan tried these lines on any credulous ticket holder.

{259} WANTED MAN

Published lyrics: Writings and Drawings; Lyrics 1985; Lyrics 2004.
Known studio recordings: Studio A, Nashville, February 18, 1969 – 1 take.

Given the dearth of new songs coming from his pen, it is somewhat surprising that Dylan should abandon this new original after a single false start at the final *Nashville Skyline* session. 'Wanted Man' was presumably already earmarked for a Johnny Cash concert scheduled in six days' time at San Quentin, having been written by Dylan as a gift to his old friend – and the 'lucky' convicts. They certainly showed their appreciation of some of Bob's lines; 'Went the wrong way into Juarez with Juanita in my lap' got so many yells that Cash temporarily lost his way.

Interestingly, Cash's introduction* at the penitentiary suggests the song had been cowritten: 'Last week in Nashville,

---

* Johnny Cash's spoken intro to 'Wanted Man' does not appear on the original *San Quentin* album, but has recently appeared on the two-CD+DVD Legacy boxed set of that fabled concert.

Bob Dylan . . . was at our house and he and I sat down and wrote a song together.' Yet the song ended up being copyrighted to Dylan alone. Presuming he didn't stiff Johnny of a song credit (unlikely), Cash probably meant he had had an idea for a song, but it was Dylan who ran with it. The song wouldn't have sat easily on Dylan's latest platter of platitudes, having some of the old sharpness in the lyrics, notably, 'I went to sleep in Shreveport, woke up in Abilene / Wonderin' why the hell I'm wanted at some town halfway between' – another couplet bound to ring a few bells with the bad boys down front. It also reached an audience for whom even *Nashville Skyline* sounded too much like pop, and that audience was a large one. *Johnny Cash at San Quentin* did what *Nashville Skyline* could not, removing *Hair!* from the *Billboard* top spot and staying there for four whole weeks.

{260} CHAMPAIGN, ILLINOIS

Published lyrics: The Telegraph #2; Words Fill My Head.

Another song Dylan donated to one of his teen idols during that February sojourn in Nashville, 'Champaign, Illinois,' was given to Carl Perkins. The author of 'Blue Suede Shoes' was now working with Johnny Cash and was probably at the Cash residence the night Dylan worked up 'Wanted Man.' And this time its recipient did get a co-credit. In all likelihood, it was left to Perkins to finish it off, after he and Dylan had a little fun writing a song about the most unlikely place in the universe. I'd like to think it was Dylan, though, who kicked off that opening verse:

> I got a woman in Morocco,
> I got a woman in Spain,
> Woman that done stole my heart,
> She lives up in Champaign.

The song was recorded by Perkins later in the year, appearing on his 1969 LP, *On Top*. Sixteen years later Dylan made it to Champaign to render aid to U.S. farmers, but he failed to make the appropriate gesture.

{261} BALLAD OF EASY RIDER

No known recording, circa April 1969.

By the spring of 1969, Dylan had seemingly got the hang of this co-writing lark. Having spent years letting unfinished songs stay that way, he now found himself collecting some nice royalty checks from 'This Wheel's on Fire' and 'Tears of Rage.' And so, when Roger McGuinn asked him to help write a ballad for the *Easy Rider* movie, he obliged. Having already demonstrated the art of bridge building, Dylan gave McGuinn another, which was then transplanted to the outset of this evocative eulogy – 'The river flows, flows to the sea / wherever it flows, that's where I want to be.' According to McGuinn, Dylan subsequently asked for his co-credit to be taken off 'because he didn't like the movie that much. He didn't like the ending. He wanted to see the truck blow up in order to get poetic justice.'

Fortunately for Dylan's accountant, the song did not become another 'This Wheel's on Fire.' However, it was recorded by the post-accident Fairport Convention for their landmark *Liege & Lief* LP – then left off, along with 'Down in the Flood' and 'Open the Door Homer' – making it the first Fairport LP to not contain a single Dylan cover. Their version has favoured a few retrospective sets by now, so hopefully Dylan has heard to what divine purpose his little lyric was put by Denny and fellow Dylan devotees.

Note: Though it is not known precisely when Dylan and McGuinn indulged in their little songwriting stint, the Byrds' recording of 'Lay, Lady, Lay' in mid-April perhaps occurred *after* Dylan played his old friend an advance copy of his latest fab waxing, curious about what the Byrd thought of his own brand of country-rock.

{262} LIVING THE BLUES

Published lyrics: Writings and Drawings; Lyrics 1985; Lyrics 2004.
Known studio recordings: Studio A, Nashville, April 24, 1969 – 6 takes [SP – tk.6].

When Dylan returned to Nashville in late April, a mere two months after he manipulated an album out of some very thin airs, he decided to reinforce his new direction by recording an album of country covers and an 'original,' nonalbum single. 'Living the Blues' was the single in question, and when he appeared on *The Johnny Cash Show* the following week – his first appearance on national TV in four years – it was with the intention of promoting both his current single ('I Threw It All Away') *and* the forthcoming one.

The song in question was a fairly weak rewrite of Guy Mitchell's 'Singing the Blues' ('Without you, you got me singin' the blues' versus Dylan's 'I've been living the blues every night without you'). And the new country twang continued to do this kinda song few favours. Presumably, it was feedback from radio stations that ultimately resulted in said single being nixed, 'Lay, Lady, Lay' taking its place. One would be hard pressed to believe 'Living the Blues' would have enjoyed similar success, even given its nonalbum status. As such, it found a more suitable slot among the covers that he crooned in June, cluttering up the *Self Portrait* smorgasbord.

1970-1

{ Self Portrait; New Morning; Greatest Hits Vol. II }

By the winter of 1970, when Dylan bought a townhouse on McDougall Street, decamping the family from Woodstock to Greenwich Village, he was desperate to rekindle the same kind of inspiration that had fueled his initial ascendance. It had been a long, long time since he had felt impelled to write songs, but he hoped that the close proximity to studios and fellow musicians might initiate a new phase. Sadly, this would not be the case. The songs just would not come. Even when that former flame did fitfully flicker, it concerned itself with aspects of the bucolic existence he had left behind or the curse of a now-dormant creativity. A commission from playwright-poet Archibald MacLeish to write songs for a new play merely exacerbated these newfound insecurities. In the end New Morning was nothing of the sort. It was, instead, a diary of what he had written while his mind was on other things. And though the few songs written in 1971 showed a greater attention to detail, only one, 'When I Paint My Masterpiece,' suggested an awareness of what he had lost, and the cost should he feel compelled to reclaim it.

Published lyrics: Writings and Drawings; Lyrics *1985;* Lyrics *2004.*
Known studio recordings: Studio B, NY, March 4, 1970 – 1 take;
March 5, 1970 – 3 takes; May 1, 1970 – 4 takes; June 2, 1970 – 14
takes; August 12, 1970 – 8 takes [NM – tk.3].

According to Dylan, 'Time Passes Slowly' was one of a handful of songs written for a play by Archibald MacLeish, loosely based on *The Devil and Daniel Webster,* called *Scratch.* He informed Cameron Crowe in 1985, 'I recorded some stuff based on what he was doing.' The three songs he cites are 'New Morning,' 'Father of Night,' and this one. When exactly he undertook the commission, and when he abandoned it, has never been entirely clear.

He claims in *Chronicles* that he was asked shortly after his father's death (in June 1968), but that cannot be the case. Initial contact took place no earlier than the summer of 1969. Using some persuasive prose, Dylan's memoir describes an initial meeting with MacLeish in which he and his wife drove over to Conway, Massachusetts, and MacLeish gave him some suggested song titles to work with, of which 'Father of Night' was apparently one, but 'Time Passes Slowly' was not. He says, 'I intuitively realized that I didn't think this was for me,' and yet he agreed to work on these ideas. But on *Biograph* he says he 'went up to see Archibald MacLeish *with the songs* [my italics], and with the producer. He lived up in Connecticut.' He also claims it was because he and MacLeish 'didn't see eye to eye on' 'Father of Night' that the collaboration never happened.

MacLeish mentions the project in a letter to his publisher dated October 7, 1970, by which time the play had been produced without any new Dylan songs. In his letter, MacLeish baldly states that Dylan 'proved simply incapable of producing new songs.' MacLeish's account, both contemporary and (originally) private, bears the stamp of authenticity. I think we can assume Dylan only came up with a couple of songs – probably 'Time Passes Slowly' and 'Father of Night.'

This would make 'Time Passes Slowly' both the earliest song written for *New Morning* and the one he worked on the longest. In the studio it gave him a fair share of headaches, attempted at all the four sets of sessions – spanning a six-month period – from which *New Morning* was culled. This was a return to a working method not really tried since *The Times They Are A-Changin'* (I discount *John Wesley Harding* because the gaps between sessions are so brief, and the songs are obviously of a piece).

In that time we can probably assume 'Time Passes Slowly' underwent a transformation, though none of these many outtake versions circulate. It remains the one credible candidate for a line quoted in a *Rolling Stone* article at the time: 'Air to breathe and water to wash in,' the song containing this line apparently being recorded at the May 1, 1970, Dylan/Harrison session. We have complete documentation of the sessions that day, and there is no such song – unless it comes from one of two *New Morning* songs recorded that day, 'Sign on the Window' or 'Time Passes Slowly,' and the lyrics were later changed. The image (which appears verbatim in Charles Williams's first published novel, *War in Heaven* (1930)), was partially reused by Dylan in conversation in 1984: 'If I was starting out right now I don't know where I'd get the inspiration from, because you need to breathe the right air to make the creative process work.'

The March version of 'Time Passes Slowly' may be another pleasant surprise, if and when it is unearthed. It could well be another song recorded with just piano and/or guitar, given that it is sandwiched between 'Went to See the Gypsy' and 'All the Tired Horses.' As it is, Dylan decided to make all subsequent versions full-band performances. As a result he spent almost the entire June 2 session working his way through fourteen takes (and a very bad cold). Finally, in August, when an LP sequence had already been approved, he used one last session to have *another* eight goes at demonstrating that time passes very slowly when you're stuck in a studio.

{264} FATHER OF NIGHT

Published lyrics: Writings and Drawings; Lyrics *1985;* Lyrics *2004.*
Known studio recordings: Studio B, NY, June 5, 1970 – 11 takes [NM – tk.11].

In *Chronicles,* Dylan says he 'composed a few things for the [MacLeish] play bearing in mind the titles that were given me.' 'Father of Night' was one song title MacLeish suggested to Dylan at their first meeting – along with the likes of 'Red Hands' and 'Lower World.' The songwriter also alleges that he took the songs up to the play's producer, Stuart Ostrow, who had an office in the Brill Building, 'and recorded them. He sent the acetates to Archie.' If so, these unique recordings have never turned up, or even been logged.

All this activity presumably dates from the fall of 1969. Yet it would be the following June before Dylan got around to recording 'Father of Night' in the studio, and when he did, it was hardly representative of a play 'full of midnight murder.' Rather, it was a solemn prayer to a Judeo-Christian deity, apparently inspired by an already ancient French-Canadian Jesuit priest who resided at the Meads Mountain church, near Woodstock. Father Francis was someone with whom Dylan had been discussing spiritual matters since 1964, when his breakup with Suze caused a great deal of soul-searching (in an April '64 letter to the lass, he admits 'the only person I've spent any time with is father francis at his church on the mount'). By 1969 his concerns had changed, but he still found solace at this 'church on the mount,' even if his first hymn was hardly a humdinger.

{265} WENT TO SEE THE GYPSY

Published lyrics: Writings and Drawings; Lyrics *1985;* Lyrics *2004.*
Known studio recordings: Studio B, NY, March 3, 1970 – 1 take; March 4, 1970 – 5 takes; March 5, 1970 – 1 take; June 6, 1970 – 4 takes [NM].

> I asked him about 'Went To See The Gypsy' and he told me it was about going to see Elvis in Las Vegas. – Ron Cornelius (guitarist on *New Morning*), *Melody Maker* 1971

In the winter of 1970, Dylan and his wife took a trip to Las Vegas, where his uncle Vernon may or may not have still been living, apparently scouting out possible places to relocate his clan in Nevada and/or Arizona (where they would settle for a while in 1972). While there, the couple caught one of Elvis Presley's shows at the International Hotel, part of a four-week residency at the famous watering hole. Elvis was one of the few living legends who could still inspire awe in the boy from Minnesota, and Dylan seized the opportunity to go backstage and meet the singer without whom – as he observed on the man's death – 'he would never have gotten started.'

Back in January, Elvis seemed to have pulled off the most difficult trick in the book – a comeback that restored his critical standing and commercial preeminence a decade after he had turned the world upside down, doing the hip shake. He had consolidated all the good press a Christmas 1968 TV special had accumulated with two albums of pure Memphis stew, while producing a pair of chart-topping singles culled from that crop: 'In the Ghetto' and 'Suspicious Minds.' So when Dylan ventured backstage, part of him was doubtless wondering how he might do the same himself.

Long before a posthumous cult grew up around the man, Dylan imbues this 'gypsy' with mystical powers – specifically an ability to 'drive you from your fear / [and] bring you through the mirror.' Afraid that he might never be able to do consciously what he used to do unconsciously, he perhaps feared a future as a Vegas act, playing the old hits to baby boomers with corporate credit cards. The result is his first song to address the creative drought that now had begun in earnest.

At least one late editor of a Dylan fanzine believed the 'mirr'r' of 'Went to See the Gypsy' was a direct allusion to Herman Hesse's *Steppenwolf*, in which the hero, Harry, another Gemini character – half man, half wolf – is shown a looking glass at a magic theatre so that he may be brought 'through the mirror' and made to face his fearful other self. Mr. Bauldie was surely right, given the two references in the song to the 'pretty dancing girl.' This pretty dancing girl is Hermine, the 'heroine' of Hesse's novel (Dylan later mimics the first meeting between Harry and Hermine in 'Tangled Up in Blue'). So when he starts writing about the kind of 'fear' that has driven him to seek out the gypsy, he is alluding to *both* a real-life meeting with the man who made all things possible in Pop and a fictional meeting with the mystical Pablo.

Not surprisingly, Dylan considered 'Went to See the Gypsy' an important song, which he was anxious to record right. He tried out the song each day of the three sessions he booked at his familiar Columbia stomping ground in early March 1970, doing it first with the pick-up band who were having to pick their way through a couple of dozen traditional songs, one or two takes at a time, and then recording it with just Al Kooper at the electric piano, a stark performance that almost lit up *New Morning*.

Though it was one of at least three originals recorded at

these sessions, 'Went to See the Gypsy' was never intended to be part of the album he was finishing off. *Self Portrait* did not show a man driven by fear or trying to break through the mirr'r; rather, it was an album of smoke and mirrors. He just wanted to see how it sounded. Ultimately dissatisfied, and returning to 'The Gypsy,' he recast it in the style of *New Morning* at sessions the first week in June. It was this phlegmatic performance that he felt finally gave him a reflection of what he had in mind.

{266} ALL THE TIRED HORSES

Known studio recordings: Studio B, NY, March 5, 1970 – 1 take [SP].

I guess if one considers 'Went to See the Gypsy' as Dylan's first song about writer's block, 'All the Tired Horses' would have to be his second. Relying on a fairly obvious pun – the words 'riding' and 'writing' sound awfully similar – Dylan set this three-minute song to a single couplet: 'All the tired horses in the sun / How'm I supposed to get any ridin' done?' Repeating this terse sentiment ad infinitum, as an opener to a sprawling self-portrait (that was nothing of the sort), is positively Warholian.

Recorded in a single take, back in New York, 'All the Tired Horses' was then layered with some eighteen musicians and female singers at two sessions later that month in Nashville. He removes himself almost entirely from his own song, leaving no vestige of his own voice on the finished recording. However, given that the song, cut in a single take at the end of the last *Self Portrait* session, is given this title (whereas other instrumental originals he recorded then, like 'Wigwam' and 'Woogie Boogie,' were given titles like 'New Song #1' and 'Piano Boogie'), one is inclined to think a Dylan vocal resides on that multitrack, underneath all the gunk plastered across the track by Bob Johnston.

Hopefully, it started as a solo performance, just a Dylan

guitar/vocal riffing – perhaps spontaneously – on this one phrase until Kooper joined in part-way through. The subsequent application of Buttrey and McCoy as a rhythm section in Nashville suggests as much, as does McCoy's comment to Bob Spitz: 'I . . . figured it was only a work-tape.' The original session log times the New York version at three minutes, fifteen seconds, longer by a minute than the released version. If, as one suspects, it began life as another 'Rock Me Mama' (see #289), it was probably a fun song before Johnston got all baroque.

{267} MY PREVIOUS LIFE

Known studio recordings: Studio B, NY, March 5, 1970 – 3 takes.

The most mysterious of the thirty-plus songs Dylan recorded over three days in March at his old New York homestead is a song listed on the studio logs as 'My Previous Life.' Recorded towards the end of a three-and-a-half-hour session and timing out at two minutes and fifty-nine seconds on the one complete take, it is followed by attempts at 'Went to See the Gypsy,' 'Time Passes Slowly,' and 'All the Tired Horses,' all Dylan originals. However, it comes after four cover versions, three of them traditional. If it is a cover song, it resembles no song title on any popular-song database I can find. Could it actually be one of those song titles suggested by MacLeish? An intriguing thought.

{268} IF NOT FOR YOU

Published lyrics: Writings and Drawings; Lyrics 1985; Lyrics 2004.
Known studio recordings: Studio B, NY, May 1, 1970 – 5 takes [TBS]; June 2, 1970 – 2 takes; August 12, 1970 – 5 takes [NM – tk.5].
First known performance: Sydney, April 14, 1992.

There are three separate Dylan recordings of 'If Not for You' in circulation. The one with George Harrison from the

May Day sessions appeared on *The Bootleg Series*, while an August re-recording made at the 'Day of the Locusts' session is the one that finally appeared on *New Morning* (after initial reports suggested he would use the version with Harrison). Aside from these, there is a bootlegged version from the pukka *New Morning* sessions in June, which was subsequently sent to Nashville to acquire violin and pedal-steel embellishments (once thought to derive from the March sessions, it was only assigned a CO number at the overdub stage, making dating it by this method impossible). Of the three, the most melodic is the June recording; the most experimental, the May version; and the least satisfying, the released take.

Dylan suggests on *Biograph* that he 'wrote the song thinking about my wife' but was reaching for something he failed to find: 'It seemed simple enough, sort of tex-mex . . . [but] it came off kind of folky.' Originally, he may even have become dissatisfied enough to consider sidelining the track, which does not feature on early *New Morning* sequences. Three weeks after he and Harrison tried to inject some life into the song, Harrison demo-ed it at Abbey Road for his own album, and found the spirit of the song solo. He presumably had Dylan's blessing to record the then-unreleased song, and proceeded to record a full-band version for *All Things Must Pass*. By then, Dylan had sent the June version to Nashville to see if they could make it sound closer to the border.

By August, he no longer seemed sure what he was reaching for, embarking on a rather cluttered reworking, against which his vocal was no match. Harrison's version, included on an album that appeared alongside Dylan's in December, beating *New Morning* to the #1 spot on the charts, generated further recognition for a song that started out as a simple serenade for Sara. There was enough of the song's simple charm in Harrison's version for Olivia Newton-John to find it, too. She recorded her own, hit-single version, released the following April. Given its Dylan/Harrison association, the song also seemed like an obvious selection when it came to the *Concert for Bangladesh* in August 1971. But a run-through the previous day with Harrison convinced Dylan to stick to what he knew. Yet this performance, which recently appeared as a bonus cut on the revamped DVD edition of the concert film, is not at all bad.

Surprisingly, Dylan continued to keep away from it in performance. Even in 1978, when the song was extensively rehearsed and appeared as an 'alternate' on set lists for a number of Japanese and Australian shows, it failed to make the final cut. It was 1992 before it was finally released from its *New Morning* prison, appearing at a number of shows that spring, occasionally with a nice harmonica intro, and delivered with a hint of country cookin'.

{269} SIGN ON THE WINDOW

Published lyrics: Writings and Drawings; Lyrics *1985;* Lyrics *2004.*
Known studio recordings: Studio B, NY, May 1, 1970 – 5 takes;
June 5, 1970 – 8 takes [NM].

> [After the accident] I started thinkin' about . . . how short life is. I'd just lay there listenin' to birds chirping. Kids playing in the neighbor's yard or rain falling by the window. I realized how much I'd missed. – Dylan to Sam Shepard, August 1986

'Sign on the Window' is one of those overlooked masterpieces that can still be found in the nooks and crannies of Dylan's lesser albums – and there's a few of them. Few, though, as gorgeous as this. For one, it surely ranks as Dylan's finest piano playing on record (his classically trained brother must have been impressed). And, as with most examples of

Dylan at the stand-up, it was almost entirely done using the black keys, where he found his own sound. As he told Paul Zollo, 'On the piano, my favorite keys are the black keys. . . . The songs that go into those keys right from the piano, they sound different. They sound deeper. . . . Everything sounds deeper in those black keys.'

Whether it sounded this good when Dylan began recording it on the afternoon of May 1, one of five originals he was working on with guru-loving George, must be in doubt. According to the *Rolling Stone* report of the session and the AFM sheet, it was producer Bob Johnston, not Dylan, who played piano at that session. I fear to suggest quite how the song would have sounded if it received the same bass-heavy, guitar-oriented arrangement as 'If Not for You' and 'Working on a Guru.' But it sounds just fine a month later, Dylan leading the band a merry march, while crooning clear through his cold, 'Sure gonna be wet tonight on Main Street / Hope that it don't *sleeeeeeeeeeet.*'

As for the song's sentiments – 'Have a bunch of kids who call me Pa / That must be what it's all about' – he had been testing the theory to its fullest extent, and finding it wanting. This was no longer the man who told a Chicago reporter in November 1965, 'Getting married, having a bunch of kids, I have no hopes for it.' He had been there, done that. And still it was not enough.

Having written a song straight out of the Brill Building, Dylan then decided to give it the full orchestral treatment – or at least allowed Al Kooper to score it to see how it sounded. Ultra-gorgeous is the answer. But the strings might have reminded folk of *Self Portrait* – freshly out and widely panned. As such, it was the stringless June original that gave *New Morning* its one uncut pearl (though it retains Kooper's little organ/flute fugue during the bridge).

So bound up with Dylan's performance was this released

jewel that few dared to cover it. It took until 1979 for Jennifer Warnes to brave these waters – and she was rewarded with an opportunity to demo 'Every Grain of Sand' with the man himself. As for Dylan, he never felt like catching the same cold again, and allowed the once-resplendent 'Sign on the Window' to fall into disrepair.

Note: Michael Krogsgaard, in his online sessionography, seems to think Dylan recorded a song called 'What It's All About' at the June *New Morning* sessions. As a result he attributes the May 1 version of 'Sign on the Window' to the album. Needless to say, the 'two' songs are one and the same, and the official version dates from June.

{270} WORKING ON A GURU

Published lyrics: Words Fill My Head; In His Own Words 2.
Known studio recordings: Studio B, NY, May 1, 1970 – 1 take.

Cut in a single take on May Day, sandwiched between 'Time Passes Slowly' and 'Went to See the Gypsy,' this sounds like something Dylan and Harrison worked up the evening before, but never quite finished. The lyrics are not so much elusive as plain elliptical. Dylan may have been 'working on a guru before the sun goes down,' but the rest of the words suggest little purpose in perseverance, a conclusion he presumably reached himself, since he ran down the song just once and then forgot it. His music publisher, though, did not. In a clearing-up exercise in January 1985, they copyrighted it, prior to its inevitable appearance on bootleg.

{271} ONE MORE WEEKEND

Published lyrics: Writings and Drawings; Lyrics 1985; Lyrics 2004.
Known studio recordings: Studio B, NY, June 3, 1970 – 2 takes [NM – tk.2].

Despite the real work on *New Morning* being assigned to begin the first week in June, Dylan didn't seem to feel he had an album's worth of originals in him, devoting the first two days of sessions to cover versions, à la *Self Portrait*, while re-recording two originals he'd already tried with Harrison in May. Even at the third session, he spent the bulk of the two three-hour sessions working on arrangements of four covers, two of which ('Can't Help Falling in Love' and 'Lily of the West') ended up on the *Dylan* LP, a spiteful spoiler released by CBS in December 1973, ahead of Dylan's real 'comeback' album, *Planet Waves*. Only at the end of proceedings does Dylan run through two complete takes of 'One More Weekend,' an innocuous, everything's-hunky-dory addition to *Nashville Skyline* part 2 – minus the twang.

{272} NEW MORNING

Published lyrics: Writings and Drawings; Lyrics 1985; Lyrics 2004.
Known studio recordings: Studio B, NY, June 4, 1970 – 3 takes [NM – tk.3].
First known performance: New Orleans, LA, April 19, 1991.

The June 4, 1970, session continued the *New Morning* pattern of covering previous songwriters, with only the odd diversion into something new. Among the things he borrowed were Lead Belly's 'Bring Me a Little Water, Sylvie,' Joni Mitchell's 'Big Yellow Taxi,' and, from a lifetime away, his own 'Tomorrow Is a Long Time.' Just two new originals were attempted, of which 'New Morning' would be the only one to suggest light at the end of the tunnel. Dylan told Crowe it was one of the songs left over from the MacLeish project, but this strikes me as unlikely. Its author is attempting to convince himself that the sun is shining again – hoping such an act of will can make everything right.

Perhaps it was some residue of such an idea – that a force of will is sometimes required to turn things around – that prompted Dylan to introduce the song live for the first time as an opener to shows in the spring of 1991, when he found himself at his lowest ebb in twenty-one years. He certainly demonstrated almost no knowledge of its lyrics. Most performances have more slurred lines than 'I'm Not There.' At a train wreck of a show in Stuttgart, he failed to sing a single intelligible syllable. Thankfully, by the fall, 'New Morning' began to mean something positive again, as he rediscovered his performing self.

{273} THREE ANGELS

Published lyrics: Writings and Drawings; Lyrics *1985;* Lyrics *2004.*
Known studio recordings: Studio B, NY, June 4, 1970 – 3 takes
[NM – tk.3].

One can usually measure the degree of faith Dylan has in a given song from this fraught period by counting the number of girl-singers he dollops on, and how high they have been placed in the mix. 'Three Angels' began life as a spoken-word piece, itself no great leap for the man. He had, after all, first made his reputation in the Village performing *talkin'* blues. And perhaps his single most mesmerizing performance given back then was a spoken rendition of Lord Buckley's 'Black Cross.' But 'Three Angels' is a very self-conscious performance of a plainly moralistic piece, perhaps inspired by the idea of putting songs in a play. The result speaks for itself.

{274} IF DOGS RUN FREE

Published lyrics: Writings and Drawings; Lyrics *1985;* Lyrics *2004.*
Known studio recordings: Studio B, NY, June 5, 1970 – 3 takes
[NM – tk.3].
First known performance: Munster, Germany, October 1, 2000.

How low can one man get? A chihuahua, perhaps? 'If Dogs Run Free' is a wretched way to start the 'final' day of work on a 'comeback' album. But what a day! Fully half of the released album comes from this single six-hour session, during which six Dylan originals were executed, mostly with aplomb (especially reworkings of 'Went to See the Gypsy' and 'Sign on the Window'). Dylan is enjoying himself so much that he even runs down a couple of takes of 'Lily of the West' at day's end, to wind down. 'If Dogs Run Free,' though, seems more like a hangover from the previous day, belabouring the point that this boy could have been a rapper and a poet. Yet even when toying with releasing another album of part covers, part originals (a common enough practice in country circles), Dylan continued to short-list 'If Dogs Run Free.'

I suspect the part-covers premise was pulled after Dylan saw the reviews dished out for *Self Portrait*. Surely word of its reception was already starting to filter back as these sessions progressed. After all, the album was ostensibly released on June 1, so it would certainly have been generating airplay and comment by the time the final session rolled around. Was it this that convinced Dylan he needed to jettison the covers he'd industriously worked on earlier in the week, and give life to whatever dog of a song he might have lying around? As for 'If Dogs Run Free,' having failed to figure in any fan polls of Dylan songs they'd like performed live, it made a wholly unanticipated appearance on the 2000 European leg of the Never Ending Tour. By then it was probably the best way to use that gnarled crag of a voice. And this time he was word-perfect. Woof, woof.

{275} THE MAN IN ME

Published lyrics: Writings and Drawings; Lyrics *1985*; Lyrics *2004 [1978 version:* Words Fill My Head].
Known studio recordings: Studio B, NY, June 5, 1970 – 2 takes [NM – tk.2].
First known performance: Budokan Hall, Tokyo, February 20, 1978.

Once again, a Dylan song demonstrates that context is all. In the context of the 1978 world tour – or the Coen Brothers' finest workprint, *The Big Lebowski* – this is one damn fine song. On *New Morning*, propped betwixt 'One More Weekend' and 'Three Angels,' it does not sound so great. The girls don't help. Nor does Dylan's cold. This time that voice breaking up all over the place sounds like someone trying too hard. There is the arid aroma of unfinished business here. However, barely has he begun to entertain doubt – 'Storm clouds are ragin' all around my door / I think to myself I might not take it anymore' – before he feels compelled to revert to the plangent platitude, 'Take a woman like you / To find the man in me.' The working title, 'A Woman Like You,' explains exactly whom he was trying to impress.

But then, as part of the unreality of the Dude's daydream existence in the Coens' celluloid vision, the sentiment seems entirely apposite. Even better is the 1978 rearrangement/rewrite. This time Dylan ain't trying; he's succeeding. Rather than worrying about 'storm clouds,' he is 'lost on the river of no return,' a wonderfully evocative way of describing both a fated affair and his 'former' amnesia. Worked up in stages during the January 1978 rehearsals, the new 'Man in Me' remained part of the set till end of summer, surprising one and all with its level-headed use of the girl-singers and a delightful duplicity underlying those lyrics. Having set the song up as a replay of the slightly sickly original, he pulls the rug away:

> I can't believe it, I can't believe it's true,
> I'm lying next to her, but I'm thinking of you . . .
> I know you got a husband, and that's a fact,
> But, ah baby, turn me loose or cover my tracks.

Perversely, though, 'The Man in Me' was not one of the songs picked for the live *At Budokan* LP, despite becoming a highlight at his first series of Japanese shows. Subsequent, sporadic Never Ending Tour performances have reverted to the original lyrics, perhaps a homage to the Dude in us all.

{276} WINTERLUDE

Published lyrics: Writings and Drawings; Lyrics *1985;* Lyrics *2004.*
Known studio recordings: Studio B, NY, June 5, 1970 – 5 takes [NM – tk.4].

I gotta think this one came quick. Dylan the wordplay merchant is back in town. Repeating the 'Santa Fe' trick, Dylan hits on a whole new word, *winterlude,* to describe an interlude in winter. Save that this 'Winterlude' is a person, a time, and a place all rolled into one – kind of like the Holy Trinity. Determined to see if he still has what it takes to make a rhyme outlandish, he goes with, 'Winterlude, this dude thinks you're fine.' And this guy was about to get a doctorate from Princeton?!?!

{277} DAY OF THE LOCUSTS

Published lyrics: Writings and Drawings; Lyrics *1985;* Lyrics *2004.*
Known studio recordings: Studio B, NY, August 12, 1970 – 7 takes [NM – tk.7].

It is hardly unusual for Dylan to continue working on new songs long after the bulk of a new album has been completed. On many occasions he has actually written the last song of the album 'to order,' thus bookending the process. Which is what he had done on both *John Wesley Harding* and *Nashville Skyline.* This time, though, when he wrote 'Day of the Locusts,' he left it so late that he had to set up a special recording session to record it, *after* sessions in New York and

Nashville had applied overdubs to the songs he recorded in March, May, and June.

Yet 'Day of the Locusts' would not be the album's closer. That, one suspects, was a position long assigned to one of the spoken-word pieces. Recording it, though, allowed Dylan to rethink what he wanted the album to say. He cast aside *all* the many covers that had occupied him at previous sessions and instead re-recorded two originals – 'Time Passes Slowly' and 'If Not for You' – both already attempted a number of times.

'Day of the Locusts' completes his account of real experiences that he drew on to make this slim volume, depicting in metaphorical terms his trip to Princeton to collect a doctorate in music in June, in much the way 'Went to See the Gypsy' had depicted the winter trip to Vegas. During the actual 'Day of the Locusts,' Dylan was in a weird frame of mind. Nerves were getting the better of him when the missus, Sara, and an old buddy, ex-Byrd Dave Crosby, convinced him to get in the car.

To calm him down, Crosby passed the would-be scholar a joint that, he says, 'we smoked . . . on the way, and I noticed Dylan getting really quite paranoid behind it. When we arrived at Princeton, they took us to a little room and Bob was asked to wear a cap and gown. He refused outright.' Dylan's account of what happened next is a feature of the song: 'I was ready to leave, I was already walkin' / But the next time I looked there was light in the room.'

Like 'Went to See the Gypsy,' this song hardly claims to be a prosaic version of the day. One presumes the man standing next to Dylan did not actually spontaneously combust ('his head was exploding'). But when Dylan says he 'sure was glad to get out of there alive,' we can probably take that assessment at 'white face-value.' As he wrote when he was over sixty, and had received more awards than he could shake a joint at, 'After whispering and mumbling my way through the [degree] ceremony, I was handed the scroll. We piled back into the Big Buick and drove away. It had been a strange day.'

What undoubtedly contributed to the surreal nature of the experience – exacerbated by the heightened sensory awareness Crosby's mighty fine weed triggered – was the din that greeted Dylan when he came to the campus, for it was year seventeen in the life cycle of that most remarkable of insects, the Magicicada. The best known of the hundreds of cicadas around the world, the Magicicada has an extremely long life cycle. Every thirteen or seventeen years they emerge in vast numbers and make a noise that is a spectacular backdrop to any summer. The summer of 1970 was one such year for the Magicicada, known sometimes colloquially as locusts, though they are nothing of the sort (true locusts are part of the grasshopper family). Dylan thought he had walked into a Nathaniel West novel, and at the end of the day he was very happy to walk out of it, too. But the Princeton 'locusts' would sing all summer long, even as Dylan returned to New York to record his latest diary entry, closing the book on another false dawn.

{278} SHIRLEY'S ROOM

Published lyrics: Isis #45 (handwritten lyrics from auction catalogue, circa August 1970).

A draft of an unfinished song scrawled in Dylan's hand, along with an envelope addressed to him dated August 25, 1970, was offered for sale at a 1992 Christie's New York auction. The telltale microscopic handwriting, with arrows and lines spiraling to the outer edges of the page, confirms it as his work. The date of the envelope – which one assumes relates to the draft lyric – suggests he was still trying to shake off this phase of forgetfulness and find some fresh thoughts to represent this particular *New Morning*.

Like 'Day of the Locusts,' this is a narrative song, but the narrative is fractured. The second verse could almost be evocative, if one were able to discern the whole thing. But what is legible is still mildly intriguing:

> It had been a long blind night,
> Lot of heavy drinking and [. . .] until dawn
> Bongos played [across?] the street from the hotel
> Where lonesome men were holed up in Shirley's room.

Shirley – the true name of his wife, Sara – is a most unexpected incursion. Whether the narrator was one of the 'lonesome men' holed up in her room is never explained (a great deal of crossing out suggests even its author may not know). In fact, the song suggests the narrator-self remembered very little after he 'woke up on the fifth in the middle of the day / [And] vowed never to pass that way again.'

Unable to decide which way to go, the narrator finally concludes, 'It didn't matter – the road wouldn't have no end.' The last image, written at the bottom of the page with an arching arrow attached, suggests this is another place he is grateful to get out of alive: 'I grabbed my rucksack and headed out of town.' Without a session, or a tour, on the horizon, and without a clear idea of where this vignette might lead, Dylan left this lyrical scrap behind, little suspecting it would be snagged by someone who knew it was a curio worthy of preservation.

{279} WHEN I PAINT MY MASTERPIECE

Published lyrics: Writings and Drawings; Lyrics 1985; Lyrics 2004 [*recorded version:* Words Fill My Head].

Known studio recordings: Blue Rock Studios, NY, March 16–18, 1971 – 11 takes [MGH].

First known performance: Academy of Music, NY, December 31, 1971 [ROA].

It was . . . very disorientating. In the early years everything had been like a magic carpet for me – and then all at once it was over. Here was this thing that I'd wanted to do all my life, but suddenly I didn't feel I could do it anymore. – Bob Dylan to John Preston, 2004

When, for the first time, Dylan booked an independent Manhattan studio to record some new song/s in March 1971, it had been more than six months since he last entered a CBS studio. Blue Rock Studios had been a suggestion of pianist and producer Leon Russell, whom Dylan had asked to help him get a new sound. The sessions, which spanned three days, only resulted in two Dylan originals, and one of those appears to have been partially composed during the sessions. So much for shaking himself from his creative torpor.

Repeating the pattern of the June 1970 sessions, Dylan started off recording a series of covers, including a supposedly magnificent 'That Lucky Ol' Sun' (a song he nailed for good fifteen years later, at the first Farm Aid).* Only after he had gotten these songs out of his system did he turn to 'When I Paint My Masterpiece,' and then, finally, to 'Watching the River Flow.'

'When I Paint My Masterpiece' was probably a song Dylan lingered over. It addressed issues that had been brewing ever since he wrote the equally troubled 'Went to See the Gypsy,' a year earlier. And like that song, it drew upon a literary model. F. Scott Fitzgerald's *Tender Is the Night* concerns itself with the writer Dick Diver, who finds himself at the end of an affair, wandering the streets of Rome, past the Spanish

---

* Recordings of a Farm Aid rehearsal on September 19 (on video); of the soundcheck the night before, September 21; and the concert itself all feature the song, and are all worth seeking out. One presumes the subject matter was chosen because of the nature of the benefit.

Stairs, coming to terms with a former love and lost inspiration. Again making such an influence explicit – 'On a cold, dark night on the Spanish Stairs' – Dylan demonstrates he has embarked on a course of reading designed to inspire and illuminate.

The narrator of 'When I Paint My Masterpiece,' though, has a far greater burden to carry than Fitzgerald's antihero – Fame. The description of landing in Brussels only to witness newspapermen having to be 'held down by big police' shows just how heavy this burden had become. And it wasn't getting any easier. When Dylan chose to visit Jerusalem with his wife, 'on a sort of [second] honeymoon,' two months after the 'Masterpiece' session, 'It was miserable for us. . . . Photographers would come up with the room service and they would catch us on the beach, and all we wanted was to relax a bit.'

This narrator has convinced himself that he might derive inspiration from experiencing some of the artistic achievements of humankind, travelling from the New World to Europe's *ancien régimes* only to find himself thirsty for a home whose greatest legacy to the world is a sickly sweet soft drink ('Oh, to be back in the land of Coca-Cola!'). Rome's ancient thoroughfares only reinforce the void in his soul. In *Chronicles*, he refuses to admit how much it hurt: 'Sometime in the past I had written and performed songs that were most original and most influential, and I didn't know if I ever would again and I didn't care.' This is not what he told John Preston on the book's publication (see above).

'When I Paint My Masterpiece' is the song of a man who cares a great deal – who longs to return to a time when it all came 'smooth as a rhapsody.' And Rome was a city Dylan knew well. The memorable couplet, 'Oh the hours that I spent inside the Coliseum / Dodging lions and wasting time,' probably drew on a real experience, if not a recent one. Back in October 1965 he had told Nat Hentoff, 'The first time I was in Rome, I was standing there and digging that Coliseum. . . . The second time I was there, it just distracted me.' That second time may have been in May 1965, when he and Sara escaped the madness of British Dylanmania by heading for mainland Europe.

Was Dylan making an incantation to lost inspiration? Spring 1965 had been a time when he had almost quit singing, unable to see a way ahead. A couple of weeks later, 'Like a Rolling Stone' came to him, and things changed. 'When I Paint My Masterpiece' rides on a similar hope – 'someday, everything is gonna be different.' But by 1971 he knew that getting back to a similar point would take more than mere willpower. As he had learned, this road was long. He famously told author Jonathan Cott in 1978, 'It took me a long time to get to do consciously what I used to be able to do unconsciously . . . and the records I made along the way were . . . [me] trying to figure out whether it was this way or that way . . . what's the simplest way I can tell the story and make this feeling real.' He is talking about 'Masterpiece,' more than any other song of the era.

By reaching for a way to 'make this feeling real,' Dylan succeeded in writing his second masterpiece of the new decade. Which he promptly gave away to his friends in The Band, as he had back in 1967, when it seemed like the tap would never be turned off. By 1971 The Band needed all the help they could get, quality songs having dried up with them, too, ever since their hugely influential first two albums, *Music from Big Pink* (1968) and *The Band* (1969).

According to Rob Bowman's notes to the expanded reissue of *Cahoots* (2000), Dylan had called at Robbie Robertson's house that winter – probably some time in late February/early March – and Robertson asked 'whether he had any material that might be appropriate for the album. Dylan proceeded to play an embryonic version of the still unfinished "When I Paint My Masterpiece." Inspired by Robbie's enthusiasm, Dylan completed the song shortly thereafter.'

One suspects the song had not come easy. As he told biographer Robert Shelton just weeks later, 'A few years ago, I would write a song in two hours, or maybe two days at the most. Now it can be two weeks . . . maybe longer.' In this case Dylan did not fully finish the song until *after* entering Blue Rock Studios – indeed not until he had already recorded the version that ended up on *Greatest Hits Vol. II*. Whatever embryonic version of the song Robertson heard, it was not the one that would provide the template for The Band's. They heard a later version, after Dylan reworked the lyrics and wrote a bridge. Absent from Dylan's released recording – but there in *Writings and Drawings* and on *Cahoots* – is the captivating couplet, 'Sailin' 'round the world in a dirty gondola, oh, to be back in the land of Coca-Cola!'

Other equally significant rewrites were also made between the *Greatest Hits Vol. II* take and the song's 'final' form. Some were just straight improvements. On *Greatest Hits Vol. II*, Dylan does not complete the thought, 'Train wheels runnin' through the back of my memory,' content to just pen something that rhymes with the song title: 'As the daylight hours do increase.' By the end of the process, though, he has returned in his time machine to Hibbing, remembering a time when he 'ran on the hilltop following a pack of wild geese.' Likewise, when caught in a scrum at Brussels airport, he initially concentrates on finding a rhyme (with 'side') and comes up with, 'Everyone was there but no one tried to hide.' Then he finds a line that truly expresses the curse of fame: 'Everyone was there to greet me when I stepped inside.'

However, one rewrite is inferior. Perhaps Dylan thought he was being too cryptic – at a time when he was still looking for 'the simplest way I can tell the story.' Having landed in Brussels 'with a picture of a tall oak tree by my side,' he changed it to a 'plane ride so bumpy that I almost cried.' The reference to the picture was a specific one – presumably the well-known story of an old man who spent his whole life painting and repainting the same tree, a tale about the kind of artist Dylan could never be. The description of the plane journey is mere fluff – though Dylan makes more of it in 1975 when he rhymes it with, 'Sure has been one hell of a ride!'

Quite why Dylan elected to include what is evidently an early take of the song on *Greatest Hits Vol. II* is not obvious. The session log reveals that there were eleven takes of the song, including five complete vocal performances. That it was a last-minute decision to use the early take is clear from a CBS tape box marked: 'Outs from *Greatest Hits Vol. II.*' Aside from the stereo version of 'Can You Please Crawl Out Your Window?' – which failed to make the final track listing – there are two separate versions of 'When I Paint My Masterpiece' on the reel, one described as 'piano version,' marked DO NOT USE, and the other described as a 'full band version.' I think we can safely assume Dylan went with the latter, since no one could describe the released take as a 'piano version,'

However, when it came time to put the song as a final entry in *Writings and Drawings*, he used what might be described as the finished lyrics, i.e., the ones The Band used – complete with the 'Coca-Cola' bridge. The Band may well have heard a slightly different version, for Helm sings about 'a date with a pretty little girl from Greece,' as opposed to 'Botticelli's niece.' Since Dylan also sang this line at subsequent performances, we can probably assume this was not a spontaneous rewrite by some Band-member, but a last-minute Dylan 'improvement.'

Nor was it the last such improvement he wrought on this

little masterpiece. In 1975 he announced a return to that plane of inspiration by opening every show on the Rolling Thunder Revue with this song. Having demonstrated why he sang 'When' and not 'If I Paint My Masterpiece,' Dylan reinforced the song's renewed relevance by opening his four-hour docudrama, *Renaldo and Clara*, with the very same song (which only compounds the criminality of its omission from *The Bootleg Series Vol. 5*, sacrificed to make a corny joke out of 'Tonight I'll Be Staying Here with You').

He also showed that the old lyrical dexterity was fully restored, making the streets of Rome full of 'trouble,' not 'rubble' – which, for the narrator, happens to be the case – and remaking the 'mighty kings of the jungle' as 'those kings of the Vatican,' a more apposite image. He also completely reordered the verses – now 1, 3, 2, 5, 6, 4 – an audacious exercise that makes for a more effective narrative.

If the 1975 performances indicated a restoration of creative powers, the song was one that could work from either vantage point – drought or flood. In June 1991, when he delighted a large Roman audience by opening a show there with it, the song was again coming from someone who was half-stepping up 'the Spanish Stairs,' wondering who turned the lights off. It survived in the set through the following year, even though no comparable masterpiece would come. Finally he decided to stop forcing it, though he continued 'sailin' 'round the world.'

{280} WATCHING THE RIVER FLOW

Published lyrics: Writings and Drawings; Lyrics 1985; Lyrics 2004.
Known studio recordings: Blue Rock Studios, NY, March 16–18, 1971 [45].
First known performance: El Paso, TX, November 21, 1978.

Two years earlier Dylan had been content to watch while 'the river flows, flows to the sea / wherever it flows, that's where I want to be.' By March 1971 he was restless again, wishing he 'was back in the city / Instead of this old bank of sand.' 'Watching the River Flow' – unlike 'When I Paint My Masterpiece' – makes light of the amnesia that afflicts its author, suggesting he might just 'stop and read a book' (a nice reference to one place he was increasingly turning for inspiration). Just the act of starting the song – both a single and an album opener in a matter of months – with the sentiment, 'What's the matter with me / I don't have much to say,' seemed intended to dispel the claims of those who, like Ralph J. Gleason, had recently proclaimed, 'We've Got Dylan Back Again.'

'Watching the River Flow' – the last song recorded at Blue Rock – appears to have come together while the sessions rolled along. A detailed *Rolling Stone* report of the session unequivocally states, 'The song was *written* and cut during the Russell-Dylan jams at Dylan's New York studios.' ('I remember Bob . . . had a pencil and a notepad, and he was writing a lot. He was writing these songs on the spot in the studio, or finishing them up at least.' – Jim Keltner, *Uncut*, October 2008.) The magazine also claimed Dylan slipped some new lyrics into his Blue Rock recording of 'That Lucky Ol' Sun.' The couplet quoted doesn't sound at all like that gospel classic; it sounds more like a starting point for this new original: 'What're you gonna do when the fence needs mending / I just can't sit around here pickin' flowers.'

Dylan was not averse to picking out lines from old favourites with which to bolster his newest song. One barely notices the way he slips in a line from 'The Water Is Wide' – 'If I had wings and I could fly . . .' – or another from 'Old Man River,' among the catalogue of desires that is 'Watching the River Flow.' But he knows he's stuck, looking at 'the river of no return,' waiting on the next wave of inspiration. A good choice for a single, 'Watching the River Flow' accentuated all the positives from his association with Leon Russell and provided fans with that old sardonic wordsmith again. Yet it was only a minor hit (peaking at #41), and Dylan did not work with Russell again.

In fact, the song's future status would be largely based on its inclusion as the opening cut on *Greatest Hits Vol. II*, an album with almost no hits, but a number of previously unreleased tracks that *were* hits, just not for Dylan. It took until November 1978 for him to remember he'd written the damn thing. But after a couple of soundcheck tryouts, he debuted it in Texas with a big-band arrangement that worked surprisingly well. And it was restored to the set in the nineties, when his very own bar band was willing to boogie on down to the river at a time when he again didn't 'have much to say.'

{281} WALLFLOWER

Published lyrics: Lyrics *1985;* Lyrics *2004.*

Known studio recordings: Studio B, NY, November 4, 1971 [TBS – tk.4].

Evidently recorded as a potential B side to the 'George Jackson' single, nothing perhaps exemplifies the dearth of inspiration that now ensnared Dylan than the reemergence of 'Wallflower' the following October, as a half-hearted duet with Doug Sahm at sessions for a Sahm Band album on Atlantic. That Dylan should even remember such an insignificant song a year after he wrote it demonstrates someone largely working from a *tabula rasa* when it came to his songwriting. Reminded about the song during a radio special to promote the first *Bootleg Series* – on which it features – Dylan described it as 'just a sad song . . . one of those pathetic situations in life that can be so overwhelming at times.'

{282} GEORGE JACKSON

Published lyrics: Lyrics *1985;* Lyrics *2004.*

Known studio recordings: Studio B, NY, November 4, 1971 [45 – tks.9+13].

Once again it took the reading of a book to inspire the songwriter in Dylan. The book in question was *Soledad Brother*, a collection of prison letters by a Black Panther named George Jackson. The fatal shooting of Jackson by a prison guard at San Quentin on August 21, 1971, while allegedly trying to escape, had prompted Dylan to pick up this collection. On finishing the letters, he apparently phoned up a CBS executive and booked a studio for the following day, aiming to record a quickly penned eulogy to the black activist.

The results were just as hastily released, as a double-sided single, at the beginning of December. Though it would appear he had originally intended to put 'Wallflower' on the B side, a friend pointed out that this might result in radio stations playing this innocuous country 'miss' as the new Dylan single, rather than a statement of support for a violent radical. As a result, Dylan put an acoustic version of 'George Jackson' on one side of the single and a band version on the other. The outcome was not any greater amount of radio play, and the single pretty much sank without a trace. No one was listening, it seemed. Just as Dylan suspected. (He had noted as much three years earlier: 'No one cares to see it the way I'm seeing it now, whereas before, I saw it the way they saw it.')

At the same time, Dylan incurred a remarkable degree of flak from those who already disparaged his civil rights record and questioned his general commitment to the Cause; they were now inquiring whether he intended to donate his royalties to the Soledad brothers' defence fund. These angry young folk saw 'George Jackson' as a sop to get them off the singer's back, not a 'return' to radicalism. The song was actually prompted by a series of conversations with filmmaker and friend Howard Alk, who had been working on a film about the Black Panthers through 1970–1, which made Dylan curious about the Panthers' goals and motives, leading to a meeting with Huey Newton and David Hilliard the previous December.

From this it was but a short step to their incarcerated brother. Unfortunately, Dylan appears to have once again bought into the counter-culture version of Jackson's 'execution.' In the song he clearly suggests Jackson was shot by the guards during a riot, not as he was trying to escape, but because 'they were frightened of his power / They were scared of his love . . . so they cut George Jackson down.' Given that the volatile inmate had told Liberation News Service reporter Karen Wald on the morning of his death, 'We've gotta . . . turn the prison into just another front of the struggle, tear it down from the inside,' they were entitled to be frightened.

The official report of the incident – which resulted in the death of three guards and two other inmates – suggests that Jackson summarily executed at least one of the guards, Jere Graham, with a smuggled 9mm pistol, as he attempted to take over his tier in the Adjustment Center. While clearly demonstrating someone who 'wouldn't take shit from no one,' one might also interpret it as evidence of a death wish. Earlier in the song, Dylan portrays Jackson as someone incarcerated 'for a seventy-dollar robbery'; the law then 'Closed the door behind him / And they threw away the key.' In fact, the seventy-dollar robbery had been back in 1959, when Jackson was eighteen, and he served just a year for what was, after all, an armed robbery of a gas station.

Jackson was soon back in jail, though, and in January 1970, he killed his first prison guard, John Mills, supposedly in retaliation for the deaths of three black activists. Quite where the 'love' comes into Jackson's philosophy Dylan never explains. He has never performed 'George Jackson,' nor has he included it on any LP or CD (save for a Japanese 3-LP set, *Masterpieces*), and he may have come to regret writing the song even more quickly than the one he wrote for another incarcerated black bruiser four years later. As for Jackson's death, it has continued to exercise conspiracy cranks, convinced that he was executed not at the authorities' behest, but at the Panthers'.

1972–3

{ Pat Garrett and Billy the Kid;
Planet Waves }

*Still in a befuddled state as far as songwriting went, Dylan
managed to write two of his most enduring songs in the wastelands
of Arizona and Mexico – 'Forever Young' and 'Knockin' on Heaven's
Door' – between the spring of 1972 and winter 1973, proving, I
guess, that there are droughts and there are droughts. But he knew
he needed to write more. And it would still be another nine months
before he had enough songs to make a ten-track album of originals.
Planet Waves, written mostly during a stint east in October 1973,
suggested he'd finally called up a familiar phantom engineer to look
at some of the internal wiring. Songs like 'Dirge,' 'Tough Mama,'
and 'Going, Going, Gone' at last suggested someone gearing up to
peer over the cliff again . . .*

{283} **BOWLING ALLEY BLUES**

{284} **FIELD MOUSE FROM NEBRASKA**

Published lyrics: Writings and Drawings *(endpapers).*

Published lyrics: In His Own Words Vol. 2.

Shortly after midnight on New Year's Eve 1971–2, Dylan joined The Band onstage at the New York Academy of Music for a rousing five-song encore that included a powerful performance of 'When I Paint My Masterpiece.' It would be January 1973 before he would be heard from again, now in Durango, playing a bit part in a Western movie by that archetypal maverick, Sam Peckinpah. In between, he somehow managed to drop off the face of the earth. In songwriting terms, he achieved much the same trick.

In fact, he had escaped to Phoenix, Arizona, with his family, where he continued to work on songs without success. According to a 1986 article by history teacher Bob Finkbine, who befriended Dylan at this time, one day he was 'sitting in Dylan's kitchen drinking coffee . . . [and] I asked him, "Bob, did you ever have a time when you had trouble writing?" Sara turned from fixing sandwiches at the counter and quipped, "Try the last two years."' The lack of any evidence to the contrary validates Sara's unguarded aside.

One way Dylan found to confront his ongoing problem of earning a living as a songwriter was compiling the evidence of a time when 'everything had been like a magic carpet,' published in the winter of 1973 as *Writings and Drawings*. Though the collection concluded with 'When I Paint My Masterpiece,' already almost two years old, the end papers to the volume included four pages of typed lyrics to what appeared to be new songs, two of which bear titles: 'Bowling Alley Blues' and 'Field Mouse from Nebraska.'

If these end papers have a lyrical equivalent, it is the 1963 Margolis and Moss manuscripts. Again Dylan seems content to let ideas fizzle out, failing to finish anything he started. A decade earlier he was taking a breather. But these half-formed lyrics were worrying evidence of stultifying stasis, either expressing the cloyingly mundane ('It was early in the evening, I was cutting up the bread / Man alive, that crust was hard') or detailing a series of vain attempts to parlay with paradoxes, which had been done so dazzlingly back at Big Pink ('When I was a boy on the Wagon Wheel / I married a false young maid / She was tender hearted and tho it showed / She kept her mood concealed'). Bookending a decade of innovation and inspiration, these unformed songs were omitted from subsequent editions of the man's lyrics.

As for 'Round and Round We Go,' this was a six-line fragment found in the Dylans' trashcan by self-styled garbologist A. J. Weberman at the end of 1971 and published in Weberman's autobiography, *A Life in Garbology*. Suffice it to say, there is a reason it was in the trashcan with all the dog shit and diapers. And there was also a reason why Dylan moved far from the crazies who were taking over the American asylum. He intended to follow the advice offered in this fragment – 'round & round the mountain / play that guitar, man' – as he headed for Arizona, where he might yet hide from 'unknowing eyes.'

{286} FOREVER YOUNG

Published lyrics: Lyrics 1985; Lyrics 2004.

Known studio recordings: Ram's Horn demo, June 1973 [BIO]; Village Recorder, LA, November 2, 1973 – 1 take; November 5, 1973 – 2 takes; November 8, 1973 – 5 takes; November 9, 1973 – 1 take; November 14, 1973 – 5 takes [PWx2].

First known performance: Chicago Stadium, January 3, 1974.

When I was living in Phoenix, Arizona, in about '72, the big song at the time was 'Heart of Gold.' . . . It bothered me every time I listened to 'Heart of Gold.' . . . I needed to lay back for a while, forget about things, myself included, and I'd get so far away, and turn on the radio and there I am, but it's not me. – Dylan to Scott Cohen, November 1985

The nine months or so that Dylan spent in Arizona in 1972 remain shrouded in the dust of rumour. Even a 1986 article in a local Phoenix paper by Bob Finkbine has done little to fill this chasm in the chronology. The one solid piece of information Finkbine does provide is confirmation that 'Forever Young' dates from this time. Dylan was proud enough to play it for his new friend, informing him, 'I've been tinkering around with a new song. I wrote it for Jesse. It goes kinda like this.' He then broke into that memorable opening, 'May God bless and keep you always . . .'

Dylan has elsewhere suggested the song had a straight-forward genesis, addressing the concerns of a family man: 'I wrote it thinking about one of my boys and not wanting to be too sentimental. The lines came to me, they were done in a minute.' He also admitted that he wrote the song in Tucson. His suggestion that it was 'done in a minute' does not tally with what he told engineer-producer Rob Fraboni when he was finally ready to record the song in November 1973: 'He told me he had carried around "Forever Young" in his head for about three years. He gets an idea for a song sometimes, he said, and he's not ready to write it down. So he just keeps it with him and eventually it comes out.'

What seems to have prompted Dylan to let 'Forever Young' come out was hearing that damn Neil Young song on the radio. 'Heart of Gold' was a song Young himself had been carrying around in his head for a year or more (the gripping piano version he recorded at Toronto's Massey Hall in January 1971 has recently been released on CD). Even Young was surprised to find the song becoming a number-one single shortly after its release in February 1972, its success proving to be a far greater curse for him than Dylan.

At a time when every label was searching for a 'new Dylan,' Young seemed to be assimilating the sound of the old Dylan. And though they may not seem obvious twins, it is clear from Dylan's comment above – apropos this song – that 'Forever Young' was his retort. He was doing Young doing Dylan. And yes, that is a pun in the title. Though it has passed most folk by, he was doing a Dylanesque Young, forever.

It must still make Dylan inwardly chuckle every time he sees the expression 'may you stay forever young' appropriated for some mushy purpose (like a sickly sweet film, a bad Rod Stewart song, and the like). For although the phrase has something of the King James Bible about it, it seems to be one Dylan can claim for his own. Yes, the song title appears in 'Ode to a Grecian Urn,' by one of his favourite poets, Keats, but in quite a different context – 'For ever warm and still to be enjoyed / For ever panting, and for ever young.'

Which is not to say that the phrase was not transmitted, along with the nightingale's code, from John to Bob; just that its purpose changed out of all recognition. And the Bible, though it is not the source of the title or sentiment, does provide its fair share of reference points in the song. When he requests his son to 'be courageous, stand upright and be strong,' it is to the book of Joshua he is sending him: 'Only be thou strong and very courageous, that thou mayest observe to do according to all the law' (1:7).

Having written the song 'not wanting to be too sentimental,' Dylan was worried lest the song be taken as evidence of someone who'd gone soft in the head. So, although he demo-ed the song in June 1973, already a full year after he wrote it, he had no burning desire to start a new chapter with it. That demo was a surprise bonus track on the 1985 *Biograph* boxed set, and it reveals a lilting, country feel and an earnest determination to hold onto the words. But still, the song sat around. He finally recorded it for *Planet Waves* in November, a full eighteen months after its composition, by which time he naturally wondered whether he had lost a handle on the song. As he admitted to engineer Fraboni at these sessions, 'I been carrying this song around in my head for . . . years . . . and now I come to record it and I just can't decide how to do it.' He had already carried the song around longer than anything written before.

'Forever Young' occupied him more than any other song at Village Recorder studios, being recorded on no less than five separate occasions, and in at least three different ways (fast, slow, acoustic). And yet, as had happened so often, the one time he found its hymnal core, it was a first take – probably on the ninth – that rendered everyone speechless. Fraboni remembers it well: 'We only did one take of the slow version of "Forever Young." This take was so riveting, it was so powerful, so immediate . . . [that] when everybody came in nobody really said anything.'

And yet Dylan was initially going to leave this take off the album. Having insisted he was fighting sentimentality all the way down the line, he was mortified by the immediate response by one person who heard it the day he recorded it. Rob Fraboni was there as Dylan found his song critiqued by some wannabe rock chick: 'Jackie deShannon and Donna Weiss came by one night and on the same night Lou Kemp and this girl came by and she had made a crack to him, "C'mon, Bob, what!? Are you getting mushy in your old age?" about "Forever Young." It was based on this comment that he wanted to leave [the slow version] off the record.'

Thankfully, Fraboni and Robertson knew that this was how the song was *meant* to sound, and they managed to persuade Dylan to ignore the opinionated outsider. Its future was thus determined – a modern hymn for anyone still 'busy being born.' Predictably, its finale status on the whole 1974 tour, and the decision to put the song on *Planet*

Waves twice – as an act of closure (on side one) and as a new beginning (on side two) – meant the song quickly got away from Dylan, acquiring a life of its own, even as he let it be.

It finally received an arrangement ornate enough for this son of 'Father of Night' in 1978, becoming one of those lighter-in-the-dark moments. But as the world tour progressed, he began to resent the way he was expected to emphasize the anthemic quality *implicit* in such a personal song, and again he sought to provide the song with the same interpretative elbow room as earlier anthems. He tried to communicate that original resonance when discussing it in September: 'It's all in your heart: whatever keeps you that way, keeps you forever young. . . . It doesn't necessarily mean that you don't grow old, but you still have contact with what put you where you are.' Shortly afterwards, he began to strip the song of some of its hand-holding elements.

Only when he found *himself* born again did he find renewed meaning in the song. That opening line invoking Jehovah no longer seemed out of place, as 'Forever Young' became one of the more applicable pre-Christian songs restored to a revamped set in June 1981. This time he drove home its kinship to 'Heart of Gold,' the song that had leaned so heavily on 'that harmonica and guitar sound' Dylan himself had 'just stumbled on.' Filling European arenas with his own swooping harmonica, separating the final verse from its tether, he rang the harmonic changes each and every night. Much to Dylan's delight, its renewed resonance was not lost on audiences. And though he has struggled to hit those same soaring notes in post-1981 performances, on the odd magical night – say, in Birmingham in 1987, at the Supper Club in 1993, or at the penultimate show of 1995 in Philadelphia – he has renewed that contact with the Lord unconsciously invoked in Arizona.

{287} BILLY (THE BALLAD OF BILLY THE KID)

Published lyrics: Lyrics 1985; Lyrics 2004 [*Recorded versions:* Words Fill My Head].

Known studio recordings: CBS Studios, Mexico City, January 20, 1973 [4 takes, inc. Billy 4]; Burbank Studios, CA, February 1973 [multiple takes, inc. Billy 1; Billy 7] [PG].

First known performance: Stockholm, Sweden, March 22, 2009.

Dylan was hardly the first folksinger to come up with a ballad about Billy the Kid, the notorious gunslinger who was shot down by his old friend, Sheriff Pat Garrett, at Fort Sumner, New Mexico, in 1881 (Garrett subsequently published *An Authentic Life of Billy the Kid*, a book he was uniquely qualified to write). Yet it was a fortuitous confluence that brought him to this place where he could write a ballad in a traditional vein about one of his childhood heroes, and then go on to play his sidekick, Alias, in a film largely based on the account given by Garrett.

The script to *Pat Garrett and Billy the Kid* had been written by a screenwriter Dylan already knew, Rudy Wurlitzer. It was a personal message from Rudy that convinced him to supply a song or two, little knowing at the time that the script he'd been shown would barely figure in the finished film. Dylan immediately responded to the challenge of writing a conventional cowboy ballad concerning a figure even more enveloped in myth than John Wesley Hardin. He was soon ready to play the result to the film's director, Sam Peckinpah, while other participants in the process sat in the adjoining room, as James Coburn recalls:

> The night we were over at Sam's house and we were all drinking tequila and carrying on and halfway through dinner, Sam says, 'Okay kid, let's see what you got. You bring your guitar with you?' They went in this little alcove. Sam had a rocking chair. Bobby sat down on a stool in front of this

rocking chair. There was just the two of them in there. . . .
And Bobby played three or four tunes. And Sam came out
with his handkerchief in his eye, 'Goddamn kid! Who the
hell is he? Who is that kid? Sign him up!'

And that was that. Dylan was onboard, as was his ballad
of Billy, one of the tunes played to Peckinpah that November
night. Whether Peckinpah realized it or not, Dylan had done
his homework. He knew that, while Garrett was giving his
side of the story, popular balladeers were already singing the
outlaw into the annals of American folklore. So although
Dylan adhered to the script more than he woud on later
'theme tunes' (*Band of the Hand*, *Wonder Boys*), he also made a
number of allusions to the traditional ballad of 'Billy the Kid,'
notably 'Gypsy queens will play your grand finale / Down
in some Tularosa alley / Maybe in the Rio Pecos valley,' a
reworking of the original third verse:

> Fair Mexican maidens play guitars and sing
> A song about Billy, their boy-bandit king,
> How ere his young manhood had reached its sad end,
> He'd a notch in his pistol for twenty-one men.

What we don't know is how many verses the ballad had
when Dylan played it to Peckinpah. According to the man
responsible for scoring the film, the irascible Jerry Fielding,
'Dylan had this song he'd written, for which he had a limit-
less number of verses that he would sing in random order.'
The various recordings and multiple excerpts used in the film
(on both its 1973 general release and 1984 re-release) partially
bear out Fielding's claim. I actually prefer some of the lost
lines. 'Laying around with some sweet senorita / Into her
dark chamber she will greet ya / In the shadows of the mesa
she will lead ya' has the edge on what he sings on 'Billy 7' and

later put in *Lyrics*. 'There's mirrors inside the minds of crazy faces' is also more Dylanesque than 'There's eyes behind the mirrors in empty places.'

Much of the confusion surrounding 'Billy' would ultimately be caused by the decision to break the song up, interspersing verses throughout the film, a subtle juxtaposition of ballad and film. By his own admission, this was Fielding's idea – not Dylan's. According to the next film director to work with Dylan, Richard Marquand, the singer-songwriter was unhappy with the idea, and very hurt 'that they took his music and they relaid it . . . so that Bob would write a piece of music for a particular sequence, and then the studio afterwards, in post-production, re-edited the whole thing.' Only at the end of the so-called 'director's cut' (put out in 1984) does 'Billy' appear in something approaching its entirety (verses 1–5, 8, and 6, in fact), as the credits languorously roll. Just as Alias intended.

{288} GOODBYE HOLLY

Published lyrics: Words Fill My Head.
Known studio recordings: CBS Studios, Mexico City, January 20, 1973.

'Goodbye Holly' was one of the songs Dylan recorded at a January 1973 all-night session in Mexico City designed to fill out the film score. Having written a central 'theme song' for the film, it seems to have been Dylan's intention (probably at Fielding's or Peckinpah's prompting) to write either a different piece of music or a variant on the central theme for each of the many murders that punctuate Peckinpah's requiem to the Old West. Thus 'Billy Surrenders' plays over the shoot-out at Billy's hideout, which claims a couple of members of Billy's gang; while 'And He's Killed Me Too' was supposed to provide the background to Billy gunning down the righteous Ollinger (it was replaced by 'Cantina Theme'). 'Knockin' on Heaven's Door' would serve a similar function for the death of Alamosa Bill. Finally, 'Final Theme' would serve as an atmospheric backdrop to the ritual killing of the last young gun, Billy the Kid himself.

As such, 'Goodbye Holly' is self-explanatory. For the death of Holly, gunned down by Garrett at Jones Trading Post, Dylan had written a song focusing on the plight of those he left behind: 'Goodbye Holly, Holly goodbye / Your wife's gonna miss you, your babies gonna cry.' Not that he forgets the larger picture (*sic*). Singing 'All your good times have passed now and gone,' he is asking, on behalf of Billy, Where have all the good times gone? It is not clear why the song was not used in the film. Instead, the forgettable 'Cantina Theme' was made to suffice twice – once for Holly and once for Ollinger – which I doubt was what either Dylan or Peckinpah intended.

{289} ROCK ME MAMA (LIKE A WAGON WHEEL)

Known studio recordings: Burbank Studios, Burbank, CA, February 1973 – 2 takes.

Dylan's habit of riffing on song ideas between studio takes has produced its share of oddities over the years. One of the more memorable is a throwaway ditty he dropped in between Billy this and Billy that at sessions in Burbank, intended to give the producer of *Pat Garrett and Billy the Kid*, Gordon Carroll, more material to work into the film. The 'song,' if we can consider it that – and it has now been covered by Old Crow Medicine Show and copyrighted as 'Wagon Wheel' – lasts barely ninety seconds the first time around, and just two minutes on a second, more spirited take, with Dylan trying to bluff a verse or two. But the song remains little more than a riff attached to the following chorus:

> Rock me mama, like a wagon wheel,
> Rock me mama, anyway you feel,
> Hey, mama, rock me.

> Rock me mama, like the wind and the rain,
> Rock me mama, like a southbound train,
> Hey, mama, rock me.

Despite this, it is one of the better song ideas he plays around with at these sessions, and the spirit of invention is one his fellow musicians – including the likes of Bruce Langhorne, Jim Keltner, and Roger McGuinn – readily accede to. The ease with which the others venture into Dylan's slipstream affirms that the song may be the singer's, but the sentiment and structure is not. 'Rock Me Mama' had long been a blues commonplace, or if you like euphemism, for, well, guess. And it is the title of at least two quite different songs, both from former talismans: Sonny Terry (found on his solo *Chain Gang Blues* LP) and Arthur 'Big Boy' Crudup. In each case they were altogether more upfront about what it is they'd like to 'rock.'

{290} KNOCKIN' ON HEAVEN'S DOOR

Published lyrics: Lyrics 1985; Lyrics 2004 [*live variants:* Words Fill My Head].

Known studio recordings: Burbank Studios, CA, February 1973 [PG].

First known performance: Chicago Stadium, January 3, 1974.

Returning to Durango, where filming continued after the Mexico City session, Dylan already knew the handful of songs recorded at the all-night session would not suffice for Sam's purposes. He also knew they would not meet with the approval of Jerry Fielding, the man brought in to score the film. Indeed, he expressed a suspicion at the Mexican session that 'this guy Fielding's gonna go nuts when he hears this!' Fielding was used to working with people who could read music, not those who liked to reinvent it. He later complained, 'Dylan never understood what I wanted.'

Dylan actually did his best to oblige, if not humour,

Fielding, who told the songwriter 'that he [had to] write at least one other piece of music, because you cannot possibly hope to deal with an entire picture on the basis of that one ballad. So finally he brought to the dubbing session another piece of music – "Knock knock-knockin' on Heaven's Door." Everybody loved it. It was shit. That was the end for me.' One must presume Mr. Fielding did not end his days in A&R.

The song Dylan had written to order was an exercise in splendid simplicity, containing one of the easiest melodies this rarely complex composer ever conjured, along with two four-line verses and a chorus that merely reiterated the song's title. Asked to come up with a song on the spot, Dylan summarized the ethos of the entire movie in two-and-a-half minutes, all the while writing something for the ages. Indeed, outside *cineast* enclaves, the film is now largely remembered for this very song, written to express everything Alamosa Bill is unable to say as he goes down to the river. According to Dylan, it was also the only song the studio used in the right place in the general release version of the film. ('The [*Pat Garrett*] music seemed to be scattered and used in every other place but the scenes which we did it for. Except for "Heaven's Door."')

Bill's 'death' scene pulls no visual punches. While the gospel choir is calling Bill home, Mama's eyes are blinded by tears of pain. As such the power of the song may have worked against the director's, and perhaps the songwriter's, intentions. When the film was reedited and rescored in 1984, the original, vocal version of the song, which works so well in context, was replaced by an instrumental take, utilized originally at a later point. One wonders whether there was evidence that Peckinpah preferred it this way, given that, in the decade separating the original from this new edit, the song had become a major selling point in its own right.

Back in late January 1973, when the song was presented

to Peckinpah, it was just another piece of his jigsaw that the studio was trying to dismantle before the director's angry eye. Only when Dylan recorded both versions at Burbank in February 1973 did *he* seem to realize how good it was, inspired as he was again by a tight deadline and a specific goal. Having assembled a who's who of L.A. session musicians to lend a hand, Dylan found himself in a unique situation, recording a song while the relevant scene from the film's rushes were projected overhead. Drummer Jim Keltner was particularly moved: 'In those days you were on a big soundstage, and you had this massive screen that you can see on the wall, [with] the scene . . . running when you're playing. I cried through that whole take.'

Though the lyrics were straightforward enough, Dylan never quite settled on a 'final' form. On the one documented vocal outtake, Dylan consistently sings, 'That long black train is comin' on round,' (or 'pullin' on down') – *not*, 'That long black cloud is comin' down.' He also seems to have consistently preferred the former image in performance, not the one he put on record. When the song received its live debut, less than a year later, it was 'that long black train' that was again pulling down the track. He had also come up with an additional verse, which could well be his one and only public comment on the Vietnam war, then entering its final stages:

Mama, wipe the blood from my face, I'm sick and tired of this war,
Got a black, lonely feeling and it's hard to trace, feel like I'm knockin' on heaven's door.

By 1975–6, when the song formed the encore to every Rolling Thunder gig, the war was over. Dylan, though, was still asking his mama to wipe the blood from his face, but for a more prosaic reason: 'I can't see through it anymore /

I need someone to talk to in a new hiding place / Feel like I'm knockin' on heaven's door.' The Revue rendition served not only as a rousing finale to every RTR show but also concluded both the *Hard Rain* TV special and that cinematic marathon, *Renaldo and Clara*.

Meanwhile, the song had been co-opted by an old friend, Eric Clapton, who inflicted a *faux* reggae arrangement on it in August 1975. This travesty was a surprising hit in its own right, so when Dylan was stuck for an arrangement on the 1978 'Alimony' Tour, he too decided to apply a lethal dose of reggae. Touring with a four-piece girl-choir for the first time ever, he denied the song its gospel heritage, instead playing it for kicks, thankfully dropping it from the set at the beginning of June.

When it was resurrected in June 1981, Dylan had found a way to blend the two strains, giving it a choppy, ska beat, but a gospel chorus. In the light of his conversion to Christianity, the song had naturally taken on an extra layer of meaning. Now, when asking Mama to remove his badge, he doesn't 'want it anymore.' And when he arrives at heaven's door, he is knocking 'like so many times before' – suggesting that the door had been closed. He also adds another new verse, which suggests he'd found heaven on the high seas while sailing his new schooner, the *Water Pearl*:

Mama, tow my boat out to sea, pull it down from shore to shore,
Two brown eyes looking at me, feel like I'm knockin' on heaven's door.

In this apposite setting, at the conclusion of a set about the struggle for salvation, it endured to year's end. It reappeared in 1986–7 when Dylan took to touring with the Queens of Rhythm, again serving as an encore that could be taken a number of ways. However, it took until August 6, 1988, at a show in Carlsbad, California, for Dylan to give one lucky audience (and author) a glimpse of how it sounded the day he played it to an unmoved Jerry Fielding and a highly emotional Sam Peckinpah as a solo acoustic valedictory. For others, the song has now become the anthem to end all anthems for *anyone* wanting to end an evening on a high moment. But only New York's seminal punk outfit, Television, has come close to capturing the true spirit of the song in concert (and on *The Blow-Up*), with a version as instrumentally expressive as anything Dylan managed back in Burbank.

{291} NEVER SAY GOODBYE

Published lyrics: Lyrics *1985;* Lyrics *2004.*

Known studio recordings: Ram's Horn demo, June 1973; Village Recorder, CA, November 2, 1973 – 7 takes [PW – tk.7].

After landing in Los Angeles in late February, worried about one of his children – who needed medical treatment as a result of the months in Durango – Dylan decided to rent a home in Malibu and settle down there for a while. He was doubtless amused to see 'Knockin' on Heaven's Door' garnering nonstop airplay, making CBS, who had effectively let him leave the label, squirm into the bargain. But the songs were still not flowing, and again he resorted to a little communal composing. When Roger McGuinn came by that spring, they decided to see if they could come up with another 'Ballad of Easy Rider.' According to McGuinn, 'We were trying to write a song together and I asked him if he had anything, and he said he had one that he started, but he was probably gonna use it himself; and he started playing "Never Say Goodbye."'

The song he had 'started' before McGuinn came along would be finished by June, when Dylan demo-ed it along with 'Forever Young' and another new song, 'Nobody 'Cept You,' at an informal session in New York for his own music publisher, Ram's Horn. That version remains unreleased, but it evidently had a verse which Dylan cut by the time he got around to recording it for his next album:

> Time is all I have to give, you can have it if you choose,
> With me you can live, never say goodbye.

The copyrighted lyrics also place the final verse's reference to 'baby blue' in the future tense: 'You'll change your last name, too.' But Dylan clearly sings 'You've changed your last name, too' on *Planet Waves*. Either way it seems safe to suggest that *this* 'baby blue' is not *that* 'baby blue.' For the remainder of the song, Dylan allows himself to go back home again in his mind. 'Twilight on the frozen lake / North wind about to break' represents a perfect evocation of Duluth in the still of winter. (As he told one local journalist in 1986, 'I don't remember much about Duluth, really. Except the foghorns.')

The childhood visions still remained, in dreams. As he informed one scribe in 2004, 'The country where I came from – it's pretty bleak. And it's cold. And there's a lot of water. So you could dream a lot. The difference between me now and then is that back then, I could see visions. The me now can dream dreams.' He told another interviewer around the same time, 'I grew up in a very isolated place and throughout my boyhood years I felt like I was like a dog hunting in dreams, always looking for something, although I wasn't sure what exactly.' Duluth was in his blood.

In 'Never Say Goodbye,' he attempts to convey those dreams 'made of iron and steel / with a big bouquet of roses.' It may have been the recent purchase of a farm in Minnesota that prompted such reflection. Or it may reflect a more psychological source, reflected in what he later said about the contemporaneous 'Forever Young': 'It's all in your heart: whatever keeps you that way, keeps you forever young

. . . hav[ing] contact with what put you where you are.' He was certainly in a nostalgic frame of mind that spring. As for 'Never Say Goodbye,' he carried it with him long enough to cut it as the first song out of the block at the November 1973 *Planet Waves* sessions. Just no further.

{292} NOBODY 'CEPT YOU

Published lyrics: Lyrics 1985; Lyrics 2004.
Known studio recordings: Ram's Horn demo, June 1973; Village Recorder, CA, November 2, 1973 [TBS]; November 5, 1973.
First known performance: Chicago Stadium, January 3, 1974.

> My work reflects the thoughts I had as a little kid that have become super-developed. – Dylan to Jon Bream, January 1978

'Nobody 'Cept You' is the second song in a trilogy of tunes that steered Dylan towards *Planet Waves*, the third one being 'Something There Is About You.' All three were written from the vantage point of someone trying to reconcile past and present through love for an unspecified muse. Connecting back to 'I Don't Want to Do It' (and maybe even 'I'm Not There (1956)'), they lead on to the quasi-mystical breakthrough he shall achieve with *Blood on the Tracks*, where past and present are allowed to constantly interchange.

On 'Nobody 'Cept You,' he seems to feel it is only 'you' who shares this connection to the past, specifically to a time when he would 'play in the cemetery / Dance and sing and run when I was a child.' He also connects the song to ones from his midsixties heyday, equating his feelings for her with a religious yearning inspired by 'a hymn I used to hear / In the churches all the time / Make me feel so good inside / So peaceful, so sublime.' In many ways, the song closes the book on songs of simple devotion from an amnesiac, and opens a new one in which desire has to be paid for with one's blood.

Which makes 'Nobody 'Cept You' the most personal of the three interconnected songs, and may explain why it was omitted from *Planet Waves*, though the song was recorded twice at the sessions – once with Manuel on drums, the other with Helm. But it would not explain why he ripped through the song at breakneck speed at the first half-a-dozen performances in January 1974, with just an acoustic guitar to guide him through. Or why at song's end he added the line, 'I'm *still* in love with you' – absent from the copyrighted version.

The song had by then been superseded by 'Wedding Song,' another protestation of constancy, but one couched in terms bound by this newer, more paradoxical framework, making it a likely replacement on the album itself. On a single night in January (the ninth, in Toronto), Dylan brought both elements together for the first and last time. After which it was left to 'Wedding Song' to reclaim the present, 'now that the past is gone.'

{293} GOING, GOING, GONE

Published lyrics: Lyrics 1985; Lyrics 2004 [1976/78 versions: Words Fill My Head].
Known studio recordings: Village Recorder, CA, November 5, 1973 – 5 takes [PW – tk.5]; November 8 – 3 takes.
First known performance: Lakeland, FL, April 18, 1976.

> Writing is such an isolated thing. You're in such an isolated frame of mind. You have to get into or be in that place. In the old days, I could get to it real quick. . . . You're always capable of it in your youth and especially if you're unknown and nobody cares. . . . But once that all ends, then you have to create not only what you want to do, but you have to create the environment to do it in, which is double-hard.
> – Dylan to Kathryn Baker, August 1988

One constant during Dylan's 'amnesia' had been a forlorn quest for a place where he could write the kinds of songs he used to manage in that old 'New York atmosphere.' However, whether he was in Woodstock, on Fire Island, in Phoenix, Durango, or Malibu, the signals continued to come through only in fits and starts. So when he committed himself to a large national tour and a new album, both to be shared with The Band, he knew he needed to get back to writing like he used to whenever an album deadline approached.

With just three songs definitely written by September 1973, he headed out for the old East Coast. According to Rob Fraboni, 'Bob went to New York *by himself* [my italics]. He stayed there for two to two and a half weeks and wrote most all the songs.' 'Most all the songs' appears to devolve down to six of the eleven originals recorded for the album, specifically 'Going, Going, Gone,' 'Hazel,' 'You Angel You,' 'Something There Is About You,' 'Tough Mama,' and 'On a Night Like This.'

He had presumably started sketching out some of these, 'Something There Is About You' being one strong candidate. 'Going, Going, Gone' would be another, with its telltale homily ('Grandma said . . . follow your heart') implying someone stuck in Malibu with the Minnesota blues. On the other hand, he could as easily have been enjoying Elvis Presley's 1969 rendition of 'Only the Strong Survive,' another possible template for this depiction of his time as a 'geographic' – someone who moves from place to place thinking the problem is location, location, location, but finds that their baggage always arrives first.

The recording of 'Going, Going, Gone' is definitely soaked in an atmosphere of acute desperation. Maybe they turned the air-conditioner off for this one, because the guy really does sound like he is 'hanging on the ledge.' And though Robertson again excels himself, it is all about Dylan's frayed performance. And yet the singer himself evidently didn't rate it very highly, because when work on the album resumed, after a two-day break, on November 8, he turned up early to record his 'first' vocal overdub.* According to the studio logs, there were three attempts, of which the DTLF (Dylan-Tape Liberation Front) recently located the third. At the end of another riveting performance, though, Dylan exasperatingly exclaims, 'We could spend all day doing this, and I don't even know if it is the right thing to do.'

Ultimately, he goes with the unadulterated take they secured on the fifth. But he clearly wasn't finished with the song, though, for now, he left it behind. He just needed to figure out where it needed to go. It did not feature on the 1974 tour, even in the early stages when he was *almost* promoting the still-unreleased album. Nor was it considered a suitable candidate for the 1975 Rolling Thunder Revue campaign.

Only in 1976, when Dylan's marriage was again teetering on the edge, and every show was a rambunctious wreck waiting to happen, did he decide to have another go, go, gone – not just toying with the arrangement but going to the song's lyrical core. This new version was worked on extensively at pre-tour rehearsals in Clearwater, Dylan bouncing from new lyric to new lyric before unveiling it at the first show in Lakeland. And though he kept the original opening verse, little else of the 1973 lyric survives. Infidelity is rife, and this time he paints himself as the innocent party:

---

* The issue of when Dylan made his first vocal overdub in the studio is fraught with contention. Two vocals on 'The Boxer' presupposes that Dylan dubbed one on to the other, but evidence is lacking. Perhaps he simply did the song twice, and left it to Johnston to sync the two. The 'Going Going Gone' overdubs were abandoned, due to Dylan's dissatsfaction with the process. Only with 'Idiot Wind,' which he recorded in New York on September 19, 1974, did Dylan actually 'punch in' a new vocal on part of the song.

> I've been sleeping on the road
> With my head in the dust
> Now I've just got to go
> Before it's all diamonds and rust.
> I'm going, I'm going, I'm gone.

Perhaps the most important change, though, comes during the bridge, where his grandma is no longer preaching constancy ('Don't you and your one true love ever part'). Rather, she dispenses a licence to pursue the unattainable ('Don't you and that lifelong dream ever part'), a line that survives every other rewrite on the month-long tour. Though the song never settled long enough to be featured on the *Hard Rain* TV special or the accompanying 'soundtrack' LP, Dylan felt there was more there, and when he resumed rehearsals for another rolling revue, in the winter of 1977–8, it was ripe for another reconstruction.

The 1978 'Going, Going, Gone' proves to be both a dry run for the 'so long, good luck and goodbye' portion of *Street-Legal* – meaning songs like 'True Love Tends to Forget' and 'We'd Better Talk This Over' – and an assertion of independence from 'true love,' in whatever shape or size it may stalk him. Included on *At Budokan*, the new lyrics were still not fully refined (nor do they resemble the ones in the LP booklet, taken verbatim from *Planet Waves*). When he finally decides he 'don't mind leaving' and he ain't 'afraid to go,' it is to Robert Johnson's 'Four Until Late' that he turns for the perfect farewell putdown:

> I've been hanging 'round your place too long,
> Feeling like a clown,
> You don't know how to do nothing
> But tear a good man's reputation down,
> I'm going, I'm going, I'm gone.

Published lyrics: Lyrics 1985; Lyrics 2004.

Known studio recordings: Village Recorder, CA, November 5, 1973 – 8 takes [PW – tk.8].

First known performance: Winterland Ballroom, San Francisco, November 25, 1976 [TLW].

'Hazel' is a song to which Dylan had been heading ever since 'I'll Be Your Baby Tonight,' with which it shares its economy of phrasing. Another captivating reaffirmation of desire for someone with 'something I want plenty of,' it seems to have come easily enough in the studio, with seven of the eight takes complete, though the thirty-two-year-old Dylan is struggling to hit those high notes on the bridge ('Oh, I don't need any reminder . . .'). On the released take, when he says he's 'up on a hill,' he sounds like someone gasping for air.

This may also explain why he has so rarely revisited one of his most affecting love ballads. And when he did attempt it at *The Last Waltz*, in 1976, he wrestled with the bridge twice, neither time entirely successfully. Indeed the song was omitted from the accompanying three-album document (though it subsequently appeared on the all-singing, all-dancing 2002 four-CD set, where we hear a new opening couplet: 'Hazel, moondust in your eye / You're going somewhere, but don't say goodbye'). And when he slipped into it at the first MTV *Unplugged* performance, in November 1994, he didn't return to it on the second night – or allow it to feature on the cut-up official CD – perhaps because he knew it sounded better in rehearsal, when he remembered it was supposed to have a harmonica break.

{295} SOMETHING THERE IS ABOUT YOU

Published lyrics: Lyrics 1985; Lyrics 2004.

Known studio recordings: Village Recorder, CA, November 5, 1973; November 6, 1973 – 3 takes [PW – tk.3].

First known performance: Chicago Stadium, January 3, 1974.

Though not demo-ed in June, along with 'Never Say Goodbye' and 'Nobody 'Cept You,' 'Something There Is About You' is the third such song to focus on a muse who is able to 'remind' the songwriter 'of something that used to be.' It is also the most unabashed in its evocation of the Great Lakes and 'old Duluth,' openly referring to 'the phantoms of my youth,' while suggesting there is something about *her* 'that brings back a long-forgotten truth,' making for three contemporary cast-iron torch ballads where Dylan harps on about this gift of Hers. Could there be a more auto-biographical relationship between such a muse, personified in his wife of eight years, and that other lifetime? Born and brought up in Delaware, it seems highly unlikely that Sara, née Shirley Noznisky, could have known Dylan before they both came to New York (at almost exactly the same time). And yet, according to a 1969 letter from a friend of hers, Sara was 'always there,' and 'they *re-met*' [my italics] in New York.

Dylan was telling English journalist Ray Connolly at much the same time: 'Sara and I grew up together in Minnesota. It wasn't love at first sight. We met again in New York where she was working as a waitress. So we married and now we've got four children.' OK, we might discount the first claim, but the last two sentences are both true. Even biographer Howard Sounes claims, albeit with his usual lack of solid evidence, that their early relationship closely resembled the account given in the second verse of 'Tangled Up in Blue' ('She was married when we first met . . .'). 'Something There Is About You,' a precursor to that tale of star-crossed lovers, strongly suggests their lives intersected before he entered the whirlwind from which she saved him.

Dylan's attachment to the song, though, proved altogether more fleeting, perhaps because he didn't feel he had quite nailed that sense of youthful wonder. It was dropped from the 1974 tour after the first week and made just a single subsequent live appearance, albeit a fascinating one, part of opening night at Tokyo's Budokan Hall in February 1978, Dylan delivering a whole new arrangement of the song.

Sung with an understatement rare for that tour, the song had been subtly changed. She does not remind him 'of something that used to be,' but rather of 'something that one time just had to be.' And he no longer suggests it would be cruel to 'say that I'd be faithful.' Rather, it would be 'tragic.' However, the most significant change is his omission of the final verse, always the weakest of the four, and probably written to highlight a single line, 'I was in a whirlwind, now I'm in some better place.' After writing (and performing) 'Shelter from the Storm,' this sentiment became superfluous. Indeed this later, greater song superseded 'Something There Is About You' on the world tour, as the *Planet Waves* song disappeared from the set on day two (though a tryout at a Paris soundcheck in early July suggests it might have been on the verge of a recall).

{296} YOU ANGEL YOU

Published lyrics: Lyrics 1985; Lyrics 2004 [*recorded version:* Words Fill My Head].

Known studio recordings: Village Recorder, CA, November 5, 1973 [*PW – tk.4*].

First known performance: Penn State, January 14, 1990.

Paul McCartney once told Beatles biographer Hunter Davies, 'The last four songs of an album are usually pure slog. If we need four more we just have to get down and do them . . . [but at least] by that stage in an LP we know what sort of songs we want.' For Dylan, all on his own in New York, fully aware that it had been three-and-a-half years since his last genuine LP, it was probably even more of a slog. 'You Angel You' was one composition borne of a basic need to find an album's worth of songs.

Using the 'Lay, Lady, Lay' formula, he offers the usual platitudes of devotion, delivering his very best 'love ya, honest I do' vocal to bolster lines like, 'You're as fine as anything's fine,' and, 'The way you walk and the way you talk / I swear it would make me sing.' He probably hoped the performance might salvage a rather slight song, and on *Planet Waves* it almost does. The Band play with all the *chutzpah* they can muster, while Dylan throws himself into the deep end of his vocal range, but his fans had already had enough of this kind of song on *Nashville Skyline* and *New Morning*.

It took Dylan sixteen more years before deciding to see whether it could stand up on stage. In the interim, he seemingly forgot the words entirely, and when he sang it one night in January 1990 at Penn State University, he was back in Big Pink, singing dummy lyrics to a song he never completed. When it made its second and last live appearance three weeks later in London, he still only seemed to know two phrases – 'You angel you' and 'I can't sleep at night for trying' – substituting lines from other Dylan songs, like 'Under Your Spell' and 'Most Likely You Go Your Way' instead.

Further evidence that he had never been entirely happy with the lyrics can be found in *The Songs of Bob Dylan 1966–1975*, in which he introduced several new lines. 'You're as fine as anything's fine' now goes with 'It sure plays on my mind'; while 'The way you smile like a heavenly child' shimmies up to 'Is the way it ought to be.' The rewriting process continued through the 1985 *Lyrics*, with the couplet 'The way you smile like a sweet baby child / It just falls all over me' appearing from nowhere. Neither exercise convinced the song's author to revisit it, and when he did, even these lyrics were but a blur.

{297} ON A NIGHT LIKE THIS

Published lyrics: Lyrics *1985;* Lyrics *2004.*

Known studio recordings: Village Recorder, CA, November 6,
1973 – 7 takes; November 8, 1973 – 2 takes [PW].

Those who can remember the hours spent waiting for
Dylan's next masterpiece in the early seventies surely also
remember how their hearts sank like a Mafia informant
when first hearing this song. 'On a Night Like This' was *New
Morning* all over again, albeit with a top-notch Band enliv-
ening proceedings. The playing swings, and Dylan's voice
sounds good, but there is nothing to suggest we'd got the
boy back again. OK, there's a witty take on Kerouac's memorable 'burn, burn, burn' phrase, used to suggest the exact
opposite of what Jack had in mind. And 'Let the four winds
blow / Around this old cabin door' amusingly cross-refer-
ences Fats Domino and 'The Man in Me.' But this was never
going to be enough. Thankfully, he was just toying with us.
Substance was just around the corner – 'Going, Going, Gone'
and, better still, 'Tough Mama.' 'On a Night Like This' was a
one-shot aperitif, not 'The Man in Me' revisited.

{298} TOUGH MAMA

Published lyrics: Lyrics *1985;* Lyrics *2004.*

Known studio recordings: Village Recorder, CA, November 5, 1973;
November 6, 1973 – 7 takes [PW – tk.5].

First known performance: Chicago Stadium, January 3, 1974.

Here, at last, one starts to sense transmission has been
fully restored. If any song sets up the splenetic rush that
culminates, ten months later, in *Blood on the Tracks*, it is
'Tough Mama.' Addressing his muse, whom he gives four
separate monikers – 'Tough Mama,' 'Dark Beauty,' 'Sweet
Goddess,' and 'Silver Angel' – in those first four verses, he
finally turns to his audience, using the fifth to disabuse them
of their own unrealistic expectations: 'I ain't a-haulin' any of

my lambs to the marketplace anymore.' Unfortunately for his muse, though, he still intended to turn up at market. As he told Maureen Orth two months later, 'I'm not standing at an altar, I'm working in the marketplace. . . . What I do is direct contact between me and the people who hear the songs. . . . It doesn't need a translator.'

Not here it doesn't. He had always considered The Band to be the best translators of his musical ideas in performance. On 'Tough Mama' they prove that they could just as easily translate those ideas in the studio. The *Planet Waves* recording is one of the very best examples of ensemble playing any Band fan could hope to find. Yet Dylan barely gave the song a chance to get out of the tour luggage before dispensing with it, performing it at just the first three 1974 shows. Perhaps it took too much out of him, early on in an exhausting two-hour set. There is no hint on the first live vocal, though, that he isn't reveling in the song. It even features a slightly manic harmonica coda absent from its studio self.

It took until 1997 for him to get around to reminding himself that he had a song here with all the wordplay, resonance of vision, and liquid lyricism of *Blood on the Tracks*, celebrating a beauty 'born of a blinding light and a changing wind,' and not yet mourning her absence. Though it took him a couple of summer months to regain a full handle on the song, when he delivered it for the last time that year, at Wembley Arena in October 1997, it was a fitting son to the original tough mama.

{299} DIRGE

Published lyrics: Lyrics 1985; Lyrics 2004.
Known studio recordings: Village Recorder, CA, November 10, 1973(?) – 1 take; November 14, 1973 – 1 take [PW].

After just four days in the studio in early November, Dylan felt he could start assembling his first album of original songs in more than three years. According to Rob Fraboni, 'Bob, myself, Nat Jeffrey and Bob's friend' all turned up on Saturday, November 10. The friend in question appears to have been actor Harry Dean Stanton, with whom Dylan had recently worked on the *Pat Garrett* film, and with whom he now recorded a version of the traditional Spanish song, 'Adelita' (also cut with Eric Clapton in 1976).

Dylan also decided he wanted to record a couple of his new songs acoustic, 'Wedding Song' and 'Forever Young' certainly being attempted. Probably also done was a song listed on a later tape log as 'Dirge for Martha.' Though the released version of 'Dirge' was not recorded until the following Wednesday, engineer Fraboni subsequently stated (in two separate interviews, given within six months of the sessions) that 'we had recorded a version with only acoustic guitar and vocal a few days earlier.' The tenth is the most logical date for this solo version. (The only other possible position for such a recording is the fifth, for which the studio logs are missing.) The tenth was the only solo session; and I tend to believe – and Rob Fraboni concurs – that 'Dirge' was written *during* the sessions.

I might even make the outlandish suggestion that he wrote it in direct response to the question Lou Kemp's girlfriend made concerning 'Forever Young': 'Are you getting mushy in your old age?' 'Dirge,' now cast as torch ballad, presents *prima facie* evidence that he was not. Whether or not Kemp's girlfriend was indeed the Martha for whom it was written (this fuller title appears only on the tape log – an inside joke, perhaps?), the positioning of 'Dirge' directly after 'Forever Young' was undoubtedly intended to be one of those classic Dylanesque juxtapositions.

In the end, the only song from the 'all acoustic' session

to make *Planet Waves* was 'Wedding Song,' as Dylan continued to brood on his new dirge for a few days more. Only on the fourteenth, as they began mixing the album, did he decide that he wanted to intercede one last time, and this time he wanted to play the piano. In fact, as Fraboni told *Recording Engineer*, 'Bob went out and played the piano while we were mixing. All of a sudden he came in and said, "I'd like to try 'Dirge' on the piano." . . . We put up a tape and he said to Robbie, "Maybe you could play guitar on this."' He then requested Fraboni get 'a kind of bar-room sound from the piano . . . rather than a majestic sound.'

There was supposedly a single rehearsal without the tape running, which was immediately followed by the recorded version that can be heard on *Planet Waves* to this day. If it really is overdub-free, then hats off to Robertson, who demonstrates a real flair for flamenco-like flourishes. Dylan is also faultless at the piano as he stabs out this song to another wanton heartbreaker. At last the circle of passion is broken, as he dissects a relationship gone sour enough to curdle cheese. When it comes to 'Dirge,' the more cryptic the lines, the better they prove: 'I hate that foolish game we played, and the need that was expressed / And the mercy that you showed to me. Whoever would have guessed?' Ouch.

One imagines Dylan had the idea for 'Dirge' when walking down Fourth Street. If he really did attempt it first on the tenth, it again demonstrates Dylan's aptitude for a little 'negative capability.' 'Wedding Song' – another new song recorded that day, again written in L.A. as an album deadline closed in – came from the other side of the picket fence. The vocal performance on 'Dirge' alone is acidic enough to strip layers of skin. Perhaps it is just too damn intense to be something he could repeat before unknowing eyes on his comeback tour. The one tour for which Dylan was really in a dirgelike frame of mind was in 1976, when Lou Kemp's girlfriend/s wasn't the problem. But Dylan left 'Dirge' back at Village Recorder in that iridescent instance when he captured it on tape. I wonder whether Martha found 'Dirge' mushy?

{300} WEDDING SONG

Published lyrics: Lyrics 1985; Lyrics 2004.
Known studio recordings: Village Recorder, CA, November 9, 1973 – 1 take [PW].
First known performance: The Spectrum, Philadelphia, January 7, 1974.

> Some songs – like 'Restless Farewell' – I've written just to fill up an album. – Dylan to Hubert Saal, February 1968

It may not be the final song *recorded* for *Planet Waves* – both 'Dirge' and 'Forever Young' being re-recorded at the first 'mixing' session – but 'Wedding Song' was assuredly the last song Dylan wrote *for* the album, and another song written to come last. His first solo closer since 'Restless Farewell,' 'Wedding Song' serves a similar purpose, though this time he assures the woman to whom he is addressing this restless farewell that he *shall* be coming back. Like the sleeve note that accompanies the album, it presents a Dylan gearing up to hit the road, writing one last love letter to deny that the lure of the road is calling:

> It's never been my duty to remake the world at large,
> Nor is it my intention to sound a battle charge,
> 'Cause I love you more than all of that,
> With a love that doesn't bend.

The intensity of the song hinges on its very immediacy. Hence Dylan's determination to cut the song rapidly and sparingly. As Fraboni recalled months later, the moment still imprinted on his mind:

> Around noon, Bob said, 'I've got a song I want to record later. . . . I'm not ready right now. I'll tell you when.' We were doing what we were doing, and all of a sudden he came up and said, 'Let's record.' So he went out in the studio. . . . Usually he wouldn't sing unless we were recording. That's the way he was. You couldn't get him to go out and just sing, unless he was running something down with The Band. . . . [This time] he asked, 'Is the tape rolling? Why don't you just roll it?' So I did, and he started singing, and there was no way in the world I could have stopped him to say, 'Go back to the top.' It was such an intense performance. If you listen to the record, you can hear noises from the buttons on his jacket. But he didn't seem to care.

The performance is so strong that one can't help but hope the guy in the song manages to win his bride over again. Yet that sense of being written in the moment, and a certain self-serving justification of his own actions, makes its closest kin 'Ballad in Plain D,' another song he wrote in haste and regretted at leisure. On *Planet Waves, it* certainly has a lot more fire than the few tepid renditions it received on the 1974 tour – its only live incarnation.

Unfortunately 'Wedding Song' – a title culled from Brecht's *Threepenny Opera* – is hardly another Song of Songs. It is not just a case of 'methinks he doth protest too much.' Hindsight – evidenced by the next song he would write – begins applying its marker pen to many lines before 'the darling buds of May' have even begun to sprout. That final line, 'I love you more than ever now that the past is gone,' appears to be a self-conscious attempt to close the book on the sense of nostalgia which kick-started the album process. But the time when he needed shelter from the storm had passed. The next song he will write about 'marriage' comes from a very different vantage point – 'I married Isis on the fifth day of May / But I could not hold on to her very long . . .'

Out now: Still on the Road – The Songs of Bob Dylan 1974–2008.

▦▦▦ A SELECT BIBLIOGRAPHY ▦▦▦

I refer readers looking for a more complete bibliography of Dylan publications to my biography, *Behind the Shades: Take Two* (published in the United States as *Bob Dylan: Behind the Shades Revisited*, 2000) and my chronology, *Dylan Day-by-Day* (published in the United States as *Bob Dylan: A Life in Stolen Moments*, 1995). The bewildering onslaught of new books on the man and his work has, of course, continued unabated since those two volumes, but so little of what I have read seems to justify the trees uprooted that I have confined myself here to the resources that have had a *direct* bearing on the text herein. Needless to say, the Internet has also provided endless opportunities for the unpublishable, self-appointed 'expert' to pontificate on the man and his art, but I have felt little inclination to fuel their self-importance with a citation here. What is here, then, is just the wheat.

1. Dylan's own writings.

'Good poem, bad poem,' c. 1957 (Morgan Library exhibition, 2005)

Bob Dylan Himself: His Words/His Music. New York: MCA Music, 1965.

Varsity questionnaire w/ handwritten answers, c. May 1965 (unpublished)

Don't Look Back. New York: Witmark, 1967.

Tarantula. New York: MacMillan, 1970.

Words to His Songs. Privately published, 1971.

Writings and Drawings. New York: Knopf, 1973.

The Songs of Bob Dylan from 1966 through 1975. New York: Knopf, 1976.

In His Own Write (ed. M. Krogsgaard). Privately published, 1980.

Lyrics, 1962–1985. New York: Knopf, 1985.

In His Own Write 2 (ed. John Tuttle). Privately published, 1990.

Words Fill My Head. Privately published, 1991.

In His Own Write 3 (ed. John Tuttle). Privately published, 1992.

Drawn Blank. New York: Random House, 1994.

Chronicles, Volume One. New York: Simon & Schuster, 2004.

Lyrics, 1962–2001. New York: Simon & Schuster, 2004.

The Bob Dylan Scrapbook, 1956–1966. New York: Simon & Schuster, 2005.

2. Dylan interviews.

The primary resource for Dylan interviews is a four-volume bookleg collection published in the midnineties by 'Dr. Filth.' Entitled The Fiddler Now Upspoke, *it covers 99 percent of the interviews given up to 1995. For more information, readers are referred to the* Behind the Shades: Take Two *bibliography.*

The post-1995 interviews also utilised are as follows (in order of publication):

September 28, 1997. Pareles, Jon: *The New York Times.*
September 29, 1997. Gundersen, Edna: *USA Today.*
October 6, 1997. Gates, David: *Newsweek.*
November 15, 1997. Jackson, Alan: *The Times Magazine.*
December 14, 1997. Hilburn, Robert: *Los Angeles Times.*
February 1998. Kaganski, Serge: *Mojo.*
March 1999. Engleheart, Murray: *Guitar World.*
September 10, 2001. Gundersen, Edna: *USA Today.*
September 17, 2001. Farley, Christopher John: *Time.*
November 22, 2001. Gilmore, Mikal: *Rolling Stone.*
September 26, 2004. Preston, John: *The Sunday Telegraph.*
October 4, 2004. Gates, David: *Newsweek.*
December 9, 2004. Scaggs, Austin: *Rolling Stone.*
February 2006. Hilburn, Robert: *Guitar World Acoustic.* [interview from 2004]
September 7, 2006. Lethem, Jonathan: *Rolling Stone.*
May 3, 2007. Wenner, Jann: *Rolling Stone.*
June 6, 2008. Jackson, Alan: *The Times* (London).

3. Dylan fanzines consulted. [* = now defunct]

The Bridge #1–8.
Endless Road★ #1–7.
Homer The Slut★ #1–11.
Isis #1–140.
Judas★ #1–19.
Look Back★ #1–27.
Occasionally★ #1–5.
On the Tracks #1–17.
The Telegraph★ #1–56.
Zimmerman Blues★ #1–10.

4. The biographies.

Heylin, Clinton. *Bob Dylan: Behind The Shades Revisited.* New York: HarperCollins, 2001.

Rotolo, Suze. *A Freewheelin' Time: A Memoir of Greenwich Village in the Sixties*. New York: Broadway, 2008.

Scaduto, Anthony. *Bob Dylan: An Intimate Biography*. New York: Grosset & Dunlap, 1971.

Shelton, Robert. *No Direction Home: The Life and Music of Bob Dylan*. New York: Beech Tree Books, 1986.

Sounes, Howard. *Down the Highway: The Life of Bob Dylan*. New York: Grove/Atlantic, 2001.

Spitz, Bob. *Dylan: A Biography*. New York: McGraw-Hill, 1988.

5. Main reference sources.

Cable, Paul. *Bob Dylan: The Unreleased Recordings*. London: Dark Star, 1978; in United States: Macmillan, 1980.

Cartwright, Bert. *The Bible in the Lyrics of Bob Dylan*. Bury, UK: Wanted Man, 1985.

Dundas, Glen. *Tangled Up in Tapes*. Privately published, various eds.

Dunn, Tim. *The Bob Dylan Copyright Files 1962–1995*. Privately published, 1996.

Heylin, Clinton. *Rain Unravelled Tales: A Rumourography*. Privately published, 1984.

Heylin, Clinton. *Bob Dylan: The Recording Sessions 1960–1994*. New York: Penguin, 1996.

Heylin, Clinton. *Bob Dylan: A Life in Stolen Moments, Day by Day 1941–1995*. New York: Schirmer, 1996.

Wenner, Jann. ed. *Rolling Stone Cover to Cover: The First Forty Years* (DVD-ROM). New York: Bondi, 2007.

6. Other reference sources.

Baez, Joan. *And a Voice to Sing With*. New York: Summit, 1987.

Balfour, Victoria. *Rock Wives: The Hard Lives and Good Times of the Wives, Girlfriends and Groupies of Rock and Roll*. New York: Beech Tree, 1986.

Barker, Derek. ed. *Isis: A Bob Dylan Anthology*. London: Helter-Skelter, 2001.

Brand, Oscar. *The Ballad Mongers: Rise of the Modern Folksong*. New York: Funk & Wagnalls, 1962.

Davies, Hunter. *The Beatles: The Authorized Biography*. New York: McGraw-Hill, 1968.

Engel, Dave. *Just Like Bob Zimmerman's Blues: Dylan in Minnesota*. Amherst, WI: Amherst Press, 1997.

Faithfull, Marianne [w/ David Dalton]. *Faithfull: An Autobiography*. New York: Little, Brown, 1994.

Flanagan, Bill. *Written in My Soul: Rock's Great Songwriters Talk About Creating Their Music*. Chicago: Contemporary, 1986.

Garrett, Pat F. *The Authentic Life of Billy, the Kid*. Norman, OK: University of Oklahoma Press, 2000.

Gilmour, Michael J. *Tangled Up in the Bible: Bob Dylan & Scripture*. New York: Continuum, 2004.

Gray, Michael. *Song & Dance Man: The Art of Bob Dylan*. New York: Dutton, 1972.

Harrison, George. *I Me Mine*. New York: Simon & Schuster, 1981.

Harvey, Todd. *The Formative Dylan: Transmission & Stylistic Influences 1961–1963*. Lanham, MD: Scarecrow, 2001.

Haugen, Larry. *Red Wing: A Year and a Day*. Privately published, 2006.

Hedin, Benjamin. ed. *Studio A: The Bob Dylan Reader*. New York: Norton, 2004.

Helm, Levon [w/ Stephen Davis]. *This Wheel's on Fire: Levon Helm and the Story of the Band*. New York: Morrow, 1993.

Kooper, Al. *Backstage Passes: Rock 'n' Roll Life in the Sixties*. New York: Stein & Day, 1977.

Lawlan, Val & Brian. *Steppin' Out*. Privately published, 1982.

Mabey, Richard. *The Pop Process*. London: Hutchinson, 1969.

Marcus, Greil. *Invisible Republic: Bob Dylan's Basement Tapes*. New York: Holt, 1997.

———. *Like a Rolling Stone: Bob Dylan at the Crossroads*. New York: Public Affairs, 2005.

McGregor, Craig. ed. *Bob Dylan: A Retrospective*. New York: Morrow, 1972.

Percival, Dave. *This Wasn't Written in Tin Pan Alley*. Privately published, 1989.

———. *The Dust of Rumour*. Privately published, 1985.

Pickering, Stephen. *Bob Dylan Approximately: A Portrait of the Jewish Poet in Search of God*. New York: David McKay, 1974.

Thompson, Toby. *Positively Main Street: An Unorthodox View of Bob Dylan*. New York: Coward-McCann, 1971.

Warhol, Andy, and Pat Hackett. *Popism: The Warhol '60s*. New York: Harcourt, 1980.

Webster, Patrick. *Friends & Other Strangers: Bob Dylan in Other People's Words*. Privately published, 1985.

Wenner, Jann S. *Lennon Remembers*. New York: Penguin, 1973.

Williams, Paul. *Performing Artist: The Music of Bob Dylan, Volume One, 1960–1973*. Novato, CA: Underwood-Miller, 1990.

Wurlitzer, Rudolph. *Pat Garrett and Billy the Kid*. New York: Signet, 1973.

Zollo, Paul. *Songwriters on Songwriting*. Exp. Ed. New York: Da Capo, 1997.

7. Folksong resources.

Bartók, Béla. *Hungarian Folk Music*. London: Oxford Univ. Press, 1931.

Bronson, Bertrand H. *The Singing Tradition of Child's Popular Ballads*. Princeton, NJ: Princeton Univ. Press, 1970.

Doerflinger, William M. *Shantymen and Shantyboys: Songs of the Sailor and Lumberman*. New York: MacMillan, 1951.

The Editors of *Sing Out!* Magazine. *The Collected Reprints from* Sing Out!: The Folk Song Magazine. Sing Out, 1990.

Guthrie, Woody (ed. Millard Lampell). *California to the New York Island*. New York: Oak, 1960.

Lomax, Alan. *The Folk Songs of North America in the English Language*. New York: Doubleday, 1960.

Lomax, John A., and Alan. *American Ballads and Folk Songs*. New York: Macmillan, 1934.

McNeil, W. K. *Southern Folk Ballads, Vol. II*. Little Rock, AR: August House, 1988.

Porter, James, and Herschel Gower. *Jeannie Robertson: Emergent Singer, Transformative Voice*. Knoxville, TN: Univ of Tennessee Press, 1995.

Randolph, Vance. *Ozark Folksongs*. Columbia, MO: Univ. of Missouri Press, 1980.

Sharp, Cecil (Ed. Maud Karpeles). *English Folk Songs from the Southern Appalachians*. London: Oxford Univ. Press, 1932.

Silber, Fred, and Irwin Silber. *Folksinger's Wordbook*. New York: Oak, 1973.

Work, John W. *American Negro Songs and Spirituals*. New York: Bonanza, 1940.

8. Miscellanous articles.

Clepper, P. M. *This Week* magazine (March 1966).

Finksbine, Bob. 'Dylan's Idaho Sojourn.' *Scottsdale Progress* (May 3, 1986).

Fraboni, Rob. *Recording Engineer* (March–April 1974).

Gerrette, Rosemary. 'Man in a Mask.' *Canberra Times* (May 7, 1966).

Helfert, Manfred. Interview with Judy Collins. www.bobdylanroots.com/anthe.html (1996).

Lang, Andrew. 'The Mystery of the Queen's Marie.' *Blackwood's Magazine* (September 1895).

Nelson, Paul, and Jon Pankake. 'Freewheelin'.' *Little Sandy Review* (Summer 1963).

Rowan, Pete. Interview, *The Journal of Country Music* (December 1978).

Svedburg, Andrea. 'Let Us Now Praise Little Men.' *Newsweek* (October 29, 1963).

Wilentz, Sean. 'Mystic Nights: The Making of *Blonde on Blonde*.' *Oxford American* 58 (2007).

9. Literary resources.

Brecht, Bertolt. *Threepenny Opera*.

Fitzgerald, Scott. *Tender Is the Night*.

Ginsberg, Allen [ed. Miles]. *Howl: Original Draft Facsimile*.

Hesse, Herman. *Steppenwolf*.

Jackson, George. *Soledad Brother: The Prison Letters of George Jackson*.

Keats, John. *The Letters of John Keats*.

Kierkegaard, Soren. *Fear and Trembling*.

MacLeish, Archibald (Ed. by R. H. Winnick). *Archibald MacLeish: Letters 1907–82*.

Rimbaud, Arthur. *Complete Works*.

Smith, Patti. *Seventh Heaven*.

Southern, Terry, and Mason Hoffenberg. *Candy*.

||||| ACKNOWLEDGEMENTS |||||

Though this kind of book requires quite a different, wider-ranging, less interactive type of research from the biography and chronologies I have produced previously, I have been delighted to find that those stalwarts of *all* serious Dylan scholarship in the past four decades have again been there to lend a hand at every turn. I am referring to Mitch Blank, Glen Dundas, and Ian Woodward, to whom every Dylan fan should inwardly genuflect for their endeavours on our behalf.

Thanks, too, to David Bristow, who has continued to compile one of the more insanely complete collections of printed matter on the man, which he not only allowed me access to, but extended loans therefrom. Many thanks, and goodwill, to Jeff Rosen and Callie Gladman, at Special Rider, for their time and professionalism. And fulsome thanks, as ever, to that generous soul Glen Korman, who has again come to my aid whenever the Sony database has caused mystification.

The manuscript of the book has been read by no less than four editors, all of whom I thank for their feedback, belief, and encouragement in the face of a perplexing inability on publishers' parts to see the need for a project on quite this scale: the redoubtable Tony Lacey, Andy Miller, Yuval Taylor, and Leo Hollis, as well as ex-*Judas* editor Andy Muir. And a final thanks to Jonathan Cott, who also believed. Enjoy.

IIIII COPYRIGHT INFORMATION IIIII

Since the completion of volume one, Tim Dunn has updated *The Bob Dylan Copyright Files 1962–2007*. In this rather weighty update are a series of song-titles, copyrighted en masse when transferred from Grossman's estate to Dylan's publishing company, in 1988. Credited to Dwarf Music, the long list (some ninety songs) appears to include some previously unknown basement-tape compositions. Aside from 'Dress It Up, Better Have It All' and 'You Own A Racehorse', it seems there were three other related titles reassigned at this juncture: 'What's It Gonna Be When It Comes Up?', 'My Woman She's A-Leavin'' and 'Mary Lou, I Love You Too'. A separate reassignment has a song called 'Baby Lou', which one suspects is simply the previous song, under another name. Further information (and maybe even a tape or two) shall hopefully emerge in the fullness of time.'

— Clinton Heylin, December 2008.

▌▌▌▌ INDEX OF BOB DYLAN SONGS ▌▌▌▌

570

IIIII GENERAL INDEX IIIIII

(see also INDEX OF BOB DYLAN SONGS, p. 568)

574

585